Business Analysis Done Right

Karolina Zmitrowicz

Business Analysis Done Right

Lessons Learned and Pitfalls Avoided

Springer

Karolina Zmitrowicz
Kamień Pomorski, Poland

ISBN 978-3-031-62193-2 ISBN 978-3-031-62194-9 (eBook)
https://doi.org/10.1007/978-3-031-62194-9

This Springer imprint is published by the registered company Springer Nature Switzerland AG
The registered company address is: Gewerbestrasse 11, 6330 Cham, Switzerland

Foreword by Karl Wiegers[1]

The caption on an old cartoon shows a manager speaking to a room of software developers. The manager says, "I'll go up and find out what they need and the rest of you start coding." I began programming computers in college more than 50 years ago. I quickly learned that it's a good idea to understand what my users—even if it was just myself—needed, and why, *before* I started coding.

That doesn't mean that I must know *everything* that *every* user would *ever* need before I begin coding. My knowledge about various stakeholders and their needs, constraints, and expectations grows and changes throughout each project. However, I found it was enormously helpful to begin by understanding the project's business objectives (*Why are we working on this?*), its key stakeholders (*Who cares about this?*), and their goals (*What must users be able to do with the solution?*).

This process of understanding the problem, business context, and stakeholder needs and then defining a solution's capabilities and characteristics has come to be known as business analysis. Business analysis encompasses the large domain of software requirements engineering, but it's more than that. As Karolina Zmitrowicz points out, the business analyst (BA) might contribute to strategic analysis of the organizational environment and business process modeling, along with stakeholder analysis, identifying business needs, and other activities. These are all foundational steps that take place before getting into the elicitation and analysis of specific requirements and structuring that knowledge into a solution description.

An effective BA accumulates a sizeable tool kit of techniques, along with the experience and wisdom to know which one to use in a given situation. We gain that wisdom through experience, remembering lessons from what we did before that either did or—more frequently—did not work well.

I love lessons-learned books like *Business Analysis Done Right*. You don't have time to make the same mistakes that every BA before you has already made. It is cheaper—and less painful—to collect valuable lessons from other people's experience and then think

[1] Karl Wiegers is the co-author of *Software Requirements, 3rd Edition* and *Software Requirements Essentials.*

about how to apply those lessons to your own work. Karolina provides dozens of insightful lessons about requirements engineering and other important aspects of business analysis. Each lesson clearly describes practical techniques that you can employ to put the lesson into action. She provides a balanced discussion of the various techniques, often based on her personal experience, to help you determine how best to apply the practice in your world.

Even if your project or product team does not include someone with the job title of Business Analyst, the team members who perform this kind of work are filling the BA role. *Business Analysis Done Right* can help all of those individuals see how they, and their work, contribute so much to the team's success.

Alternatively, your developers could just start coding based on what they think they know and see where they end up. Good luck with that.

Process Impact
Happy Valley, OR, USA

Karl Wiegers

Foreword by Tom Gilb

Business analysis, the importance of properly identifying business problems.

A "business problem" is primarily to competitively improve organizational, product, and service qualities and costs.

These competitive problems apply to public service organizations too.

These problems can be articulated as requirements for the qualities—to get better, on time, and for the costs to be more competitive.

Everybody can articulate simple ***cost*** reductions clearly: though there are some improvements most people can learn, like specifying prioritized cost improvements in high-priority locations and stakeholders. But this is the same advanced specification knowledge we need to apply to the organization/product/service, as found in the Value Requirements (Planguage) book (Gilb 2019).

The *art of mastering costs* is a deep management-and-design art, and I would like to give readers a textbook on the subject 'Cost Engineering' (Gilb 2023). You need to design the cost levels, that you need to have. Just like you need to design the "*quality* levels you need to have."

But, to the main subject. The articulation of the many quality requirements we need to satisfy to be a success (Gilb 2021c).

There are two main problems in current practice.

Point 1. We are not good enough at analyzing our large range of stakeholders and their needs. We focus too narrowly on "customers and users," and forget critical stakeholders, like competitors and laws (Gilb 2021b).

Then, point 2, we fail to articulate quality requirements usefully. We use a series of ambiguous words ("competitive security levels") rather than quantification, and other specifications (such as when, where, who). This clear measurable articulation of all critical qualities is absolutely necessary for achieving competitive quality levels in practice. And it is always possible to quantify all critical qualities (Gilb 2021a). But most professionals do not know how, and have never been trained. So, they ignore quality requirements specification, and consequently fail to achieve necessary and critical qualities. They fail at their business analyst job.

It is unlikely that your organization will train you to do requirements properly, and unlikely that a university will train you. They are not competent. They are in denial (these are difficult and "soft" requirements). So you have to initially teach yourself using this book. Then teach others. Preferably, by example and by successful delivery, of critical competitive qualities.

References

Gilb, Tom. 2019. *Value Requirements: Critical Stakeholder Objectives Engineering.*
——. 2021a. *Quanteer. How to Quantify Values.*
——. 2021b. *Stakeholder Engineering.*
——. 2021c. *SUCCESS: Super Secrets & Strategies for Efficient Delivery in Projects, Programs, and Plans.*
——. 2023. *Cost Engineering.*

Oslo, Norway Tom Gilb

Preface

This publication is based on observations and insights from projects carried out by myself and other individuals active in the field of business analysis. The motivation behind writing this book was that while there are many publications on the theoretical foundations of business analysis and requirements engineering in the current publishing market, there is a lack of publications describing the practical aspects of analysis—the application of specific tools and techniques, dealing with typical challenges encountered in IT projects (and not only IT projects).

The purpose of this publication is not to provide a comprehensive compendium of business analysis knowledge. It is not another handbook or guide, or an inventory of techniques and tools. The purpose of this publication is to bring together in one place observations, experiences, practices that work and that don't work in different areas of analysis. The reader will no doubt have noticed that the content of the publication does not cover all the practices and activities of business analysis—as this is not my goal.

The main idea of this publication was to provide readers with suggestions, ideas, and conclusions regarding selected aspects of business analysis—in particular, discussing challenges and recommendations regarding the application of specific methods and practices in specific usage contexts. The publication is aimed at readers who have a basic understanding of the fundamentals of business analysis and will be able to relate this theoretical knowledge to practical examples of project applications. The publication will be most beneficial to readers with some project experience, as the majority of the examples and situations described relate to specific projects and initiatives.

Readers who are just entering the field of business analysis can benefit from the publication by gaining insights to avoid basic mistakes made in ventures, thus making their entry into the world of business analysis smoother and less burdened by business risks than readers with only theoretical knowledge.

The tips, suggestions, and recommendations contained in the publication are based on the author's 20 years of experience in the field of business analysis, requirements engineering, and quality management, enriched with suggestions and reflections from other experts with whom the author consulted on specific topics and issues.

The content of the book does not cover the entire field of business analysis, understood as a path from defining business needs, through developing solution concepts and designing this solution to implementation and evaluation of the solution. In this publication, I focusprimarily on areas that pose the greatest project challenges, the most frequently occurring problems in the work of a business analyst. These areas—agreed upon with experts—include:

1. Strategic analysis
2. Business analysis process planning
3. Requirements engineering activities
4. Solution implementation

These areas constitute the main chapters of this publication. Each chapter begins with a brief introduction explaining the essence of the respective process area and presenting the most important information. Chapters are divided into subsections describing specific areas, while specific tips and recommendations are presented in the form of sections. Most sections begin with a guiding thought—a quote provided by an expert or a short tip developed by the author of the publication. At the end of each chapter, the reader will find supplements in the form of case studies and/or checklists facilitating the planning and implementation of business analysis practice in a project.

From this publication, the reader will learn:

- The modern definition of business analysis
- What competencies a person performing business analysis tasks should have
- That business analysis is not a practice limited solely to IT projects—its application scope is universal
- The basic concepts within business analysis and how they are interconnected
- Why understanding the organization's context is a necessary condition for effective business analysis
- The significance of business goals and organizational strategy for effective acquisition of business needs
- How to define business needs to meet basic criteria
- How to validate business needs for their adequacy in the context of organizational strategy
- The benefits of business modeling
- Who the project stakeholders are, how to identify them, and how to manage their involvement
- Why communication planning is so important
- What factors influence business analysis activity planning and how to incorporate these factors when developing a business analysis framework
- How to plan analytical activities—step by step

- How to plan information architecture in a project, especially the structure of requirements
- The types and purposes of requirements
- How to specify and validate requirements
- How to use templates and create custom documentation templates
- How to combine different methods and approaches to requirement specification and modeling
- The key requirements management practices, especially tracking dependencies and managing change
- How a business analyst can support the project team—at different stages and in different organizational setups

For most of the topics discussed, examples and analyses of possible solutions are provided depending on selected project and organizational factors. The publication also includes case studies based on real project situations. Additional assistance for readers includes checklists that make planning analytical activities, requirements management processes, and specification development easier and minimize the risk of omitting essential steps.

While working on this book, I realized that it was impossible to include all the relevant tips and thoughts on business analysis practices in one volume. Therefore, I made the decision to focus on the practices of business analysis planning and solution concept development, starting with the proper identification of the business area and ending with requirements specification and management.

The solution design and system analysis aspects are minimally covered in this publication, as this is a topic for another, larger publication.

In selecting material for this publication, I prioritized topics based on their popularity and the frequency of occurrence of a particular problem. It is worth noting that many of the topics discussed may seem trivial. However, during discussions with experts, it turned out that we often make mistakes not during the implementation of advanced, mature practices requiring expert knowledge and experience. Many mistakes are of a basic nature—related to activities considered standard, obvious, such as stakeholder identification or the selection of the right template for business needs, business processes, or requirements. As a result of haste, routine, and lack of reflection, we make trivial mistakes at the beginning of the project, which, of course, leads to the emergence of further problems in later stages.

Hence, this publication contains recommendations and tips regarding more advanced practices, as well as suggestions regarding basic business analysis activities. For this reason, this publication begins with defining the concept of business analysis and discussing the areas covered by this discipline.

In preparing the materials for this publication, I spoke with a number of experts whom I appreciate for their powerful knowledge, substance, and experience, and at the same time their modesty and humility, their ability to admit that one cannot be an expert in all areas.

Almost every one of these experts stressed the importance of planning the work properly—properly, that is, starting with a thought process, thinking about goals, expected results, and not getting into the execution mode right away. Hence, in many places in this publication, the issue of planning, proper analysis of information, gathering data before making decisions, comes up. Proper planning, according to me and many experts, is a key factor in the success of any initiatives and projects.

Another major problem identified during interviews with experts is problems in expressing thoughts precisely and translating them into a documented record. Initiatives' notorious problem is vague, imprecise requirements, business needs described in a way that makes it virtually impossible to properly evaluate them and decide on the planned solution. It seems that in many cases we are unable to evaluate the information collected, prioritize it, and express it in a measurable and verifiable way. This is why so much of the publication is devoted to the issue of requirements engineering, particularly specifications.

I would like to point out that requirements engineering practices regarding specification, ensuring measurability of requirements, apply to all areas of business analysis. Goals and business needs should also be defined in a measurable way, allowing the selection of appropriate measures to meet these goals and needs, and the subsequent evaluation of their fulfillment. Goals, needs, and requirements that are not precise, measurable and perceivable are just wishful thinking. They cannot provide a solid basis for making decisions that are often crucial to the organization's strategy.

In this publication you will find a set of practices, tips, and suggestions developed on the basis of my experience and that of experts with whom I have had the pleasure of working. If, thanks to this information, even one person avoids making obvious and less obvious mistakes, I will count it as a huge success.

If you are a business analyst who is just starting your career and would like to avoid basic mistakes and learn from the mistakes of others, if you are a business analyst who is already actively involved in projects and would like to improve your work practices, if you are someone who has basic knowledge of business analysis and wants to develop this knowledge with practical tips from a range of experts with years of experience.

This publication is for you.

Kamień Pomorski, Poland Karolina Zmitrowicz

Acknowledgments

The creation of this publication would not have been possible without the support of many people. In particular, I would like to thank the following people:

Tom Gilb and Karl Wiegers—for their valuable comments and guidance, and for the vast amount of knowledge I had the chance to absorb from you. My approach to business analysis is largely shaped by your work.

Michal Bartyzel, Radoslaw Grębski, Robert Kozlowski, Niels Malotaux, Grzegorz Skrzynski, Tomasz Tomaszewski, Elena Zhukova—for your support at every stage, consultations, and discussions—often at non-standard times of the day and under non-standard circumstances.

Piotr Biernacki, Rainer Grau, Sylwia Kopczynska, Jussi Mäkelä, Howard Podeswa, Jaroslaw Zelinski—for valuable feedback, inspiring discussions and challenging the status quo.

Special thanks to my IREB® colleagues. Stan Bühne, Martin Glinz, Kim Lauenroth, Hans van Loenhoud, Norbert Seyff, Hans-Jörg Steffe, Stefan Sturm—thanks to you, I am not only a better analyst, I am a better person, and that means so much more.

Thank you to the other friends who contributed in various ways to this publication. Talking with you was a pleasure.

Anna Kochanowska, Ewelina Eggert, Fabricio Laguna, Filip Hendrickx, John Wisner, Katarzyna Nowak-Rybka, Laura Brandenburg, Małgorzata Kusyk, Marcin Żmigrodzki, Martin Daliga, Mariusz Nagięć, Michał Buczko, Rafał Jasiński, Ross Apostoł, Thando Jacobs, Witold Egiertowski, Yulia Kosarenko.

Contents

Introduction 1

1.1 What Is Business Analysis?

What is business analysis?

The concept has been around for some time. Probably the most popular definition of business analysis is from the IIBA (International Institute of Business Analysis) organization in its publication *BABOK®* (*Business Analysis Body of Knowledge*) *Guide* (IIBA® 2015):

> BUSINESS ANALYSIS IS THE PRACTICE OF ENABLING CHANGE IN THE ORGANIZATION BY DEFINING NEEDS AND RECOMMENDING SOLUTIONS THAT DELIVER VALUE TO STAKEHOLDERS.

This definition is based on six core concepts of business analysis: change, need, solution, value, stakeholders, and context. These elements make up the Business Analysis Core Concept Model™ (BACCM™) described in the aforementioned *BABOK® Guide*.

Business analysis enables changes to be made—and these changes may involve various elements of the organization and its environment.

- Business motivation
- Strategy
- Policies and rules
- Members of the organization—both those running the organization and employees
- Customers
- Partners and suppliers
- Processes and operations
- Value proposition (services and products of the organization)
- Systems and other infrastructure elements
- Culture and value system

K. Zmitrowicz, *Business Analysis Done Right*,
https://doi.org/10.1007/978-3-031-62194-9_1

There are a number of practices and areas within business analysis, which are thoroughly described in the aforementioned guide. Each area and practice is supported by a comprehensive set of methods and tools.

Personally, I perceive business analysis as a discipline that supports the creation and development of business systems. After all, every organization is a system of interrelated components operating in a certain environment, pursuing a specific goal. This system is subject to change, evolution—natural or forced. This results in the need for changes. Business analysis deals, among other things, with understanding such a system, the factors influencing it, and determining possible directions for change.

Business analysis is a discipline that provides the competence necessary to understand the principles of any business system (organization) in a specific context in order to identify areas for improvement.

The end result of business analysis activities is the delivery of a change proposal amounting to measurable business value for specific stakeholders within the defined scope of the subject business system.

The term "system" should not be understood as a technical solution, but as a set of components, elements that make up a specific logical whole, providing specific services and capabilities and serving a specific purpose.

An organization understood as a system consists of a number of components: stakeholders, organizational structure, business processes, services and products, and external and internal factors affecting the functioning of the organization.

An organization viewed in this way behaves like a typical system—it operates in a specific environment (context) that significantly affects its functioning. It can limit the ability to achieve business goals, or it can become a catalyst for changes in the subject organization due to changes in the environment forcing the system (organization) to respond to these changes.

In order to carry out effective business analysis, it is necessary not only to have the right competence understood as knowledge and the ability to apply certain practices, methods, and tools, but also to have a certain mindset—a way of thinking. Thanks to this way of thinking, a person engaged in business analysis is able to perceive the surrounding reality as a system of interconnected elements, carrying out specific functions and objectives, providing specific benefits to various groups of stakeholders, controlled by various influential factors.

In order to effectively carry out the tasks of business analysis, one must also possess the right character traits such as empathy, courage, curiosity, or inquisitiveness. The right combination of competence, mindset, and personality traits allows one to perceive the surrounding reality in a different way than the rest of the members of a given organization.

A person with a business analyst mindset views any organization or specific initiative, as well as its environment, as an ever-changing ecosystem whose functioning and performance is affected by various factors, including those that can be predicted and those that cannot be controlled. A person with the mindset of a business analyst is capable of identifying changes in such an ecosystem and predicting or proposing possible directions for changing the way it functions, including responding to changes in the environment, in order to keep the operation of the system stable.

If we were tempted to develop a kind of manifesto for business analysts, in my opinion it could read as follows:

IN CHAOS WE FIND ORDER

WE TURN INFORMATION INTO KNOWLEDGE, ON THE BASIS OF WHICH UNDERSTANDING ARISES

WE TRANSFORM UNDERSTANDING INTO CONCLUSIONS

WE ORGANIZE AND CONSOLIDATE KNOWLEDGE ABOUT THE FUNCTIONING OF THE ORGANIZATION

WE OFFER SOLUTIONS FOR PROBLEMS

WE SUPPORT IN DELIVERING VALUE

To be able to achieve the above objectives, business analysts must:

- Evaluate the impact of the environment on the operation of the business system.
- Identify opportunities and possibilities, but also risks and threats.
- Get to the root of the problem, rather than stopping at the symptoms.
- Draw probable conclusions based on incomplete information.
- See the connections between the organization and the context, stakeholder needs and business objectives, processes and operations, and strategy.
- Obtain information from a variety of sources, assess which information is relevant to a given context, and make choices about which aspect to focus on.
- Support stakeholders in accurately defining their needs and expectations.
- Support stakeholders representing different goals and differing viewpoints in reaching consensus.
- Identify problems with a view to solving them.
- Spot the optimal one among the many solutions.
- Anticipate the consequences of proposed changes—on business, technology, people, and the environment.
- Evaluate the business value of the proposed changes.
- Present change as an improvement and an opportunity for the development of the organization and individuals, not a threat.

It is worth noting that a business analyst doesn't only have a specific set of competencies. He should also be characterized by a certain mindset. Having competencies without the right mindset does not make us effective in business analysis. This mindset makes it possible to perceive reality in a defined way, to see connections between seemingly unrelated objects, to be able to analyze and draw conclusions based on incomplete information, regardless of the object of interest. A person with the mindset of a business analyst views the environment, especially business systems, holistically, so he or she can determine where to focus efforts and make improvements and changes to achieve the best results. He or she will substantively question the status quo, asking questions that no one has asked before—resulting in discovering ways to improve business system performance.

A person with the mindset of a business analyst will seek to make improvements on both professional and personal grounds. He or she will strive to discover the causes of problems, rather than focusing on proposing solutions without knowing the full context. A person with the mindset of a business analyst will ask questions that no one has asked before, which will make those around him or her think about the status quo, the meaningfulness of the tasks being performed, and opportunities for process and product improvements. A person with the mindset of a business analyst will not focus on problems, but on solutions.

The essence of the business analyst's mindset is brilliantly explained by Fabricio Laguna, known as the Brazilian BA (business analyst) (Laguna 2023):

> THE BUSINESS ANALYST MINDSET IS A DYNAMIC SET OF ATTITUDES, BEHAVIORS, BELIEFS, EMOTIONAL TENDENCIES, MENTAL MODELS AND VALUES THAT CONTINUALLY DRIVE BUSINESS IMPROVEMENTS.

Yulia Kosarenko, in turn, points to the critical importance of the human aspect in the business analysis area (Kosarenko 2019):

> THE BUSINESS ANALYST MINDSET IS ABOUT YOUR ABILITY TO DEAL WITH THE HUMAN ASPECTS OF A PROBLEM AND THE PEOPLE WHO MAY BE PART OF IT.

Without the right mindset, even knowledge of many techniques, tools, and specific subject matter competencies will not make a person effective in the field of business analysis.

1.2 What Does a Business Analyst Do? What Is His/Her Role?

What does a business analyst do?

A business analyst is a person involved in the execution of activities that are quite broad in scope. Business analysis encompasses both the strategic, conceptual aspect of determining the business problem and the business requirements relating to it, the design and implementation of a solution that delivers business value, and the evaluation of that solution after it is delivered. Performing the various tasks in these areas requires specific competencies and skills.

Various sources precisely define the basic responsibilities of a business analyst, but it is worth knowing that these responsibilities may vary depending on the company and its organizational structure, the requirements of a particular project, and whether individual arrangements are made within the team. As a rule, however, there is a set of certain activities typical of a business analyst's work. In the most general terms, the business analyst's job is to support stakeholders in identifying business needs and proposing solutions to meet those needs. This means that a business analyst may be involved in the following activities:

1. Analysis of the organization's operations, both internal analysis and external analysis, such as competitive analysis
2. Analysis of business objectives and the ability to meet those objectives, taking into account the organization's circumstances and external and internal constraints
3. Identification of business needs and business requirements, with related relevant information, such as business constraints, risks, and assumptions
4. Identification and analysis of stakeholders directly or indirectly involved in a given change initiative
5. Analysis of the feasibility of solving a given business problem, identifying potential solution proposals and analyzing the feasibility of individual proposals
6. Supporting prioritization of initiatives in terms of the business value delivered as a result—portfolio management
7. Defining the scope of the solution by an established method, for example, by developing a product or determining simple necessary changes in business processes or organizational structure
8. Supporting the production of the solution by communicating business information to the team
9. Evaluating the produced solution or parts of it in the case of iterative or incremental production
10. Supporting the smooth implementation of the solution into production, which may include providing training to end users
11. Analysis of the functioning solution to identify possible improvements

This is a fairly general list of tasks potentially performed by a business analyst. It's worth noting that not all tasks need to be performed by the analyst alone—on the contrary, they shouldn't be. Many of these tasks are business-critical, requiring informed decisions based on facts and juxtaposing the perspectives of different people, not just one business analyst.

Laura Brandenburg of Bridging the Gap explains the role of the business analyst in this way (Brandenburg 2009):

> Business analysts lead teams from the inside out. We create positive change for our organizations. We inspire others to follow us on our path toward positive change. We help everyone understand exactly what that change is and how they can contribute to it. We help teams discover what the change should be.

My definition of the role of a business analyst assumes that a person in the role of an analyst helps to obtain certain information through the use of appropriate methods and techniques, and supports stakeholders in identifying needs, communicating and making a joint decision about the problem and possible decisions. The analyst, on the other hand, does not have "God Mode"—he does not have the authority and decision-making power to decide on his own whether or not to implement a solution, does not decide on the company's strategy, does not decide on the course of action. At most, he can provide information that can help decision-makers make informed business decisions. In my opinion, the analyst's role is to support stakeholders by providing information and recommendations, which they can then use according to their needs.

A business analyst is a person who is able to see structure in chaos, evaluate facts, and draw conclusions based on information from different, often conflicting sources. He or she is a person who sees the organization as a constantly evolving system. A business analyst is capable of using information to determine what changes could make the system more efficient and attractive to the environment.

In different organizations and projects, a person in a business analyst position may be responsible for carrying out different activities. On the other hand, it is not necessary to call oneself a business analyst to perform tasks in the area of business analysis.

Business analyst tasks can be performed by people who hold positions seemingly unrelated to business analysis. For example, in agile teams, members of the development team may perform tasks related to requirements analysis and validation of business needs.

A tester performs some analytical activities, developing test cases and analyzing product risks.

A project manager performs some analytical activities, assessing the scope of the project to develop a schedule and budget.

Business analysis is such a broad discipline, encompassing a range of practices that are somewhat universal and can be used by people working in different fields, in different areas, in different positions, that at least some business analysis practices and tools should be familiar to people who are not in a business analyst position.

People involved in creating new business solutions, business development planning, and business strategies should have at least some competence in the area of business analysis. Certain business analysis practices and tools are used by managers, product owners, board members—in a word, all people involved in running a business.

Whether or not the name of the position I hold is "business analyst" seems less important than establishing the range of competencies required to successfully perform the tasks of a specific job or according to the role definition established by the team.

LET'S MOVE AWAY FROM DEFINING ROLES. LET'S FOCUS ON RESPONSIBILITIES.
RAINER GRAU

> On every successful project you'll find a business analyst. Their title might be director of technology, product owner, product manager, requirements analyst, business process engineer, VP of operations, development lead, team lead, project manager, or CTO. The title is rather irrelevant. The activities of creating alignment around a clear understanding of 'done' that creates positive change is what it means to be a business analyst. (Brandenburg 2009)
>
> *Laura Brandenburg, Bridging the Gap*

Of course, the definition of business analysis itself implies that people performing tasks in this area are able to perform certain activities and have certain competencies. This allows us to create a definition of the standard responsibilities of a business analyst. However, it is important to note that depending on the needs of a particular organization or initiative, this basic scope of responsibility can be expanded or reduced.

Based on recognized sources such as the *BABOK® Guide* (IIBA® 2015), we can therefore define a certain range of responsibilities for a typical business analyst. On the other hand, we can define a list of things that a business analyst should definitely not handle. Among such "out of scope" tasks we can highlight:

1. *Micromanaging* and assigning individual tiny tasks to team members. The analyst is not a person who acts as a task distributor. This is, unfortunately, a problem that arises in many projects styled as agile (Agile) projects. People working in supposedly "agile" projects need to be micromanaged, assigned specific tasks with all the details necessary to develop software design and code, in order to be able to complete the work. This is not the analyst's job. The analyst determines what needs to be done, and the development team determines how to do it—other competencies are needed to carry out this work, which is one aspect that justifies the need to separate the business area from the technology area.
2. *Documenting* every piece of information that comes along, regardless of its criticality and relevance. Unfortunately, this is a trait of novice analysts who fail to prioritize. They spend long hours on discussions that contribute nothing to the business, or they create fat volumes of documentation that no one will ever use anyway, because it is simply worthless from the point of view of the audience's needs.
3. Determining *technical details* and implementation. The business analyst basically works at the level of the business layer, answering the question of what we want to achieve. The business analyst does not go into the details of implementation, technology, or solutions, and does not answer the questions of the technical solutions with which we intend to achieve the desired results. This is the job of those with technical competence. Of course, there are exceptions to this rule. If we determine in a given organization or project that the business analyst is actually a business analyst with competencies as an architect, designer, or system analyst, the responsibilities can be tailored to the specific need.

4. *Project management.* Project management, understood as defining the budget and schedule, is the typical task of a project manager. Of course, the business analyst contributes to this task—in some circumstances, he or she may even perform it independently, relying on information provided by team members. However, this is an extension of the business analyst's primary responsibility and one should be aware of it.

The role and responsibilities of a business analyst are relatively broad. Depending on the needs of a particular organization, the business analyst's responsibilities can be tailored to meet specific needs, but it is important not to cross the line beyond which the analyst ceases to be an analyst and becomes a project manager or member of the technical team. While crossing this boundary may seem sensible and tempting from a project perspective, it is important to keep in mind that doing so can introduce unnecessary conflicts of interest and negatively impact the analyst's ability to do his or her job effectively, making it difficult to maintain the appropriate distance needed to effectively execute the business analysis and work effectively.

Moreover, unconscious and unchecked expansion of the business analyst's responsibilities can lead to a situation in which management, stakeholders, and team members expect a person in the business analyst role to have competencies that in reality should belong to several team members. As a result, we ourselves create unrealistic expectations that we will not be able to meet. Therefore, even if we agree to expand our scope of responsibility, let's communicate clearly and explicitly that the task we accept goes beyond the standard area of business analysis.

1.3 Business Analysis: IT Only?

The concept of business analysis is quite strongly associated with the IT environment. There is a reason for this—business analysis as a practice has evolved and gained a place in the public's consciousness with the development of information technology. The publicly available source of the genesis of the term business analysis sees it in the 1940s, with the running of the first computers (Hermes 2014). In the 1990s there was a significant development in this field. With the spread of IT solutions, the development of technology, and a kind of revolution in access to IT services, software solutions began to be used by normal citizens, students, lecturers, ordinary people carrying out the tasks of everyday life.

With the spread of technology in almost every area of life and business, there was a need to organize the practices by which business needs could be understood and transformed into technological solutions. This field was called business analysis. Many of the tools and techniques described in business analysis are those associated primarily with the software development industry (such as data flow diagrams, interface analysis, sequence diagrams, and user interface prototyping as presented in one of the better-known sources of business analysis information, the *BABOK® Guide*).

However, it is worth realizing that the very practices of business analysis, the competencies and mindset characteristic of analysts, are domain-independent, universal—they apply to all areas of business and life. Business analysis can be applied not only to software production or other technological solutions. Many of the practices and tools of business analysis provide invaluable support in planning your own business, organizing your time, including leisure time, and supporting professional tasks.

If you are planning to start your own business, for example, to provide training services, you will most likely intuitively start by analyzing the market, checking your competitors' offerings, identifying the needs of potential customers, and finally, creating a training offer that will give you any chance of success in the market. You will most likely use business analysis methods and tools without even realizing it.

If you want to plan a birthday party for a child, you will probably start in a similar way—from understanding what might appeal to children of a certain age, determining the desired number of guests and their preferences, restrictions such as food allergies, contacting the parents to make the necessary arrangements. You will carry out an analysis of possible solutions—starting with organizing the party in your own home, and renting a venue with the ability to accommodate a certain number of guests. You'll estimate the costs of this endeavor, consider the risks, and, as a result, develop a plan based on the remaining information.

If you have a day off from work, you think about how to spend it productively. You'll probably develop in your mind a list of things you could potentially do, determine which of them are attractive, valuable, desirable to you, which of them are feasible given the circumstances (e.g., walking during a thunderstorm might not be a very good idea). Finally, you will choose a solution that meets your needs and capabilities.

The above examples show the application of business analysis practices in areas completely unrelated to technology. The discipline of business analysis is so beautiful because it is versatile—it fits into different contexts, it is useful for solving different problems not necessarily related to technology, and it helps to come to meaningful conclusions and develop solutions to problems, regardless of what those problems are.

Any person who wants to make informed decisions and be able to predict the consequences of those decisions will benefit from having knowledge of business analysis practices and tools.

Any person who is involved in running a business in any way should have at least basic analytical competence.

Any person who leads an organization should have the mindset of a business analyst.

Any person who wants to make decisions based on information rather than guesswork or gut feeling should take an interest in the area of business analysis.

1.4 Problems with Analysis

Among other things, the idea for this publication was born out of discussions with people involved in business analysis and working with analysts. As a result of these discussions and observations, a whole series of typical problems related to the implementation of business analysis emerged.

The concept of business analysis has been around for at least several decades. There are plenty of sources of knowledge on the subject, including training courses, postgraduate programs, and publications. However, despite the availability of knowledge, similar mistakes continue to be reproduced. It also appears that those in the role of business analyst still lack certain key competencies. Here is a subjective list of identified problems.

1. *Lack of analytical skills.* This is one of the critical problems—if we would like to perform business analysis tasks properly, to deliver solutions that bring value, we need to be able to think analytically. This means, among other things, the ability to decompose a problem, to think in terms of cause and effect, to see the organization as a system of interrelated elements. Lacking this skill, we very often focus on a slice of reality, completely ignoring its surroundings. As a result, the developed solution either fails to deliver real business value—the reason for which may be that a business need has been poorly identified, for example—or it may be ineffective—because it does not take into account the conditions of the organization or its area.
2. *Focusing on solutions* rather than on the need and problems. In my opinion, this is the aftermath of a lack of analytical thinking skills. If we can't see the source of the problem and get to the real root cause, we will focus on the solution rather than the real need. As a result, instead of thinking about the business problem, its impact on the organization as an ecosystem, and possible solutions—not only technological, but also process or organizational—we will focus on developing a solution. As a result, we may miss the fact that the solution does not solve the business need at all, or solves it but at too high a cost. The means will obscure our goal.
3. *Lack of relationship-building skills*. This problem was pointed out by Piotr Biernacki, among others. A large part of a business analyst's job is working with people—getting information, synthesizing information, agreeing on solution options, explaining benefits—everywhere we interact with people. Without the ability to build relationships, we can't build engagement either. Without engagement, stakeholders will not feel the need to support change initiatives. It is not enough to communicate effectively. It's not enough to work with someone to be able to build a relationship with that person that enables effective and enjoyable cooperation. To paraphrase an expert statement: "If you don't like people and working with them, choose a direction other than business analysis."

4. *Pride and lack of humility.* Another critical problem flagged by people in management positions often stems from a belief in one's own infallibility, an exaggerated notion of one's role and the responsibilities that come with it. The analyst's role is primarily to support change initiatives. This includes working with people, supporting them in identifying needs and making decisions. The analyst does not design change, set strategy, or decide on solutions—the analyst supports others in achieving these goals. This means listening to others' opinions, even if they contradict our own, and accepting that we do not have full knowledge of the organization, its context, and may be wrong. Our ideas and suggestions are not necessarily right—our role is not to push our ideas, but to develop solutions that will benefit the organization and its stakeholders. We won't develop these solutions ourselves; we need the cooperation and involvement of others to do so. Hence, a lack of humility goes hand in hand with a lack of relationship-building skills.
5. *Lack of ability to express information accurately.* An example would be requirements documentation that does not meet basic quality criteria. Another example could be defining business needs that are not specific; the expected results of the change and the rationale for the need are not known. To quote the words of Tom Gilb, "Some requirements are not requirements but poetry." A requirement should provide information about the purpose we intend to achieve with it. If there is no delivered business value from the requirement statement, then such information does not meet the conditions for being a "requirement."

A business analyst should be very deliberate in his use of words—because every word can have a critical meaning in a given context. Lack of precision may be due to lack of ability to formulate sentences precisely, lack of ability to quantify information, or lack of knowledge or lack of standards. In the area of business analysis, there is no single standard that provides a template to support requirements specification, for example. As a result, in almost every organization, each analyst uses his or her own approach to accomplish the task.

For some reason, methods that enable precise expression of information, such as modeling languages and notations, based on quantifiers in requirements specification templates, are seen as relics of the past, not applicable in the current world.

In the pursuit of quick results, we rely on less formal ways of communicating, often neglecting the written form of communication, assuming that direct communication is enough. The problem with direct communication is that it is ephemeral—today we understand each other; tomorrow we may have a different interpretation of a discussion just concluded. Moreover, verbal communication is impossible for us to validate, check, review. As a result, we lose the precision of the message and this leads to a situation where the individual activities of the change initiative are carried out not on the basis of precise specifications, but on the basis of general agreements.

6. *Lack of ability to see the organization holistically*. A business analyst looks at an organization as a system—a collection of elements that are interrelated and serve to achieve a goal. When considering a system, he or she must be aware that a change in one parameter of a specific system element affects the entire system. Making changes without analyzing their impact on the rest of the environment can lead to improvement of one part of the organization while introducing chaos in others. Stefan Bossuwe, among others, points this out—"a holistic mindset should be part of an analyst's DNA."

   Even if our role boils down to coming up with a solution to a specific problem, we need to be able to step back and look at the problem and its environment. We need to see the Big Picture—regardless of the scope of the issue we are dealing with. For this reason, the first stage of the analysis should be a kind of audit—through which we have a chance to see how the organization works, its context, to get to know the organization as a business system.
7. *Lack of ability to manage expectations*. This is a problem that Ewelina Eggert, among others, points out, citing her years of experience. Too often we make assumptions: that our work plan is clear to team members, that our thinking is the same as that of stakeholders, and that the business analysis process is known to stakeholders. We don't manage expectations properly, which very often results in frustration, misunderstandings, and conflicts. We promise stakeholders to deliver solutions without checking current capabilities and constraints, which builds expectations that we are unable to meet. We plan a meeting and expect stakeholders to guess at the course and anticipated results of that meeting, and if the actual results obtained do not meet their expectations, we often blame the stakeholders, not errors in our approach. One of the key success factors in implementing any initiatives is effective expectations management, which starts with identifying the expectations of individual stakeholders, then assessing the possibility of meeting those expectations and identifying viable options.
8. *Lack of reflection*. This is another significant problem highlighted by many experts. We enter a project and begin to implement the planned tasks. We focus our efforts on providing the output to the production team as quickly as possible, to provide a solution. We don't ask questions about whether this solution is the right one, whether it is based on sensible assumptions, whether these assumptions are still valid. We take the status quo for granted, we don't challenge the status quo, we don't ask questions because we fear they will be trivial and undermine our credibility and professionalism. As a result, we very often focus on the wrong aspects, desperately trying to provide a solution, not recognizing that this solution does not add any value. As Michal Bartyzel notes, business analysts often focus on their area of responsibility, failing to see the correlation between the current state and decisions made in the past. They often don't think about how to deliver real business value, but how to do their jobs.
9. *Form over substance*. We fail to select the right methods and tools for specific goals and needs. We focus on tool issues, not on meeting real stakeholder needs. As a result, we create complicated models, elaborate documentation that, instead of helping us solve a business problem efficiently, only generates often unnecessary costs. This problem

often stems from the fact that we simply fail to listen—stakeholders try to explain to us the essence of a given problem, what they really care about, but we, convinced of our own infallibility, know better. As a result, we fail to prioritize information properly, to focus on the aspects that really matter—instead, we generate huge amounts of data, often packaged in a visually pretty form to give the impression of professionalism. This problem also applies to the solutions we develop—unfortunately, we relatively often devote enormous resources to developing a solution that provides a plethora of functions and capabilities, a solution that no one uses because it doesn't solve a real business problem. Mariusz Nagięć aptly summed it up: "Down-to-earth customer interest and real user needs over complex models that no one understands and fancy software that no one will use."

This publication is intended to provide some assistance in eliminating some of these problems and developing competence. The publication is not an exhaustive compendium of knowledge in the area of business analysis, but it provides tips and thoughts on selected aspects and practices so that we can avoid making basic mistakes.

1.5 What Can I Learn From This Publication?

This publication contains thoughts, suggestions, practices, and conclusions from the practical experience of the author and experts who contributed to this book.

The book is not a comprehensive handbook in the area of business analysis. You will not find here basic definitions and descriptions of individual activities—these aspects are described in sufficient detail in other sources.

The book does not cover the entire area of business analysis—the identification of business needs, the development of the solution concept, the design of the solution—because then its volume would be several times larger.

In selecting the material for this publication, I was guided primarily by priority, which is based on the popularity of the topic and the frequency of problems in the area. Interestingly, many of the issues raised initially seemed to me to be too trivial to be a valuable part of the publication. However, in talking with experts, I realized that very often we make mistakes in areas that are considered standard, obvious—we don't perform basic practices, we don't take into account obvious impact factors, we skip tasks that seem obvious to us, we miss the big picture, and we focus on the details. As a result, we make mistakes at the very beginning of the initiative. Hence, the publication includes issues that may seem obvious—but as practice shows, in many cases, as obvious as we think they are, they are not at all.

I think this could be a pretty good keynote of this publication. If we want to build advanced solutions, and support organizations to grow and build competitive advantage, first of all, we need to make sure that we have done a kind of grassroots work.

If we want to build an organization's strategy, change reality, provide innovative solutions, we need to remember that the first step is to properly identify the need, assess it, express expectations in a measurable and precise way, recognize the context of change, understand the organization as an ecosystem of complex interrelated elements. Without this—without this foundation—the entire initiative of implementing business change will most likely collapse like a house of cards.

1.6 Conceptual Model

This publication addresses a number of issues. These are related to certain concepts found in the field of business analysis and related areas.

The business motivation model developed by Object Management Group (OMG) organizes the concepts used at the strategic level (Fig. 1.1).

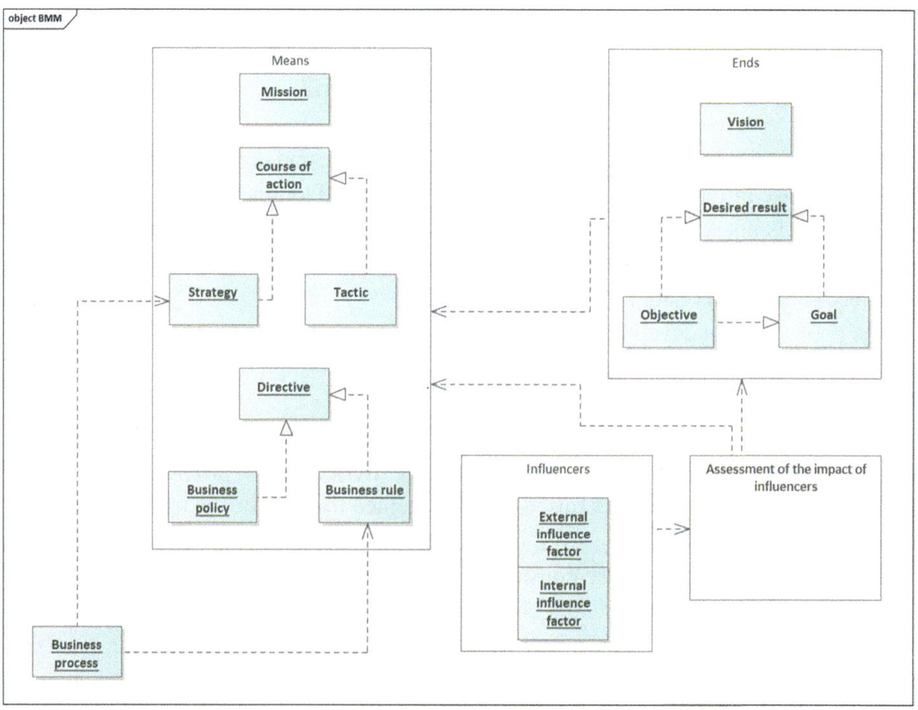

Fig. 1.1 Business motivation model—general concept (own elaboration based on OMG 2015). © 2015, OMG

Definitions and a thorough explanation of the meaning of these terms are provided in the BMM standard (OMG 2015).

Understanding the strategic domain is important to properly identify business needs. The crux of business analysis is to identify business needs and develop a solution for them that delivers value. To do this, we again operate on a number of different concepts, interrelated in different ways (Fig. 1.2).

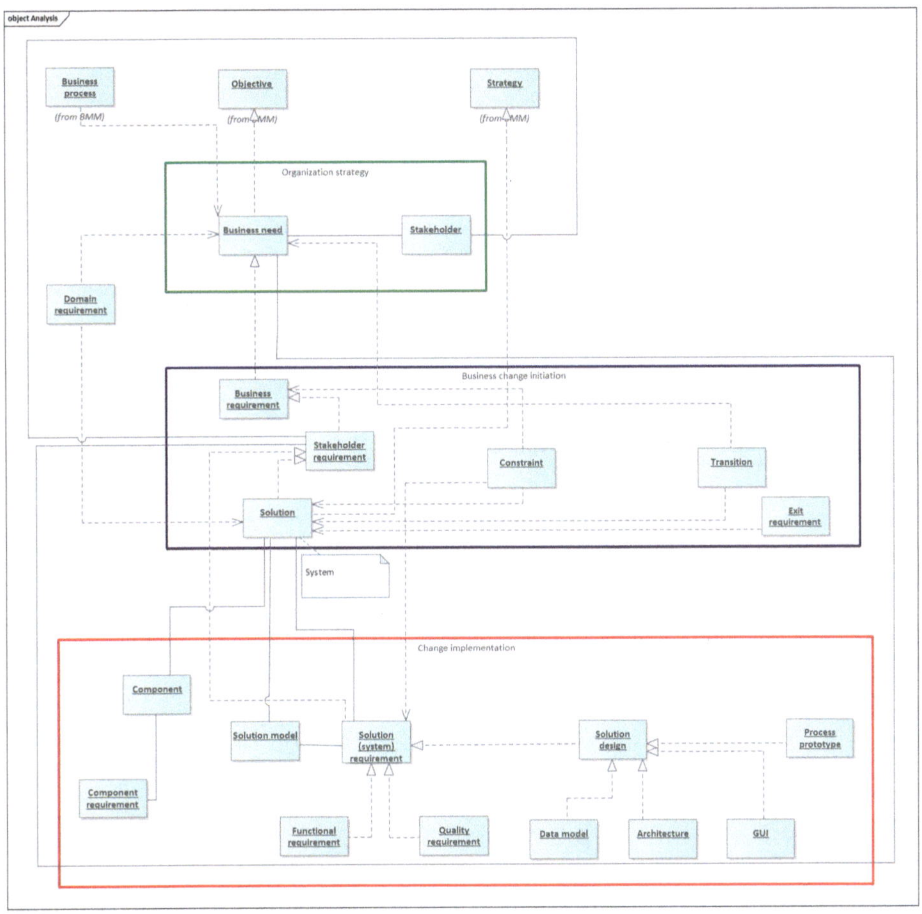

Fig. 1.2 A general metamodel of the main concepts used in business analysis

A particular concept found in many levels of business analysis is requirements. We can distinguish different types and kinds of requirements that describe information at different levels of abstraction. Regardless of the type, requirements should be characterized by certain quantifiers to ensure their measurability (Fig. 1.3).

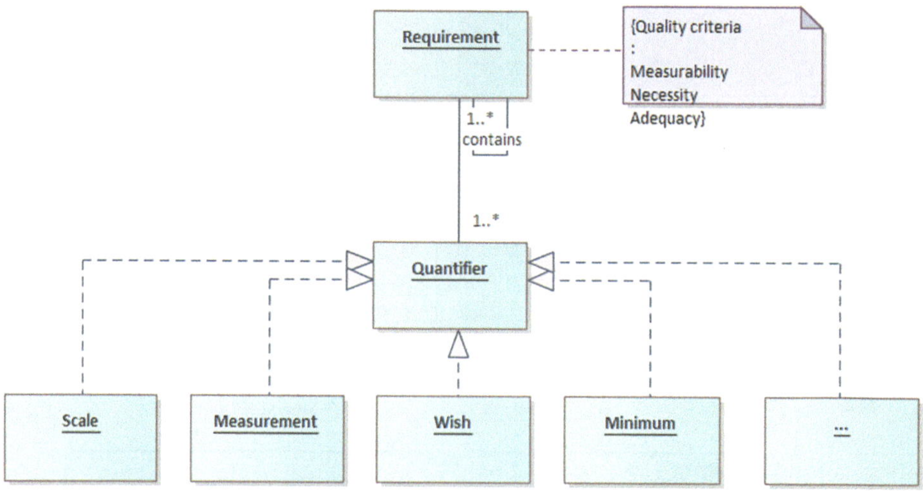

Fig. 1.3 General metamodel of a requirement

2 Strategy Analysis

PROBLEM, NEED, SOLUTION, STRATEGY. THESE ARE THE KEY ELEMENTS OF STRATEGY ANALYSIS.

STRATEGY ANALYSIS ENABLES US TO SET A STRATEGY FOR IMPLEMENTING SOLUTIONS TO ACHIEVE BUSINESS GOALS.

What is strategy? In the simplest terms, it is a way of using an organization's resources to achieve defined business goals. As explained in the *BABOK® Guide* (IIBA® 2015), strategies can apply to a specific project, product, organizational department, or region.

What is strategy analysis?

According to the *BABOK® Guide*, it is an area of knowledge that defines the business analysis work that needs to be done to "work with stakeholders to identify needs of strategic or tactical importance" (IIBA® 2015; Weese and Terri 2000).

Strategy analysis is an area of business analysis that focuses on understanding the business problems and resulting needs that are critical to the continued effectiveness of an organization's operations. It is a fairly key component of business analysis because it provides the context for a specific change initiative. This context represents knowledge of the organization's current operations, its environment, its stakeholders, especially customers, challenges, and problems the organization faces.

The starting point for a strategy analysis is usually an identified business need or business problem. In other words, an organization has identified a problem to be solved or an opportunity to be addressed. The identification of a business need triggers the strategy analysis process, allowing us to understand the relevance of that need to the organization, the impact of potential changes, possible solutions, and associated constraints and risks.

From the perspective of development projects, strategy analysis provides the context for eliciting and analyzing requirements and defining a solution for a given change—it provides information about the reason and rationale for the change, so that we are able to

K. Zmitrowicz, *Business Analysis Done Right*,
https://doi.org/10.1007/978-3-031-62194-9_2

select the right solution, that is, one that will optimally ensure the fulfillment of specific business needs in a given organizational and technical context.

At what point does strategy analysis begin? It can start when a business need is defined. For example, a new competitor appears in the organization's environment offering similar products, but which are far better rated by customers. At this point, we can identify a business need regarding the need to look at our offerings relative to the competition and possibly improve the level of quality of the products provided. To address this need, we should know:

- How we create our products and what are the quality assumptions made for the products.
- How are the products delivered to customers? A lower customer satisfaction rate is not necessarily related to the quality of the products themselves; it can be caused by problems in the delivery of products to the customer.
- What are the expectations of the target group and how are they currently being met by our organization?
- How are customers' needs being met by the competition? What in the competitors' offerings is better than ours? What can we do better to retain existing customers and attract new ones?

These are just a few examples of issues that may interest us at the strategy analysis stage. The activities usually performed at this stage can be classified as:

1. *Analysis of the current state of the organization*, including analysis of the external environment, study of the way the organization operates, and identification of internal and external stakeholders. As a result of the current state analysis, we are able to identify problems and areas for improvement, which in effect allows us to define business requirements. This is a kind of inventory of knowledge about the current way the organization operates.
2. *Analysis of the target state*, in other words, defining how we would like to operate, given the identified business requirements. The changes that need to be implemented in processes, in the organizational structure, any other aspect of the company's operations, in order to achieve the expected results. External factors that may significantly affect our definition of the target state should also be considered at this stage. The analysis of the target state may include an analysis of the risks that may affect the approaches and scope of the solution to make the organization function more effectively.
3. *Determining the change and its implementation strategy*. Once the target state and risk analysis have been established, possible solution approaches and the scope of the solution itself should be identified. Approaches to the solution may include changing the organizational structure, streamlining processes, developing a technical solution, or introducing new services or products. The scope of the solution results from the business requirements identified at the current state analysis stage, identified as the difference between the target state and the current state, and the risk analysis.

It is worth noting that strategic analysis is not a one-time step in the life cycle of an organization. This practice is repeated every time a new business need arises. This is pointed out by Anna Kochanowska, Business Analyst & Product Thinking Advocate, among others:

> Strategy analysis is not a one-time task, it is an ongoing process. Strategy analysis strengthens the feedback loops, so that the strategy is built continuously and coherently, based on experiences, lessons and conclusions. The task of strategy analysis is to provide these lessons, conclusions from different sides.

Anna Kochanowska points out another aspect that is often misunderstood and causes a number of misunderstandings: "there are many dimensions of strategy analysis, but it does not take place at the 'strategic level'—this is a misleading and rather abstract term." Strategy analysis as defined in the *BABOK® Guide* is not about setting directions for the entire organization. It is not about shaping business service strategies or product strategies. Strategy analysis focuses on developing a strategy for implementing a solution to a specific business need. Of course, developing an effective change strategy requires coordinating that change with other areas and directions of the organization—but this is not usually strategy shaping at the organizational level.

In my opinion, strategy analysis should start from understanding the context. Why? If you want to understand a system well, you need to know its context. An organization is nothing more than a business system. It operates in a certain environment—external and internal—which explains the rules of its operation and is a source of influencing factors. So context analysis is one of the crucial steps in understanding business needs and defining the change needed.

2.1 Context of Organization

2.1.1 To Speak the Same Language: Establish a Dictionary

> Communication is the exchange of information by means of contractual symbols. If you do not define the meaning of certain symbols, there will be no understanding.

Where do we start with an analysis aimed at understanding the functioning of a given organization? How do we begin a project that is expected to result in developing a solution to an identified business need? Can we start by establishing the basics of communication?

Whatever goals we set for the business analysis, we will have to communicate with many people, process huge amounts of information to draw meaningful conclusions, and be able to propose next steps toward solving the problem at hand. We will have to acquire information, interpret that information, process it, and communicate it to others. Without a standard of communication, it is difficult to count on the success of such an endeavor. One of the pillars of effective communication is a dictionary.

A dictionary, a glossary, is a work product familiar to all those involved in the field of project management. It is a tool with which we can explain the meaning of business terms, technical terms, terminology specific to a particular field, abbreviations used in a particular organization, words that we use every day, but in a particular company have their own specific meaning.

Developing a dictionary is such a basic, obvious task that in many cases it is completely overlooked; precisely because it is seemingly so trivial, we neglect it. We make the assumption that since we communicate in the same language, in the same business area, with people representing a more or less equal level of knowledge, we don't need a dictionary.

As a result, we may fail right from the start—making unsuccessful attempts to interpret acquired information according to our own state of knowledge, trying to communicate with stakeholders using our own vocabulary, trying to convince others to take certain actions or decisions with words that do not convince them because they are not the right words.

Many project failures and problems are often due precisely to the neglect of these basic practices, the abandonment of doing seemingly trivial and obvious things. And developing, or rather working out, a vocabulary is one such activity.

We may assume that our vocabulary and the vocabulary of our stakeholders are no different—and sooner or later we will find out that we were wrong. We may assume that the business nomenclature in a given area is the same everywhere—and we will also suffer the consequences of this assumption at some point. When starting analytical work in a given organization or project, starting any work in an environment that is unfamiliar to us, let's make sure at the very beginning that we speak the same language. You may find that misunderstandings arise over the simplest words—such as the words customer, process, product, operation, or system. Each stakeholder or each group of stakeholders in the organization may interpret these words in their own way, based on the specific activities performed, experience, or knowledge of the subject. Often organizations have their own terminology, incompatible with the "standard" nomenclature.

I will cite an actual example of using one's own interpretation for a term widely known in the IT industry.

An organization providing solutions to the automotive industry uses the concept of a user story during development projects. This concept is well known to those working in agile projects and is used to capture information about requirements, usually functional (although there is no rule), from the point of view of a specific user role. The form of the user story is strictly defined:

As [role] I want [description of need], in order to [justification].

When establishing cooperation with this company, the first thing I asked for was the opportunity to learn about the organization's product design and manufacturing processes. An analysis of the current state—the way the process is implemented, the form and content of the artifacts being developed—showed that the user story functioning in this particular organization has nothing in common with the user story known from agile projects. Indeed, artifacts classified as user stories described the operation of the system at the level of software components. An example of such a story would be the initialization of a software update when a USB drive is placed in a port.

There is no agreement on the user's role here, and no mention of the business case for this requirement. With the user story known by Mike Cohn's definition, this had nothing to do with it. So why the idea to call these objects user stories? The answer to this question turned out to be surprisingly simple—the company was simply using software that allows the creation of objects called stories. Their "stories" referred to software requirements created using this software.

We clarified this issue at the very beginning of the work implementation. And thanks to this, at later stages I was aware that when we talked about a user's story, we did not mean requirements representing specific needs of stakeholders, including users—we meant a description of software requirements.

What could be the consequences of not clarifying this situation at the beginning? For example, such that without knowing what we are really talking about, at the moments when the team mentions user stories, I could assume that we will be specifying requirements at the stakeholder level. In the case of this particular project, this would completely miss the point, since the stakeholder requirements were already obtained—the company was responsible for developing the software based on predetermined requirements.

Examples of such misunderstandings and differences in interpretation of terms can be multiplied. It may turn out that we interpret the concept of a system differently—which happens very often, by the way. Many people, hearing the word "system," implicitly add "information system" and assume that we are talking about software. And yet a system is a much broader concept—it is a collection of components and elements that carry out a specific purpose. Without establishing a common, agreed upon nomenclature among project participants, we ourselves generate a powerful project risk. The effects can be manifold:

- Making wrong decisions based on misinterpreted information
- Wasting resources on developing documentation of pleasing work results that do not meet the expectations of the audience, who expect something completely different
- Making wrong assumptions leading to the implementation and deployment of a solution that does not solve the real problem at all
- Frustration and loss of trust among stakeholders resulting from communication problems, difficulties in understanding each other, the need to return to topics already discussed.

So what can we do?

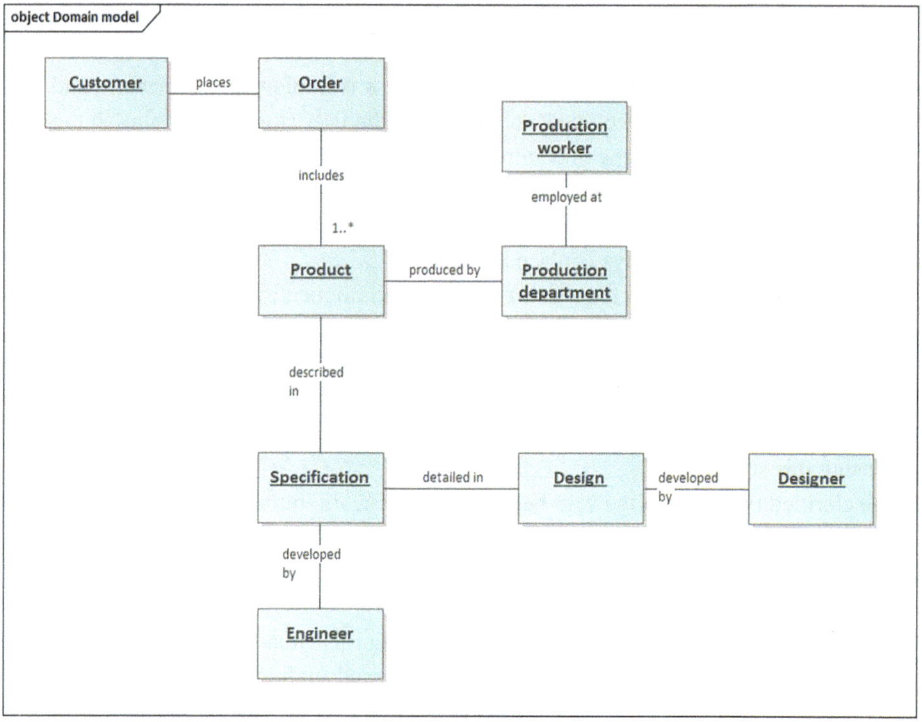

Fig. 2.1 Excerpt from a simple conceptual model (domain diagram)

Develop a dictionary—just that and so much more. It doesn't have to be a comprehensive text document. Sometimes a conceptual model (also called a domain model) is enough, through which we are able to understand what business concepts within an organization we are talking about, and how they are related to each other (Fig. 2.1).

I recommend the practice of trying to understand and organize the functioning of an organization using single words before going into deep analysis.

For example, if we are talking about a company that provides corporate customers with various types of products and services to service those products, we know that our conceptual model should include the following terms: corporate customer, target market, product (this concept can be decomposed into types of products, as there will likely be different types of products depending on the type of customer or market), and service. Identifying these terms as key to understanding a company leads to further conclusions and a concomitant deeper analysis: since a company produces certain goods and delivers them to customers, we need certain processes to do so. And these processes need to be named. Processes are performed by specific people in specific departments of the organization—this too needs to be named. To produce and execute other processes, we need specific resources, specific information—name them. Otherwise, we won't know how the organization delivers value to customers.

In this way, we can develop an initial vocabulary, a domain model, so that we know in which area of interest we are moving. Each of these terms needs to be defined, as each can be interpreted differently by each stakeholder. For example, to a production worker, the word "product" may be synonymous with an intermediate product, a final product, a product component, while to a sales or marketing representative, "product" is a complete commodity prepared for use by the customer, including instructions for use, warranty cards, etc. Such doubts—crucial in understanding the essence of business needs, the impact of changes, and defining the scope of a potential solution—should be clarified at the beginning of the project, not during the work.

2.1.2 Understand the Organization's Environment

Every system operates in a certain environment. If you don't understand the environment, you won't understand the system.

An organization does not operate in a vacuum. It operates in a certain context—the environment. Understanding this environment is essential to understanding the conditions in which the organization operates, including the constraints and specific factors affecting the business. Planning a solution for any business need requires an understanding of these conditions.

Let's consider an example.

An organization sells handicrafts produced by local artists. Currently, sales are stationary, carried out through two outlets located in one region. There is a demand for this type of product in the market, as evidenced by sales statistics. In addition, the organization is receiving signals from the market that customers from outside the region and even outside the country are interested in purchasing items.

The organization's business goals include increasing the market, that is, selling its products not only in the regional market, but nationally and perhaps even globally. A business need has been identified to open new sales channels and a second need to increase production.

Without knowing the organization's environment, it would be difficult to talk about any sound strategy analysis and develop a solution that will actually deliver value. This is because the following information would be missing:

- How many artists does the organization currently work with, and how many artists would be interested in collaborating?
- How does the process of producing and selling goods currently work—does the artist create a product and then inform our organization of its availability? Or does the organization place specific orders and the artist fulfills them?
- Is it possible to make a special order for customers? What would the lead time be?

- What products would be attractive in markets where the organization does not currently have a presence?
- Does the organization have partners who could support in the distribution of goods?
- Does the organization currently have any means of marketing and electronic sales? Given the nature of the products being sold and the fact that it is not mass production, would online store-type solutions make sense? Are there any special risks associated with shipping handicrafts?

The elements of the organization's context are:

- Partners and suppliers
- Business processes
- Stakeholders
- Market segment
- Market trends
- Technology
- Information
- Constraints, such as standards and regulations

The environment of an organization can be presented in graphical form. An example of a simple context diagram for a manufacturing company is shown in Fig. 2.2. Figure 2.3, on the other hand, shows a simplified map of the processes carried out in a specific department of the organization. The context diagram provides an understanding of the company's environment; the process map, on the other hand, shows the general business functions carried out within a specific department of the organization.

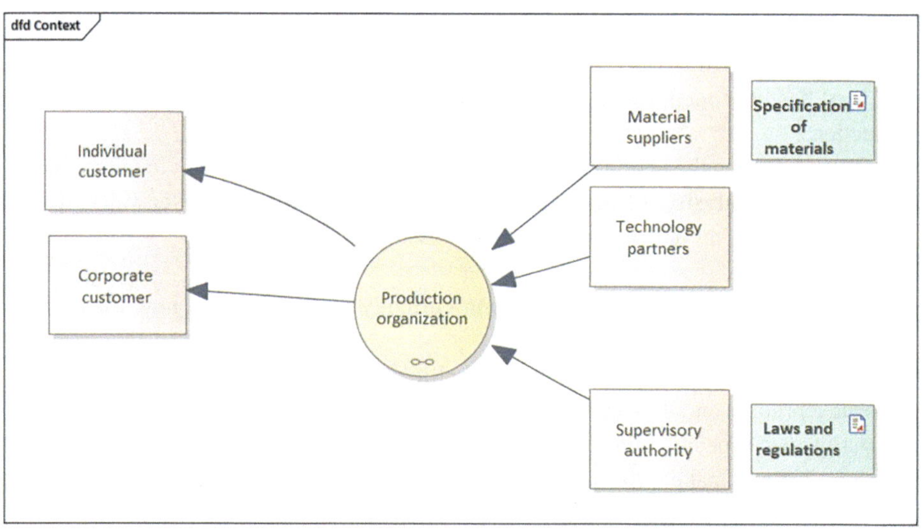

Fig. 2.2 Simple model of the organization's context

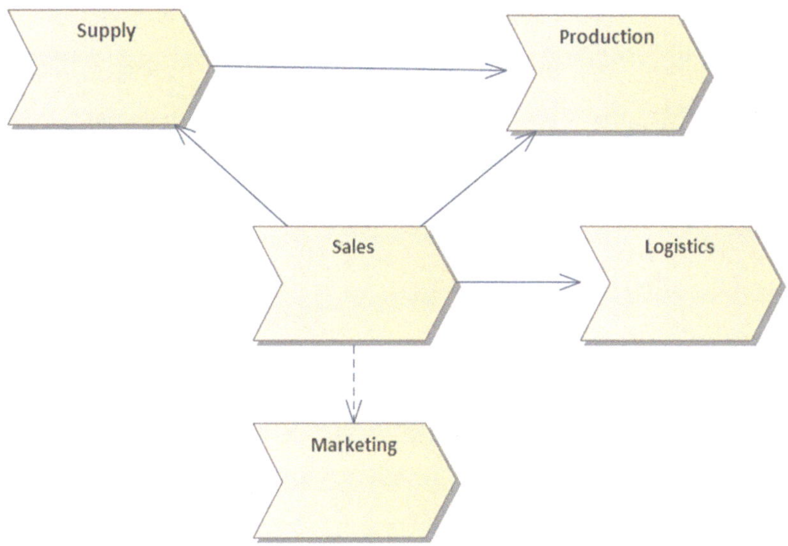

Fig. 2.3 Simplified map of processes carried out in a specific department of the organization

2.1.3 Business Motivation Model and Strategy Analysis

The functioning of the organization is driven by the Business Motivation Model. If you don't understand this model, you don't know what changes will deliver business value.

The primary goal of business analysis is to make changes that will bring value to the business. In order to be able to propose changes that will actually bring value, it is necessary to understand the basic motivations of the organization's operations, such as the vision, mission, and goals, and the way the business is implemented, that is, among other things, the strategy. A number of different factors influence an organization's operations, its ability, and the way it achieves its goals, so it is important to identify the influencing factors, both internal and external.

An excellent aid in analyzing an organization's business is the Business Motivation Model (BMM) developed by OMG (2015). A detailed specification of this model can be found in the standards document. For the purposes of this publication, I will quote a brief summary (Fig. 2.4).

A proper business motivation model consists of four concepts: ends, means, influencers, and assessments. Ends define what the organization wants to be in the future—an outcome can be, for example, a change in the services or products delivered to the market, the introduction of new products or services, as well as the maintenance of the current position given the company's external environment (especially the competition).

The specific elements of ends are vision and desired outcomes, which include business goals that are familiar to business analysts. Means are the actions the organization has taken to achieve its goals. Means are otherwise known as tools, the specific mechanisms

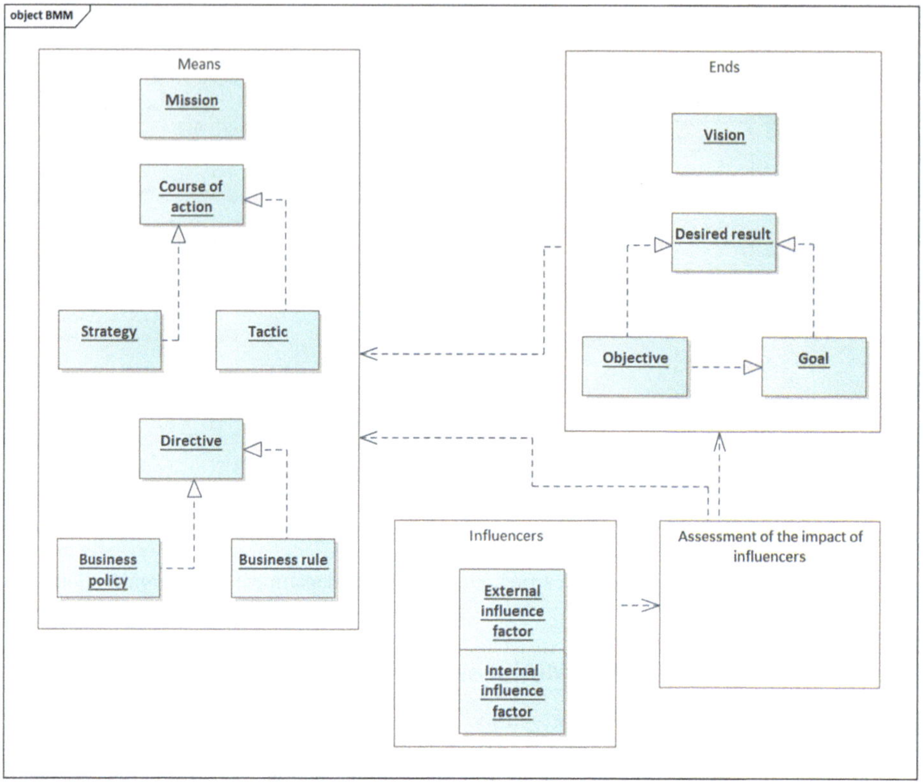

Fig. 2.4 Business Motivation Model—general concept © 2015, OMG (2015)

by which the organization intends to achieve the desired results. It is worth noting that in the BMM's interpretation, the means are not business processes, which define how specific activities are carried out to achieve specific goals. Business processes also include the definition of responsibility for the implementation of specific tasks. In the Business Motivation Model, measures include mission, course of action, and directives.

Influence factors affect the organization in a specific way—they can cause changes in the ability to achieve results or the use of resources. Influence factors can be external, coming from outside the organization's boundaries, and internal, if they affect the organization itself, its business assumptions, and the way it operates. It is worth noting that, according to the Business Motivation Model, impact factors are neutral, meaning that they function as facts. They are neither bad nor good—it is up to the organization how to respond to these factors and what decisions to make with knowledge of their existence.

The final element of the Business Motivation Model is assessment. Assessment is performed by specific individuals, with the goal of obtaining information about how specific influencers affect ends and means. Through evaluation, decision-makers can decide how to respond to influencers, and whether it is worth responding to them at all. An example of a tool that can be used for assessment is a Strengths, Weaknesses, Opportunities, and Threats (SWOT) analysis.

That would be a brief introduction to the Business Motivation Model according to OMG. How do you use the information in a business model to support strategy analysis?

Strategy analysis, as defined in the *BABOK® Guide*, includes several key practices: analysis of the current state, analysis of the target state, analysis of risks, and identification of strategies for change.

Analysis of the Current State ("AS IS")

Recall that the starting point of strategy analysis is a specific business need. The as-is analysis provides information on the organization's current way of doing things, its organizational structure, business context, and other considerations. The result of the current state analysis is business requirements, defining changes that bring value to the business. The Business Motivation Model can help analyze the current state as follows.

The ends and means identified as part of the Business Motivation Model indicate what the organization's goals are and what measures are provided to achieve those goals. This gives information about the current strategy and direction of the organization. When identifying business requirements, we should be aware of the strategy; otherwise, we may define changes that will not necessarily bring value to the business. Influence factors that are part of the Business Motivation Model will allow us to understand the organization's environment, both external and internal. They can represent both a source of risk and opportunity for the organization. Some of the impact factors can realistically affect the ability to meet business objectives. And since business requirements should enable the fulfillment of business objectives, this can have a significant impact on our definition of business requirements.

Target State Analysis ("TO BE")

The goal state analysis is to define how the organization is to operate—what processes and conditions need to be in place to achieve the fulfillment of specific business needs. The result of this activity is a description of the target state along with an indication of how business value will be delivered. The definition of the target state also involves an indication of the business objective, since any change made in the structure, operations, or principles of the organization should make it possible to meet the specified business objectives. How can the Business Motivation Model help us define the target state of the organization?

Ends indicate in which direction the organization is moving—so this is the starting information for developing the concept of the target state. Means, according to their current definition, are also input information, telling us what instruments and tools we have at our disposal at the moment. In the course of defining the target state, it may turn out that we need different measures than those currently available. Their provision may therefore be the extent of the potential solution. Influence factors are another input to the target state development process. For example, if we have identified an evolving technology as an impact factor, this fact should be taken into account in planning the target state. Technology can be part of the planned change.

In both the analysis of the current state and the target state, evaluation is important—because the results of the impact factor evaluation may determine the scope of the planned change.

Risk Analysis

When designing any organizational change, a risk analysis is necessary. Risks can arise both from the change itself and from operating in the target state of the organization. Examples of common risks associated with change include:

- Inability to accurately estimate the scope of the change to be implemented
- Resistance from stakeholders reluctant to change
- The need to make changes in multiple processes and business areas
- Volatility in the business environment, potentially rendering obsolete the business need that initiated the change initiative even before the implementation is completed.

An excellent source of risk in the Business Motivation Model is the influencers and the assessment of their impact on the ability to achieve business goals. It is also worth noting that risks from internal factors are controllable to some extent, while risks from external factors are often beyond the organization's control, such as changes in legislation.

Defining a Change Strategy

The primary purpose of defining a change strategy is to identify possible approaches to a change initiative, evaluate them, and then select a recommended approach. This includes clarifying the context for the change, derived from an analysis of the current and target state, and developing a change strategy with tools, assumptions, and expected results. The change strategy should include how it will be implemented, areas of impact on processes and stakeholders, as well as organizational aspects such as the team working on the change, time lines, etc.

The Business Motivation Model can be an input for developing assumptions about the change strategy. For example, the rules or business policies defined as elements in the Business Motivation Model represent certain constraints that should be taken into account when designing a change strategy approach.

Below is an example of how Business Motivation Model information can be used in the context of strategy analysis for a company whose core business is providing a sales platform.

Vision: To be the most recognized sales platform in the country.
Goals:
D1 Maintain high customer satisfaction.
D2 Offer high-quality customer support services.
D2 Offer high-quality products.
Objectives:
C1.D1 By the end of 2025, achieve a customer satisfaction rate of at least 4.5 on a scale of 5.
C2.D2 Within 6 months from today, provide a customer case resolution time of less than 5 min.
C3.D3 By the end of 2026, achieve an average product quality rating by customers of no less than 4.5 on a scale of 5.
Mission: Provide high-quality product sales services to individual and corporate customers in the domestic market.
Strategy (in various areas):
S1 Implement a customer and supplier relationship management system.
S2 Develop product offerings according to customer needs.
S3 Implement a quality management system.
Business rule: Withdraw the offer of suppliers whose products are rated below 4 on a scale of 5.
Business policy: Personally contact each customer who has made a complaint.

The above information can provide valuable insights for the business analyst.

For example, if a company aims to be the most recognized sales platform, any business changes under consideration should therefore be in line with this vision. Goals related to customer satisfaction and product quality, on the other hand, can give clues about areas for improvement, such as customer service processes.

The company's mission statement indicates target groups and may suggest the need to tailor offerings to individual and corporate customers. The company's strategy informs planned steps, such as implementing a customer relationship management system. This can be a starting point for an analysis to determine which areas of customer relationship management need improvement. Business rules and policies define how an organization should operate in certain areas, such as automatically withdrawing an offer from a substandard supplier.

A business incentive model is therefore an excellent source of information for a business analyst, enabling the identification of areas for analysis and potential improvements. In the absence of a predefined model, business analysis can begin by obtaining information about the organization's business motivation.

At the same time, it is worth noting that business motivation can change—the company operates in a changing environment that forces constant evolution. This evolution touches not only the goals, but also the vision of the organization itself.

2.1.4 Identify Products and Services

PRODUCTS AND SERVICES DELIVER KEY BUSINESS VALUE.

Every organization offers products and services to its consumers, regardless of whether it operates commercially for profit or nonprofit. A specific offering is directed to the market. If you are working on a strategy analysis of a company, trying to identify potential business problems and opportunities to solve them, an important part of this analysis is to understand the company's offerings.

In understanding the current state and identifying possible directions for change, it will be useful to get answers to the following questions:

- What products and services does the company produce?
- What market are these products or services aimed at?
- What are the characteristics of the target audience?

Understanding these aspects will allow us to determine how an organization delivers value to consumers. This is a key aspect of a company's business—the realization of its vision and mission. If we are thinking of making changes that amount to business value, we should focus first on analyzing the organization's operations and possible improvements.

Therefore, let's determine:

- For which audience or customer segment are products and services created? What needs do they meet? What benefits do they deliver?
- How are products and services delivered to the market, and how are they produced, advertised, and delivered to customers?
- How is feedback on the quality of these products and services collected? Is it collected at all? If not, this is likely to be one area to address and improve.
- Which products and services are critical to the operation of the organization, and which are ancillary?

It may be helpful to develop a visual map showing products, related services, distribution and marketing channels, and groups or segments of customers (Fig. 2.5). If it is within the scope of our analytical work to propose improvements to specific processes related to the realization or distribution of particular products, we will probably need to determine in what environment the product or service operates, what other products it is related to, what processes enable its manufacture and service, and what departments are involved in any

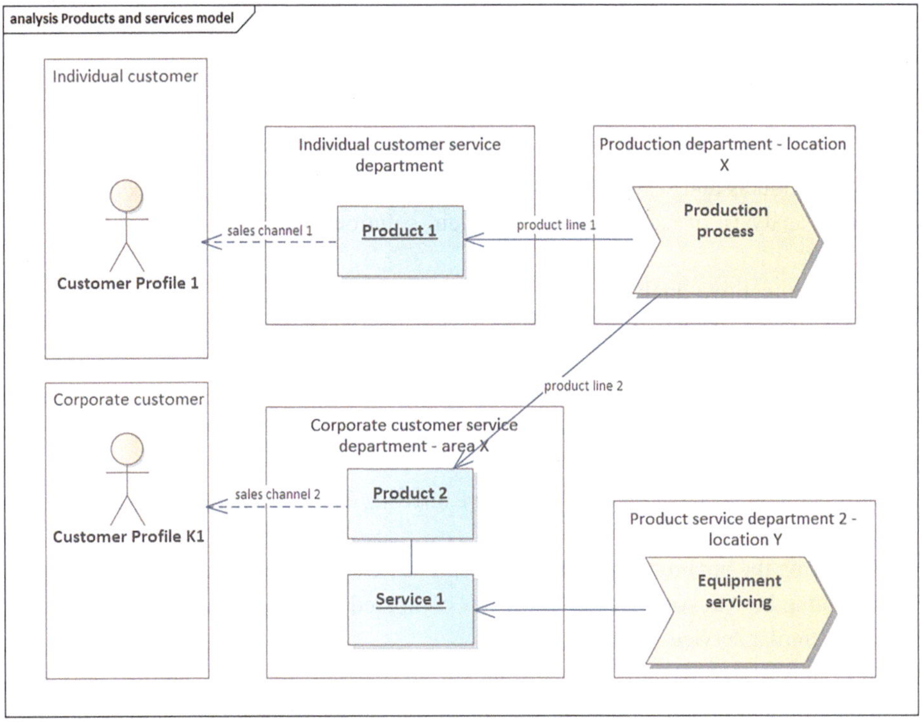

Fig. 2.5 Example of a simple product and service map

way in the creation and distribution of the product. This will enable us to determine the impact of the proposed changes.

An additional benefit of knowing what the organization offers is the ability to assess business needs. Identified business needs should be analyzed for priority and feasibility. Linking the business need to the organization's portfolio can help in performing such an assessment.

2.1.5 Learn About Your Competitors' Offerings

How can you provide a competitive advantage to the organization if you don't know what the competition is offering?

Organizations operate in a specific business environment. Its element is competition, an aspect all the more important because it is difficult today to find an area or branch of business in which there would be no competition. In order to maintain a competitive advantage and ensure the attractiveness of the business offer to consumers and customers, people involved in creating the organization's strategy should have knowledge of the competition and its offerings.

Having this knowledge allows us not only to assess how our products and services compare to the competition, but also to avoid mistakes made by the competition. In addition, it allows us to consciously shape our business offerings, drawing inspiration from observations of competitors and their customers.

If our task is to determine business needs, help shape the organization's strategy, introduce new products and services to the market, or develop a solution to specific business problems, analysis of competitors and their solutions can provide important input information.

A full competitive analysis, or market analysis in general, can be outsourced to an external company specializing in this type of research. However, it is not always necessary to invest resources in such solutions. Valuable competitive analysis can be carried out in-house, using standard business analysis techniques, such as SWOT analysis, or information extraction techniques, such as observation, documentary analysis, and system archaeology.

At the strategy analysis stage, competitive analysis can be particularly useful for:

- Comparing the organization's offerings with those of other companies
- Evaluating how the organization operates compared to competitors or companies providing similar services
- Analyzing risks, especially threats from the strengths of competing companies
- Comparing our company's target audience and that of our competitors

Obtaining this information can be useful in determining directions for improvement and areas for improvement. In other words, it provides support in determining the target state of an organization or its specific area or process.

To conduct a simplified competitive analysis, you can:

- Determine what specific aspect you are interested in and what information you want to obtain, as well as what problems to explore.
- Create a list of competing companies, and then make a selection of companies for deeper analysis. Apply specific comparison criteria, such as convergence of business offerings or target market.
- Determine the comparison criteria and the scope of the comparative analysis. Determine which aspects are prioritized so that the analysis is focused on the most important issues.

When conducting a competitive analysis, it is worthwhile to:

- Compare the competitor's products with our company's products.
- Analyze how the competitor operates in comparison to our organization's processes.
- Focus on specific areas, such as the marketing strategy pursued by the competition.

It is a good idea to document the results of the competitive analysis so that you can present them to stakeholders, discuss them, and determine further actions.

An Example of Competitive Analysis

A company doing business in a certain region of Europe wanted to expand its operations throughout Europe. Before making any concrete decisions, the company asked for support from the consulting firm where I was working at the time. We launched a Discovery Project to determine:

1. Which of the company's products and services are likely to succeed in the broader market
2. What strategy it can adopt to scale the business

As a first step, we understood the functioning of the company itself. Together with the client's stakeholders, we selected processes, products, and services worthy of deeper analysis. At the same time, it was decided to perform a general market analysis to determine:

- The size of the target market for the client's services and products
- The existence of competitors and the nature of their offerings
- Risks and constraints associated with entering new markets

The competitive analysis was carried out as follows:

- It was determined which organizations provide similar services to the client's company, using information available on the Internet and interviewing business stakeholders, particularly in marketing and sales.
- The dimensions of the competitive analysis, that is, the specific aspects to be analyzed, were proposed to the client. The client accepted these proposals.
- Publicly available information about the competition was analyzed, especially on Web sites, social media, and industry forums. In parallel, an analysis of the competitor's products was carried out by installing and using publicly available mobile applications.

As a result of the activities carried out, previously established aspects were analyzed, and a preliminary SWOT analysis and risk assessment were performed. The results were included in the market research report. As a result, the client, before deciding whether to enter new markets, was fully aware of the competition and their position. The client's company, realizing the global importance of one of its competitors, decided to try to partner with it, following the principle of "if you can't beat them, join them."

Competitor analysis can therefore be a very valuable part of analyzing a company's environment, and providing information about competing players, their offerings, as well as their strengths and weaknesses. These factors are important when planning a business strategy, to avoid a situation where the strategy is doomed to failure while still in the development stage.

2.1.6 Understand the Organization's Strategy

A good strategy is one that allows you to make decisions. Strategy implementation is the process of iterating the strategy, verifying assumptions in the shortest possible time.

Elena Zhukova, co-founder of OKR Poland

An important aspect of strategy analysis is the identification of business needs and solutions to meet those needs. These solutions should take into account the organizational context, including constraints, assumptions, and defined directions of the organization. And this is where business strategy comes to our aid.

In the context of business analysis activities, understanding the overall strategic assumptions of an organization is important, because this allows us to determine how the organization wants to develop, how it responds to the environment, and how it achieves the established goals, both at the level of the whole organization and at the level of individual initiatives, products, and departments. Strategy defines the approach adopted to achieve business goals—taking into account the constraints and factors arising from the organization's environment. It can be an excellent source of high-level business needs and assumptions, but also risks. Knowing the strategy enables us to identify the right solution options in a given context—right, that is, in line with the strategic assumptions.

In what specific ways can strategy help us identify a business need? Here are some examples:

- Strategy is a way to *achieve business goals*—goals are the basis for identifying business needs. In the simplest terms, in order to achieve a given goal, we need to do something, change something—so we identify business needs. For example, if the goal is to increase market share, we should ask ourselves what we need to do, to know, in order to be able to achieve this goal. And so, for example, we may need to expand our business offerings in such a way as to meet the needs of a new group of customers.
- The strategy can *address many areas*—not only the direction in which the entire organization is heading, but also the development of a specific product line, a marketing strategy for a particular customer segment. There can be many such areas—so the organization must identify strategic priorities. Those areas that will be identified as high-priority areas are those on which attention should be focused. This may mean that as a result of analyzing a specific area that is a priority at a given time, we identify a whole set of business needs that are triggers for change.

For example, if an organization is for some reason determined that a strategic priority is to improve its employee recruitment process, a business need identified as a result of the analysis of this issue could be to change the way it communicates externally, or to define clear requirements for particular positions.

- Strategy is how an organization *responds to changes in the environment.* Changes in the market, such as the emergence of competition, changes in legislation, or changes in the geopolitical situation, are very typical triggers of business needs and changes necessary for an organization to adapt to changing market conditions. For example, a company's strategy might be that if a competitor offering very similar products emerges, our response will be to change our business offerings. This can generate needs in the form of having up-to-date information about the competitor's offerings, ensuring that production processes are flexible enough to be able to quickly change the business offering for a specific customer segment.
- Strategy describes how to *use resources*, including internal and external resources, such as technology. If the strategic premise is to use technology to innovate, business needs may be to have up-to-date knowledge of new technologies in a particular area and to improve existing processes using innovative solutions.

Business strategy thus provides the context for identifying business needs. When undertaking a specific business initiative, we should be aware that strategic assumptions are a kind of overarching requirement—they provide a framework for the entire analysis, and help orient our efforts to areas and aspects whose improvement will contribute to the organization's success.

It is worth noting that strategy is not constant over time—it changes as the context of the organization changes. A strategy that is current this month may no longer be effective in a few weeks. To be able to identify the right needs and approve a solution with the potential to deliver real business value, the analyst should keep abreast of changes in the organization's environment and how the organization responds to those changes.

The very concept of an organization's strategy is often associated with bound documents, a huge amount of information difficult to process and understand. However, this is not always necessary or desirable.

> A 50-page strategy with dozens of sophisticated goals is a recipe for communication failure. How much time is needed to coordinate so many goals? Well that's exactly it—such a practice is almost a guarantee of inefficiency. For each strategy, therefore, it is worth creating a one-pager—a clear and readable document with several clear and measurable objectives and an indication of the hypothesis that these objectives verify. This will minimize misunderstandings about where we are going as a company.
>
> *Elena Zhukova, co-founder of OKR Poland*

An example of a one-page strategy for a training company is shown in Fig. 2.6.

Having knowledge of the goals, the links between them, the expected results, and the initiatives already undertaken or planned is an excellent support for our strategy analysis process. With this knowledge, we will know on which areas to focus efforts and strive to maximize business value, and which areas have a lower priority at any given time.

2.1.7 Understand the Business Objectives

Business objectives are top-level requirements.

Properly defined business objectives can be a significant support for strategy analysis. Objectives define the desired future state of an organization or some area of it. Thanks to this, we are able to determine in what direction the organization is heading, what future state we are aiming for, what results we want to achieve. Based on this, we are able to think about what is needed to achieve the goals, taking into account the organization's capabilities, the external environment, and various types of influential factors.

Let's imagine that in a given organization, the following goals have been defined as part of the Business Motivation Model:

- Increase the level of customer satisfaction.
- Expand the target market.
- Increase the quality of products and services offered.

What are the benefits of having knowledge of these goals in the context of business analysis?

Imagine that an organization has a practice of constantly monitoring the environment to identify business needs and possible organizational improvements.

If the organization's goal is to increase customer satisfaction, one of the first steps for a business analyst would be to find out what the customer satisfaction rate is at the moment, what elements make up customer satisfaction, what factors may be reducing customer satisfaction, and what can be done to prevent this from happening. The answers to these questions will probably allow us to formulate business needs, which will be the input for the strategy analysis process.

If we have determined that customer satisfaction is predominantly a result of the perception of the quality of the services offered by the company, in order to maintain a high customer satisfaction rate, it is necessary to make sure that the services offered are of high quality. To make sure they are high quality, we need to understand what level of quality they are currently at. And here comes the question: How do we measure this quality, and do we measure it at all? If we don't have a defined measurement process, we don't have specific indicators by which we can decide which service is at a sufficient level of quality and which is not; this will be the first area to look at. As part of the status quo analysis, we will also look at the process of service delivery and probably develop a process for quality control, including collecting customer feedback.

The prerequisite for such a procedure is, of course, to have a definition of the business goal. And this is where the problem arises, because many organizations notoriously confuse goals with means. Instead of focusing on establishing where they are going and what they need, organizations tend to point to specific tools and means. And so, for example, goals are defined in terms of the need to implement a new system, launch a new product in

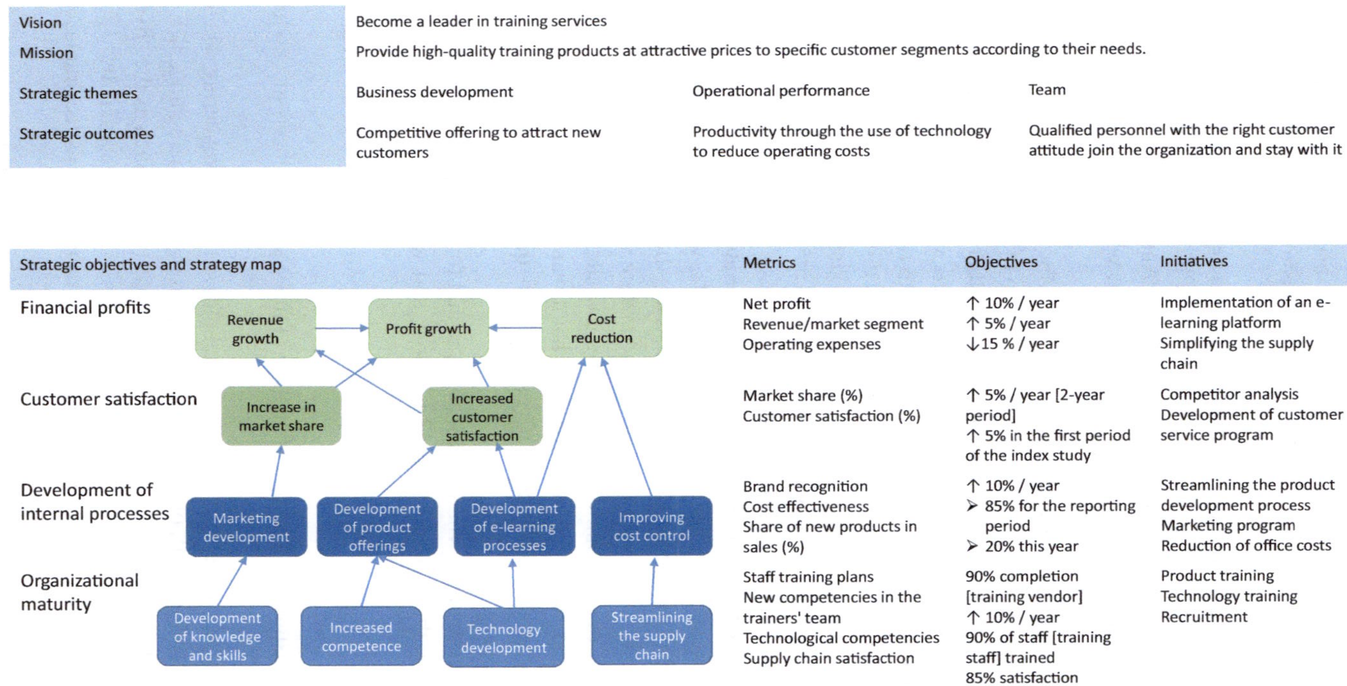

Fig. 2.6 Example of a one-page strategy for a training company

the market, or open a new sales channel, without justifying what these means are to be used for.

The mere implementation of a new system will not bring any benefit if we have not defined what the system is to be used for, what problems to solve, and what areas to support and how.

If we don't know for whom and why we are creating a new product, simply implementing a new product will not change much—at most we will incur the cost of designing and producing a product that will not succeed in the market. And it won't succeed for a simple reason: we launched the product without thinking about who it is for and what audience needs it addresses.

Opening a new sales channel without determining why we want to open this channel, what target group it is aimed at, and how it enables us to meet the needs of this group can be doomed to failure in advance. Imagine, for example, that an organization that has so far conducted stationary sales decides that sales of products will be carried out exclusively online. Such a solution is supposed to make it possible to reduce operating costs. Making such a decision without understanding how it affects existing customers could result in us cutting off access to our products to a sizable group of existing customers who do not use the Internet. The purpose of opening a new sales channel and abandoning an existing channel remains unclear. The purpose may be to reduce costs and to be able to reach a larger group of customers. Without understanding the goal, we are unable to determine whether the measure used—switching to an online sales channel—will be appropriate.

In practice, we may encounter a variety of situations—both one in which the organization describes its business goals in a conscious and mature way, and one in which they are described incorrectly or not at all. In the latter case, I would suggest starting by first determining what the organization is aiming for and what it wants to achieve.

If the company wants to implement a new system, ask questions:

- Who needs this system, by whom will it be used, and for what purpose will it be used?
- What problems is the system supposed to solve, and what benefits is it supposed to provide?
- How common are the problems the system is supposed to solve, and what are the effects?
- How will we measure that the implementation of the system has been successful?

Sometimes asking these questions causes stakeholders to start wondering whether the system is really the end in itself, or whether the problem lies elsewhere altogether.

At this stage, tools familiar from Root Cause Analysis (RCA), such as the "five times why" (5 × Why) technique or cause-and-effect diagrams, come in very handy.

Let's consider an example of the application of root cause analysis techniques and the resulting benefits.

An organization that produces and sells medical equipment initiated a project to develop a new project structure for IT, in particular to introduce a business analyst role. The rationale for the project was that business representatives complained about the quality of the technology teams, in particular the long wait times for implementing business changes, and that the changes made did not bring enough business value—technology changed systems, but this did not improve processes and operations at all.

The project, as initially requested by the client, had to look at the current project structure and establish a new division of roles and responsibilities within the project teams.

When asked what problem the outcome of this project would solve, the client said: "The products delivered to customers are of good quality, but we have problems with the production, storage, and distribution processes of the products. Sometimes we take orders from customers for products we no longer produce, because the procurement department has no knowledge of what the company's current offerings are." Another question was how would changing the structure of the project team help achieve these goals? The client answered that introducing the role of business analyst would result in a person responsible for determining the right business needs, solutions, and the impact of the change on existing processes, departments, products, and having someone in this role, the company will avoid identified problems, the results of this project affect a certain department, while this department is not aware of the consequences of the change.

In the course of further conversation we came to the following conclusions:

- Business representatives of a given company understand their areas of responsibility, but are not familiar with other areas—often they do not even have basic knowledge of other areas. Thus, for example, the warehouse knows little about sales activities.
- Business representatives do not communicate with each other, and very often report needs for change that are in clear contradiction to the needs of other departments. In the current configuration of project teams, the problem with conflicting requirements and needs is very often revealed only at the production stage—when the change has already been implemented and the affected departments begin to escalate the problem.
- The company's business representatives confuse the means with the ends—instead of reporting business needs, they report specific changes to specific systems, which, coupled with the fact that they often have no knowledge of what system the change should be implemented in in order to maintain consistency at the process level, leads to results such as implemented changes that do not deliver any business value. On the contrary, they disrupt the continuity of other stakeholders.
- Business representatives are unable to justify the changes they report. They are unable to determine the impact of the change on business processes, other aspects of the organization.

In the context of the above information, the client's idea of introducing a business analyst role turns out to be quite misguided—the problem is the lack of business strategy, lack of communication, and lack of knowledge of how to implement changes. Adding one project role will not solve the problem here—because it lies elsewhere.

After several discussions involving all the stakeholders involved, both on the business and technology side, the client and I came to the conclusion that introducing new roles would not change anything in the current ways of working. The project was divided into the following stages:

1. *Education stage*—at this stage, all people involved in the delivery of business services will receive training in the basics of business analysis, in particular in determining business needs, analyzing the impact of changes, and modeling business processes.
2. *Production process improvement stage*—at this stage, the business and technology teams will jointly develop a new approach to implementing the change project. In particular, they will determine the required work products and the key activities required to achieve these work products.
3. *Competency structuring stage*—at this stage, a new structure of project teams is established. Specific roles will have defined competencies. Competency gaps will be filled.

The above method illustrates how initially set business goals can be wrong. If we implemented the project according to the client's assumptions, it is likely that the results obtained would have zero business value—the client would only bear the costs of implementing the new role and the consequences of that implementation. Instead, we put the idea up for discussion and came to a completely different conclusion.

2.1.8 To Make the Objectives Worthwhile...

> Understand the context of the objective, determine why the objective is important, why exactly now we want to pursue it.
>
> Do you know what problem you want to solve? What is not working today? What do you want to change? How will you know it is better?
>
> What will change when the goal is realized?
>
> What changes in stakeholder behavior do you expect?
> *Elena Zhukova, co-founder of OKR Poland*

Business objectives, to truly provide valuable information and support the development of the organization, should be defined in a specific way. The information they contain should be a precise indication of the result we want to achieve, and should provide a measure to meet the objective and a time frame.[1] It is worth noting that the objectives should be relevant to the organization—Which means that if we define objectives whose the

[1] Note that sources such as BMM distinguish between two types of objectives—some are quite general and set aspirations, while others should be specific, measurable, and time-bound.

achievement of which will not result in the real growth of the organization, will not contribute to the realization of the vision, and which will not be in line with the strategy, it is likely that such objectives have been defined incorrectly.

A well-defined objective meets the SMART[2] (Specific, Measurable, Achievable, Relevant, Time-bound) criteria and enables the realization of the vision, and its achievement represents a significant step in the development of the organization, a specific department, or another aspect of the organization's functioning.

Unfortunately, practice shows that in many organizations objectives are defined incorrectly. It's not even the mere fact of mixing objectives with measures, as we mentioned earlier, but the very definition of an objective.

Consider the following examples:

1. Improvement of the production process
2. Increase in customer satisfaction
3. Reduction in the number of reported complaints

These are real-life examples of objectives set in organizations. The first objective for improving manufacturing processes is neither specific, providing no information about which processes we want to improve and what we mean by improvement, nor measurable, as it lacks any measure that would allow us to say whether this objective has been achieved. The time horizon is also unknown, meaning we don't know when we will achieve this objective. We don't know how the business process improvement will deliver value and what that value is. It is therefore difficult to assess whether it is a real business objective or just a means to an end. Such an objective is practically worthless; it does not contain any specific information about the target state we would like to achieve, nor does it explain why achieving it would deliver business value.

If we make the assumption that improving production processes is important because it will reduce production costs, improve quality, or ensure that products are delivered to customers faster—such assumptions allow us to reveal that the objective is not process improvement itself—it is "merely" a means, a tool.

The problem is that process improvement in itself (even if we define what exactly this "improvement" means) does not necessarily deliver any value. For example, if the objective for a specific area of the company's operations is to improve product quality, the means to achieve this objective would be, for example, to ensure that the materials used in production come only from reliable suppliers and meet certain quality standards—"streamlining" the process does not provide any tangible benefit.

[2] A method that supports the development of high-quality objectives—which means, among other things, ensuring that they are measurable and specific.

For the second objective of increasing customer satisfaction, the first problem that is immediately apparent is the lack of measurability of this objective. We don't know by how much we want to increase customer satisfaction, we don't know what the current level of satisfaction is, and we don't know what kind of customer we are talking about. We don't know in what area we want to increase customer satisfaction—whether it's satisfaction with the quality of the products purchased, customer service, or perhaps other aspects. Such an objective gives some idea of the organization's aspirations, but does not provide concrete information to envision the target state.

The third objective is to reduce the number of reported complaints. Again, we don't know by how much we want to reduce the number of complaints, and we don't know how many complaints are currently being reported and over what period of time, which makes it impossible to assess the feasibility of a given objective.

We don't know what kinds of complaints we are talking about, whether they apply to all possible products and services, or whether they are limited to a certain scope. This is important because we don't always care about reducing the number of all complaints. It could be that we care more about reducing the number of complaints from key customers or about key services or products. When analyzing the very core of the objective, i.e., reducing the number of complaints, we need to consider why we care about reducing the number of complaints, and what benefits we will achieve. We may come to the conclusion that simply reducing complaints doesn't bring any real benefits other than relieving the burden on complaint handling staff. To understand the essence of this objective, we can conclude that the objective is not to reduce the number of complaints, but, for example, to reduce operating costs, of which complaint handling costs are a part. Another objective may be to increase customer satisfaction by providing quality products and services, leading to increased revenues, strengthening the brand in the market, and potentially expanding the company's market share. So the question arises: What is the objective, reducing complaints, or providing customers with quality products and services so the company can grow?

Of course, objectives can be defined at different levels—at the level of the organization, at the level of a specific department or business function, and at the level of the development of a specific service or product line. The specification of the objective should also include such information that the recipient is able to understand what level of objectives we are talking about, what they concern, and their potential scope of impact. Setting objectives of the type optimizing processes, increasing employee satisfaction, and improving the customer service process is at best the first step in developing appropriate, measurable, and valuable objectives.

From a business analysis perspective, objectives are one of the important inputs. Understanding strategic objectives enables us to identify business needs, and on the other hand, the identification of business needs may bring with it the need to set new objectives.

In this context, it becomes particularly important to ensure that the objectives are appropriate, measurable, and specific.

I believe that business objectives, like business needs and further requirements, should be specified according to the principles of requirements engineering. Objectives, needs, and requirements at different levels are in fact very similar work products; they define what we want to achieve and the desired results. The only difference between them is that they involve different levels of abstraction. Objectives and business needs operate at the strategic level, and requirements at the level of the change initiative and later the solution production project. However, the principles of developing these work products, in my opinion, are very similar, and the objectives, needs, and requirements must be measurable and precisely formulated, both their objective and expected results. The business value that is delivered through the implementation of these artifacts must be known, and it must be possible to analyze the impact of the proposed change on other aspects of business system performance. There must be measurable acceptance criteria that we can use to verify that an objective, need, or requirement has been achieved as intended. Thus, when analyzing business objectives in particular, pay attention to the following aspects:

- What is the objective referring to and do I understand what the objective is?
- Why is the objective important? For whom is it important and for what reason?
- What will happen if the objective is not achieved? If nothing happens, it is probably not important enough to the functioning of the organization to invest in its implementation.
- What value will be gained by achieving the objective? Who will get the value?
- Who or what will be affected by achieving the objective? What will be the positive impact, the negative impact, and the unknown impact (if unknown, it may mean that there are specific risks in achieving the objective)?
- How will we check whether the objective has been properly achieved? When should we check the achievement of the objective?
- What do we check? What parameter or metric will enable us to verify the achievement of the objective?
- Does the declaration of the objective dictate how it should be achieved? If so, we are probably dealing not with an objective, but with a means to achieve it.

2.2 Business Process Modeling

Modeling is never used to determine who is at fault—modeling is used to determine what the cause is.

Piotr Biernacki, MGX Infoservice

2.2.1 Depict the Operation of the Organization in the Form of a Business Process Model

An organization is a business system. Every system can be modeled.

If you can't model an organization, it means that you don't understand how it works.

When considering the topic of strategy analysis, especially the analysis of the current state and the target state, it is impossible not to mention business process modeling. Process models are an excellent visual representation of how certain activities are carried out, how business participants communicate, and the results of performing activities.

We can use modeling to achieve various objectives, including documenting the current and target states.

In documenting the current state of an organization, business process models allow us to depict not only the sequence of execution of certain activities, tasks, and communication between process participants, but also the dependencies between different processes. This allows us to better understand how the organization delivers value to consumers. If we already have a model describing the current state of the organization, it is easier to identify weaknesses and areas for improvement—because we have a visual picture of reality, which is usually easier to understand than a textual description, which also makes it easier to identify potential problem areas. From there, we are close to identifying desired changes and trying to model the target state of the organization.

When modeling business processes, there are several aspects worth noting.

First of all, we need to determine the *scope of the organization we want to model.* Usually we do not have the resources or the necessity to model all the business processes implemented within the organization. Therefore, it is necessary to define precisely the scope of the processes we will model. For example, if the objective of the analysis is to identify possible improvements in the area of customer service, this area will be the main focus, encompassing processes related to customer service, such as order placement and processing, after-sales service, or general customer relationship management. By analyzing these processes, we can come to the conclusion that production or logistics processes can also affect customer satisfaction, so it is worth looking into them as well.

It is also necessary to determine *what we want* to model—the current state, the target state, both? Of course, you can model both—and that's the way it should be done according to the art. To be able to determine the target state, we must first understand the current state. Through modeling, we can achieve this understanding.

However, in many cases, due to design constraints and the objectives of the analysis, we do not have the ability to fully analyze the current and desired states. We may simply not have the resources to do so.

Thus, for example, if the objective is to improve the organization's performance in a certain area, documentation of the current state (if it doesn't exist) is in many cases ignored—because the stakeholders believe that the value is provided by documentation of the target state, which includes the proposed improvements and the target way to accomplish tasks. From the perspective of decision-makers, the current state will soon become history, so there is probably little point in documenting it. Rather than devote resources to documenting the current state, they prefer to focus on understanding how the organization operates and the opportunities for improvement, and then documenting the desired target state.

Such a decision is, of course, associated with a whole host of risks—among which is the risk of building a target state without having a sufficiently deep knowledge of the organization's current way of doing things.

If, on the other hand, the objective of analytical activities is to understand the organization's operations and document this knowledge, we will most likely be limited to modeling the current state. In addition to documenting the current state, it is also a good idea to document current issues and challenges—which will almost certainly be identified when analyzing the organization's current operation. This will provide input for any subsequent change initiatives.

It is also important to consider *who will be the recipients of the results* and for what objective they will be used. If the business process models are to be used to explain to a potential solution provider how the organization functions, care should be taken to ensure that the form of modeling and the information content of the models can be understood by external organizations. If, on the other hand, the models are to be used for the organization itself, for example, to organize knowledge of how tasks are performed, to provide information to employees, or to provide a basis for possible process improvements, the information content of the models should be tailored to explain in sufficient detail how the organization operates.

Let's consider an example. Figure 2.7 shows how to handle an order placed by a customer and is intended for customer service personnel.

As it stands, the diagram provides at most an overview of the order handling process. If it were to be a diagram dedicated to customer service employees, it should be detailed enough to explain:

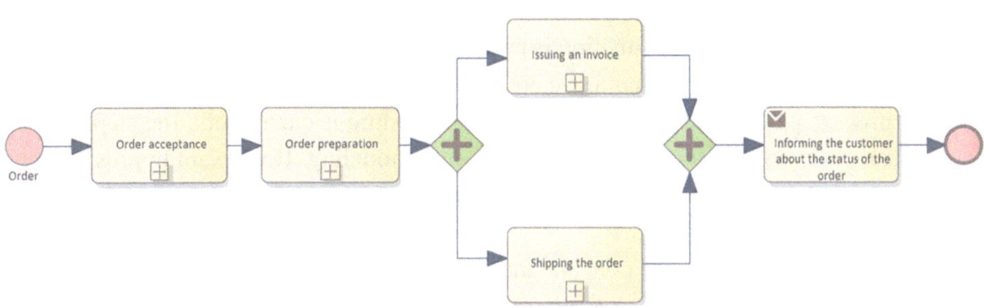

Fig. 2.7 Example of an order handling process model

1. Who is responsible for carrying out specific activities and tasks. At the moment, the diagram does not clarify the responsibilities in any way, since there is no information about the allocation of resources to specific activities.
2. How exactly the tasks should be performed. The diagram shows sub-processes and a single task (informing the customer about the status of the order). Using the sub-process mechanism in this context would only make sense if the individual sub-processes were supplemented with additional diagrams explaining exactly how the tasks should be performed. Without these additional diagrams, using the information contained in the presented diagram, it is impossible to understand exactly how operations are performed. For example, the way the sub-process "order acceptance" is carried out is completely unclear—it is not clear who is supposed to accept the order, how it is accepted, or whether it is recorded in any way. Accepting an order can also mean rejecting an order in case of an emergency. Such information is not included in the diagram. If the one and only diagram were to explain how to handle an order to the organization's employees, it would unfortunately fail in this task, except for a very general overview of the steps involved in the process. If a new employee were to learn how to handle an order based on this diagram, he or she would unfortunately not be able to.

2.2.2 Process Mapping vs. Process Modeling: Don't Confuse the Terms

A PROCESS MAP IS A LIST OF PROCESSES CARRIED OUT IN A CERTAIN AREA OF THE ORGANIZATION, ALONG WITH THE RELATIONSHIPS BETWEEN THEM.

A PROCESS MODEL IS A DESCRIPTION OF HOW A CERTAIN PROCESS WORKS.

"In our project, we are mapping processes in BPMN."

"Process mapping allows us to understand how a specific task is performed."

"Process maps represent how business functions are performed in our organization."

Sound familiar? If so, we have reason to worry. If you are mapping processes in your project or organization using BPMN, be aware that nowhere in the BPMN standard does the concept of process mapping appear. If we think we can use process mapping to explain how a specific task or business function is performed, we are probably confusing mapping with modeling. If, on the other hand, we are concerned with depicting the communication between process participants, the way a certain procedure is carried out, the step-by-step flow of tasks, we most likely mean business process modeling. If we want to present a list of processes that operate in a given organization along with the links between them, then we probably think of a process map.

The differences between one concept and the other are brilliantly explained by Robert Kozlowski and Piotr Biernacki:

> Process map can be compared to a map of the country—it shows the cities and the links between them (understood as roads). However, you do not know how to get from one city to another. You see the points, but not the way to accomplish the journey. A process model explains how to get from one city to another city—it explains the details of a journey started in a certain place, with the objective of reaching the destination.

In terms of business processes, a process map will show what processes exist in an organization and how they are related—for example, the output of one process is the input to another. With a process map, we are able to understand the overall scope of the organization—the business functions performed in it. However, a process map will not show how individual business processes are performed. That's what business process models are for.

The problem is that in many organizations the two concepts are confused—and so, for example, when talking about a process map, the analyst simply means a diagram showing one particular process. The difference in meaning between the two concepts can be compared to confusing the concepts of user stories and story mapping. We are talking about completely different levels of detail, because these concepts are used to represent different information, for different objectives.

Process mapping is the first step in understanding how an organization works. Before we start modeling individual processes, it is useful to understand in what context these processes function. Let's determine what processes within an organization we are talking about at all, and how these processes are related to each other. Developing a process map can also help you establish the boundaries of individual processes—because if, while creating a process map, we identify a process called "manufacture and deliver a product to the customer," already a preliminary analysis of the naming of this process can make us realize that we are actually dealing with several processes: product design, production, quality control, warehousing, preparation for shipment, and shipment to the customer. In this way, we will be able to establish the boundaries of the process even before it has been accurately modeled—at the process map stage. As a result, we will avoid the fairly typical mistake of having a business process model cover several processes.

Having a map of the processes, explaining in some aspect the functioning of the organization, we can make a choice as to which of these processes will need to be detailed in the form of a process model, and at what level of detail. This choice will be determined by the objective of the analysis, the business needs that were the trigger for the strategy analysis, and the needs of the stakeholders, especially domain experts.

If we have already determined which of the specific processes listed on the map will be the subject of modeling—in other words, we have determined the "Table of Contents" of the initiative—we can proceed with process modeling. Again, the process map will be an excellent facilitator for us, since the process map shows inputs and outputs and dependencies with other processes. This is information that is often missing from business process diagrams.

The differences between a process map and a process model are shown in the following figures. Figure 2.8 shows an excerpt from the process map; we see three processes and the

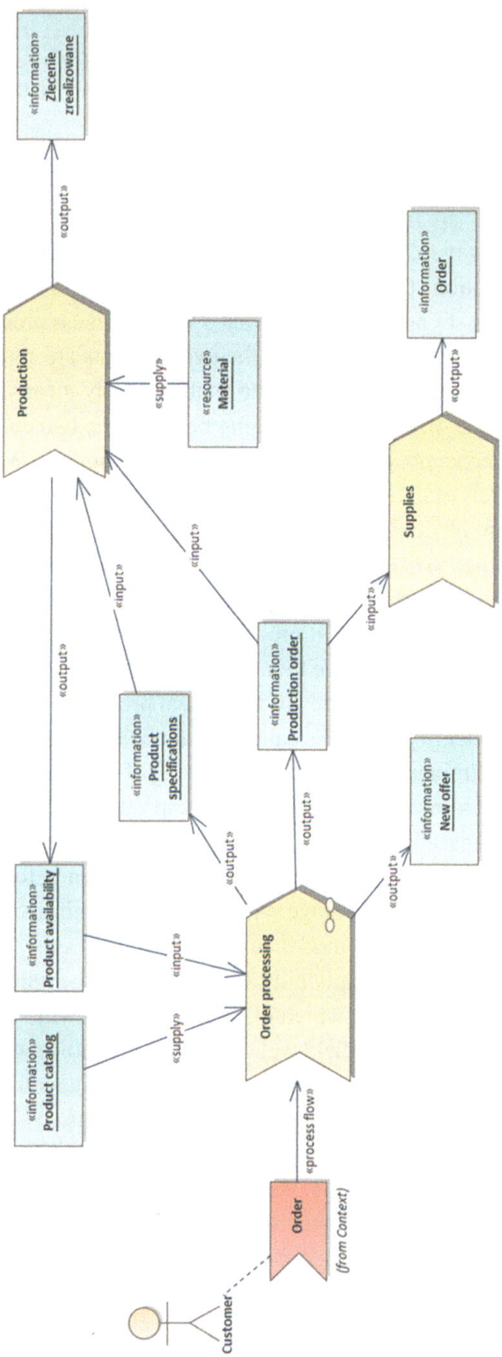

Fig. 2.8 Excerpt from process map

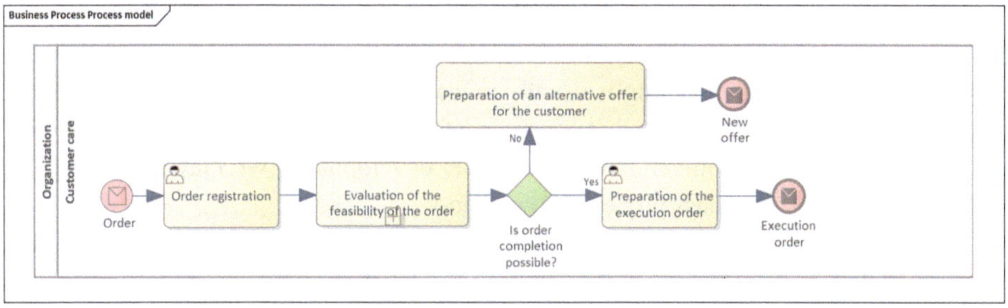

Fig. 2.9 Business process model: "Order processing"

relationships between them. Figure 2.9 is a simple business process model, "Order Processing"; it explains how a specific process is implemented.

The terms mapping and process modeling mean different things. Let's be aware of the difference before we put the nomenclature into practice.

2.2.3 Learn the Principles of Creating Business Process Models

> REMEMBER THAT MODELS ARE NOT FOR OURSELVES. THEY DO NOT HAVE TO FAITHFULLY REPRESENT REALITY TO ACHIEVE THEIR OBJECTIVE, BUT THEY SHOULD ALWAYS COMPLY WITH THE DECLARED MODELING STANDARD.
>
> *ROBERT KOZŁOWSKI, BPMN COACH AND BUSINESS PROCESSES IMPROVEMENT CONSULTANT, MPB INFOSERVICE*

There are many approaches, techniques, and notations for business process modeling, among which it is worth mentioning BPMN, Integrated DEFinition Methods (IDEF), Universal Process Notation (UPN), suppliers, inputs, process, outputs, and customers (SIPOC), and flowcharts (OMG 2010; (Knowledge Based Systems 2023). Unfortunately, familiarity with a notation or a given technique does not necessarily mean that the modeling results will be at the right level of quality. Knowing how to use a given notation is one thing; knowing how to model it is quite another. Diagrams can be correct from a formal point of view, that is, built according to the syntax of the notation, but incorrect in terms of semantics, that is, meaning a reflection of the reality being modeled.

How to avoid typical mistakes?

Identify the *objective of the modeling*. Starting by defining the objective seems a fairly natural step. Models serve various purposes. They can be created to consolidate knowledge about the functioning of the organization, to explain how a certain process is carried out to the organization's employees, or to analyze how a certain task is carried out for possible improvements. Determining the objective of modeling and the expected results is necessary to decide on the level of detail of the model, the audience and their expectations, the notation or approach to modeling, and many other aspects.

Understand the *reality being modeled.* Without understanding the object, the process we are modeling, knowing the notation is not enough to create a valid model. For this reason, business process modeling is usually preceded by a series of interviews to obtain information about the process and its participants, results, and objective. Let's involve stakeholders, especially domain experts, in model development. We may have modeling skills; they may have business process knowledge.

Determine the *level of detail* of the model. Processes can be modeled in general, or they can be modeled in great detail, going down to the level of individual atomic activities, modeling all possible alternative and unique paths. The level of detail of our diagrams depends primarily on who they are intended to serve and for what objective. If the objectives of the modeling are general, serving, for example, to clarify the functioning of the organization in the context of the processes being implemented, high-level modeling may be appropriate. If we are modeling to accurately describe the procedure for performing a certain task, this suggests putting detailed information on the model.

It is worth noting that different levels of detail can be applied within the same model. For example, if we are modeling an order handling process, some activities may be detailed tasks, while others may be presented at a higher level of abstraction, since they are not the ones we want to focus on within a given model.

Identify the *subject of the modeling.* As a general rule, business modeling should model business-level objects and interactions. In practice, I have more than once encountered "business process" models, which showed the steps an actor performed in an information system (other than workflow systems, allowed in the BPMN standard). In such a case, it's worth asking ourselves what we really want to model—the business process or the way a particular system is used. If the latter, let's use the right technique and the right standard, and let's not call it business-level modeling. The business layer and the implementation layer are different; their modeling serves different objectives and focuses on representing different aspects—these layers should not be mixed together.

Don't make it more complicated than necessary. A good model is one that represents reality in a way that is appropriate to the objective of the modeling. In many cases, it is not necessary to create very complex, extensive models that attempt to represent all possible paths and ways in which business participants interact. Models, by definition, are a simplified representation of reality—they are not intended to describe everything. Let's keep this in mind when modeling. The model should include what is relevant to the objective of modeling and the needs of the target group. Irrelevant information can at best obscure the model and cause problems with understanding and interpretation.

To understand what a piece of information or element contributes to the model, let's ask ourselves the following questions:

- What is the relevance of the element to understanding the overall process?
- For whom will this information or element be relevant and crucial to interpreting this model?

- Without this element, will the completeness or readability of the model, with respect to the defined objective, suffer? If not, do we really need to put this element on the model?
- Should the element be modeled on this diagram or on another?

Identify *recipients of models*. Piotr Biernacki, an expert in business process modeling, says: "the model should always be audience-oriented". In order to create a model that will be understandable and useful to the recipient, we need to know who the recipient is, what information they need, and for what objective they will use the models you develop. Keep in mind that the recipients are not only the people who are currently helping us develop the model and will use it in the near future. Recipients are also the people who will be using the models in a few years—and for these people our results should also be understandable and readable.

In many cases, the principle of simplicity works. We model not to demonstrate our expertise of knowledge of a given notation; we model to communicate, to express a given process in visual form in order to consolidate knowledge, to explain how a process works, to educate. A model that is built according to the syntax, but is incomprehensible to the recipient, is a model that is simply useless.

In practice, the principle to model as simply as possible often works, assuming that the recipient will be able to understand the model without advanced knowledge of notation. Of course, I'm not talking about situations where the objective is to model the reality of the organization perfectly according to the rules of a given notation and for some specific objective (e.g., the purpose of later implementation of ERP systems). I'm talking about situations where our models are mainly for communication—to understand the operation of the organization, areas for improvement, and the possibility of ways to improve the process. For such objectives, fairly simple models will most likely suffice.

Develop a *modeling methodology*. Before you begin to create models and present the results of your work to stakeholders, develop a modeling methodology that explains which elements of the notation you intend to use, what they mean in a given context, and how to interpret them. From the set of elements of a given notation, let's select those that will be used in a given modeling project—and explain how to use them to stakeholders. Such a methodology can also clarify certain elements of project management, such as the key activities performed in the modeling of expected results and how to involve stakeholders, especially domain experts. Developing and clarifying the assumptions of the methodology will achieve a number of benefits—one of which is to increase the comfort and sense of security of the stakeholders, since the methodology will clarify the principles of cooperation, rather than put them before the fact. You will also avoid the risk that those familiar with the notation may interpret the use of the notation in a way that is inconsistent with your intentions. Keep in mind that the same aspect of a process can be presented in several different ways. The methodology should explain what the modeling approach is for your project. An additional aspect that justifies the need for a modeling methodology is that by doing so, you will create a contract that clarifies the subject of acceptance. The customer has commissioned us to develop a process model. This information is not enough to determine what result the customer really wants. At what level of detail the model should be, for what objective it is being built, who it is intended to serve, what approach/notation and its various elements we are to use to develop the model, what information the model should contain—all these details should be explained so that both parties are clear about the expected results of the work. Otherwise, we accept the risk of delivering a product that will not meet the expectations of the recipient (because we never agreed on those expectations and how to achieve them).

Stick to the standard. If we use a specific notation and would like to claim that our models are built according to that notation, stick to the standard. For example, in BPMN, each element has its own specific meaning and can only be used in combination with specific elements. These rules are described in the BPMN standard.

If we break these rules and adopt our own modeling rules, our model is no longer a model built according to BPMN, and we should be aware of this. Of course, this may in no way affect the completeness and readability of a given diagram, but it may generate some undesirable consequences. If, for example, the recipient is a person who is perfectly familiar with the notation in question, this person may be misled by the "modifications" of the notation rules made by you. As a result, he will understand the diagram differently than was our intention.

Keep your models *consistent*. Quite a common mistake is that we selectively model a few processes and create quite good-quality diagrams, but they are not related to each other. In other words, we don't know if and how these processes relate to each other. This may be a deliberate procedure; unfortunately, in many cases it is simply a mistake in the art. As a result, we have individual diagrams that represent single processes, but we don't know what the flow of information is in a given organization or department. For example, let's imagine we are modeling the process of order processing, order invoicing, and order fulfillment by the warehouse. These processes are clearly interrelated—the result of the order handling process, for example, an order accepted for processing. If the new order were to have an invoice, this would be a trigger for the invoice process. In addition, the acceptance of an order for fulfillment is a trigger for the order fulfillment process by the warehouse. Between the processes of order processing and order fulfillment by the warehouse, there is thus a link at the data level. Our models should express these linkages; otherwise we can at best conjecture what the relationships between the processes in question are. This example is trivial, but if we assume more complicated processes and a more complicated organizational context, the problem becomes significant. We have models representing individual processes; we do not have a view of the operation of the entire organization.

2.2.4 How to Properly Document Business Processes?

A BUSINESS PROCESS IS NOTHING MORE THAN A FUNCTION. DOCUMENTATION OF THE FUNCTION MUST INCLUDE INFORMATION ABOUT THE OBJECTIVE, INPUT AND OUTPUT, THE RESULT, AND THE EXECUTION ALGORITHM ALONG WITH THE RESPONSIBILITY.

As we already know, there are many ways to describe business processes, such as scenarios, models, or mixed forms, using textual forms. Regardless of the form chosen, let's make sure that the process documentation is complete. Good business process documentation should include:

- Defining the objective of the process
- Defining inputs and outputs, i.e., input information and output information—the state at the end of the process
- Assigning resources to activities
- Definition of initial conditions and end conditions
- Describing how the various activities in the process are carried out

Some help in defining the process may come from familiarity with the very idea of function—as a transformation of input data into output data (Fig. 2.10)—and models such as Input, Control, Output, Mechanism (Knowledge Based Systems 2023).

Sometimes, when describing a business process, we focus only on one aspect, such as the flow, resulting in only defining the workflow itself in the form of a flowchart or other type of diagram. Unfortunately, we often leave out other information that is important to understanding how the process works. A process description in the form of a flowchart can be inadequate when there is no information about who performs the activity, how it is triggered, and what the result of the process is. This makes it impossible to properly assess the correctness of the model.

To make sure you are describing business processes properly and completely, let's make sure that:

1. We have clearly defined the objective of the process, which should be to achieve the stated business objectives. If we can't define the objective of the process, let's hold off on modeling because we probably don't fully understand the business area or scope of the model. An example of a process objective might be to handle an order placed by a customer.
2. We have defined the inputs for the process, that is, the information provided by another process or a specific business participant. Inputs for the process should come from specific sources, allowing us to clearly identify the output information for the process we are documenting. An example input could be an order for a specific product from a specific customer.

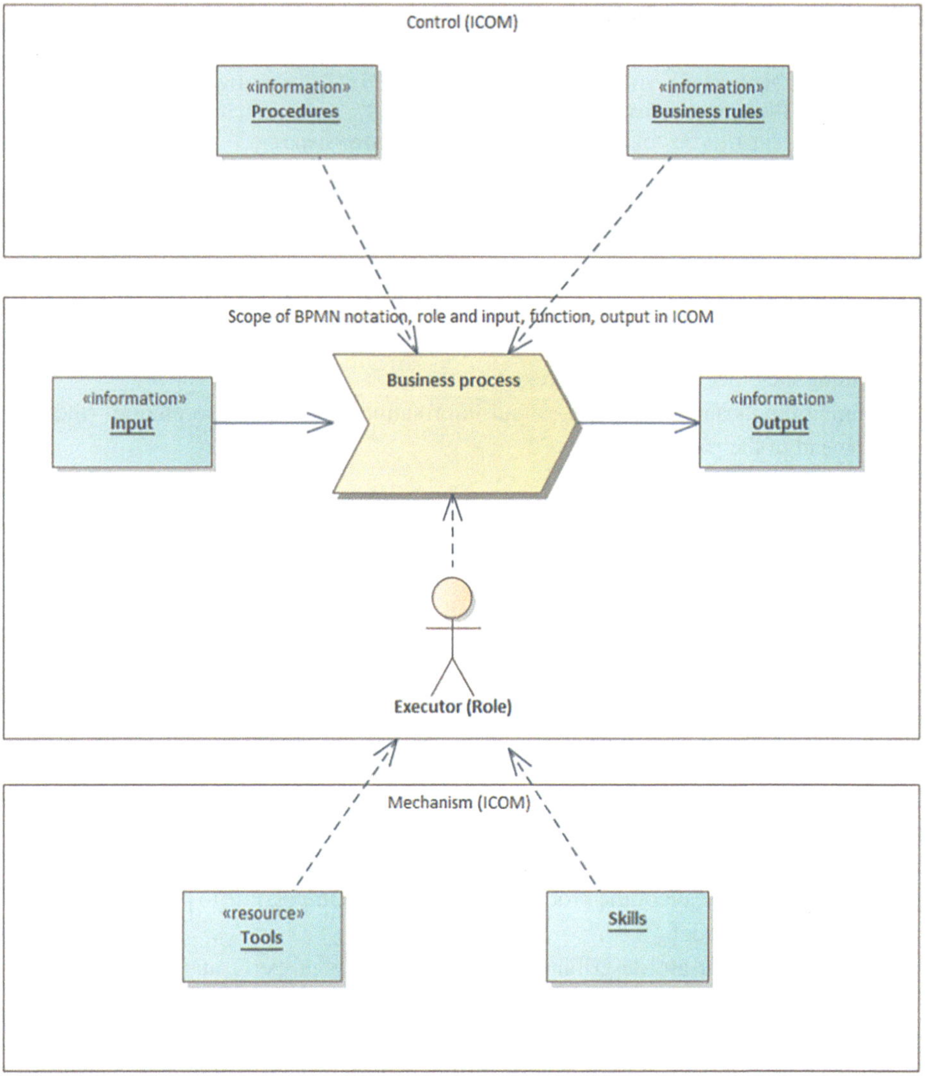

Fig. 2.10 Concept of business process, ©2015 Żeliński (compiled on the basis of Żeliński 2015)

3. We have defined the outputs for the process. In our case, the output of the process is the information about the order ready to be transferred to the customer. Note that the output of one process can be an input for other processes. Our process documentation should be consistent, and the definitions of inputs and outputs should be unambiguous and consistent in terms of nomenclature so that the links between processes can be identified.
4. We have identified the consumers of the process, i.e., the people, stakeholders, departments, or other processes that benefit from the outputs of the process we are

documenting. In our case, the consumers of the process may be the logistics department responsible for transferring the finished order to the customer, as well as the customer himself, who will receive information about the order that is ready to be shipped.

5. We have defined the order of activities. In our example, the sequence of activities may include assessing the feasibility of the order, transferring the order to be completed at the warehouse, preparing the documentation necessary to release the order to the customer, and preparing the order and documentation for transfer to the customer.
6. We have identified resources for each activity. The primary resource needed to carry out the activities in a business process is people. In other words, when defining a business process, you need to determine who is responsible for carrying out the activity. In our example, the resource assigned to the activity "order preparation" may be a warehouse employee.
7. We have defined the roles and powers of the people involved in the execution of the process. Certain roles perform certain activities in the process, others support their execution, and still others may be informed when an activity is completed. This information should be included in the process documentation; for example, you can use the RACI(S)[3] matrix to complete the information about the business process being modeled.
8. We have identified relevant alternative flows and exceptions. Relevant flows are those that are relevant to understanding the model. All scenarios necessary to understand the operation of the business process should be included in the documentation. In our example, an alternative scenario might be a negative result of an order feasibility assessment. In such a case, we can inform the customer that the order cannot be fulfilled and cancel the order, agree with the customer to change the scope or subject matter of the order, or—if the inability to fulfill the order is temporary—inform the customer of the delay and temporarily hold off on fulfilling the order until we can take it up again.

Regardless of the form adopted and the modeling notation chosen, some general guidelines for the information content of business process documentation can be identified.

Here is a sample template of a business process description document. Note that whatever form the information documentation takes, the following information should be included in it. The template below was developed based on the SIPOC method, ICOM (Knowledge Based Systems 2023), the definition of a business process according to the BPMN standard (OMG 2010), and discussions with experts in the field of business process modeling.

[3] Responsibility matrix; the name is an acronym derived from the definition of key responsibilities occurring during the implementation of the initiative: Responsible, Accountable, Consulted, Informed. The RACI matrix is relatively often expanded to include S—Support. There are also other variants of the RACI matrix.

1. Name of the process
2. Objective
3. Input criteria/conditions
4. Inputs
5. Process model—flow diagram
6. Activity descriptions
   (a) Initial conditions
   (b) Metrics
   (c) Roles and responsibilities
   (d) Result
7. Exceptions/alternative flows
   (a) Initial conditions
   (b) Final conditions
   (c) Business rules
   (d) Outputs
8. Consumers/recipients of process results
9. Termination criteria/conditions
10. Related processes

2.2.5 If You Use a Standard, Use It Correctly

A STANDARD USED INAPPROPRIATELY CEASES TO BE A STANDARD. INSTEAD OF IMPROVING COMMUNICATION AND UNDERSTANDING, IT DISRUPTS THEM.

If a decision has been made in our organization to use a business process modeling standard, a particular notation or language, let's make sure that we apply the standard correctly. Otherwise, we may end up with a situation where the models we create should theoretically comply with the standard, but practically do not. This can cause difficulties in understanding and interpreting them.

Let's consider with examples the consequences of not adhering to the standard.

Figure 2.11 shows a process model built not in accordance with the principles of BPMN. The customer-side process has started, while there is no termination.

The process on the store side has an ending, but no beginning. The diagram in this form can be interpreted as follows: the customer starts the process; the process then moves from the customer to the store and ends on the store side. This is inconsistent with the principles of business process modeling according to the BPMN standard. Each business participant, in this case the customer and the store, has a process. The process on each participant's side should have an explicit start and end marking, or we abandon such markings altogether. Using them selectively (in the "Customer" pool the start and end events are there; in the "Store" pool they are no longer there) is not prohibited by the standard, but it introduces inconsistency and can cause problems with the proper interpretation of the digraph.

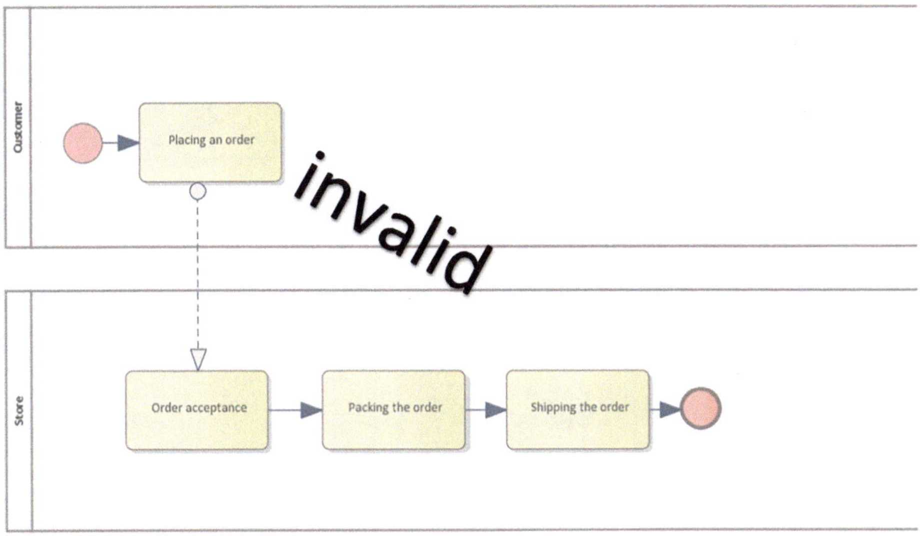

Fig. 2.11 Example of order handling process model (BPMN)

Figure 2.12 shows a model of the complaint process. This model, like the next model, contains elements of BPMN—indicating that it is intended to be compliant with the BPMN standard. Unfortunately, it contains at least a few significant problems.

First, we see pools: "Customer" and "Complaint Department Employee." These pools (Pool) are adjacent to each other, which can be interpreted not as two independent pools, but as two lanes (Lane) occurring within a given business process participant—the organization. The logic of the diagrams indicates something else, namely that the customer is a participant in the business process, and the complaint department employee is another participant, i.e., we are dealing with two pools. If so, then the two pools should be clearly separated. They cannot have a common edge.

The phrase "Complaints department employee" indicates that this is a track within a pool, rather than a pool in itself.[4] Therefore, in the first instance, the diagram should be corrected, separating the process participant under the title "Customer" from the process participant "Store" (example name).

The concept of pools and lanes is shown in Fig. 2.13.

---

[4]According to the BPMN standard (OMG 2010),

"A Pool (Pool) is a graphical representation of a Participant in a collaboration. A Participant can be a specific EntityPartner (e.g., a company) or a more general RolePartner (e.g., a buyer, seller or manufacturer).

A Participant represents a specific EntityPartner (e.g., a company) and/or a more general RolePartner (e.g., a buyer, seller or manufacturer) who are participants in a collaboration.

Track, (Lane)—a partition that is used to organize and categorize activities within the Pool. A track extends the entire length of the Pool, both vertically and horizontally. Tracks are often used for such things as internal roles (e.g., Manager, Employee)...."

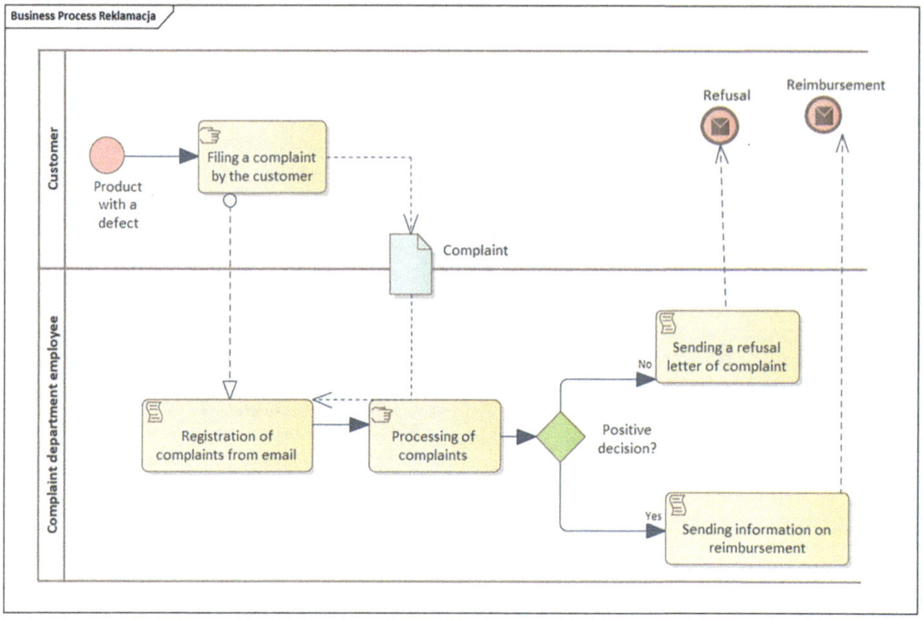

Fig. 2.12 Example of a complaint process model (developed by the author on the basis of an erroneous diagram from the network)

Fig. 2.13 BPMN—process participants and roles

Another very visible problem in this diagram is that on the customer side the process starts and ends—the start and end events are visible—but the continuity of the process is missing. After the action of "filing a complaint" by the customer, the process stops, and the final events never happen. The diagram in this form for those familiar with BPMN is simply wrong.

Another problem is the use of the "script" tasks "Sending a refusal letter of complaint" and "Sending refund information" as tasks that were probably intended to represent the task of sending information to another process participant (the customer). If in the diagram we want to represent a situation in which one process participant sends a message to another participant, we should use the task type "message." This mistake in the use of notation has resulted in the fact that from tasks of type "script" it is impossible to send a message to end events in the pool "Customer." Please note that the dashed line connecting tasks to end collisions is not a flow of "message" but a relationship of dependency because the tool, which has some control over the syntax of notation, has blocked the possibility of placing a message flow here.

Figure 2.14 is an extension of the previous model. On this model, we see (most likely) a participant in the business process called "Customer" and a participant in the business process called "Complaint Department Employee" (which, as we already know, is not a participant, but a track). The tracks within each participant, or organization, are on the model systems. And this is where the fundamental problem arises.

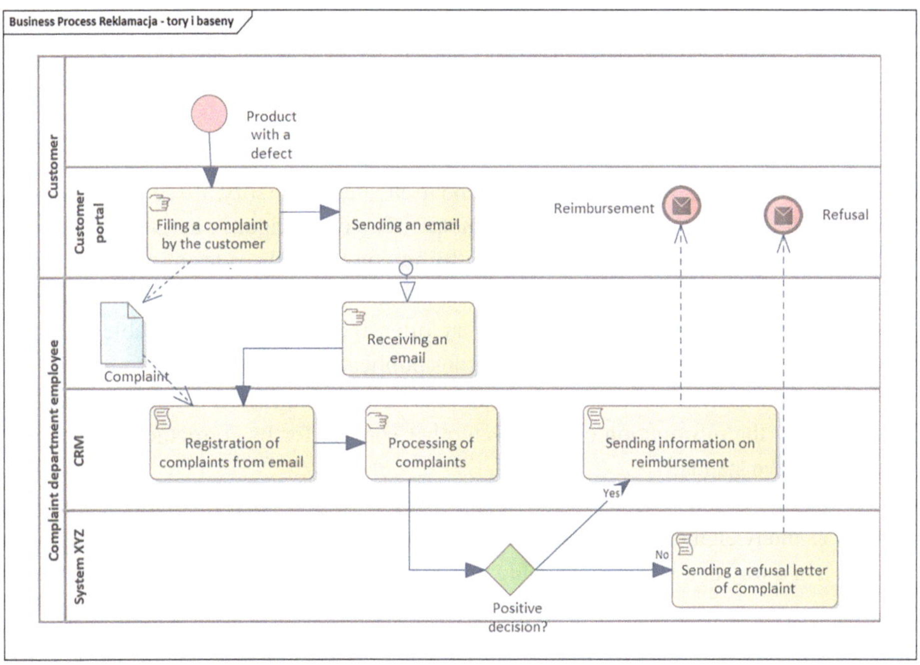

Fig. 2.14 Example of complaint process model 2 (developed by the author on the basis of a wrong diagram from the network)

First, business process models are not used to determine what we do in individual systems. That's the technology layer, not the business layer. Systems can be thought of as resources assigned to individual activities, an implementation layer, but not roles in business processes. Unfortunately, this is one of the common mistakes in business process diagrams. Business modeling focuses on the interaction of business participants. For some reason, on a business process model we show the interaction of a participant with the system. From the point of view of the business process, it is irrelevant in which system this interaction takes place. What is important is the interaction between business participants. The system is a resource, a tool, not a business participant.

Even if we assume that the representation of the system on the process model makes sense and brings some value, it does not change the fact that the logic of the model is disturbed, to say the least. For example, the activity "processing a complaint" is a manual task. According to the standard, a manual activity is "… a task to be performed without the help of any business process execution engine or any application" (OMG 2010). How, then, do you interpret a model that shows that this task is performed in the CRM track?

The tasks "Receiving an email" and "Sending a refusal letter for a complaint" are not assigned to any track inside the "Complaint department employee" pool, unless the track is there, but not named (which is a modeling error). If we use the mechanism of tracks inside the pool, then each task and each model element should be assigned to a specific, named, track.

Business process models with glaring errors, not just errors related to not following specific notations, are plentiful on the Web and other sources. It is therefore worth treating the available sources quite carefully, especially if we care about the compliance of our models with specific notations.

What can be done to avoid similar errors?

- *Learn the notation.* While this recommendation sounds cursory, it seems that there is indeed a lack of knowledge about the standard of a given language notation. Personally, I believe that the best source providing information about the rules of a given notation is its specification, or standard. I realize that reading standards is not very engaging, but it is a reliable source of information. Very often the information available in a more accessible form, on the Internet or in various publications, is inconsistent with the standard[5]—so in order to avoid factual errors, it is best to either learn from the source or at least verify the information contained in other sources for its correctness and compliance with the standard.
- Use notation *as much as necessary*. Typically, business process modeling is not about using as many elements of a particular notation as possible, but about presenting information in a way that is understandable to the audience. If this means that we can use the

[5] As Robert Kozlowski vividly put it, paraphrasing Eric Roth's words spoken in the movie *Forrest Gump* by Tom Hanks: "Analyst blogs are like a box of chocolates—you never know what you're going to end up with."

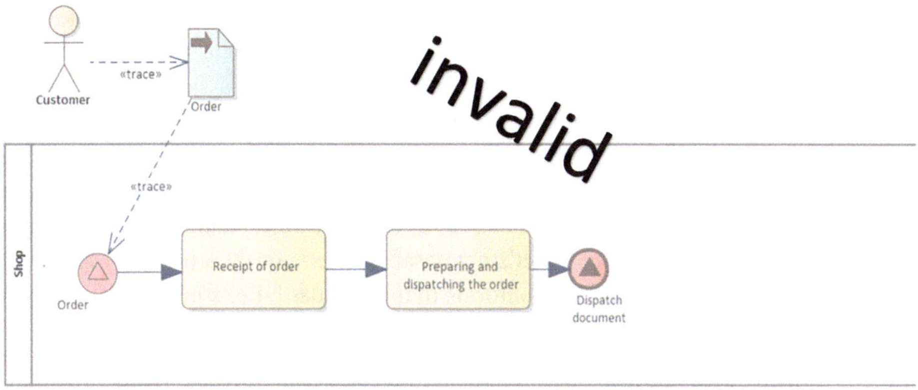

Fig. 2.15 Example of a model with incorrect use of BPMN

simplest elements of the notation, let's use them—correctly. The use of advanced notation mechanisms, as a rule, requires quite deep knowledge of the standard—in this case, it is really easy to make a mistake. The scope of notation used within a given modeling project should be defined in the modeling methodology, which can narrow and clarify the context of the symbols used.

- Don't add *your interpretation* inconsistently with the standard's assumptions. Many times I have seen models on which elements of a specific notation and language were used, but these elements were according to the interpretation adopted by the author, not according to the definition in the standard. Figure 2.15 shows a diagram in which elements of various notations were used quite freely.

On the model, you can see BPMN elements—see the "Shop" pool, UML elements, and the "customer" actor— and a fairly loose handling of the relationships between these elements. The first problem may be the practice of placing elements from several language notations on one model. This generates potential problems with understanding such a model, since we do not know quite how to interpret the resulting diagram. In the example above, we can see the relationship between the elements "Customer" and "Order"—this mechanism is not defined in either the BPMN or the UML language, from which the actor element (i.e., Customer) is derived. So we have to conjecture what the author of the diagram had in mind. By the method of deduction, we can reason that Fig. 2.15 attempted to represent the following logic: a customer places an order, which is the input information (and also the trigger) for the order handling process.

In the order handling process itself, in the "Shop" pool, another free use of BPMN appears, namely the start and end event types. The types used are signals. The situation modeled in the diagram does not justify the use of this type of element—if the input for the process is an order, this suggests that the start event should be a message type event. The final event is a dispatch document—which also indicates a message type event. The author of the diagram adopted his own interpretation of the event type, considering that the order receipt and shipping confirmation events are signals.

It is worth noting that BPMN is an open standard, which means that you can define your own artifacts. In this way, we can develop "analytical" diagrams that show not only the business process model itself, but also its context. Under this assumption, the above diagram is correct. However, if the assumption were to develop only the business process model according to the BPMN standard, Fig. 2.15 might generate unnecessary confusion.

If we are already, for some reason, using elements of the standard in our own way, let this be clearly communicated to the audience so as not to mislead them. What exactly does this mean? In the case of Fig. 2.15 , let's not describe it as a process model in BPMN—because it is in no way a model that conforms to this standard. Let's just call it a process model using elements of BPMN and other elements.

2.2.6 You Don't Always Need BPMN

THE TOOLS ARE SELECTED ACCORDING TO THE OBJECTIVE AND AUDIENCE—NOT THE OTHER WAY AROUND.

The internationally recognized standard for business process modeling is BPMN. However, it is not the only way to document processes, as we mentioned earlier. BPMN is a standard, which means that each element of this notation has its own defined meaning, and the combination of elements is strictly defined and should be used as defined in the standard. The notation itself offers extensive possibilities for modeling business processes, both at a high level and at the level of very detailed flows, exceptions, and specific conditions that trigger particular flows.

However, there are risks associated with using a particular notation or modeling language. Not every stakeholder is familiar with the notation, which means that not everyone will be able to understand the diagram and properly interpret the information it contains. Also, not every model developer is familiar with the notation. It sounds paradoxical, but I repeatedly see examples of diagrams, developed by professional business analysts, that purportedly follow BPMN, but have glaring deviations from the notation standard. If we are already using a particular notation or language, let's either use it in accordance with the standard, or let's not mislead the audience by claiming that the model we have developed is a BPMN (or any other standard)-compliant business process model.

As a general rule, there is nothing wrong with deviating from the standard and making your own assumptions, as long as your audience is aware of this, as well as aware of the consequences of such deviations, namely potential difficulties in interpreting the model by outsiders who will try to interpret it according to the notation standard.

Every notation and language has its limitations, which means that not everything can be easily modeled using a notation with limited syntax. It is worth being aware of this. There is, of course, a simple solution—nothing prevents diagrams and models from being supplemented with textual explanations. There is a dedicated mechanism in the BPMN standard, namely annotation—an element through which we can explain the meaning, special conditions, or other information relevant to understanding the diagram or its specific elements.

When is it worth using BPMN?

- When we care that processes are modeled according to the standard. This can be relevant when we model processes as a basis for later implementation of ERP or similar systems. An argument can also be made when the results of our work—the documentation of the models—are intended for others, who will not necessarily be able to correctly interpret models developed using the “proprietary” method.
- When the recipients know and understand the notation at a sufficient level to avoid potential misunderstandings. This means that when developing simple process models, it is not necessarily required to use the full capabilities of the notation. In many cases, a very limited set of elements is enough to create complete and accurate models.
- When we do not want to incur unnecessary costs. There are people in the market who are familiar with the BPMN standard (as well as other modeling standards). If an organization would like to use its own approach to modeling, one should expect that one’s own standard has to be taught to new employees—in many cases an unnecessary cost.

When is it not necessarily appropriate to use a standardized notation?

- When our objective is mainly to communicate and agree on how processes work. When the audience does not care about models that conform to standards, but about structuring knowledge so that people without specific competencies are able to understand and interpret them. When there is no need to model specific aspects, such as communication between process participants or the definition of conditions for triggering exceptional and alternative flows. When you care about simple flow models, then you can choose other ways to model processes, such as simple flowcharts.
- When we do not know the notation or know it at an insufficient level, then there is a risk of creating processes that do not conform to the standard, which can introduce information chaos. In such a case, the solution may be to use a simpler method of process documentation that does not require knowledge of an elaborate standard with many rules. Examples of such a technique might include SIPOC or simple block diagrams.

Alternatives to BPMN may include the following:

- Workflow diagrams (flowcharts)
- Universal Process Notation (UPC)
- Data flow diagrams (DFDs)
- IDEF—a family of process modeling techniques developed by the United States Air Force. Includes various versions such as IDEF0, IDEF1X, etc.
- Event-driven Process Chain (EPC)

2.3 Stakeholder Analysis

CRITICAL STAKEHOLDERS ARE THOSE WHO CAN DETERMINE THE SUCCESS OR FAILURE OF A PROJECT.

IF YOU DON'T FIND CRITICAL STAKEHOLDERS, THEY WILL FIND YOU.
TOM GILB, CONSULTANT, METHODS INVENTOR.

2.3.1 Understand the Concept of Stakeholders

A STAKEHOLDER IS ANY PERSON OR ORGANIZATION THAT IS INVOLVED IN ANY WAY IN THE IMPLEMENTATION OF A CHANGE INITIATIVE, OR THAT WILL BE AFFECTED BY THE CHANGE. THIS IMPACT CAN ALSO BE INDIRECT.

A project stakeholder is not only the customer and end users (Paul and James 2020). Sometimes we forget this and focus mainly on analyzing the needs of these stakeholder groups only. As a result, we have no knowledge of other stakeholders who may be as critical as the customer. And since we have no knowledge of stakeholders, we also have no knowledge of their expectations and needs. Consequently, we don't have the information that may be critical to determining the right solution option. Stakeholders are important because we don't just work with them to identify requirements, develop a solution, and validate it later. Stakeholder identification and analysis are critical to the success of any endeavor, as stakeholders are the source of constraints as well as risks.

How to approach stakeholder identification?

- Understand the very idea of a stakeholder. Stakeholders are all individuals and organizations that affect and can be affected by a project and its results. Stakeholders are, for example, institutions that provide industry standards, regulators, tax authorities, etc.
- Remember that stakeholders are not just the people who will directly use or benefit from the solution. Stakeholders can be and are connected to the project or the change initiative in general in an indirect way. People who are affected by the change through a change in work practices, procedures, or organizational change are also stakeholders. Project team members who will produce the solution and can provide suggestions on how to implement the requirements are also stakeholders.
- Use tools to help classify stakeholders, such as *Alexander's onion diagram* or *stakeholder wheel*. These tools will help you understand the different levels of stakeholders and how they relate to the project you are implementing. Thus, we will reduce the risk of overlooking stakeholders who are not directly related to the designed solution.
- Classify stakeholders. There are many ways to classify stakeholders, starting with the simplest methods, dividing stakeholders into business and technical. According to another approach, you can divide stakeholders into internal and external. Such a

classification will make it easier to later analyze stakeholders and establish rules for working with them.
- Remember that stakeholder identification is only the first step. The next step is to analyze them, determine their importance in the project, their level of decision-making, and their competence and areas of expertise. And this, in turn, is the starting point for managing stakeholder expectations, managing stakeholder relationships, and planning communications.

Already identifying a stakeholder can provide information about additional stakeholders. Unfortunately, it happens that we stop identifying stakeholders when we obtain a list of people and organizations that we know are involved in the project in some way. What we often don't know is that these stakeholders can provide information to identify other stakeholders that we don't know about because they are not directly involved in the planned change.

Let me provide an example of extended stakeholder identification.

The initiative is about improving product storage processes. Stakeholders were identified: people operating the warehouse, business process owner, logistics. Interviews with people working in the warehouse revealed that warehousing processes are closely linked to sales and production processes, which consequently means that the stakeholders of the change are also those involved in sales and production processes. At a minimum, stakeholders associated with related processes should be consulted on any changes proposed to warehousing processes, as they may affect how tasks are performed in other departments. Thus, the pre-identified stakeholders became a source of information regarding other stakeholders.

2.3.2 Stakeholder Analysis Is Not Just About Identifying

> The stakeholder list is just the beginning. The key information for the success of the initiative will give us only stakeholder analysis.
>
> It's like building a project team. If you gather a group of people around you, but don't understand who has what competencies and what contribution they can make to the project, if you don't determine who should do what given their skills, needs and motivations, you don't have a team, you have a group of people.

Stakeholder is a concept widely used in the field of project management in business. As a rule, we are familiar with the definition of this word, also known as the concept of stakeholder analysis. The problem is that, relatively often, we view stakeholder analysis only as stakeholder identification.

To effectively collaborate and manage stakeholder engagement, it is not enough to simply develop a list of people involved in a project. An analysis needs to be done to understand:

- Their positions in the organization
- Their level of decision-making
- Their motivation toward the project, and their attitudes
- The extent of their expertise
- Expectations regarding communication and information provided

In fact, stakeholder identification is only the first step in the stakeholder management process itself, which includes stakeholder analysis, prioritization, and engagement planning and monitoring.

At this point, one may ask why it is not enough to know that there are certain stakeholders, and they have some influence on the tasks we carry out. Let's consider the example of a company providing property security services—alarm systems for residential and commercial premises. The organization plans to provide customers with an application through which they will be able to monitor the status of the alarm system anywhere and anytime. With the help of cameras, they will be able to have a remote view of what is happening at the premises and react accordingly.

Let's imagine that for a project to develop such an application, we have identified the following stakeholders:

- End user—the owner of the premises with an alarm system or a resident of the premises or an employee of the company where the premises has an alarm system installed
- Business representatives of the organization
- Alarm system installers
- Property security agency
- Police

The above information is the result of preliminary stakeholder identification. How to use this information for further analytical activities? We might be tempted to interview each representative of the stakeholder groups and get information about what they would expect from such an application. The problem is that stakeholders like the asset protection agency or the police probably don't know what we're talking about at all—because they are in no way interested in the application we are developing, have no opinion about it, and are unable to provide any meaningful and valuable information, except what they are able to determine by playing the role of the end user of such a system.

So let's try to take an interest in the type of stakeholder "end user"—the resident of the premises. Again, we can spend some time conducting pleasant interviews with this type of stakeholder, learning about their pains, needs, and expectations.

Can we treat the information we get from them as confirmed requirements? Absolutely not. Why? Because these stakeholders, in the context of our project, are most likely not decision-making stakeholders—any information, suggestions, insights obtained from them should be discussed with the decision-making stakeholders who will decide whether to implement such proposals.

Without stakeholder analysis, there is a high risk of making mistakes of the kind described above. This is because we don't know the importance of the various stakeholders, we don't know who the decision-makers are, we don't know who cares about the project and who is willing to help us, we don't know who are the stakeholders whose opinion will be binding on our decisions, and finally, we don't know who are the stakeholders who can impose restrictions on us. In a word, there is a lack of stakeholder analysis, without which:

- We are unable to identify key stakeholders who will be the source of requirements.
- We are unable to determine the levels of decision-making in the project.
- We are unable to identify the source of constraints and overarching requirements that will have to be met, regardless of the opinions of other stakeholders.
- We are unable to identify who will be allies of the change and who will be opponents—speaking more generally, taking away information about potential project risks.

Identifying stakeholders without analyzing them can be compared to trying to make a cake, having a list of ingredients, but without a recipe. Probably by trial and error, after some time we will come to a reasonable conclusion and manage to produce a reasonably good-quality cake. This will take some time and consume some resources (when producing a cake for personal objectives, this is probably an acceptable risk). In the case of business projects, the cost of such experiments and mistakes is usually enormous—so it's better to avoid them by properly managing risks. And in this case, the source of risk is the lack of stakeholder analysis.

One interesting tool that can help a business analyst understand stakeholders is the so-called Stakeholder Circle. This tool identifies stakeholders belonging to specific groups and categorizes them into stakeholders internal and external to the organization (Fig. 2.16).

Examples of stakeholder groups are:

1. Owners—internal stakeholders (e.g., founders, directors)
2. Managers—internal stakeholders (e.g., executives)
3. Employees—internal stakeholders (e.g. staff, teams, departments, groups)
4. Competitors—external stakeholders (e.g., competitors operating in the same industry or similar industries)
5. Customers—external stakeholders (e.g., buyers and users of products/services)
6. Partners—external stakeholders (e.g., allies, partners)
7. Suppliers—external stakeholders (e.g., suppliers of materials, parts, services)
8. Regulators—external stakeholders (e.g., regulators and supervisors)

The use of the Stakeholder Circle technique, on the one hand, supports the identification of stakeholders, providing an almost ready-made checklist for identifying the groups influencing the organization, while at the same time making it possible to classify them according to the approach taken.

Fig. 2.16 Stakeholder wheel

Another very valuable tool is the salience model, developed by Ronald K. Mitchell, Bradley R. Agle, and Donna J. Wood (Mitchell et al. 1997). This model is already years old—it was developed in 1997, but the passage of time does not at all reflect on its value and usefulness. Among business analysts, a fairly popular stakeholder analysis technique is a simple power and interest matrix. The importance model is an advanced development of this concept.

According to this model, the attributes against which we can classify stakeholders are:

1. Power—the ability of a stakeholder to influence an organization or project. In other words, the likelihood that a particular stakeholder will be able to pursue its objectives and its will even despite resistance.
2. Legitimacy—the general perception or assumption that a stakeholder's actions are desirable, appropriate, or suitable within a given organizational or project context. Empowerment gives the stakeholder the right to influence the organization's decisions and actions.
3. Urgency—the degree to which a stakeholder's claims require immediate attention.

Each stakeholder may have a different level of value for these attributes—as defined by the salience model (Fig. 2.17). For example, stakeholders who have only one of the

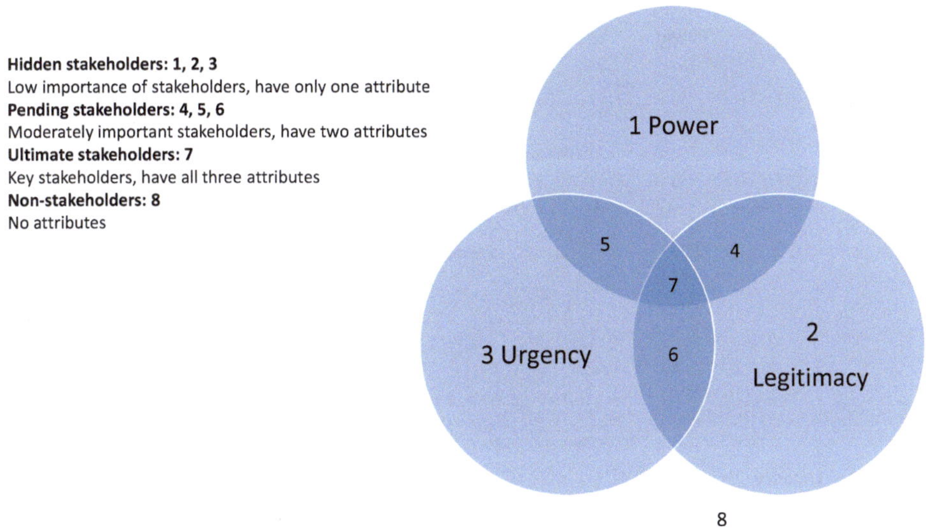

Fig. 2.17 Salience model, adapted from Mitchell et al. (1997)

attributes (e.g., only power) are referred to as hidden stakeholders. Given the project constraints, the relationship with these stakeholders is not managed in a special way, as they are unlikely to have any interest in the project and the results achieved. Hence, in the importance model, the importance of these stakeholders is described as low.

On the other hand, stakeholders who have high power and legitimacy are referred to as dominant stakeholders—they have considerable influence in the organization or in the project. Relationships with them need to be managed especially carefully and engagement needs to be built, because their expectations are reasonable; they are decision-makers, so they are key project stakeholders.

Another very interesting type of stakeholder mentioned by the importance model is the dangerous stakeholder. These are those stakeholders who have some power; their needs are urgent, while they lack legitimacy. Such stakeholders may use some coercive means or may be aggressive, as long as they achieve their objectives. They may act to the detriment of both the project and the organization itself.

The salience model defines several other types of stakeholders (Fig. 2.18). Personally, I think it is worthwhile to at least familiarize yourself with this model and the assumptions made in it, because in many cases they explain certain behaviors and situations related to stakeholder relations. There are many other techniques and methods of stakeholder analysis. The choice of a particular tool depends on what information you want to obtain and what objectives you want to achieve. What is important at the stage of strategy analysis, studying the functioning of the organization and identifying business needs, is to understand who are the potential beneficiaries of the change, how they will be involved in the process of implementing the change, and what that involvement manifests itself as. It may consist in the fact that they will provide information, make decisions, and use the solution.

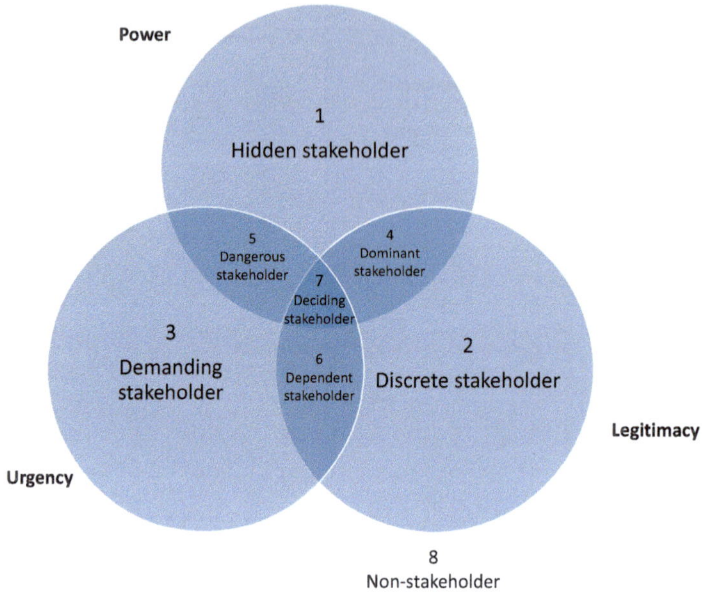

Fig. 2.18 Salience model—stakeholder types, adapted from Mitchell et al. (1997)

It is worthwhile to understand what characterizes each stakeholder group, so that we will be able to manage their involvement more easily, without overlooking the relationship with them as well.

I would summarize the stakeholder analysis identification activities as follows:

- Identify stakeholders (using any technique that fits the context).
- Identify stakeholder characteristics, such as level of decision-making, level of interest, area of expertise.
- Identify the objectives of the stakeholders in relation to the change initiative—this will enable you to identify potential conflicts of interest.
- Identify attitudes toward the change initiative, so you will know who potential allies are and who opponents are.
- Get information that will allow you to plan communications with stakeholders—availability at a certain time, preferred channels and forms of communication.
- Remember that already identified stakeholders are a source of information about subsequent stakeholders.

An example of an excerpt from the result of stakeholder identification and analysis is shown in Table 2.1.

Complementing the above information can be information related to communication planning (Table 2.2).

Table 2.1 Excerpt from stakeholder documentation

Area	Name	Position	Domain	Decision-making	Interest	Attitude	Goals
Business	Tomek	Director of production department	Production	High	Medium	Neutral	The change must not affect the way production workers work
Business	Dorota	Director of procurement department	Sales	High	High	Positive	Obtain information on production capabilities to support sales and customer services
Business	Anna	Customer service employee	Customer service	Low	Medium	Neutral	Access to information on the status of order processing
Business	Jan	Customer service employee	Customer service	Low	Medium	Positive	Ability to check the feasibility of an order within a certain time frame

Table 2.2 Excerpt from stakeholder documentation on communication requirements

Name	Position	Location	Time availability	Communication channel	Comments
Tomek	Director of production department	Warsaw—Office Building 1	8:00–16:00	Phone	SMS before making a phone call
Dorota	Director of procurement department	Gdansk—Office building 12	7:00–15:00	Phone, email	
Anna	Customer service employee	Remote	Shift mode	Mail, corporate messenger	

2.3.3 Understand Stakeholder Motivation

When planning and then implementing change in an organization, the support of stakeholders is essential. Even if they have no formal authority, their involvement and active participation significantly facilitate the implementation of change. Therefore, it is worth involving stakeholders as early as possible and taking into account their needs and expectations. If we give them the feeling that they are participants and not just objects of the change, they will accept it much more easily.

Radosław Grębski, Business analyst, Coach, Mentor, ITability

Stakeholders are, in many cases, one of the main sources of requirements and information about the operation of an organization. It is from the stakeholders that domain expertise about a given area comes—the business analyst is "merely" a facilitator of discussions and a person who coordinates the work toward determining business needs and developing solutions. It is the stakeholders who have the knowledge of how the organization functions, what problems it faces, and what the consequences of those problems are—consequences that are very often invisible to those in management.

Stakeholder analysis is done, among other things, to understand who we will work with on a given change initiative, and who will provide us with the information we need to carry out our tasks. However, it's worth realizing that we also analyze stakeholders to determine what impact the planned change will have on them—on their tasks, position in the company, and other aspects. We need to realize that identifying business needs means that we start working on an initiative that changes the current state of affairs in the organization—not everyone sees change as something positive.

So we will be dealing with stakeholders who see change as an opportunity for growth, an improvement in the processes in which they are involved, and a chance for advancement. Their attitude and expectations regarding the results of the initiative make them our allies. These stakeholders care about developing an effective solution, changing the way the company operates, even if it means changing their own work style. These will be stakeholders who are likely to absorb new knowledge, learn, and want change because they see it as a benefit to themselves.

From the point of view of business analysis and the objectives set before it, it is important to understand what benefits stakeholders see in the change. This is important because stakeholder motivation can influence their perspective, needs, and expectations of the planned solution. For example, if a stakeholder's motivation is to implement process automation so that he or she sees an opportunity for a promotion, we should realize that this stakeholder will be very involved in identifying possible improvements and bringing about their implementation. From our point of view, this is both beneficial and a risk—because it may turn out that the highest business value will be obtained not by automating the process, but by abandoning it altogether (because during the analysis it turned out that in the target state of the organization the process is unnecessary).

A stakeholder who has specific objectives related to the implementation of the solution and will try to achieve them can be, to some extent, a threat to the success of the initiative, as he may try to push his point of view and his needs.

Consider another example of the potential impact of stakeholder motivation on analytical activities. We are working on improving the manufacturing process. At the moment, the production process is carried out by employees, the operators. The employees don't necessarily care about the financial success of the organization, improving processes, or increasing organizational maturity—they just want to do their job and get paid for it. Since we analyze their processes, it is natural that they are our stakeholders with expert knowledge of how to execute the process. However, we know that their motivation to support change may be relatively low—on the contrary, they may care about maintaining the status quo (i.e.,let's not change anything).

If we planned analytical activities in such a way as to involve these stakeholders in the process of identifying possible process improvements, we must realize that the information obtained from them may be very biased. For example, we may receive information indicating that there are no opportunities to improve certain processes—not because such opportunities do not exist, but because these stakeholders do not want any changes. The question remains, then, whether it makes sense to involve stakeholders with such attitudes in activities aimed at identifying opportunities for change.

We can probably identify stakeholders who would be better suited to support this objective—the production manager, the owner of production processes. These stakeholders have different motivations, different needs and expectations due also to their different position in the organization. They are most likely to care about making changes that increase the efficiency of the production process. So they will be motivated to work on identifying real opportunities for improvement.

Does this mean that we should completely ignore the existence of process operators? I think not at all—they are an excellent source of knowledge about how the process is being implemented at the moment. We can get this knowledge from them by asking questions about how the work is being carried out or by using observational techniques. However, given their attitudes, we would be unlikely to involve them in developing a proposal for change.

If we want to properly plan stakeholder engagement, we need to understand not only stakeholder characteristics, such as their expertise or position in the organization, but also their motivations. By doing so, we will be able to determine who we can see as an ally in the change design process, and who is more of an opponent. Stakeholders with a neutral attitude, those who see neither benefit to themselves nor special harm in the change, we can probably consider as a relatively objective source of information. However, we should be aware that because they do not see the change as a benefit to themselves, we should not expect them to be particularly involved in the process of determining the change. They are likely to help us when we ask them to, but they are unlikely to come up with the initiative on their own.

Understanding stakeholder motivations will help us determine how and on what topics to communicate with them, to what extent the information we get from them can be seen as reliable. It will also help us evaluate the changes they suggest—whether they are changes that have the potential to deliver value to the organization or only to that particular stakeholder. Of course, understanding the motivation of stakeholders is not a trivial task, because very often this motivation is hidden. Stakeholders rarely overtly reveal their motivations, aspirations, and plans. Very often we have to guess this motivation on the basis of certain symptoms and information obtained from other sources. That's why it's so important in the analysis process not to suggest the opinions of one party, but to gather information from various sources, confront this information, and evaluate the reported business needs and proposals for change for convergence with the organization's objectives. Of course, this requires knowledge of the organization's business objectives and strategy—but if we don't have knowledge of the organization's motivations, we won't be able to determine whether the changes deliver value to the business or to individual units.

2.3.4 Explore Stakeholder Perspectives

SINCE EACH OF US PERCEIVES REALITY IN A DIFFERENT WAY, ANALYZES INFORMATION AND DRAWS CONCLUSIONS FROM A DIFFERENT PERSPECTIVE, WHY DO WE ASSUME THAT STAKEHOLDERS HAVE A CONSISTENT VIEW TOWARD CHANGE?

Any change initiative touches a range of stakeholders representing different business areas involved in different aspects of the organization. Stakeholders, who are key to realizing and implementing a solution that meets specific business needs, may have different attitudes about the initiative; and so there are stakeholders who will support the change, as well as potential opponents.

Stakeholders are one source of requirements and needs, so it is worthwhile to know their perspective before moving on to the information acquisition processes.

As Anna Kochanowska, Business Analyst & Product Thinking Advocate, notes, one of the objectives of strategy analysis is to generate information flows between different areas of the organization's operation. Stakeholders representing different areas usually have different attitudes toward change.

For example, top management is responsible for setting business objectives and business development strategies. These stakeholders rarely see the issues and needs relevant to stakeholders at lower levels in the organization, because they have neither the need nor the space to delve into such details. They are mainly interested in the organization's layer of business motivation, courses of action, and challenges and problems relevant to business development.

Middle and lower-level management, on the other hand, is responsible for implementing the established strategy. At this level, problems may arise in interpreting how to implement the strategy, setting measurable objectives, and defining responsibilities. Resistance to change can also arise at this level, as change undermines the status quo, can be perceived as a threat to the position of individuals in the organization, and can reveal competency gaps. There are also often internal conflicts of interest—stakeholders at this level are often driven by their own interests, without delving into the organization's business development strategy.

Employees, i.e., the people who will be affected by the planned change, often do not see the need or justification for the changes. From their perspective, the planned changes do not solve real problems (real, i.e., visible from their point of view) but only change the way the organization operates, and cause information chaos and the need to adapt to new procedures. From the perspective of the rank-and-file employee, the strategy set at the management level often does not add any significant value or solve the problems that employees face on a daily basis. What's more, the needs and problems flagged by rank-and-file employees are very often classified by them as critical, while from management's perspective they are not significant to the way the organization operates. As a result, employees often perceive management and the strategic layer as something detached from reality. However, employees are the ones who perform the tasks whose results deliver specific value to consumers, so their perspective and insights should be important in verifying the improvement of the change strategy.

Understanding stakeholders' perspectives is important not only to understand their attitudes toward change, but also to determine what kind of information these stakeholders can provide.

A rank-and-file employee can provide detailed information about how a particular process is being implemented, the problems and challenges that are occurring, and their suggestions for improving that particular process. The rank-and-file employee often does not see the interdependencies between the organization's various departments, and other processes and business functions, and views the organization through the lens of his or her limited slice of reality.

Middle management is responsible for implementing the strategy set by the organization's authorities. They have set objectives that often conflict with their personal goals and objectives. Therefore, it is very important to pay attention to potential conflicts of interest and the conscious or unconscious sabotage of change initiatives. These stakeholders often care about implementing certain strategies with minimal effort and risk. Like rank-and-file employees, middle management may not see the connections between different areas of the organization. Therefore, when working on a given change, it is important to involve stakeholders representing different areas and business functions, so as to simultaneously help them understand the impact of decisions on other elements of the organization.

Top executives often see the organization as a business system and its context. They do not delve into the details or know the problems occurring at the operational level. Nor do they see the correlation between problems at the operational level and the performance of the organization as seen from their perspective. They may set objectives and strategies that are unworkable or high risk, given the organization's circumstances. That's why it's important not only to elicit information from stakeholders during strategy analysis, but also to enable discussion among stakeholders operating at different levels in the organizational hierarchy.

Interestingly, this discussion is often hindered by biases and stereotypes.

To cite an example, a certain manufacturing organization initiated a business process improvement program. Management representatives were involved in the initiative—they were to be responsible for determining the desired changes and developing a target state concept for selected business processes. Already at the early stages of the discussion a problem arose in the form of lack of detailed knowledge of the current way of implementing the processes. Stakeholders representing management had never been production employees, so they had no knowledge of how certain processes are performed, and what challenges might be involved in improving them. Documentation explaining some aspects of process execution was available, but it did not cover all areas of interest.

To suggestions to engage production employees in communication to determine the current state and identify opportunities for improvement, management responded by stating that production employees certainly have nothing of value to say, as they are focused solely on getting their work done, and any improvement initiatives certainly do not interest them. This statement was not based on facts—conversations with representatives of production workers, feedback received from them. It was simply an opinion expressed by management.

The question I asked regarding if and when anyone had talked to employees about this issue was answered in the negative. The same answer was given when they were asked about the availability of feedback from production employees on proposed process improvements. There was no feedback—not because employees didn't provide it, but simply because no one asked for it. The problem was not a lack of motivation for employees to get involved in the change initiative, but the lack of any attempt to build that involvement.

A decision was therefore made to change the way of working.

As a first step, management was to inform employees about the initiative launched, and its objectives and goals. Next, we selected employee representatives who were to be involved in understanding the current state and identifying opportunities for improvement. These included both long-serving employees and those new to the company. This was a completely intentional procedure—we wanted people who had just started work and had not yet managed to develop any habits and routines to provide a fresh perspective.

At the next stage, we developed target state models of the processes with the production staff. This was a valuable exercise for both sides—employees and management—because both sides learned their perspective at the same time. And so the employees learned what the processes they were implementing were for, and the management learned details of process implementation that they were previously unaware of. Interestingly, management and production employees in many places had completely different opinions about how processes should be carried out—management thought that according to procedures a certain task should be done like this, while employees straightened out this information and explained that for years tasks have been carried out in a completely different way, established within the organizational standard.

Ultimately, we developed models of the current state, a list of possible improvements that would actually bring business value, from both the employee and management perspectives, and models of the target state. In addition to these tangible results, we also achieved shared understanding, knowledge sharing, and employee involvement in the business change initiative, which translates into a reduced risk of staff resistance when the change is implemented.

Thanks to this approach, management has understood that rank-and-file employees often have very valuable information to share, their insights and suggestions allowing for actual improvement of processes and business results. On the other hand, employees understood that their opinion counts—they have a real impact on the way the company operates. And that's what business analysis is all about, too—to arrive at a solution in a way that involves stakeholders, rather than by themselves.

2.4 Identification of Business Needs

What the customer identifies as their needs is usually not what they really need.
Niels Malotaux, Project Coach, N R Malotaux, Consultancy

The essence of the analyst's role is to ask, listen, understand.
Robert Kozłowski, BPMN Coach and business processes improvement consultant, MPB Infoservice

2.4.1 Ask. Obtain Information. Draw Conclusions

At every stage of the project, let's keep in mind what our role is and the objectives we have set for ourselves. The business analyst's role is to gain information, support stakeholders in identifying problems and making decisions, and use his knowledge and experience to present options and alternatives. The role of a business analyst can be compared to that of a meeting facilitator—we aim to gather information from stakeholders and other sources, such as the business context, and then analyze and synthesize this information, suggesting some directions for change.

The analyst's role is not to impose solutions before identifying the business problem, understanding the scope and impact of potential changes. I would say that the role of an analyst is not to impose any solutions at all—we perform an advisory function, connecting the business world with the world of technology. With this in mind, let's remember to:

- Ask questions about problems, needs, pain points. Let's not ask "What kind of system do you want to implement?" "What changes do you expect?" "What requirements do you have?"—our role is to understand the current situation and the problems that exist and areas that can be improved. Let's refrain from asking questions about what stakeholders expect solutions. The time to choose a solution will come when the business problem and possible ways to solve it are known.
- Listen to suggestions for changes and improvements. In many cases, stakeholders have insights into the current state of the organization. Listen to these opinions—it is not uncommon for them to be ready suggestions for changes that should be made to a particular process or product. It is the stakeholders who perform certain processes, use systems or products on a daily basis—they are the ones who have the best knowledge

of what is not working and what can be improved. Our job is to gather this information and translate it into specific business needs. Let's not see ourselves as the only people empowered to determine changes—if only because we most likely lack the information and understanding of the business context to be able to propose changes that will actually bring value to the business. Instead of relying solely on our own knowledge and our own understanding of the situation, let's use the knowledge that exists in the organization—the knowledge that people have.

- Use the information available to determine business needs together with stakeholders. Stakeholders are not the only source of information. A great deal of valuable data can be obtained from market analysis, especially competitive analysis, studying trends and solutions implemented in other industries. Let's conduct such an analysis, and consult the results obtained with stakeholders. This will give us more data before making any binding decision on the planned solution.
- Not be afraid to ask questions, in case of doubt. Let's remember to ask for additional information that can help clarify the problem. Unfortunately, quite often in case of doubts, missing information, or inconsistencies, we ignore this fact and move on to the next steps. We count on the fact that problems will solve themselves over time. Unfortunately, as a rule, they do not solve themselves at all, but grow to critical status. If at any stage something is unclear to us, let's ask questions, even if we think the questions are "stupid." If we are unable to understand certain information, let's ask questions. If we are missing some information, let's ask questions. Let's encourage stakeholders to do the same—let's explain what the objectives of the initiative are, why it is important to them, and what the consequences of decisions made on the basis of wrong assumptions might be. Let's explain why it's better to ask 100 questions and revisit the same topic several times to clear up any doubts, rather than rely on assumptions or guesswork.
- Accept the fact that stakeholders are entitled to opinions different from ours. In no way does this justify trying to undermine those opinions and prove your point.

Our job is not to prove to others that we are professionals, experts, and have deep knowledge of a particular business area.

Our job is to identify solutions that will bring value—with the active participation of stakeholders. It's not our opinions or preferences that are critical in deciding on a course of action—so let's not focus on individual opinions, including our own, but on the business, the organization and what will bring real benefit to it.

Obtaining reliable information from a variety of sources, from stakeholders representing different points of view, getting information that we don't question and evaluate through the prism of our own opinions and experiences—this is the starting point for analyzing it and drawing conclusions. Note that only if we keep an open mind and simply acknowledge the information that stakeholders give us will we be able to determine the real business needs. This is a prerequisite for defining the right solution options.

2.4.2 Root Cause Analysis as a Source of Business Needs

If you don't know what the source of the problem is, how do you want to solve the problem permanently?

Too often we focus on the symptoms and don't get to the root of the problem. As a result, we put out fires instead of preventing them.

There are many approaches to identifying business needs. One of them is interviewing stakeholders to identify problems affecting them during the execution of the work and the possibility of ways to solve these problems. Business needs can arise from the business environment, such as changes in regulations, competition with similar offerings, and changes in customer preferences. An interesting approach to determining business needs is also the use of Root Cause Analysis. Root Cause Analysis, in a nutshell, involves examining a specific problem to identify the cause of its occurrence. Through Root Cause Analysis, we are able to understand what is the real source of problems—such as complaints, decreased customer satisfaction, delays in production—and, going forward, eliminate that cause.

Improving a process or product, improving the quality of a specific focus by removing the source of the problem, sounds like a fairly obvious practice. However, despite appearances, it is neither obvious nor particularly widely used. In many cases, unfortunately, we focus not on addressing the source of the problem, but rather the symptoms—and it's the source of the problem that we don't get to at all. Consider a simple example.

A tester checks the operation of a system. As a result of the testing activities, he reports a large number of faults. The defect at this point is a problem, specifically a problem related to the poor quality of the system under test. However, is it really a problem, a root cause, or merely a symptom of a real problem? If, in this particular case, we take the trouble to analyze the situation and find out where the problem is coming from, we can come to the following conclusions: the tester reports a large number of defects because the system is not working according to specifications. When asked why his source code does not comply with the specification, the developer replies that the source code was implemented according to the provisions of the specification. At this point we already see the problem of conflicting opinions from two sides. Analyzing the topic more deeply, we should look at what is clearly the point of disagreement here, namely the requirements specification. An analysis of the requirements specification can show that the provisions of the specification are so vague and ambiguous that they can be interpreted in different ways. So, in a sense, both the tester and the programmer are right—of course, this is a contractual statement, pointing out that if the requirements specification is not unambiguous, there will be discrepancies in interpretation and each party will be convinced that its interpretation is correct.

The source of the problem we have just discovered, therefore, is an imprecise and ambiguous requirements specification. We have stated a fact, based on analysis of information. What is the result of this fact? Nothing yet, beyond the fact that we know there is a problem with the quality of the specification. However, we still don't know what the source of the problem is. And here we come to the bottom line—what could be the cause of an imprecise requirements specification?

The reasons can be various:

- Lack of requirements quality control practice—for example, there may have been a lack of reviews in the specification development process, and the analyst was not even aware of the mistakes he made.
- Workshop deficiencies of the analyst, who does not know the principles of developing requirements in such a way that they are precise, measurable, and unambiguous.
- Insufficient time for specification, resulting in the analyst's hurried, time-pressured focus on describing the requirements in a reasonably complete manner, rather than on describing them well enough.

If the cause of the requirements specification quality problem is a lack of quality control, the next question we could ask is why the project lacked specification reviews. And here we could discover the real reason—because reviews are not standard in the organization's product development process, particularly requirements development, and therefore were not planned as part of the design work. A solution to this problem could be to include reviews as mandatory quality gates in the requirements development process. With this solution, we reduce the risk of requirements being released for implementation that have not passed mandatory quality control, and as a result there is less risk that both the developer and tester create their work products based on imprecise requirements and are forced to make some interpretations and rely on assumptions.

In summary, in the specific situation under discussion, the root cause is the lack of requirements quality control practice. The solution could be to implement reviews as a mandatory design practice.

It is worth noting that when trying to get to the cause of a problem, it often turns out that there may be several sources of problems. In our specific example, the problem could be both a lack of reviews due to a lack of a process standard, and the analyst's workshop deficiencies, which in turn could be due to a lack of proper training or preparation for the job, and a lack of requirements specification standards in the organization (in other words, each analyst "writes" the requirements as he or she sees fit). All these reasons put together increase the risk of delivering poor-quality requirements to the next stage of system implementation. Wanting to eliminate the problem, or at least significantly reduce the probability of its occurrence or potential consequences, we should aim to eliminate those causes that contribute most to the end result (in our case, the end result is a large number of defects reported for the product under test). In our particular case, we could conclude that the key source of the problem is the lack of a process standard—both in the sense of lack of review in the manufacturing process and lack of an analyst's work standard. In a way, the problem of lack of training is a consequence of the lack of an analyst's work standard—because since we don't have a work standard, we have no basis for requiring people to be adequately prepared to carry out project tasks.

The above example shows in a simplified way a simulation of Root Cause Analysis using the "5 × Why" technique. This technique involves asking questions thanks to which we are able to refine the answers we have already obtained and systematically get to the root of the problem. At the same time, it is worth noting that, as in the above example, I did not overtly use the question "why"—it is not necessary; questions can be asked in any form. In many cases, it is also not necessary to ask as many as five questions—we can get to the root of the problem with the second or third question.

The specific questions we could ask in the above example are:

- Question: What is the reason for such a high number of defects?
- Answer: The requirements are vague and ambiguous; the programmer has to make his own interpretation.
- Question: What is the reason that the requirements are vague and ambiguous?
- Answer: The analyst does not have adequate competence including in developing high-quality requirements.
- Question: What is the reason that the analyst does not have adequate competence in developing requirements?
- Answer: The analyst was assigned to the project without proper training, there is no knowledge sharing practice in the organization, and there is no standard for requirements specification.

If we used specific tools such as Ichikawa diagrams for Root Cause Analysis, we could apply the Pareto principle to identify the 20% of causes that generate 80% of effects. By the same token, we do not invest resources in eliminating all possible causes, because eliminating many small causes will not translate into any real benefits—we focus on eliminating those aspects that most determine the end result.

How can Root Cause Analysis be applied in strategy analysis, particularly in identifying business needs?

Imagine that you are conducting an analysis of the current state of a specific one from the scope of the organization's operations. The activity stems from a business problem, which is that customers make a lot of complaints (of course, it is worth specifying what "a lot" means in this context—probably a value above a certain rate; for simplicity I omit this aspect). Complaints relate to defects in the product delivered to the market by the company. To identify the right business need—that is, to determine what needs to be changed to improve the situation—we need to understand the source of the problem. The source of the problem could be, for example, that customers are expecting a completely different product, having been misled by the product description on the store's Web site, which gives incorrect information about the product.

The source of the problem may also be that indeed the product is defective, and the defects are due to defective material used in production. Defects could also result from inadequate product manufacturing technology—if, for example, we were considering a clothing or footwear product, the problem could stem from improper sewing of the product.

Until we determine the actual cause of a problem that manifests itself as a complaint on the part of the organization, we can neither determine what change should be made and where, nor select the right solutions for the problem.

And so, considering this example further, if, by way of Root Cause Analysis, we determined that the complaints are due not to design defects, but, for example, to poor-quality material from a particular supplier, we would be able to narrow the search area and slowly approach the core of the problem. And the crux of the problem could be that in our procedures for sourcing materials from suppliers, there is a lack of mandatory quality control of each batch of materials delivered to us. This problem, in turn, could have arisen from the fact that at the very beginning of an organization's operations, the list of contractors was very small. They supplied materials of very high quality, so the organization assumed that this level of quality would be maintained. Over time, the situation may have changed, the number of suppliers may have increased, and their methods of sourcing materials may have also changed, resulting in a situation where even the most trusted suppliers happen to deliver low-quality material.

Having such information already, we are able to identify possible ways to eliminate the problem, for example

1. Ceasing to order material from a particular supplier (which, from the point of view of business relations, can be a rather drastic measure)
2. Introducing mandatory quality inspections of each batch of material from the "problematic" supplier
3. Introducing mandatory quality controls on every batch of material from every supplier

The latter proposal implies that the change will be implemented at the level of the entire supply control process, not limited to specific suppliers. This means that there is likely to be more work involved in receiving deliveries, but on the other hand it reduces the risk of similar mistakes being repeated in the future with other suppliers.

In summary, we can therefore use Root Cause Analysis to identify the sources of problems, such as production failures, customer losses, complaints, service delays, and so on. By identifying the causes of specific problems, we can conclude that there are multiple causes, among which some are key and others are minor. In this way, we can determine the scope of the proposed change.

2.4.3 Technology as a Trigger for Change

The development of business entails the development of technology. Technology serves business. But also the opposite: the development of technology causes changes in business.

Can technology be a trigger for change?

It has been said that business should be in some way detached from technology—that business development triggers the development of technology, which is a means to achieve specific business objectives. When I say detached from technology, I mean that business development should not be determined solely by current technical capabilities, which have many limitations.

When we plan the development of an organization, we very often plan it as if technological limitations did not exist—because we realize that the development of a business over time will entail the development of the technology that serves that business. Of course, this does not mean that we will develop a specific technology in a month or a year—it often takes several months or several years.[6] However, the very fact that business objectives and strategies set specific directions for technology development gives us the opportunity to create new services and shape the future.

Is it possible that the reverse is true, that technology causes business change? In other words, is it possible that a business need arises from technological capabilities, the existence of certain tools and means that give an organization a chance to achieve better business results?

Of course it is, and there are many examples of this. The business services and products available on the market are constantly evolving—they evolve because new business needs arise from, for example, new customer needs, but they also evolve because the technology available makes it possible to provide new services and modify existing ones in ways that increase consumer satisfaction.

Technology developed in one organization, by a measure, in a region, becomes available to other market players over time. They can use it with the objective of developing their business offerings, providing customers with a better user experience. An example is the use of biometrics in various business areas. The concept of recognizing people through individual physical characteristics has been known for many years. Biometric technology has been developed by many companies, including technology organizations and research centers. Today, many business areas are using this technology, including financial services, healthcare, security, education, and industry. The availability of technology is creating new business needs—as new opportunities arise to provide services, to deliver value to recipients. In the context of the biometrics under discussion, such value could be the

[6] For example, James Cameron, the director of *Avatar*, waited a dozen years to develop enough technology to realize his vision.

facilitation of a way to authorize access to certain devices through space without the need for users to log in, enter access codes, or use access cards.

Currently available technologies support business in many areas, such as data analytics, through which organizations—on the basis of analysis of huge amounts of data—can draw conclusions, thanks to which they make decisions about new strategies and development directions. Another area of technology application is the digital transformation of organizations, which entails the need to revise the entire structure and business processes of the organization, to establish a new way of doing things, new solutions and rules. This development of technology has caused many organizations to go from a "paper" mode of operation to a digital mode of operation, including customer service via the Internet, using bots, or other solutions that allow the customer to solve the problem himself with the support of a virtual consultant.

The development of new technology can initiate many changes in the way of doing business, which from the point of view of business analysis translates into new business needs, new opportunities for solutions, but also new risks. Such a risk could be, for example, the issue of maintaining data security.

How can we take advantage of the fact that business and technology are linked in the work of a business analyst?

Knowledge of new technologies can help identify business needs. Such a need may be, for example, to provide a new channel for communicating with customers via the Internet.

Knowledge of new technologies can help identify solutions to any business problem. There are many solutions available. Some of these solutions take advantage of technologies already available within an organization, while others may be based on technology that is commercially available but not within the organization. The choice of these solutions can, of course, involve increased business risk, but on the other hand, it can also give the company additional opportunities—since we are already running a certain technology to the organization, in a certain area and scope, this gives us the opportunity to test the technology at home. And this, in turn, can be the first step toward implementing the technology in a larger scope, so we can improve the organization's operations to a greater extent.

Technology is a tool, a means to achieve certain objectives. It is worth realizing that the use of a particular technology in a given context will not necessarily be a good choice.

For example, if we would like to streamline the customer service process in a small restaurant, serving an average of 200 customers per day and employing three employees, implementing a complex IT system based on biometrics, using tablet devices and signaling to customers that a dish is ready for pickup, may be counterproductive—because until now the stability of the system has been based on the effective cooperation of these three people, direct communication, and maintaining contact with the customer.

The implementation of the system may disrupt communication, or it may cause the process to slow down instead of speeding up, because employees, instead of focusing on quickly handling customer orders, will be forced to learn new technology, in running order data into the system, instead of transferring it directly to fulfillment.

The example is simplified and does not take into account many factors, but I want to show that technology is not the solution to all problems and pains of stakeholders. Sometimes the best solutions are the simplest ones, involving, for example, changing the way of communication or the order of pleasantries in the process. This is also worth keeping in mind when considering technology support.

2.4.4 Learn to Specify Business Needs, Just as We Specify Software Requirements

Vision, objectives, business needs—these are all requirements. Refer to other levels of abstraction, but define stakeholder requirements for different dimensions of the business.

"A business needs information from production."

"The courier company needs information on the number of shipments."

"The customer needs the ability to pick up shipments at any time."

Here are examples of several business needs. Business needs, as a rule, are formulated by so-called business people, thinking as stakeholders representing the business perspective, involved in the operation, owners of processes or given business areas. These people are rarely requirements engineers, are not always competent in the area of business analysis, and are not always able to properly document business needs. They have the right to do so—we are the experts with the right competencies; they have the business knowledge.

Needs specified as above are, unfortunately, completely unmeasurable. The business needs information from production—but what information? How do we verify that this need has been properly met? The same questions can be asked for the other needs in the example above.

We don't know what we really need. To say that we need information, capabilities, is not enough—to understand the essence of a business need, we need to understand what result we expect. At this stage we are not interested in how to get to the result—this will be the subject of developing the solution concept. However, at the stage of defining and evaluating a business need, we need enough information to be able to analyze the need, evaluate it, prioritize it, and decide whether the need will be implemented or not.

Referring to the above examples, another problem is also striking, namely the lack of any justification or contextual information so that we can understand why these needs are important, what problem they solve, who needs them, and for what objective. What business value do they bring and to whom? This information is not there—nor is there any way to determine whether it is worth committing any resources to further analysis of these needs.

Objectives, needs, requirements—all of these artifacts should have similar characteristics: they should be measurable, specific, relevant, and be defined in a way that allows you to assess the extent to which they are being met. They should be SMART. The SMART method has already been mentioned when discussing business objectives—in combination with SMART requirements these can take a slightly modified form. A need, a requirement, should be specific, measurable, achievable, relevant, and testable (SMART).

Requirements that are unmeasurable are ambiguous, leading to problems with implementation, testing, and acceptance of the solution. Requirements that are not relevant do not add business value. Similarly, in the case of business needs, if they don't meet SMART or other organization-defined quality criteria, they most likely don't provide information about the expected results—so we don't know what value their implementation is expected to bring; we don't even know if it's worth investing in undertaking their analysis and developing a solution concept.

Implementing solutions for specific business needs generally requires devoting a significant amount of resources. Before an organization decides to invest these resources in analyzing a given need, developing a solution concept for it, we should ensure that the documentation of the business need provides enough information to make such a decision consciously. And we will not make it if the business need documentation does not provide the following information:

- A clear, precise definition of the business need, for example, in the form of [who] needs [what] for what [objective].
- An explanation of the rationale for the business need, for example, by reference to the current state and related problems.
- A general description of the desired state. At the stage of defining the business need, we don't know what the solution will look like—and that's a very good thing, because the solution should be developed through analysis, taking into account different perspectives, constraints, and capabilities of the organization. We don't know what the solution will look like—but we know what business results we want to achieve. These results should be documented. Otherwise, we will not be able to assess whether the implementation of a business need will significantly benefit the organization.
- The risks of not making any changes from the status quo. With this information, decision-makers will be aware of the consequences of maintaining the status quo.
- Information about the overall scope of the change resulting from the realization of the business need. At this stage, it is not a matter of specifying the exact scope of the change. However, in order to assess the business need, it is necessary to know what area it touches, which business functions or processes, company divisions, and stakeholders and their groups are affected by the business need and the implementation of the change.

A business need specified in this way may look as follows:

Description: The sales department needs information about the capabilities of the production department for products defined as [company's main products].
[Company's main products]: ABC line products for the European market.

Current state: The sales department currently has no information on the capabilities of the production department. The sales department is informed after the production of certain products is completed, and there is no way to check the production capabilities before accepting an order from a customer. As a result, it often (on average 10 times per quarter) happens that a product is sold that production is not able to deliver in the declared time to the customer when the order is accepted.

Target state: The production department is involved in the process of evaluating the feasibility of the order. The sales department and the production department analyze the possibility of delivering the product within the time defined in the terms of service. If the order cannot be delivered within the defined time, the customer is informed of the extended lead time. This may result in cancellation of the order.

Acceptance criteria: The sales department receives monthly information about the capabilities of the production department, broken down by product line. The information makes it possible to determine how many products from a particular line we are able to deliver to customers in a given sales period (quarter). Based on the information provided, the sales department is able to determine the realistic lead time for customer orders.

Business benefits: Prevention of situations in which the sales department accepts a customer order for fulfillment, which the production department is not able to deliver within the agreed time. Supporting the achievement of the business objective of customer satisfaction (Business goal 01) and reducing the cost of lack of quality (BG 05).

Risk analysis of maintaining the status quo:

Risk: Decrease in sales value

Criticality: High

Consequences of not being able to deliver products on time may include an exodus of customers discouraged by prolonged lead times and a strengthened negative reputation in the market, which could lead to further customer churn and a decline in sales.

Impact of change—preliminary analysis:

Business processes or business opportunities: Production planning

Stakeholders who will be affected by the change:

- Production department
- Procurement department

Those involved in implementing the change:

- Production process owner
- Owner of the procurement and sales process
- Owner of the customer service process

This approach to documenting business needs means, of course, that the change initiator must provide more information if he or she wants the business need to be analyzed. I use this practice intentionally—among other things, to stop poorly thought out changes, unwarranted changes that do not add business value, but are simply the wishes of a particular stakeholder. Using the right template will result in the requester of a business need having to provide specific information, and to do so in a way that is as measurable as possible. Otherwise, the business need will not even be analyzed. It is therefore in the interest of the submitter to provide at a level sufficient for those evaluating the new idea.

The proposed approach imposes an obligation to provide information at the proposal stage of a business need. However, it does not mean that it is the stakeholder submitting the need who must provide and formulate this information himself—supporting the process of forming a business need fits perfectly into the responsibility of the business analyst. An example procedure for developing a business need document could be as follows.

The requestor formulates the essence of the business need, defines the current state and desired outcomes, and identifies known areas of impact of the potential change.

The business analyst verifies the information provided, supplementing it as needed and according to the state of his knowledge.

The submitter and the business analyst jointly complete the document until the information content is sufficient for the needs of the team evaluating the new ideas.

It is worth noting that assessing business needs, especially their impact, requires knowledge of how the organization operates and the interrelationships between different functions, works, and so on. Business models such as process maps and business process models can be an excellent support here.

2.4.5 AI in Strategy Analysis

Today's artificial intelligence, with its full freedom of data mining and algorithmic information processing, is becoming an invaluable ally in the field of strategy analysis. Its ability to quickly process massive amounts of data allows it to identify key patterns, trends and hidden dependencies, enabling decision-makers to better understand the business environment and make more informed decisions.

Ross Apostoł, Data Science Architect, Machine Learning Trainer

Artificial intelligence has been a hot topic of any discussion in the business analyst community for some time. Conferences, meetings, articles—much of it focuses on the topic of AI and how artificial intelligence can help us in our work.

Indeed, new technologies can help us in many areas. They can also hurt in many others—every technology has its pros and cons, as does every tool. What is noteworthy when perusing various publications is the notorious confusion of terms. Artificial intelligence, machine learning, data science—many authors treat these concepts interchangeably. Just as many over-dramatize the subject, attributing human-like thinking abilities to algorithms. At the current stage of technology, artificial intelligence is far from being truly intelligent. However, this does not change the fact that in many areas this technology is able to improve our work quite significantly, including in the area of business analysis.

For example, in strategy analysis, data science and AI can help point out new directions for business development. This is possible by analyzing large amounts of data identifying business-relevant patterns. For example, analyzing historical data on sales of specific products and juxtaposing it with factors that influence sales—such as political conditions, market trends, or fashions and lifestyles—can provide information useful for forecasting future sales. Algorithms can, for example, provide information that an offering containing certain products, targeting a specific market and customer segment, is more likely to be financially successful than an offering with other parameters. Algorithms analyze data, compare it, and draw conclusions based on certain parameters, allowing humans to make decisions based on data rather than their own intuition.

Another example of the use of algorithms in strategy analysis is business process improvement. A fairly typical problem in organizations is that business processes, designed and monitored by process owners, are performed in a way that is "out of specification." In many cases, an employee skips certain steps in the process, takes shortcuts, or performs tasks differently than defined. It would be extremely time-consuming to manually collect information about such deviations and analyze them further. Algorithms can help in this regard as well—by collecting information about how the process is currently being executed and by whom, which steps are executed according to the pattern and which are not, and which are executed differently than the model predicts. The collected information is then analyzed and grouped, so that we can conclude, for example, that certain activities envisaged in the process are unnecessary because employees do not perform them on a recurring basis and they do not affect the efficiency of task execution or the achievement of objectives. From there, a business need for process simplification may arise.

In this particular case, algorithms undoubtedly save us time. They can also avoid the risks that would likely arise if we chose to collect this information through direct observation of employees. An employee, aware of being observed, would likely be tempted to perform the process "according to the art," fearing unpleasant consequences for himself. If the algorithm is run in the background, the employee is not even aware that his operations are being recorded.

Artificial intelligence can also prove itself in the automation of certain activities, for example, in the banking or insurance area. Such solutions have existed for a long time—the algorithm analyzes the received data to detect potential fraud. The employee receives notifications of supposed fraud attempts and makes a decision based on the data and his expertise.

However, even if artificial intelligence helps us by providing information, the final decision, in my opinion, should be a human decision, made by a domain expert. Artificial intelligence algorithms provide information and make decisions based on the data they were taught on. This data is unlikely to be complete—as a result, the suggested decisions do not necessarily take into account many factors. Artificial intelligence will make it easier for an expert to make business decisions by providing compiled data, but decisions, especially those of strategic importance, should, in my opinion, at least at the current stage of technology development, be left to humans.

What else can artificial intelligence help us with? It can provide some support in identifying business needs. Here, the recently fashionable generative artificial intelligence, which provides information in response to a user's query, is particularly applicable. So, for example, a business analyst could use generative artificial intelligence to get guidance on proposed improvements, opportunities for the development of a specific business, or organizational or technological changes. This has some potential because a business analyst working to identify business needs or solutions has a limited amount of information at his disposal—his knowledge from education and experience, stakeholder knowledge, and available documents. Generative artificial intelligence may have access to much more information, which means that the hints and suggestions it provides may be new to the analyst. This opens up a whole new perspective—we no longer have to rely solely on our knowledge, perspective, and experience to suggest possible improvements, courses of action, or solutions to a business problem to stakeholders. With generative artificial intelligence, we can have access to broader information, and learn about solutions to other similar business problems available on the market, although of course with certain limitations. This opens up new possibilities and enables us to make more accurate decisions.

However, it is worth being aware that we should not take the "hints" of artificial intelligence for granted and as a reliable source of information—the quality and usefulness of data can sometimes vary greatly.

Areas of application of artificial intelligence are plentiful. Another interesting example is the use of algorithms to create models based on text. For example, an algorithm analyzes a document, identifies certain keywords in it, and creates a process model based on this. The quality of the generated results still leaves much to be desired, but the technology itself is again opening up new possibilities.

Personally, I see some potential for using artificial intelligence in the following areas:

- Identifying business needs and opportunities for change based on analysis of data processed within the organization and available to the public
- Assessing the feasibility of achieving business objectives
- Support for determining the organization's development directions
- Identification of opportunities for solutions to business problems
- Supporting gap analysis, in particular, providing information on the shortage of resources needed to implement the change
- Supporting quality control of key work products, e.g., analyzing the completeness of specifications of business needs and requirements, which will enable the reduction of risks associated with making decisions based on incomplete information
- Presentation of information in various forms, which includes generating diagrams based on text, generating text specifications in a specific format based on incomplete information, images, etc.

In my opinion, artificial intelligence is a tool that supports certain activities, and will probably support them better and better. However, it is not a replacement for human competence and experience. Of course, new technologies are a trigger for change—and similar changes can be expected in the field of business analytics. Thanks to advances in technology, business analytics will probably evolve. Instead of doing tedious manual analysis, gathering data from various sources, verifying that data, and filling in gaps, many of our competencies can focus on providing relevant data and algorithmic content, in building business rules. This will enable much faster data analysis and conclusions. As a result, we will be able to focus on building rules and models, shaping the organization's business architecture, and then interpreting the data processed by the algorithms. We will be able to propose new solutions and business offerings and identify points for improvement in a more efficient way, based on a wider range of data. Of course, as long as business exists and relies on people, there will be a need for the role of business analyst and the soft skills provided by this role.

2.5 Identification and Evaluation of Solution Options

First define the problem, then the solution, and only then its implementation.
Niels Malotaux, Project Coach, N R Malotaux, Consultancy

2.5.1 Innovation—Portfolio—Development

If every business need raised was implemented, the organization would be stuck in chaos. Business needs have different priorities and contribute in different ways to the implementation of the business strategy.

What is the path from idea to solution? The starting point is the emergence of some factor that triggers the need for change (business need) in the organization or in a specific area of the organization. These factors can be internal or external, such as changes in the market. The business need triggers a process of analysis, during which we try to understand the current state of the organization's operations and establish a target state. Achieving the target state involves doing something, making decisions, providing the necessary resources or processes. We then develop a solution concept that addresses a specific business need. The solution concept is subjected to analysis, the objective of which is, among other things, to understand the costs to be incurred to implement the solution, the benefits we plan to achieve, and the risks associated with the change initiative. Generalizing, then, one can assume that the typical path from idea to solution is as follows:

Factor—Business Need—Solution Proposal—Solution Recommendation—Solution Design—Solution Implementation.

Briefly:

Innovation—Development

Such a sequence seems consistent and logical. Assuming that a given change initiative is the only one or one of the few undertaken by a given organization, in the reality of many larger, and not only larger, companies, more than one need, or even dozens or hundreds, are reported over a given period of time. Analyzing these business needs, developing a solution for them, and implementing them would be, first, time-consuming, and second, completely ineffective from the point of view of the organization's strategy. Not all of these business needs are of equal priority—not all of them will contribute business value in a significant way. An element of business analysis should therefore be an assessment of business needs in terms of their priority for the success of the organization and their ability to be realized, which is based, among other things, on the availability of resources. It is difficult to imagine a situation in which an organization undertakes all legitimate business initiatives without regard to business priorities and available resources. Even if such a situation were possible and the organization had the necessary resources at its disposal, there would be a question about the wisdom of such an approach (Scaled Agile, Inc. 2022). From a business point of view, we don't implement all possible changes—we implement those that will significantly help achieve established objectives and realize the organization's strategies.

From the point of view of business analysis activities, this is important insofar as it implies the need to evaluate both the business needs themselves and the proposed change initiatives (Fig. 2.19). This essentially means that in the strategy analysis process we need a step, a checkpoint, to evaluate the reported business needs in terms of their relevance, priority, and benefit to the organization; we also need a similar step in the process of deciding on the implementation of initiatives. Instead of an "Innovation—Development" sequence, we therefore need:

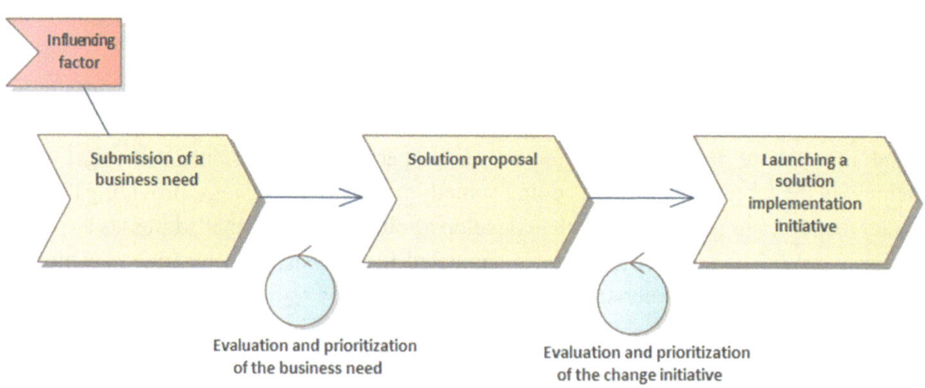

Fig. 2.19 Visualization of the overall process of handling a business need

Innovation—Portfolio—Development

Evaluating improvement proposals and deciding whether to implement an initiative is one of the biggest challenges in the work of a business analyst and in business development in general. After all, on what basis do we decide to implement a certain business need and reject another? The evaluation criterion concerning the attractiveness of the idea itself, the potential business value delivered by the change, is unfortunately insufficient—because it lacks the aspect of assessing the feasibility of the need. In other words, there may be a situation in which a business need for a desired change in certain processes, a need whose implementation delivers real business value to certain stakeholders and the business itself, may not be feasible from the point of view of the organization's capabilities at any given time. Otherwise, we may end up with a situation in which the organization invests significant resources in implementing improvements and innovations, at the expense of the continuity of core business functions.

Deciding which business ideas to pursue and which not to pursue should not be the responsibility of one person—and in no case should it be the responsibility of a business analyst alone. Such decisions require that the people responsible for the organization's strategy, for specific areas and initiatives, meet regularly, exchange information on the current state of affairs, discuss possible courses of action, agree on business priorities, and together make decisions on the ideas to be implemented. At the same time, it is worth noting that such meetings should indeed be held regularly, since the organization is in constant evolution. Ideas that were targeted for implementation because they offered the potential for high business value at a given point in time may turn out to be "obsolete" at some point in time—because, for example, a particular business need has expired or been replaced by another. Continuing an initiative started on the basis of already outdated assumptions is, in many cases, a completely unnecessary waste of time and resources.

We therefore need mechanisms for managing a portfolio of initiatives. With them, we gain the ability to maximize business value—a prerequisite for which, of course, is defining what that business value is. And this is where another problem arises, since, in principle, each stakeholder in an organization may have a different definition of business value, which makes it all the more important for ventures aiming to deliver business value to first define the concept of business value. They should also define how we will determine whether a certain value has been achieved—so we need metrics. A metric is not simply the fact of delivering a certain solution in a certain time. This information only tells us that we have performed certain tasks and delivered certain results. It does not in any way allow us to verify that the results obtained are the ones we wanted.

We need metrics that can be provided, for example, in the form of acceptance criteria, or as a definition of the key results of our work. Various tools come to our aid here, among which we can mention Objectives and Key Results (OKR). According to the OKR Framework, an objective is a meaningful, specific, clearly defined goal, and key results (of which there should be no more than three to five) are measurable success criteria used to

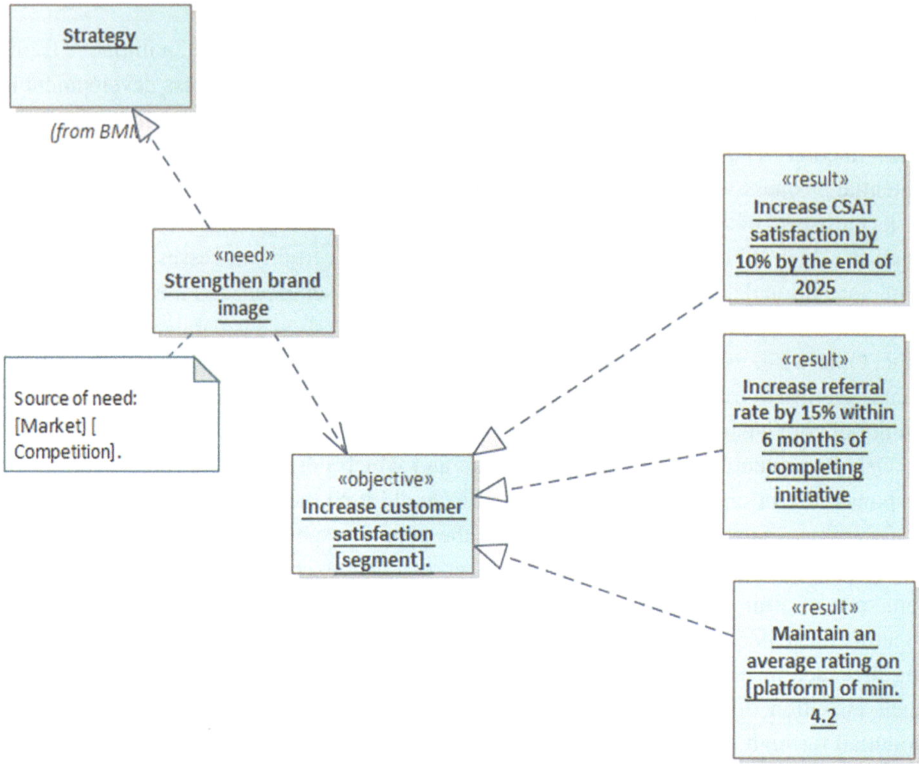

Fig. 2.20 OKR and business need

track the achievement of that goal. This concept can be successfully applied to strategy analysis. A business need defines a certain opportunity, a business opportunity that enables the implementation of a certain strategy. The need tells us about a certain target state that we want to achieve, thus enabling the definition of an objective. For a given objective, we define key results that allow us to determine whether we have achieved that objective. And it is these results that become the criteria for evaluating the results of the solution implementation initiative, rather than the fact of implementing the solution itself. Determining key results in relation to business needs and solutions helps us understand how the initiative and its results are relevant to the company's strategy.

An example of the use of OKR to establish a strategy for meeting business needs is shown in Fig. 2.20.

At the strategic level, the objectives allow us to choose between different initiatives.

So what is worth paying attention to when deciding on the implementation of change initiatives? As a rule, we implement those initiatives that are beneficial. In assessing what is beneficial and what is not necessarily beneficial, the following questions can help:

- What will really help the organization? How is the proposed initiative going to improve business operations, people's work, product development, etc.?
- What strategic objective supports the identified business need? How relevant is this objective on the organization's strategy map?
- What factors affect the operation of the organization? How can these factors affect the business value obtained by implementing a solution for the business need?

2.5.2 One Need, Many Solutions

Hesitate to choose a solution. By choosing it too quickly, you may lose sight of other, potentially better options.
Radosław Grębski, Business Analyst, Coach, ITability

For every business need, there are many possible solutions. Even if during the analysis of a business need a particular solution comes to mind on its own and seems attractive and appropriate to us, let's not rush to make a decision and lock ourselves into that one solution. The first thought in this case is not necessarily the right one—so let's refrain from identifying solutions until we have enough information to be able to identify and consider multiple options from different perspectives (Robertson and Robertson 2018).

Good results can be obtained by first gathering information about the business need, the stakeholders, and the business areas it affects. You need to know the context of the need, such as the specifics of the business process to be improved, the characteristics of the customer segment you want to reach, and so on. With the necessary information, we can use brainstorming or another technique from the group of creative techniques[7] to identify possible solutions. There are a number of techniques for identifying solution concepts—one of them is the Value Proposition Canvas (VPC), through which we can identify potential solutions based on an analysis of several factors.

In simple terms, VPC is about developing solutions—products or services—that allow us to eliminate the so-called pains of stakeholders and increase their level of satisfaction. Developing a VPC requires gathering and organizing information about the tasks performed by the stakeholders affected by the problem that is the source of the business need, about their pains and the factors that cause satisfaction. We then proceed to the stage where we try to determine what could eliminate the pains and increase the satisfaction of the recipient. Having this information, we are able to generate a list of ideas for solutions—this could be, for example, a new process, product, service, or organizational change.

Another interesting technique to support solution identification is benchmarking. If our business need relates to an aspect, area, or process that is also found in other organizations, we can identify solutions used by other organizations and draw inspiration from them. The

[7] By creative techniques, I mean information generation and creative problem-solving, detailed in the International Requirements Engineering Board (IREB) Certified Professional for Requirements Engineering (CPRE) certification program, among others.

prerequisite for applying this technique is, of course, to have knowledge of the market and the players operating in it, and the solutions and technologies they use. However, this technique is interesting in that it not only allows us to identify solutions in a relatively simple way, but also gives us information about what our position is in relation to companies that are leaders in the industry.

Still another method of developing solution concepts is an ordinary workshop meeting, involving representatives from different areas and specialties. Very often, the best solutions come not from observing the market and being inspired by other companies, but from the employees of a given organization. After all, they are the ones who have knowledge of how the organization functions and what could be improved. They also have knowledge of the relationships between processes, departments, and regions. Very often they also have thoughts on how a problem could be solved. And even if there are no such ready-made suggestions for solutions, they are very likely to be identified during a meeting where we gather the knowledge, experience, and perspectives of various stakeholders, confront them, and conceptualize possible solutions.

It is worth noting that many of these solutions may not be feasible in a given business context. Others may be feasible, but deliver relatively little business value. Still others have the potential to deliver very high business value, but their implementation is fraught with risk. It is therefore worth identifying possible solution options and subjecting them to a preliminary analysis, which will result in a preliminary classification.

Such classification can take the form of a pyramid of solutions.[8] This pyramid includes three levels:

1. *Perfect solution*: This solution concept is the result of a mindset that assumes there are no constraints—not budgetary, cultural, or technical. The result is a perfect solution that delivers excellent business value, but at the same time is unattainable under the current internal and external constraints of the organization.
2. *Feasible solution*: This solution concept takes constraints into account. The feasible solution addresses a business need and delivers some business value, but significantly less than the perfect solution. However, the implementation of this solution is often associated with relatively high costs.
3. *Minimum solution*: This is the solution that the organization is able to implement given its financial capabilities, existing constraints, and business priorities. It does not provide excellent business value and does not solve problems comprehensively—it is the so-called minimum version.

When deciding on the solution we will implement, we usually choose between a minimum and a feasible solution. We choose the solution that provides the greatest benefit while minimizing risk and limited cost.

[8] I learned about the formalized concept of different levels of solutions from Piotr Biernacki and Robert Kozlowski, who point to the authorship of Dr. Tadeusz Lis.

One may ask what is the point of defining the ideal solution if we won't implement it anyway, since we normally choose between a feasible and a minimal solution. The objective of taking the time to conceptualize the ideal solution is justified by the fact that organizations are constantly evolving, their context is changing, and constraints are changing. This can cause the levels of boundaries between the different levels of the solution to change. In other words, if there is an organizational change that removes some constraints, and we actually have knowledge of what is defined as the ideal solution, it opens up new possibilities. We can conclude that the ideal solution is becoming feasible. This, in turn, enables us to modify the change strategy accordingly.

Let's consider an example.

A production company provides services to customers around the world. The organization includes several locations, in different regions of the world, with some locations operating according to their own local regulations and standards. The company's product offerings depend on the region—the characteristics of the products offered to the European market are slightly different from those offered to the Asian market. The company does not have a global standard for production, logistics, or customer service—as a result, a product produced by a factory in one location, according to local procedures, is delivered to the customer in a slightly different way than a product produced in another location.

The organization's business objective in the area of customer satisfaction is to reduce the level of complaints. Currently, the number of complaints is relatively high, and most complaints are related to inconsistent service delivery. Sometimes customers are served by different factories, different distribution centers, and different customer service departments. For example, it happens that an order handled by one factory is delivered within a month, while an order handled by another factory is not finalized until several weeks later. Sometimes the customer is informed of the status of the order, sometimes not.

The organization has identified a business need related to standardizing customer service procedures in the region.

The *ideal solution* would be to develop a global standard for the operation of the organization—meaning that every location, every department regardless of region, would function in exactly the same way. This solution is not feasible at the moment due to local regulations in different countries.

Feasible solution. This solution takes into account the constraints of the company's specific operation. Instead of developing a global standard of operation, the organization implements an analysis of the current state, and determines feasible changes in processes so as to standardize as much as possible. Business rules are established to ensure customer satisfaction at the maximum level. An example of such a rule would be that, regardless of the region, no more than 3 weeks must elapse from the time an order is placed until it is delivered to the customer. Such a business rule enforces that orders placed by customers are handled by locations that are able to meet the business rule deadline. This solution is feasible and comes at a very high cost due to the change in the way the organization operates to a large extent.

Minimum solution. The organization takes a kind of inventory of the processes currently in place. It then organizes the procedures in place in specific regions as needed. When an order is placed, the customer is informed that his order will be processed by a particular location and the order processing procedure is explained to him. The processes are still not consistent, but the customer is aware of possible differences in the process of fulfilling his order. The change mainly comes down to informing the customer of the procedures, which to some extent reduces his frustration level and provides him with a sense of security. The very way the factories and distribution centers operate does not change.

The solution indicated as ideal is impossible to implement in the current reality of the organization. However, in the future, this state may change. After all, let's imagine that the company makes quite far-reaching changes and all factories, distribution centers, and logistics are located in one geographic area. Customer service is transferred to a remote mode. Thus, the operating conditions in the organization have changed. Some limitations have been eliminated. The boundary between an ideal solution and a feasible solution has changed—a previously unfeasible solution is becoming possible to some extent.

Therefore, it is worthwhile to make a full analysis of the possibilities, and to identify solutions, not only the obvious ones that are easy to implement, but also those requiring more effort, those with high risk or high implementation costs. Keep in mind that all analysis is done under certain assumptions. These assumptions are true for the moment, but we have no knowledge of how they change over time.

2.5.3 Which Solution Proposal Is Best? Build a Business Case

For every need and every requirement, there are a number of different solutions. If you don't analyze these solutions against specific criteria, you don't know which solution is optimal. So how do you identify the recommended solution?

We already know that for each business need there can be multiple solution concepts. In order to enable decision-makers to choose the best solution proposal in a given context, it is necessary to provide information that makes it possible to compare different proposals. Such information can be:

1. The cost of implementing and maintaining the solution
2. The potential benefits of choosing a particular alternative—both measurable and non-measurable benefits, such as the opportunity to test a new technology in practice
3. Implementation risks, including operational risks, business risks, technical risks, and so on
4. The impact of the solution proposal on other elements of the organization's infrastructure—existing systems, business processes, personnel

The above information, as well as many other types of information, is usually provided in the form of a business case designed to demonstrate the rationale for undertaking the change implementation project. If the business case shows a positive return on investment, in other words, it is worth implementing a particular solution, this suggests a positive decision regarding implementation. However, it happens that even in the absence of a positive return on investment, the project will be implemented because it is necessary for the continuity of the organization's operations. An example of such a situation may be legislative projects aimed at adapting some area of the organization to legal changes. By themselves, these changes have no measurable benefit; they are a cost that must be undertaken in order for the organization to continue to function smoothly, in accordance with the current law.

The business case for several solution proposals can show a summary of costs, benefits, and risks for each proposal. In other words, we prepare something like a comparative analysis, so that we can evaluate the various options according to the defined criteria for comparison and, based on the information presented, choose the recommended solution.

Many times, however, I have seen business justifications in which several alternatives for a solution are listed. For each alternative, a general description of the benefits and cost components was provided, while accurate estimates were provided only for the proposal recommended by the team developing the business case.

Such a practice can be seen as a more transparent solution for the audience, because we do not burden them with a vast amount of information; we present only recommendations based on sound (at least I assume) analysis. On the other hand, limiting the information provided to only that which pertains to the recommended solution may lead the attention of decision-makers in the wrong direction. For example, it may turn out that decision-makers accept the recommended solution without having detailed information about alternatives that, from their point of view, could prove more beneficial.

My view is that if the team developing the business case has reasonably complete information about the interrelationships between the various initiatives, the business strategy, management's priorities, and the organization's overall approach to risk tolerance, the practice of explaining the possible options in general terms and accurately sizing the recommended solution can be a significant management improvement. Otherwise, if the team has limited knowledge, I believe it makes more sense to provide a full analysis so that decision-makers are able to consult the relevant stakeholders on the feasibility of the various options with the associated level of risk before deciding which project to pursue.

It is also worth noting that one of the solution proposals should be a "do nothing" option, i.e., make no changes. Practice shows that in many cases the best decision will be to leave the organization in its current state, since making any changes would mean incurring negligible costs and providing meager benefits. It also happens that the proposed solutions indeed have great potential to deliver high business value, but the risks associated with their implementation are too great, and the organization does not agree to accept them. In such situations, it may be a wise decision to refrain from making changes at all. Considering the "do nothing" option may seem ridiculous—because for some reason we have made the effort to propose a solution at all—so there is a real business need that we are trying to address. The "do nothing" option means that we have conducted an analysis, and spent a lot of time and resources gathering information, developing a solution concept, and evaluating the feasibility of the various solution proposals, probably involving a lot of people in developing estimates, and as a result, a decision has been made not to pursue any of the solution proposals. The very fact that we made such a decision based on data, the results of the analysis, and not under the influence of the moment or intuition in itself is a benefit.

By performing the analysis and presenting the results to decision-makers, we gain knowledge, better understand the area of interest, and learn and draw conclusions based on the information obtained. If this conclusion boils down to the fact that at the present time the organization's operation is optimal, or that our proposals for change will not bring significant benefits at all, then this is the right conclusion at the time. Without analysis, we would probably not be able to arrive at it and would make a hasty decision based on limited, incomplete data.

Is the development of a business case the responsibility of the analyst? By no means is it the responsibility of one person. As a rule, a staff of people—representing different areas and having access to information of different types—works on developing a business case for major changes. For example, in order to estimate the cost of implementing a solution, it is necessary to estimate not only the cost of production, but also the cost of implementation, maintenance, and withdrawal in case of abandonment of the solution in the future. This requires the identification of individual cost elements, which may be beyond the competence of a typical business analyst. Working on the business case is the effort of the entire team.

What if we come to the conclusion that we do not have the information necessary to create a convincing justification, for example, that we have no knowledge of how much it might cost to implement the solution? The very fact that this gap is found at the stage of creating a business case, and not during development of manufacturing projects, is a wild success. Since at this stage we have no knowledge of how much the solution is expected to cost to implement, we are unable to develop budget assumptions for the proposed project. We can at best make a guess. Since we don't know how much the project is expected to cost, on what basis are we able to conclude that the results of the project, the solution, will provide benefits in excess of the cost of implementation?

If, at the stage of creating a business case, we find that we lack information, it is worth asking for this information before asking decision-makers for permission to implement a project whose assumptions we ourselves do not know. Viewing the business case in this way is a kind of sanity check—before we go any further, before we decide that we want to implement a particular project, let's make sure we know why we are implementing it, what risks we are taking, what budget is needed for it, and what our plan is and what results we expect.

In the ventures I participate in, I encourage business representatives to start using a similar mindset when defining business needs. Before declaring a business need that must be analyzed, taking specific steps to develop a solution for it, involving a lot of people and often significant resources, let them answer the following questions: What benefits do you want to obtain? How will you determine that these benefits have been obtained? What problem do you want to solve? Who is affected by this problem and what areas are affected? If the business is unable to answer these questions, it probably means that the business need has been poorly formulated or is unfounded, adding no business value.

2.5.4 Consider the Risks

THE OBJECTIVE OF RISK ANALYSIS IS NOT TO PRODUCE ANOTHER DOCUMENT WITH A LONG LIST OF POSSIBLE RISKS.

THE OBJECTIVE OF RISK ANALYSIS IS TO DETERMINE THE RESPONSE TO PROBABLE EVENTS THAT COULD LEAD TO THE FAILURE OF THE INITIATIVE IF WE DO NOT DEVELOP DEFENSE MECHANISMS. IF SUCH EVENTS OCCUR DURING THE EXECUTION OF THE WORK, THEY WILL NOT SURPRISE ANYONE AND WILL NOT PARALYZE THE PROJECT BECAUSE A CONTINGENCY PLAN HAS ALREADY BEEN DEVELOPED.

When developing a solution concept that addresses an identified business need, it is important to consider the risks associated with implementing a business change. These risks can relate to a number of areas, for example:

1. Business risks
2. Organizational risks
3. Technical risks
4. Risks related to the human aspect

An example of a business risk might be the risk of delays in delivering products to the market due to the introduction of a process change and the need to train staff on the new procedures.

A typical example of organizational risks are those related to the flow of communication—relatively often the objectives and course of planned initiatives are not properly communicated to the employees of an organization, which can result in resistance to change.

Technical risks may arise, for example, from the need to introduce new technologies unknown or not previously used in a given organization. In addition to the risks arising from the assimilation of knowledge about the new technology, there may be the risk that the technology, theoretically suitable for achieving certain objectives, will not work in a given organizational context or will cause unexpected side effects.

Risks related to the human aspect include, for example, potential resistance to change, attempts to sabotage the change initiative, and issues of cooperation and commitment—or rather, lack thereof.

Implementing change is often a long-term initiative. The success of the endeavor depends, among other things, on considering the risks and addressing them appropriately.

Consider an example. We are developing a solution concept for a business need related to improving service delivery processes. One of the proposed solutions is to make changes to the stack processes, changes that will affect multiple departments of the organization and hundreds of stakeholders. The likely risks associated with this initiative are:

- Operational risks resulting from the lack of coordination of changes in different departments of the organization
- Risks resulting from the lack of proper communication between the owners of different processes, which can result in mutually exclusive process changes
- Risks of staff resistance resulting from the lack of knowledge of the objectives of the change initiative and the consequences of the change for their work and position in the company
- Quality risks concerning the deterioration of the quality of services delivered to the market resulting from improperly designed process changes

We subject the identified risks to a standard risk analysis aimed at determining the level of risk, and on this basis we can plan appropriate mitigation actions. Yes, for example, we can minimize the risk of staff resistance by planning proper communication regarding the planned initiative. The strategy for implementing the change should include informing employees about the objective of the initiative, how it will be implemented, what the consequences will be, and what is expected of employees, with an emphasis on the benefits of the change. Risks associated with a lack of communication among process owners can be reduced by developing an appropriate plan for communication and coordination of work on the change, especially in the early stages when decisions are made on the scope of process changes. Risks can also be mitigated by designating a business owner responsible for coordinating changes across processes, with an emphasis on maintaining process consistency.

Of course, a business analyst cannot identify all possible risks, so risk identification and analysis should be a team effort—all key stakeholders, representing both the business and technical areas, should participate.

The basic questions to answer when designing any change are:

1. What is the scope of the impact of the change?

The answer to this question can indicate specific risks associated with, for example, coordinating the change in different areas of the organization. It also indicates potential stakeholders involved in the implementation of the change or who will be affected by the change—they too can be a source of risk information.

2. What factors influence the definition of change?

Impact factors will allow us to understand potential areas of risk. For example, if a regulatory change may alter the business need that was the starting point for developing the solution concept, this is a project risk for us. If the success of the project to implement the change depends on budgetary issues in the organization, again, this is a risk factor for us.

3. What can go wrong?

The change relationship is an undertaking—a project. As part of the project, we will have to carry out a number of activities. For each of these activities, for each expected work product, it is worth asking ourselves what can go wrong, what could be the obstacles to the task, to the development of a specific work product in achieving the objective.

4. What do we not know?

As a rule, almost all areas of uncertainty are potential risks. For example, if our solution is process changes, but at a given stage we are unable to indicate what the scope of these changes will be, this is a risk. This is because it may turn out that the scope is much larger than we initially estimated, which will affect the duration and cost of the entire project. It may also turn out that the scope of the process changes is impossible to implement, given the current conditions of the organization.

Identification and analysis of risks can be supported by a number of techniques, such as brainstorming, workshops with stakeholders, or interviews with experts. The use of historical information is also a very great support in identifying risks. In most cases, we or stakeholders have already implemented a number of initiatives. It is worth asking ourselves what risks were present in previous projects and how they were handled, since some risks are quite generic and occur in different initiatives regardless of their type and scope.

We can also approach risk identification in a structured way, with the help of specific checklists or tools. An example of a checklist to support the identification of risks is provided in Table 2.3.

Table 2.3 Checklist template for identifying uncertainties and risks

	What do we want to achieve?	Who do we need to engage?	What do we need to do?	What resources do we need?
	Measurable results of the initiative	List of stakeholders, departments, partners	List of activities	Information, tools, resources needed to meet objectives
What do we know?				
What don't we know?				
What do we need to check?				

2.5.5 Business Model in Solution Concept Development

Developing and implementing a solution is a business initiative, such as launching a new service or delivering a new product to the market.

And can be planned in a similar way.

Business change can be compared to a proposal for new business. Any change should deliver some value to specific customer segments (whether internal or external). We need partners to implement the change, and the change itself is delivered through specific channels. The implementation of the change and its subsequent receipt are specific costs. On the other hand, the decision to implement the change and deliver value is based on the estimation of potential benefits.

Designing a business change can therefore be compared to designing a business—and using dedicated tools, such as the Business Model Canvas (BMC). With a slight shift in perspective, we can find an analogy between developing a solution proposal and developing a business plan.

If we want the business we plan to launch to be successful, we should consider a number of factors and estimate the risks associated with our idea. We take a similar approach to analyzing business needs and developing solution concepts.

A solution that does not deliver the right value to specific stakeholder groups is an inadequate solution. A solution whose cost of implementation exceeds the estimated benefits is also unlikely to be a very good choice. A solution proposal that provides value, but we can't identify to whom, is probably a good proposal, but not for a specific business need.

If we think of our solution as a business initiative, a new service, in a process, a business, we will find that in developing a rationale for the value of the solution to the business and formulating its specific measurable attributes and assumptions, guidelines for developing a business plan can be an excellent help. When planning a business, we should identify:

- For which customers, for which market segment, company department, or stakeholder group, we are targeting our offer (i.e., the value proposition—the proposed solution)
- What this offer is—what value it delivers and what benefits it provides to customers
- What activities need to be performed to deliver the offer to specific market segments
- How we want to communicate with customers and deliver our offer
- Who we need to deliver the business offering—who are the business and technology partners
- What costs we need to incur to deliver the value proposition
- What benefits we expect to receive

The same way of thinking can be successfully used to develop the assumptions of our solution. Our solution is to deliver specific value to specific stakeholders in a specific way.

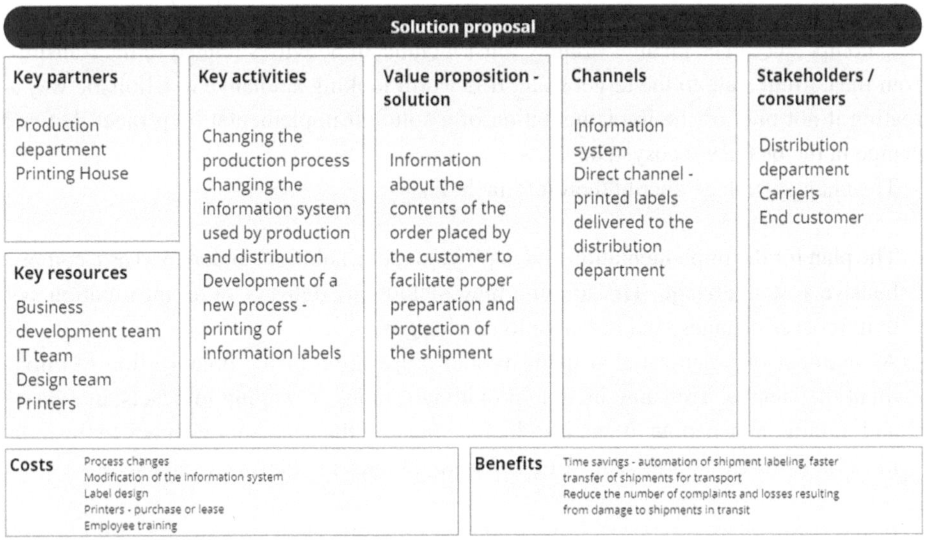

Fig. 2.21 Example of a solution proposal in the form of a canvas—developed by the author on the basis of the BMC concept

This value will be delivered through specific channels, for example, through a new business process or communication channel within the organization. We will need partners to deliver the value—such partners could be stakeholders involved in other company departments or technology providers. Implementing the solution will require certain work on both the technology and business side. Similarly, in the form of costs and benefits, without the development of a business case outlining the financial assumptions, there is no basis for accepting the project to implement the change.

The information gathered during the development of the solution proposal can be presented in the form of a canvas, based on the BMC (Fig. 2.21).

2.5.6 Develop a Change Strategy

A BUSINESS OBJECTIVE WITHOUT A STRATEGY TO ACHIEVE IT WILL NOT BE ACHIEVED.

CHANGE WILL NOT HAPPEN WITHOUT DEVELOPING A CHANGE STRATEGY.

Change strategy—how to develop it to be effective? Is it enough to plan the undertaking of implementing the solution? Is a schedule, a project team, and a lot of motivation enough? Sometimes yes, sometimes unfortunately no. A change strategy is not just about executing and implementing a solution, but also about properly preparing the organization to adopt the change. This does not only include informing people that the change is being initiated, how it will be implemented, and what the results will be. The change strategy must also include adjusting procedures, ways of carrying out work, supplementing people's competence. The change strategy must include all activities related to the transition from the current state to the target state. It is worth looking at change in a holistic way—treating it not only as the implementation of a solution implementation project, but as a change in the business ecosystem.

The change strategy should therefore include:

- The plan for the implementation and deployment of a solution, understood as a comprehensive system change. The solution may include the delivery of an information system, process changes, and organizational changes.
- Assessment of organizational maturity and preparation of the organization to implement the change. This may include providing training, changing mindsets, and hiring and training new people. It can also include making the necessary changes to the organization's infrastructure—adjusting software, purchasing hardware, and so on.

It is worth paying special attention to the fact that the change strategy should include the definition of so-called transition requirements. Transition requirements are necessary to achieve the target state. They are not a final component of the designed solution—they are needed to make the solution work. An example of transition requirements might be the provision of training and education, and the transfer of data from an old system to a new one. A related problem is that very often they are completely overlooked. We focus on defining the business requirements, understanding the needs of the stakeholders, and then developing the solution concept. We specify the requirements of the solution and the solution delivered—but we often don't consider whether this solution will be able to function smoothly and deliver the expected business benefits. Overlooking the issue of transition requirements can result in an organization implementing a solution that employees are unable to use effectively. And they are unable to use it effectively because training has not been provided. They are expected to seamlessly change from their previous way of working to working with the new solution. As a result, the implemented solution, instead of making work easier, helping to achieve certain benefits, can generate losses and delays and cause human error. This is not because the solution is bad, but because employees are not prepared to work with the solution.

The transition requirements are important because they affect the scope of work to be done. With reference to the previous example, employee training must be planned and delivered. Depending on how you define the training needs and what solution you find, training can be delivered in the form of lectures, presentations, video training, or user manuals. Each of these options requires specific tasks and resource allocation. This not only affects business assumptions, including budget, schedule, and risk analysis, but is also an important part of the change strategy. Overlooking transition requirements can lead to the failure of the entire change implementation initiative.

Transition requirements define what is needed for an organization to move from the current state to the target state. However, it is worth noting that similar transition requirements should also be provided for the end-of-life of the solution. Let's conventionally call them exit requirements.

A solution that meets a defined business need has a defined life cycle. At some point the solution may cease to be useful or be replaced by another. It is useful to anticipate such situations and take a long-term view to avoid the risk of not being able to move from the current solution to a future one.

Consider the example of an organization operating in the public administration sector. For many years, the organization stored information in analog form—on paper. At some point, the need to make information more accessible was identified. The solution to this need was to implement an information repository, where paper documents were scanned and saved in a specific format.

The transition requirement, identified at the beginning of the initiative, was employee training, especially instruction on how to scan documents, describe them, and organize them in a repository.

Now consider what the "exit" requirements could be. At some point, an organization could decide to retire the document repository. There could be various reasons for this, such as outdated technology or implementation of another comprehensive system. When discussing potential options, the question will arise of what to do with the documents stored in the old repository. And this is where the question arises as to whether the information collected over the years in the repository is in a format that can be handled by the new solution, for example, if scans were stored as image files, and the new need includes searching documents, including archived documents, not only by title, but also by content. How would the image file support this objective? Will the new solution be able to use image files migrated from the old repository? Will it even be possible to migrate files in a specific format?

If not, the consequence could be that a significant amount of information would be lost. The analogy of CDs can be invoked here. At one time, many organizations stored data on CD media. The technology was popular and stable at the time. Over time, CD media was replaced by DVD media, followed by USB media and cloud solutions. Information stored on CD media in many organizations is now completely inaccessible because the devices used in the organization do not even have a CD reader.

When developing a change strategy, it is therefore important to consider not only how to implement the change, but also how to "roll it back" when the time comes.

3 Planning the Business Analysis Process

How do you know that an initiative is successful and the results are of value to the target audience?

How do you know that the activities you are doing are actually needed?

Setting a plan is like developing a strategy to achieve an objective—it allows us to determine what we want to achieve and how it can be done given known constraints.

A problem affecting many initiatives is assuming that certain practices are self-evident—and overlooking their proper planning. We assume that certain things are obvious, known to everyone, are a kind of standard—and we make a mistake. What is obvious to us, what is a basic standard of work, for other team members will not be obvious at all. Proper planning is an element of expectation management, enabling a significant reduction in the risks arising from making wrong assumptions and, consequently, wrong decisions. By setting a plan of action, regardless of what the plan is about and what the results of the initiative are to be, we will be forced to analyze certain topics, discuss them with other team members, and make a decision. As a result, we will not only establish a course of action acceptable to the team, the expected results of implementing the plans, but also ensure proper communication and transparency. Planning is one of the basic practices of implementing any project or initiative, and it is often overlooked. We jump into an initiative, start executing tasks, without considering for what objective we are performing these tasks, and to what extent they translate into the success of the initiative.

Business analysis activity planning enables us to organize information about the desired results of our tasks, the activities to be undertaken, and the relationships between them. With proper planning, we are also able to identify the competencies that are needed to perform specific tasks and deliver agreed-upon results.

K. Zmitrowicz, *Business Analysis Done Right*,
https://doi.org/10.1007/978-3-031-62194-9_3

Business analysis planning also includes establishing procedures that allow us to work efficiently with stakeholders, which is one of the critical success factors. It is by establishing rules for communication and cooperation that we are able to monitor on an ongoing basis the fulfillment of stakeholder expectations in terms of how project work is carried out and the results achieved.

Effective planning should take into account a number of factors that can affect our approach to the work. Such factors are, of course, project constraints such as time and budget, stakeholder requirements, requirements arising from standards, and the adopted project delivery method.

A less intuitive part of planning analytical processes is determining how to manage information, which includes, among other things, developing the structure of artifacts and organizing the analytical repository.

Specific aspects of planning business analysis activities are:

1. Planning the *business analysis approach*: Determining how we will perform the tasks, what the results will be, what methodologies we will support, and what tools and techniques we will use.
2. Planning *stakeholder involvement*: We do not carry out projects alone—we collaborate with stakeholders at every stage. The effectiveness of this collaboration depends on how we plan it. Hence, it is necessary to plan how we would like to involve stakeholders in analytical activities, how and to what extent to communicate with them, how to manage their expectations, how to motivate them, and how to communicate the consequences of the designed change.
3. *Information management planning*: In projects we create huge amounts of information. Unfortunately, very often this information is collected but not managed. As a result, we do not know what information is available, where it is available, and how to use it. To avoid such consequences, when we initiate analytical activities, we should also establish ways to manage information.

3.1 Planning the Approach to Analysis Work

> Business analysis techniques do not belong in frameworks. Who said you can't create user stories in a waterfall approach? It is up to us to choose the tools and techniques that fit the context of the work we are doing.
>
> Business analysis is still business analysis, no matter what framework you work in.
>
> *Thando Jacobs, Business Analysis Consultant, host of the Inside Business Analysis podcast*

> Managing software development through cost and deadlines is only half the truth.

It comes naturally to us. It's so concrete.

On the other hand, value is something intangible and impossible to define. Unless it is.

Value is the main objective of the entire development process—it defines our success.

Jussi Mäkelä

3.1.1 No Best Practices, No Best Methodologies

With the current complexity of business, transformation processes, manufacturing initiatives, there is no question of "best" practices. There are no practices, methods, tools that "always" will work and achieve certain objectives.

There are good practices.

Which will be good in a given situation—it depends on the context.

When observing an industry related to solution design, software production, and project management in general, one often comes across publications and articles that scream in their headlines "10 best practices for project management," "Business analysis in seven steps," "Five best practices for requirements management." With all due respect to the authors of these publications, in most cases they miss the truth. I would venture to say that there are no best practices, no best tools, no best methodologies, techniques, and approaches. In the area in which we work, an area of changing business, ever-changing technology, and constant challenges, an area that by definition involves the uniqueness of each venture and is not mass production, it is impossible to say that any practice is the best or the worst. There is no rule that a particular methodology for one project will achieve spectacular results, and we will repeat that success in subsequent projects. The only rule that really works is that everything depends on the context.

Agile approaches for some organizations turn out to be a hit; for other projects, on the other hand, they are a ready recipe for failure. Tools used successfully on one project will not necessarily be the right choice in another initiative. The five business analysis best practices preached by an industry-renowned self-proclaimed expert on your project may turn out to be completely useless. For what reason? The reasons are many.

Every project is different. This is due to the very definition of a project as a unique endeavor. Projects are implemented with different objectives, by different teams, in different environments, with different factors affecting the projects and different constraints. We work for different clients with different expectations, organizational maturity levels, and communication styles. In an environment of constant variability, we would like to ensure that any practice or method will produce 100% repeatable results. We confuse means with objectives. We don't think about what the objectives of our work are, or what we want to achieve, focusing very often on tool issues. We don't examine project constraints and other considerations in the context of choosing the right method or technique. Instead, we make a premature choice of methodology, usually wondering later why a particular method doesn't work, and blaming not ourselves and our hasty decisions, but the methodology.

We lack knowledge. Yes—I would venture to put this thesis in a world that promotes quick results, experience over theory, bravado over caution. Very often we focus on getting started on tasks with the objective of getting to any result quickly. We want to apply techniques and tools we have just learned about as quickly as possible, without knowing in what context these methods and tools work. In many cases, we lack a solid theoretical foundation, which, in my opinion, is necessary to make the right choice of tools and work methodologies. I have repeatedly encountered the belief boldly proclaimed by "long-time experts" that it is best to learn by doing. Investment in knowledge, education, training, and books is, according to these experts, completely misguided. The best results are obtained by practicing.

In a way, I understand the intentions—people who are pure theorists very often can't put theory into practice; they don't know what the real challenges of using given methods are. On the other hand, only relying on practical learning without a theoretical basis can end up in such a way that we have learned practices.... bad. Worse, we don't even realize that these are bad practices because we lack the knowledge to evaluate the effectiveness of our actions. As a result, we get stuck in these bad practices, constrained by our own lack of knowledge, in our focus on carrying out work that very often amounts to nothing of value, and not realizing that there are many areas that we could improve if only we were aware, first, that there is something to improve, and second, that we had knowledge of the means that could help us.

Let's consider an example.

In one of my projects, I noticed that the analyst was creating a requirements specification using user stories. Personally, I consider this approach to be a pretty good method for describing functional requirements, mainly from the perspective of specific stakeholders. It is one of many methods for describing requirements at the stakeholder level, a method that is valuable in that it allows requirements to be described in a way that non-technical stakeholders can understand. However, the use of user stories to describe the behavior of a system in which many of the requirements are quality requirements, there is no direct interaction of the system with the end user, and most of the system's functioning is reduced to interactions between software components seems puzzling to say the least. When asked by the analyst where he got the idea to use user stories for specifications, he replied, "Because that's what we usually do." There is an argument to be made; I do not hide it. Drilling into the subject, I learned that the practice of using user stories stemmed from the fact that some time earlier they had been recommended as the "best technique" for describing requirements, universal in its application and recommended as the basic form of requirements description for information systems. Since most of the analysts working in this organization were people with relatively little experience, people just learning, they did not yet have the knowledge and experience necessary to verify certain assumptions. As a result, they thought that since user history was a universal and expert-recommended method, it had to be that way and that was the way to go. As a result, they developed "requirements" as follows:

1. As system x, I want to send signal to system y.
2. As camera, I want to receive xyz signal from central unit.
3. As database, I want to receive data from x, y, z module.

The above examples look a bit bizarre. It is a complete distortion of the user story concept as understood by the authors of this concept. The very name "user story," user, not system story, indicates what the main focus of this method is.

The reason for the use of user stories in describing requirements was primarily the analysts' lack of knowledge that there are many other ways to describe requirements—ways that are much more appropriate for the type of system for which they specified requirements. There was a lack of knowledge and a lack of reflection.

My recommendation would be this: practice, to be effective, should be supported by some theory. It is not my intention to deny the value of empiricism, to undermine the importance of practice. However, I am pointing out that without theoretical knowledge, we cannot assess whether the practice we are currently doing is being done properly. Nor can we assess whether we are choosing the right tools and methods, because we lack knowledge of what tools and methods are generally available. It is also worth remembering the aspect of self-improvement and development. If we focus only on getting more and more practice, we may miss whether practicing in a particular direction helps us grow or improve our approach to work and the results we get. By having knowledge in a particular area, following certain trends or new technologies, we are able to consciously shape our development and education. I believe that conscious and systematic expansion of knowledge is the key to self-development and a prerequisite for ensuring that the results of our work are at the right quality level.

3.1.2 Understand Your Role

Think about what specific values and benefits a business analyst can bring to a project, and also where their value will be negligible.

The extent of the business analyst's involvement in different projects can vary significantly—so consider how the analyst can streamline activities to deliver the greatest possible business value.

Consider the tasks and objectives for the analyst in a given initiative, and support open communication about them. Otherwise, both the client and the person in the analyst's role will not see the value in this engagement.

Katarzyna Nowak-Rybka, Head of Business Analysis, Objectivity

The standard definition of a business analyst's role and responsibilities is fairly well defined by commercially available sources. However, in our organization or project, our role may be, and probably will be, not quite in line with the standard. It may turn out that within a specific project our tasks are not those of a business analyst, but rather those of a systems analyst—in other words, a solution designer. We will not be involved in defining business needs, since they are already established, or in determining solution concepts, since the solution has already been selected. Our role will be to develop a detailed solution specification, which will be the basis for implementation.

In another project, our role may be to understand and model the business processes implemented in the client organization. We will not be involved in identifying changes in these processes and improving them—as this is the scope of another initiative. Our role will be to analyze available information about the processes, obtain information from available sources, including stakeholders, organize this information, and present it in the form of coherent business process models.

In a given organization, our role may not only be to support clients in identifying business changes and developing solution concepts, but we will also be involved in bidding. We will be involved in initial discussions with clients about the objective of the planned project and provide input for estimating and pricing projects.

In another organization, our task may be—in addition to developing requirements based on customer information and supporting the implementation of the solution—project management in the sense of cost and schedule control.

Keep in mind that "business analyst" is a term used to describe people who perform various tasks. When proceeding to plan analytical activities for a given project, we first need to understand what the expectations are for our role in the project. It may turn out that the responsibilities set for us in a given project go beyond the standard definition of business analysis. It may also turn out that the responsibilities are much smaller than the standard scope of the business analysis definition. When we start working on a particular initiative, we probably don't know what the expectations are for our participation—so we need to set them. Until we establish them, we don't know what our role in the initiative is, what objectives we will help achieve, what results are expected of us—so we won't be able to plan the work properly.

Before we start planning the work, we should obtain the following information:

- What are the expected results of the project? What artifacts (work products) should be delivered? What tasks should be completed? This will tell us what outputs should be delivered as part of the work performed.
- What output information is available? What is its level of completeness? The answer to these questions will give us the information we need to understand from where we are starting—what information is available, and what we will need to obtain in order to achieve the expected results of the project.
- What is the projected composition of the project team? With this information we will be able to understand what competencies should be available within the team. We will

contrast the expected results of the work with the competencies required to realize those results, and will thus be able to determine how to involve individual team members in the implementation of specific tasks.
- How is my role defined? Of course, it may be that the client, project manager, or other person responsible for leading the initiative does not have a clear definition of the business analyst's role, as well as the roles of other team members. If the responsibilities for individual project roles are not defined, it is a good idea to agree on them in consultation with the rest of the team. This will minimize the risk of later misunderstandings, disappointed expectations, and frustration resulting from lack of clarity. It is worth touching on the topic of roles and responsibilities in the case of so-called agile projects.

It is worth raising here the topic of roles and responsibilities in the case of so-called agile projects. I have repeatedly encountered the statement that in agile projects we should not define the roles of team members, because it causes individuals to lose their sense of responsibility for the project as a whole and focus only on the implementation of tasks for their area. In agile projects, the team should be selected in such a way that it includes all the competencies necessary for the realization of the product. This is undoubtedly true—in a team, to add from ourselves, whether it is agile or not, we should have the competencies necessary to achieve the objective of the project.

Should we define the roles and responsibilities of individual team members? If we don't, I see the following risk. We have competencies in the team, but we have not determined how these competencies will be used. The result could be that a person is directed to perform a task for which he or she does not have the right competence. Another risk could be that team members are unwilling to voluntarily take on tasks that they don't like, that they don't find developmental or satisfying. Of course, in theory, an agile team should be sufficiently motivated to achieve a common objective, sufficiently responsible and able to coordinate its work effectively so that such risks do not occur. However, I find with regret that such teams are relatively few.

So, if I'm dealing with a team that I haven't worked with before, whose members don't know each other and who work in conditions that are not conducive to intrinsic motivation, my personal preference is to prevent potential problems through proper risk management. Setting expectations for individuals, dividing tasks, at least initially, I consider one of the mechanisms of risk management. Nothing prevents us from changing the way the work is done as the project progresses and allowing team members to choose tasks flexibly, but for this to happen, we should get to know each other as a team and work out the ground rules for cooperation.

In the course of establishing responsibility for completing specific tasks and delivering specific results, it may become apparent that we, as business analysts, are expected to perform tasks outside the standard area of analysis. Such a task may be, for example, the specification of the system architecture, the design of realistic user interface mock-ups, the development of system tests, or the monitoring of team members' progress.

In most cases, we cannot afford to agree to perform only a certain part of the tasks and reject the rest as incompatible with the standard business analyst's area of responsibility. This serves neither us nor the objectives of the project. If we are competent enough to perform tasks that are not the typical tasks of a business analyst, and there is no other person on the team who is better qualified to perform such tasks—or such a person exists, but is already burdened with a large number of responsibilities—I believe that with the agreement of both parties, we can take on this responsibility. In doing so, we clearly communicate that this goes beyond the standard area of responsibility.

For example, when joining a project in the role of a business analyst and taking on the task of developing system test specifications, we should communicate very clearly that these tasks are not in the standard of an analyst's work. We can, and will, perform them to the best of our ability, given the competencies we have, but they are not standard activities that can be expected of a person in a business analyst position. I believe that setting such boundaries is very important, because it informs others, including executives, where the limits of responsibility of each role end.

Why is this important? Imagine the following situation. In a given project, we have taken on the responsibilities of analyst, project manager, and designer without a word of comment. If we are competent enough to perform the tasks arising from the responsibilities—excellent. However, if we are not competent enough in the relevant tasks, we generate a problem for ourselves. We have undertaken tasks without informing stakeholders that we are not competent to perform the task. If the results we obtain are of poor quality, stakeholders may rightly question our professionalism. Rightly not because as business analysts we should be able to manage the project and design the system—rightly because we have not put up boundaries and communicated that these tasks are beyond our scope of responsibility and beyond our competence.

In addition, if we undertake tasks well beyond the standard areas of business analysis, we may lead those around us to believe that this is the standard of an analyst's work. Consequently, other analysts, engaged for other projects, will suffer the consequences of our actions. The expectations placed on them will be inflated—because we were the first to unknowingly define an inflated standard for an analyst's scope of work. This will lead to a situation where business analysts engaged in projects will be assigned analysis, project management, and design tasks by default.

So I recommend clear communication and setting boundaries. If I am hired as a business analyst, the standard of my responsibilities includes activities in the area of business analysis. If I take on other tasks, I clearly communicate that I go beyond the standard. It is absolutely not my objective to rigidly set the boundaries of individual roles, as I am well aware that role definitions vary from organization to organization. However, if an organization has a definition of a role and documented expectations of the tasks performed by that role, expected competencies, typical work products, we either stick to that definition or modify it as needed and communicate it to all concerned.

3.1.3 Understand Constraints

> Constraints explicitly and intentionally try to directly restrict any system or process.
>
> *Tom Gilb, Consultant, Methods Inventor.*

> Constraints inform you that certain options and capabilities are not available.

In most cases, the initiatives we take part in are subject to certain constraints. When planning the analytical process, it is necessary to take these constraints into account. Examples of constraints include budget, deadlines, stakeholder availability, location of team members, and technical infrastructure.

How do you incorporate these constraints into your process? Let's consider an example.

We are planning analysis work for a project where there are fairly strong constraints on the duration of analysis activities. Given these constraints, we will not be able to prepare full documentation of the planned system, according to our previous assumptions. The solution to the above situation may be, for example, to reduce the documentation to the minimum necessary (which, of course, implies the need to talk about what we consider the minimum, from the point of view of the project implementation and from the point of view of the subsequent maintenance of the system), or to involve other team members in the creation of the documentation.

Constraints can affect task completion decisions in a variety of ways.

Time and budget constraints may result in the abandonment of certain activities or the delivery of less important artifacts.

Constraints related to the team's competence or skills may result in inadequate execution of tasks, requiring planning to reduce the risk of lack of competence, such as hiring outsiders or outsourcing some activities to experts.

Stakeholder availability constraints may require proper planning of analytical processes, such as requirements sourcing and analysis, taking into account these constraints and reducing the need for stakeholder involvement to the minimum possible. For example, Instead of scheduling extensive stakeholder interviews to obtain requirements information, you can try to obtain requirements from other sources, such as documentation or competing systems.

Unfortunately, in many cases we plan analytical processes without considering constraints at all. This is due to various factors, including a lack of knowledge about constraints, relying only on our own knowledge, and not consulting other team members. Another reason for not taking constraints into account is simply a lack of awareness of how important these factors are to the scope and execution of the work. In a word, there is simply a lack of awareness.

How can you support the planning of the analytical process by taking into account the constraining factors? Let's start by asking questions:

- What are the time constraints for the project or initiative?
- What are the budget constraints of the planned analytical activities?
- What is the composition of the team, both business and technical, and how is the team expected to work (remote, on-site, hybrid)?
- What are the characteristics of the team members, who has what competencies, and are the competencies possessed sufficient to perform the tasks?
- What is the availability of team members and stakeholders? Are vacation plans and other planned absences known?
- Are there known specific rules regarding channels and modes of communication, affecting the way of working (e.g., communication with the client only possible through the project manager)?
- Are there established rules regarding response times to questions posed to stakeholders?
- How are other processes and areas organized, related to business analysis, such as design, implementation, testing, and change management?

This list of questions can be expanded as needed. It is important, when planning the analytical process, to think not only about how to organize the work, but also about what can affect it, what can limit our capabilities, and what factors can affect us—both positive and negative. A project risk analysis can be very helpful at this stage.

3.1.4 Framework for Planning the Business Analysis Process

Planning analysis activities is quite a challenge. Before we begin the actual analysis, we need to consider what to implement and how to achieve the desired results and meet the client's needs. This is problematic because we conduct planning in the early stages of an initiative—when much information is not yet available, and we rely heavily on assumptions. Sometimes we don't have the full picture, we don't know the scope of the project or all the participants, and yet we need to plan our activities.

How can we approach this subject? Of course, we can use a technique familiar from project management, namely the Work Breakdown Structure (WBS), and decompose high-level analysis activities into smaller tasks, going down to a level that we can estimate.

The Work Breakdown Technique is very popular, but unfortunately, in my opinion, its use as the main and only method of task planning carries a serious risk—the risk of planning tasks that don't really add any value. On more than one occasion, I have encountered plans, not only for analysis activities, that assumed the execution of a number of activities that were unnecessary to the core objective of the project—not bringing business value, not serving stakeholders, and not providing valuable feedback. They were planned only because they constituted a project routine and were part of a kind of standard project plan. The unreflective application of such a method leads to project planning in a template fashion, with no consideration of specific business needs and limitation of a given project.

Instead of the typical decomposition of activities into smaller tasks, I propose an approach based on establishing first the objectives of our project and then the expected work products. Only after this stage is it worth considering the activities required to achieve these work products. Developing an effective action plan, not just analytical, requires a fairly holistic view of the initiative and its environment. Analytical work provides results that will be used not only by the initiative's participants, but also by other stakeholders—it should therefore provide value to all involved. In addition, business analytics, like other areas in the implementation of the solution, is not done in isolation—so we should consider the interdependencies with other areas and disciplines.

Start planning by setting an objective. Then determine what will allow you to determine that you have achieved that objective. Define metrics and key results.

Without an objective and results, your plan is not a plan—it will only indicate a direction in which you will go, without really knowing why.

As part of my approach to developing a process framework, I propose to identify the following information:

1. The *objective* of the analysis work: What do we want to achieve by implementing analysis activities? Provide a basis for system manufacturing? Define the business change strategy? The objective determines the approach, methods, and results.
2. Results and work products clearly define the products that should be delivered as a result of our analytical work. Products both final—those that stakeholders care about, and intermediate products that we need to be to develop final results.
3. *Tasks and activities*: From the definition of objectives and results come the activities to be performed. Let's define specific tasks and activities, and the links between them. This will make it easier to coordinate activities and avoid chaos.
4. *Roles and responsibilities*: Failure to define responsibilities is one of the more common project problems and causes of misunderstandings and disappointed expectations. In a project, do you know in advance what everyone is doing? Not necessarily ... so let's define who is responsible for each task and decision in the project. With this exercise, we can also discover competence gaps—we have certain tasks to perform, but lack the competence to complete them at the appropriate level of quality. At the same time, it is worth remembering that analytical work does not have to be the work of one person—in many cases, the team can assist us, and many activities can be (and are WORTH being) carried out together. Team cooperation can bring better results, and at the same time there is an exchange of knowledge.
5. *Techniques, methods, and tools*: Let's think about specific tools and methods that will be suitable for achieving the objectives. The choice of tools should be based on a prior needs analysis. If it is necessary to use specific tools (which may be due to organizational or project constraints), let's adapt the tool to our needs.

The above approach is illustrated in Fig. 3.1.

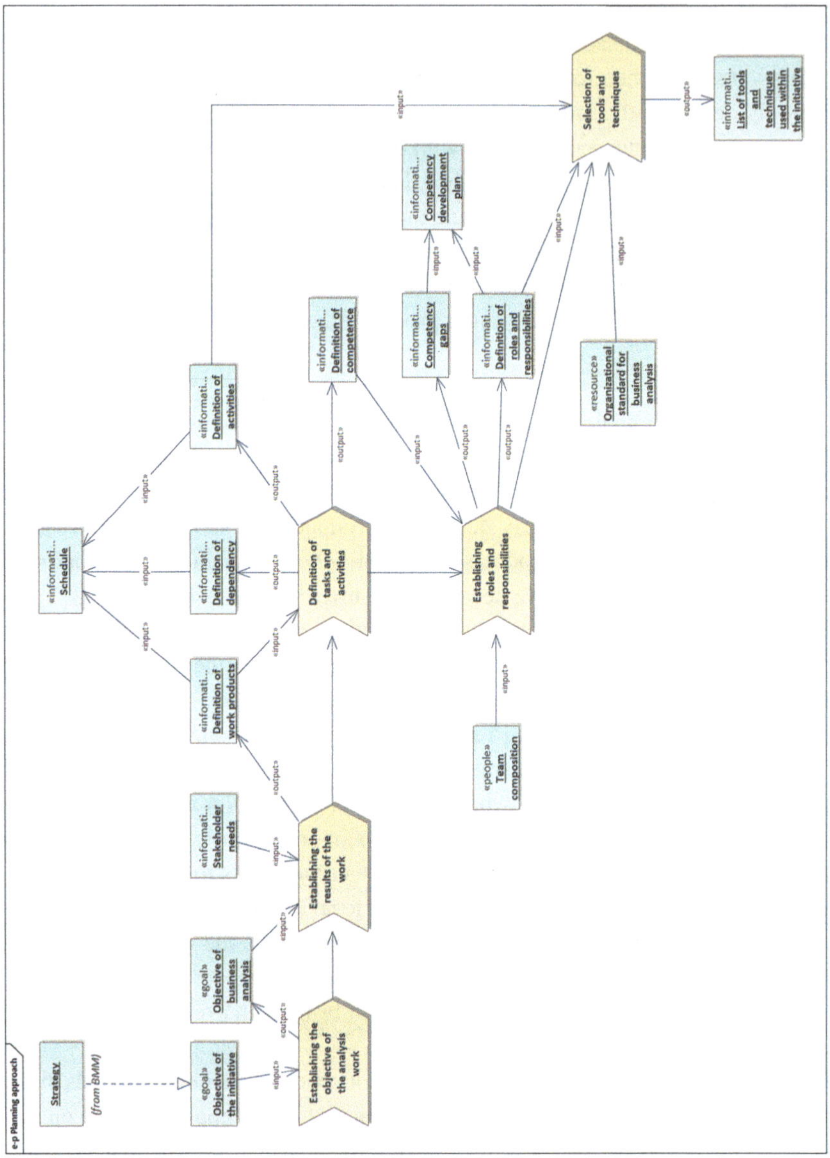

Fig. 3.1 Approach to planning analysis work

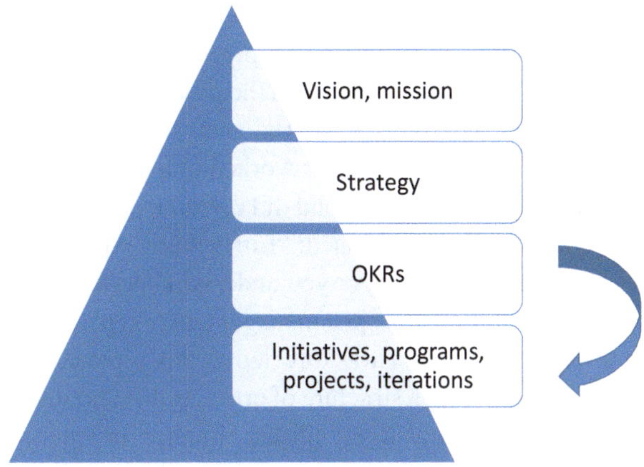

Fig. 3.2 OKR in planning initiatives (compiled from Tomaszewski and Matt 2023)

To plan analytical initiatives and ensure their alignment with strategic objectives, the OKR framework can be successfully used—and in at least two ways.

Establishing OKR, on the one hand, enables us to understand how our initiative should support the achievement of specific objectives—what we should deliver to make the results of our work valuable to the organization.

On the other hand, we can apply OKR to plan our work (Fig. 3.2). Each business analysis initiative should serve a specific objective. And to ensure that these objectives are met, we need to define key deliverables. So, for example, if the objective is to develop the basis for producing a solution, the key deliverables could be, for example, the definition of the scope of the solution expressed as a list of system requirements, a conceptual model of the solution, and the definition of interfaces with other solutions.

Planning based on a systematic analysis of needs and desired results will allow us to avoid unpleasant consequences in the form of:

- Implementing a process that does not meet the expectations of the team and the customer because it does not enable the delivery of the desired results
- Execution of tasks that do not deliver valuable results
- Execution of tasks by people who do not have the right competencies—resulting in low-quality results
- Lack of coordination of activities and tasks, resulting, for example, in duplication of work or long waits for others to complete work, which can be avoided by planning activities in a different way

In some cases, mistakes at the planning stage can put the success of the entire project in question. Let me cite an example of a project situation.

The customer of a certain consulting company asked for consulting services to determine the strategy for entering a new market. The company's management, without analyzing the customer's real needs and determining what should be provided as part of the work undertaken for implementation, assigned an analyst with systems competence (an analyst with experience in software design) to the project. The very first discussions and workshops with the customer revealed the problem of a complete lack of understanding between the customer and the analyst. The analyst was unable to understand the customer's point of view because he had never worked at a strategic level, did not understand the vocabulary used by the customer, and did not understand the customer's objective. As a result, at one point the customer stated: "Either I am expressing myself imprecisely and you don't understand what I mean, or you understand perfectly, but think you know better." This was a clear signal for the project management to react immediately—clearly the customer was at a loss. As a result, I was directed to this project to support the analyst in the work. We began by preparing a structure of artifacts that should ensure that the customer achieved its objective, which was to establish a strategy for entering a new market. The artifact structure included the various work products, the links between them, and the definition of the steps to be taken to generate a given work product. We presented this artifact structure, along with an explanation, to the customer to present our proposal for implementing the work. Only at this point did the customer believe that we were the first to understand their needs, second to know which ones to address.

Fortunately, in this particular project, the management reacted very quickly and did not escalate the problem. We managed to fix the situation before it became unrepairable. Remarkably, further cooperation with this customer was excellent, and the project results achieved were of great value to the customer (in his own words, not only did we help understand the directions of strategic change, but we also succeeded in causing the customer's employees coming from different areas and with different experience to work as one team, with one objective).

The final success of this project does not change the fact that a cardinal mistake was made at the initial stage—the lack of proper planning.

When proceeding to plan analysis activities in a project, you can apply some guidelines. The following checklist is an example.

Objective of analysis work:

- Identify the measurable objective of the initiative.
- Determine how the stated objective enables the business objective and supports the selected business strategy.
- Verify the validity of the stated objective with relevant stakeholders.

Results and work products:

- Identify a list of analysis work products to achieve the objectives.
- For each work product, identify:
  - What measurable value does it deliver and to whom?
  - How does it contribute to the objective?
- Identify which products are final, key to stakeholders, and intermediate, necessary to develop final results.

Tasks and activities:

- Identify the specific tasks and activities necessary to develop the planned work products and achieve the defined results.
- In the case of several possibilities for achieving results, define options.
- Define the initial conditions that must be met in order to start the defined tasks.
- Determine the links and dependencies between the different tasks, in particular the input–output relationships (the result of a task is the input information for another task).
- Determine which tasks and activities can be performed in parallel.
- Determine what competencies are required to perform each task.

Roles and responsibilities:

- Identify/confirm the roles in the project.
- Determine what competencies are possessed by people involved in projects in specific roles.
- Determine who is to be responsible for completing specific tasks. Not all "analytical" tasks need to be performed by a business analyst. Not all business analysis work products are delivered by an analyst.
- Determine competency gaps. How many skills and competencies are required to achieve project objectives, and which are currently lacking?
- Develop a proposal to fill the competency gaps:
  - Hire people with the desired competencies.
  - Obtain temporary support from people involved in other initiatives within the organization.
  - Provide training and other forms of education.
  - Provide mentoring from individuals with the desired competencies.
  - Outsource the work to an external company/consultants.

Techniques, methods, and tools:

- Establish a list of specific tools and methods that will be appropriate to accomplish tasks and deliver specific results.
- Identify limitations and other factors that may affect the selection of tools.
- Determine which tools and methods can be used in a given project context.
- Select techniques and tools based on previous needs analysis and, if necessary, adapt them to the specific requirements of the project.

Coordination:

- If your activities have a direct impact on the work of other project team members, consult with them about the proposed approach.
- Take into account comments from team members.
- Present the assumptions of your planning to stakeholders; explain why you have made the assumptions you have and not others, and how they will affect the course of the work. Get feedback.

3.1.5 Plan the Results of the Work

IF YOU CAN'T EXPLAIN TO STAKEHOLDERS WHAT MEASURABLE VALUE COMES FROM THE RESULTS OF YOUR WORK, IT PROBABLY MEANS THAT WHAT YOU'RE DOING DOESN'T MAKE SENSE.

Every activity we plan should generate measurable results. These results, in turn, provide tangible value—either to the analysts, as they are used to achieve specific objectives, or to other members of the project team, or to business stakeholders. An activity that does not generate a valuable result probably should not be performed at all.

A common problem in analysis projects is that we perform a series of activities routinely, without thinking about their meaning and benefits of their execution. That's why one of the basic tenets of my approach to planning, described in the previous section, is to define first the objective and then the results to achieve that objective.

The typical result of an activity is information—a concrete work product that we are able to define and the meaning of which we can explain to stakeholders. In doing so, it is worth noting that most of the work products created and used in an initiative are interrelated. For example, the specification of system requirements is dependent on individual system requirements. Therefore, when planning analysis activities, we first need to understand what results we are aiming for and the dependencies between them, so that we are able to plan the optimal sequence of individual tasks.

Accordingly, one of the first steps in planning analytical projects (but not just analytical projects) that we take is the so-called establishment of an artifact structure. This is usually a visual form of information representation showing a kind of map of artifacts and the connections between them. This allows us to understand what we want to achieve and how best to get there. An example of such a structure is shown in Fig. 3.3.

Developing an artifact structure requires the following steps:

- Determining what indirect and direct work products need to be developed as part of the initiative to meet a specific objective.
- Determining which artifacts provide input information for other artifacts. By doing so, we are able to establish rules for the order in which individual artifacts should be developed.
- Determining the dependencies between artifacts, including implementation and containment dependencies. For example, the work product "business requirement specification" is linked to "business requirement" by a containment relationship. The work product "solution requirement" is linked to the stakeholder requirement by an execution relationship.
- Establishing responsibility for the development of individual artifacts. By determining who is responsible for developing a particular work product, we are able to establish a potential area for collaboration. For example, if we know that the system requirements are linked to and provide input to the test cases for the system tests, we can decide that

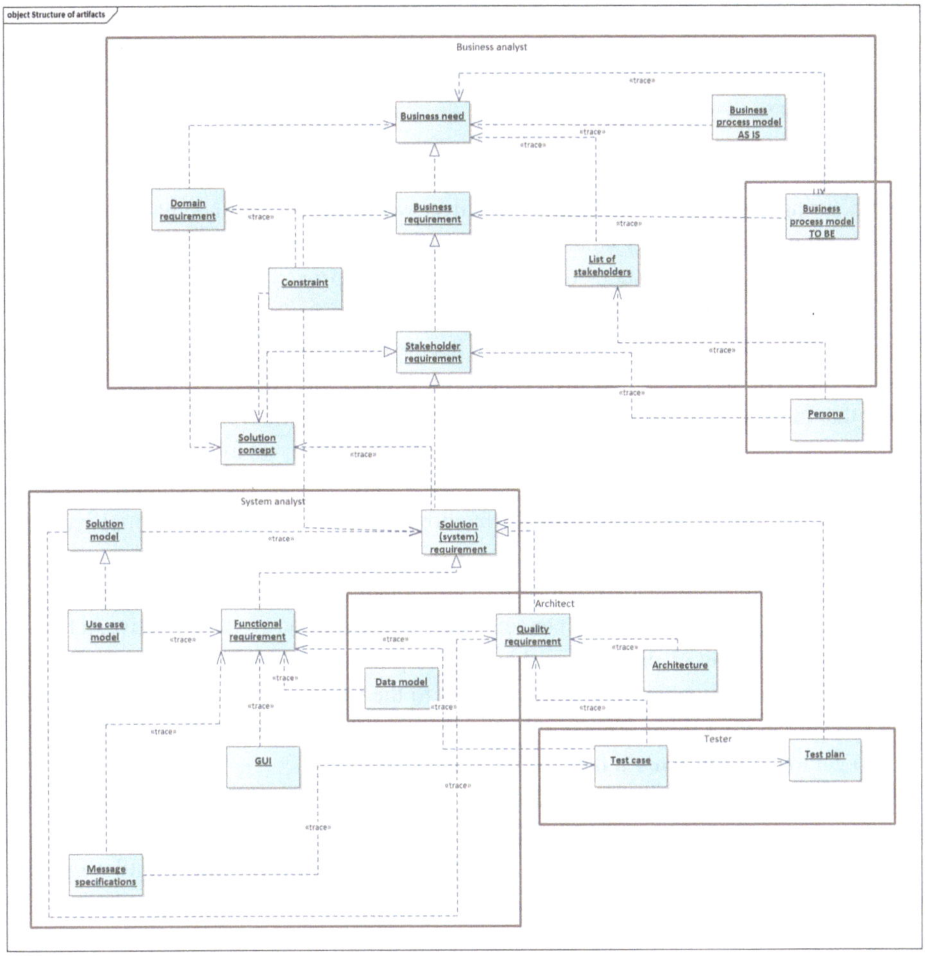

Fig. 3.3 Example of structure of development artifacts

certain activities in the development of the system requirements will be carried out jointly with the test team. This will reduce the risk of overlooking information that is important to the testers and at the same time ensure a smooth flow of knowledge.

By developing an artifact structure, not only will we clearly define the results we want to achieve, but we will also have the ability to plan optimally. In addition, we will be able to explain to stakeholders and team members our approach to achieving the objective of the initiative, including linkages at the level of activities and work products. This will make it easier to explain why the implementation of a specific task is important and what purpose a specific artifact is intended to serve.

3.1.6 Plan as Much as Needed

EFFECTIVE PLANNING IS PLANNING THAT GIVES YOU THE ABILITY TO RESPOND TO UNFORESEEN FACTORS.

Without getting too deep into philosophical discussions about so-called traditional manufacturing methods vs. agile methods, it is worth noting an undeniable fact: many businesses operate in a highly volatile environment. This can mean changing requirements and business needs, adding scope during the course of a project, having to suddenly adapt to unexpected technological changes, etc.

Planning in itself is a very good practice, because without a plan we have no idea how to get to the expected result and what that result is in the first place. However, it is worth noting that in many cases very detailed advanced planning misses the objective. Operating in a highly volatile environment, we have to expect that a plan set today in a month's time may change. Consequently, devoting significant resources to detailed planning is simply pointless. Does this mean that we should abandon planning altogether and simply respond to emerging needs and signals? No, not at all. Planning is needed no matter how big a project we are implementing. Even for small jobs, planning is the basis for success. It's not about developing a plan document per se; a plan is just a means to an objective, a tool. In my opinion, the value of planning is the thought process itself that enables us to understand what we want to achieve, the ways to get to the result, the risks that arise, and possible ways to address them. This is the value of planning—information about where we want to get to, and what might happen along the way.

If we know that along the way there may be a myriad of factors that can change the direction of our project, its scope, the approach to carrying out the work, then it becomes a logical conclusion that it is not worth planning too carefully. So what should we plan to make it worthwhile?

- *Specific results* of the work: If we do not know what products, intermediate and final, we want to achieve, we will not be able to determine what work to plan. Work outputs are the scope for which we contract with stakeholders. Identifying the work products will not only allow us to determine the current scope at a given time, but also to handle changes in this scope when they occur.
- Initial *schedule of activities*: I don't mean detailed schedules accurate to the day and time, but identifying work steps, plotting work elements and the relationships between them on a roadmap, will not only help us understand what we are aiming for and how, but also make us aware of the relationships that exist between the various tasks.
- *Communication*: I believe that regardless of the size of the project, and regardless of the level of variability in the project, it is a good idea to plan for communication. This means determining who will communicate with whom in the project, on what topics, what the channels of communication will be, and preferences for means or manner of communication. The scope of the project may change, but established ways of communicating will help us keep it under control.

- *Competencies*: Planning is the determination of activities and work products. Someone will perform these activities. To do them in the right way with the right level of quality, he or she should have the right pledge of competence. I believe that an essential part of planning is to determine what competencies are needed to achieve the desired results. If there is a shortage of competencies, we should plan appropriate activities that will enable us to fill the gaps, such as training or hiring people with such competencies. Determining the necessary competencies will also allow us to properly select the composition of the project team (in our case, the analytical team). In my professional experience, I have encountered several times a situation where people were assigned to a project not based on their competencies, but on their availability. In other words, people were assigned to projects who were free at any given time, not necessarily competent to properly perform the tasks planned under the project.

The formal approach to project management has taught us to create elaborate, highly detailed project plans. However, it is not always necessary to create such documents. The result of planning can be "light forms," such as checklists or mind maps showing the basic assumptions of our plan.

An example of an overall plan in the form of a mind map is shown in Figs. 3.4 and 3.5, which show an overall view, and in Figs. 3.6, 3.7, and 3.8, which show close-up views of individual areas.

3.1.7 Planning Is a Team Effort. Don't Plan Alone

In projects, initiatives, or programs, you are not working alone. So don't plan as if you are planning only for yourself.

The planning of analysis activities, like the planning of any other project, should be coordinated with the work of other team members. Business analysis is not done in isolation, in a vacuum—it is linked to design, project management per se, testing, and other areas in the process of developing and implementing a solution. So we can't plan our activities as if we were completely independent of other project areas. Therefore, it is worth ensuring that business analysis planning is effective and tailored to the realities of the project?

First of all, it's worth understanding the connections between business analysis and other areas. Let's view business analysis like any other process that has inputs and outputs. Let's determine what provides input to the analytical processes, and for which other areas and processes the business analysis results provide input. For example, if we determine that business analysis provides input to the design of the solution architecture, by the same token, we will conclude that our analytical work plan should at least be consulted by those involved in architecture design. This will ensure that our work results will provide valuable input to others.

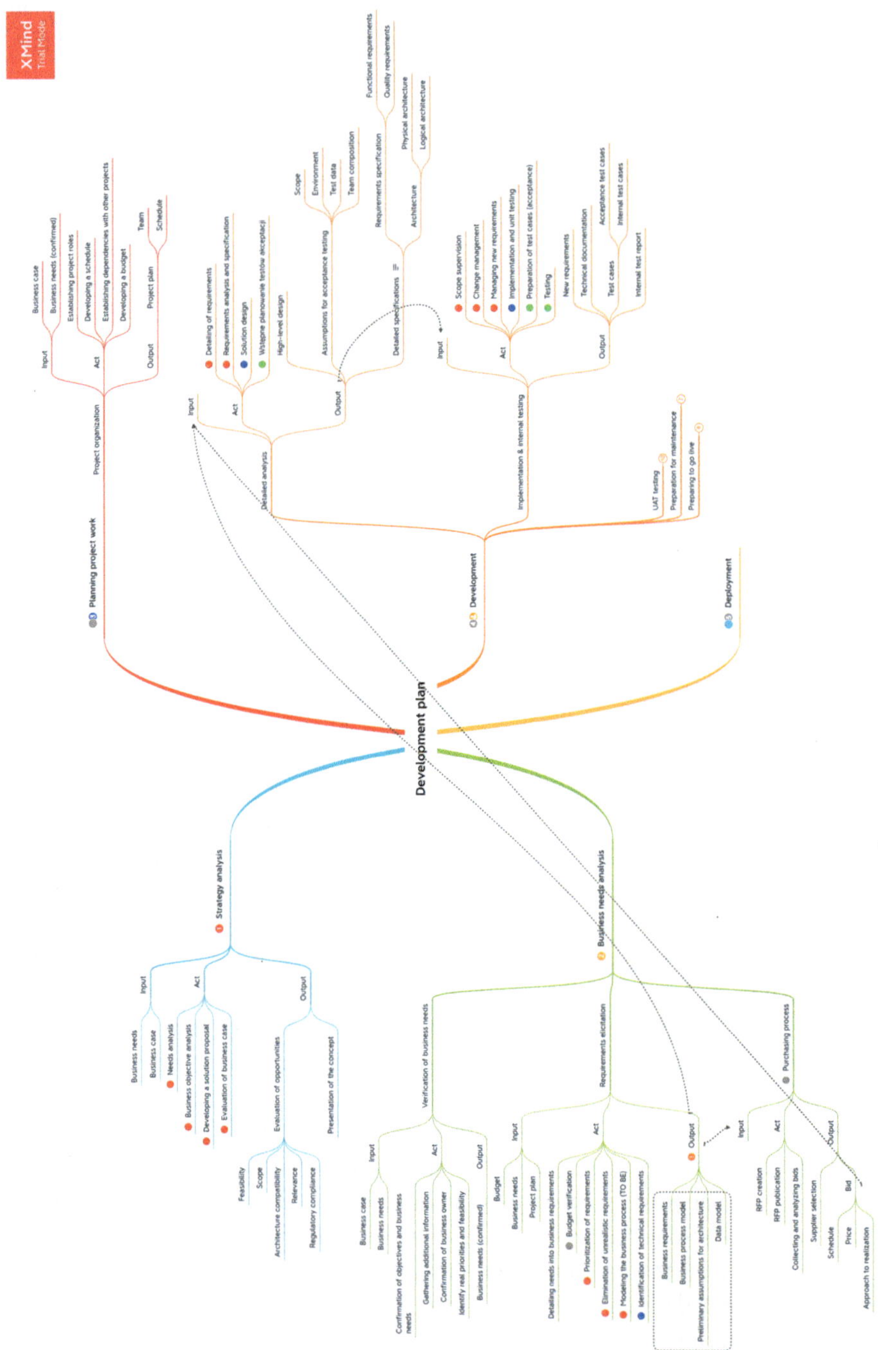

Fig. 3.4 Example of a work plan in the form of a mind map

Fig. 3.5 Example of a work plan in the form of a mind map—simplified view

Fig. 3.6 Example of a work plan in the form of a mind map—strategy analysis

Let's determine the results of the business analysis work and the results of work generated in other areas. You may find that some of the work can and should be done jointly with other specialties in the project. For example, analysis work products can overlap quite a bit with user experience (UX) work products. In fact, it often happens that a business analyst and a UX specialist work on the same task. It's half bad if they analyze a topic from different perspectives and the results of their analysis differ; it's worse if the work is duplicated. However, I have seen such situations many times in projects where the analytical work was planned as a separate project, and the UX work was treated as an area independent of the analysis and planned completely separately. As a result, both the business analyst and the UX specialist partly did the same work, and developed personae, value propositions, and the definition of business problems. The results were partly congruent, partly contradictory, the product of different assumptions made during the execution phase of the work and discussions with others on the customer side.

Remember that our processes provide results for other processes. So it's worthwhile for those results to be of value to the people who will use them. What exactly does this mean? Since we know that the results of analysis work, such as business requirements or stakeholder requirements, will be the starting information for the system analyst, who will develop system requirements based on business and stakeholder requirements, let's make sure that the information gathered from the high-level requirements is sufficient for the

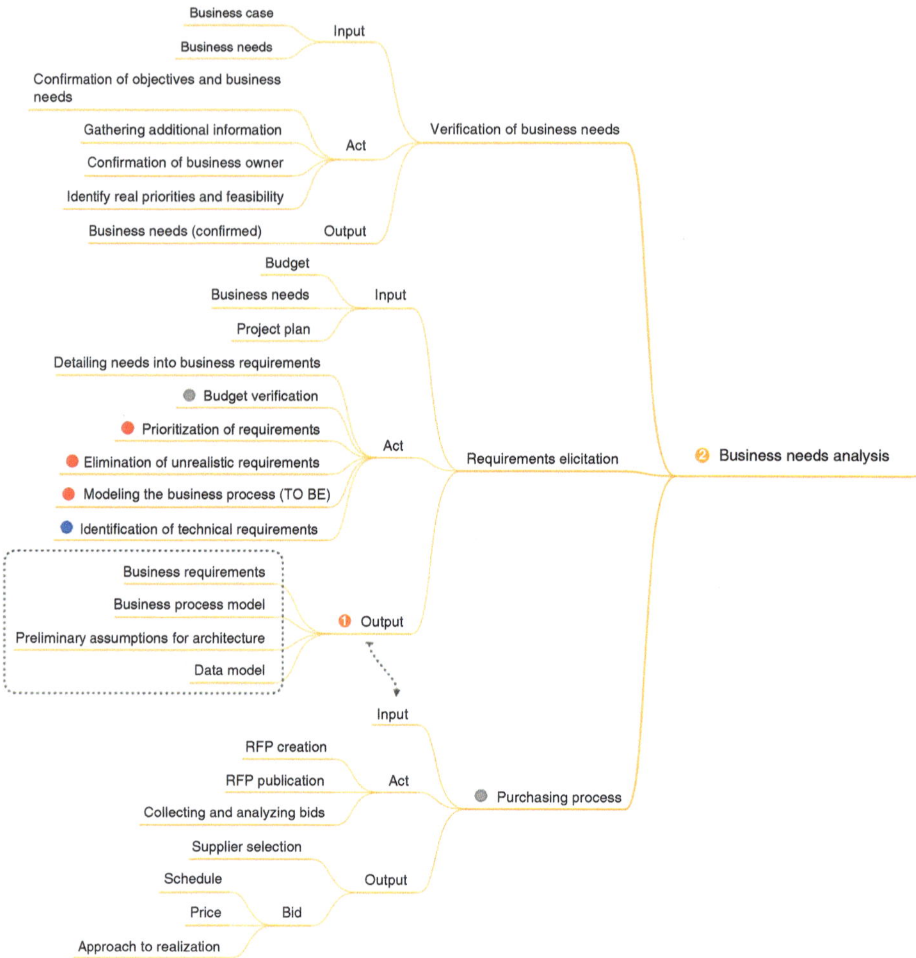

Fig. 3.7 Example of a work plan in the form of a mind map—business needs analysis

system analyst to get started. If we don't know what information the system analyst needs, let's ask about it. Nothing prevents us—before we start work—from seeking information from people who will use our work results, who will rely on them, in a word, who will be the recipients. Nothing prevents us from asking system analysts or designers, programmers, or testers what input they need, how they plan to carry out their tasks, and what they will need from the business analysis. In this way, we will avoid a situation in which we feel we are doing our job well, while the results obtained will not meet the expectations and needs of the other members of the project team.

Consultation with other team members should not be optional during planning—it should be part of the work standard. Let's plan together—otherwise we are back to the concept of organizational silos. This is, unfortunately, a fairly common mistake made by

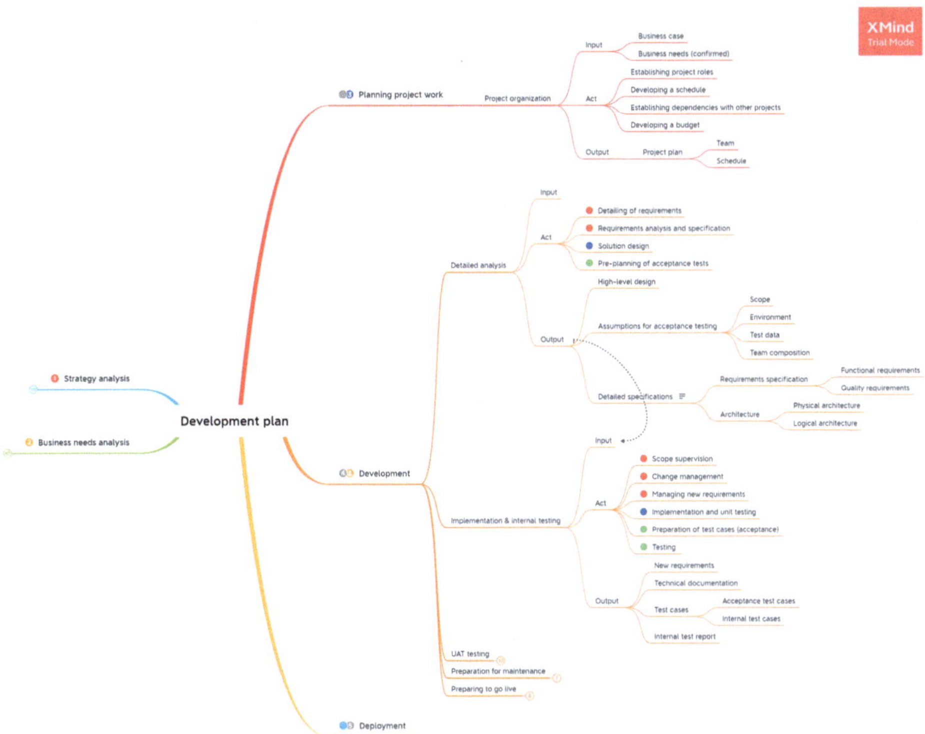

Fig. 3.8 Example of a work plan in the form of a mind map—analysis work planning and development

business analysts (and others)—planning based solely on one's own point of view. As a result, we develop a work plan that meets our needs, meets our expectations, while it neither meets the needs of others involved in the project nor delivers results that are valuable to the objective and goals of the project.

Filip Hendrickx, Innovating BA, author, trainer, President IIBA® Brussels Chapter, also provides valuable planning tips:

> Really listen to your stakeholders. Before challenging them, make sure you understand their reasoning on how the proposed solution will work and create value.

> Clearly describe the goals of the change initiative: when will your stakeholders consider it a success? Make sure the goals are specific enough to guide your actions, yet independent of how you may achieve those goals.

> Specify how the proposed solution will enable your stakeholders to achieve their goals. Describe these enablers in a solution-independent manner, in order to prompt alternative solution options.

HIGHLIGHT THE ASSUMPTIONS ON HOW THE SOLUTION CONTRIBUTES TO THE GOALS. TURN THESE ASSUMPTIONS INTO FALSIFIABLE HYPOTHESES AND SPECIFY HOW YOU WILL VALIDATE THEM.

3.1.8 Don't Rush Into Choosing Tools

IF YOU DO NOT KNOW WHAT PROBLEM YOU WANT TO SOLVE, WHAT OBJECTIVE TO ACHIEVE, WHAT RESULTS TO ACHIEVE, NO TOOL WILL BE A GOOD CHOICE.

START BY DEFINING THE OBJECTIVE AND NEEDS—CHOOSE TOOLS TO HELP ACHIEVE THE OBJECTIVE AND ENABLE YOU TO MEET THE NEEDS.

A common mistake in planning is that instead of thinking about what we want to achieve, what objectives and aspirations we want to achieve, we focus on choosing specific tools and techniques. By this I mean both CASE[1] tools and a variety of techniques and methods.

Examples can be multiplied. We do not yet know how we will work, but we already know that we will choose JIRA for "requirements management" (putting requirements management in quotation marks is intentional because it is difficult to talk about professional requirements management in a workflow tool).

We plan the requirements elicitation activities and instead of thinking about what information, to what extent, and from what sources is to be elicited, we predetermine that it must be a workshop. In agile projects, very often any planning related to requirements comes down to "since we are working in Agile, we will use user stories."

Planning any work done in such a way that the starting point is the selection of tools is, in my opinion, a complete confusion of means with objectives. Tools and techniques are means—if we don't know what objectives we want to achieve, on what basis do we select tools?

To illustrate the problem let's use a very trivial example. Let's compare planning processes and analytical tools to an interior decorating initiative. Our task is to select the tools necessary to decorate the interior of a house.

To put a decoration on the wall (let's make it a painting for simplicity), we need a hammer.

Does this statement make any sense? On what basis do we conclude that we need a hammer to place a decoration on the wall, if we do not know what kind of decoration it is, how it can be placed on the wall, what we want to achieve (where, at what height, if any, the decoration should hang, if it should hang at all)? After all, no one said that the decoration, let it even be our conventional painting, has to be hung on the wall. If we don't know what we want to achieve, how do we know what tools will help us achieve it?

[1] Computer-aided software engineering.
CASE tools automate methods of designing, documenting, and structuring program code.

The example with the wall decoration almost immediately shows the absurdity of the situation and the mixing of objectives with resources. Note that this is a trivial example—the provision of resources in the form of a hammer, which will potentially turn out to be unnecessary, does not involve particularly high costs and risks. Transferring the same situation to the project and organizational setting, the costs and risks of premature decisions already present themselves on a completely different scale.

For example, if we choose a tool that in no way supports the process we would like to implement, the cost could be that:

- We purchased licenses for a tool that does not help us (theoretically, it has no right to help us, because it was not chosen on the basis of any analysis, but on the basis of a momentary want).
- Since the tool does not help us, some of the work will be done manually. The result may be that we do some work in the tool, some manually, some in a completely different tool that was implemented in the project because the first tool did not work.
- We use the tool and use it with satisfaction—the tool generates the kinds of results we would like to achieve. The problem is that these results from the tool cannot be easily transferred to other tools, and in many cases this turns out to be necessary.

Let me cite an example at this point. One project used Miro as a tool to support communication, conducting workshops, business modeling, and solution design. In simple terms, the tool resembles a virtual whiteboard, where you can place graphic elements, text elements, and to some extent organize information in the form of frames.

The project had to provide the customer with:

- Models of specific business processes along with an identification of needed changes
- Initial product backlog—user stories with business acceptance criteria
- Initial mock-ups of the solution screen—mock-ups covering basic business scenarios

The team decided that the results of all business analysis would be stored in the tool. The reason was very simple—the tool is easy and fun to use, and designing and modeling solutions using this tool does not require special skills (in simple terms, it is enough to put cards on a virtual board and connect them using lines). In addition, since the organization had a commercial license to use Miro, all team members had access to it.

The analysis was therefore conducted using the tool. The results of the work, such as business process models, screen designs, and the product backlog, along with the requirements specification in text form, were posted on Miro. Up to a certain point, everyone was satisfied. I'll admit that the resulting board was impressive.

The problem arose when the results of the work had to be transferred to the customer. Communicating the results in the work in the form of a link to the Miro dashboard might be a certain solution, but not when, for the customer, these work results are input information for preparing a request for proposal. The customer's logical expectation was that they would receive results in a form suitable to their needs as part of the project. The needs were known from the beginning—the customer clearly communicated that the results of the Discovery project would be input information for the request for a proposal.

Unfortunately, for some reason, the project team ignored these needs, perhaps failing to foresee the consequences of their decisions, and decided to use Miro as the primary tool for both implementing the workshop and recording the results of the work.

As a result, all key work results stored on Miro had to be "rewritten" to the format expected by the customer. To some extent, therefore, the same work was done twice. And the reason was that there was a lack of reflection on the suitability of the chosen tool in terms of specific needs and objectives.

3.1.9 Don't Be Afraid to Use Metrics

If you don't have a reference point, you don't know if the results obtained are as expected. You don't know if the progress of the work is within the expected standard. You don't know when you should react because something wrong is happening in the project.

Part of planning is defining metrics that will allow us to assess the progress of the work and the quality of the results obtained. In other words, we need to define metrics. For some reason, we are often afraid to use metrics. We fear that metrics impose certain quality objectives that we will have to achieve, even if unexpected circumstances arise. Another problem may be that in order to set meaningful metrics, we need to have some knowledge and experience; otherwise we will set metrics that may not be achievable. The same effect will take place as in the case of defining objectives that are too ambitious and therefore unattainable—motivation will drop significantly even before work begins. Other concerns that I often encounter in organizations and projects related to the use of metrics arise from the fact that metrics are defined and used in inappropriate ways.

For example, I once encountered the following use of metrics. A company determined, based on historical data, that when reviewing a requirements specification, five defects are expected to be found per page of text. The metric in itself is not bad—it only tells us that based on the information obtained in the past, we are forecasting the average density of defects at such a rate and not another. With such a metric, we are able to assess whether the review is being carried out correctly, as intended and expected, or whether the results obtained may indicate some problems that need to be looked into. For example, if the review yields information that on average we found not five defects per page of text, but three, this result may indicate the need to look at the review process. The result doesn't say at all that the reviewers didn't put in the work; in fact it doesn't say anything concrete; it doesn't give a basis for making any decisions until we look into the topic and get more information, and based on that we can take steps.

That's the logical theory. In practice, in this particular organization, there was the following rule: since it was established that in a review of a requirements specification five defects were found per page of the specification, this value had to be obtained; this meant that if the document was "good" and fewer defects were found than expected, both the author of the document and the reviewer had to expect management control. Control was not about looking at the review to possibly point out problems in the process; control was about using various methods to "force" an admission that there were, in fact, more defects. As a result, a kind of cooperation developed between the documentation developers and the review team—if the reviewers found too few defects, the author artificially added them, just to get the expected result of the review.

The described situation sounds improbable; however, this is not the only example of such use of metrics. Can it be said on this basis that the metric in itself is bad? Absolutely not. What is wrong is its application, drawing far-reaching conclusions on the basis of single data taken out of context. It is wrong to make decisions based not on data analysis, but on a wrong interpretation of the situation. Metrics are a kind of auxiliary tool; in themselves they are neither good nor bad—good or bad can be the application of the tool.

The above example shows a rather drastic misapplication of metrics. Fortunately, this is not and should not be the rule. The use of metrics does not have to involve special challenges, frustration, or fear of the results obtained and the resulting consequences. Metrics can be applied in a completely noninvasive way.

First, let's establish a few, not many, metrics that will actually be useful in our situation. For example, if stakeholders expect us to provide them with information about the progress of requirements development, let's consider metrics to assess progress. Such a metric could be, for example, information about the status of requirements at a given time. If stakeholders expect information about the quality of requirements, let's choose metrics related to assessing the quality of work products. Such a metric could be, for example, the number and criticality of bugs found in requirements at the review, implementation, and testing stages.

Second, let's acknowledge that a metric is a number—a number that, without context, without its interpretation and juxtaposed with other information, most often says nothing.

For example, let's imagine that as a result of the measurement we get the following information: out of 300 requirements, there are currently 50 in the analysis.

What does this measurement result tell us about? About nothing; it informs us that out of a set of 300 requirements, we currently have 50 in the analysis. What does it tell us? Nothing. To make the measurement result a metric, we should have some kind of benchmark. For example, if historical data indicates that at a certain stage of analysis, we expect the percentage of requirements analyzed to be no less than, say, 80%, then the measurement result can help us assess progress against the plan. By itself, the measurement result, without a benchmark, does not provide such information.

Third, let's set the right value for the metric. If we set the value level inappropriately, it can generate negative consequences for our ability to monitor progress and make decisions. For example, if we define a metric that says a requirement can be considered of good quality if fewer than 15 defects are reported to the requirement during a review session, the consequence may be that poor-quality requirements will "move on" to further stages of manufacturing. Fifteen defects is a relatively large number. A requirement can be of very poor quality even if only one or two defects are reported for it. This is because the severity of the problem depends not on the number of defects, but on their criticality and impact on the quality of the object being evaluated.

It is worth noting here that without historical data, without some experience, it is very difficult to determine a reasonable value for a metric. For example, if you have never performed a review in your life and don't know what values to expect, you will certainly have problems in determining the right level of metrics. What to do in this regard? You can consult data from industry standards. There are sources that provide general values for certain metrics. You can consult colleagues from other teams, other projects. The fact that we ourselves do not have experience in a particular area does not at all mean that such knowledge does not exist in the organization. Finally, we can make some assumption about the expected value. This assumption will be verified during the execution of the work, and if together with the team we find that the metric should be changed because it does not properly cover your expectations and does not provide information that carries value, we will make the appropriate changes.

What specific metrics can be used in an analytics project? Here is a list of selected metrics.

1. Progress metrics
   - Percentage of work completed against plan: This metric can give information about whether the current progress of the work is in line with the plan. If we notice deviations from the plan, this is a signal to get more information to determine whether the plan should be modified because it was too optimistic, or whether the scope and execution of work should be revised because we are performing activities that may be unnecessary. It could also mean that factors have emerged that have a negative impact on our work progress—in other words, we have just identified a hitherto undiscovered project risk.
   - Percentage of completeness of results against plan: This metric measures not so much the percentage of work completed, but the completeness of the work results, for example, the percentage of completion of requirements specifications. With this information, we are able to inform stakeholders when we plan to complete a work product and when it will be ready for review or approval.
2. Coverage metrics
   - Coverage metrics are a rather interesting type of metric that can be categorized as metrics to assess the level of quality of work products, but also the progress of tasks. For example, a coverage metric can be the coverage of high-level requirements with system requirements. If we get a score lower than 100%, it means that not all high-level requirements are "covered," that is, not every high-level requirement is detailed with a lower-level requirement. Now if we do not complete the coverage, ensuring that every high-level requirement is detailed by a lower-level requirement, we can expect problems of the following form: stakeholders will not accept the designed system because it does not cover all the defined needs and requirements.

3. Quality metrics
   - The number of defects, along with an indication of their criticality, found in the work product against estimates. In doing so, it is worth noting that the total number of defects found in the work product during its entire life cycle should not be estimated, as such a metric will be impossible to verify. Let's set a specific time frame within which we will control the quality of the product.
   - Number of defects by type: This metric can give information about problem areas that need to be improved. For example, if the defects found are mainly defects related to the business logic of the planned solution, this may suggest a problem with the understanding of the business domain. Another example is if the defects found in the requirements specification are errors related to mental shortcuts, workshop deficiencies in the requirements specification, it may suggest insufficient training in the requirements specification area.

There are many other metrics that can be applied to your projects. Personally, I recommend choosing a relatively small number of metrics, but choose them judiciously—only those that are really needed and provide valuable information. Otherwise, you may find that you are collecting a massive amount of information as part of your design activities, spending a lot of time ensuring that this information is collected, but not using it in a meaningful way.

3.1.10 Learn from Mistakes. Preferably Someone Else's

FAILURE IS NOT A FAILURE IF THE LESSONS LEARNED FROM IT ALLOW YOU TO GROW.

Learn from mistakes; draw conclusions. This advice sounds trivial, but for some reason many analysts don't follow it. In theory, we know the rules and good practices; we know what practices to avoid—and yet we don't follow certain rules. In practice, of course, this can be due to a number of different factors, among which we can list the rational ones and those that I would simply call excuses.

For me personally, such excuses are "We don't have time to develop good-quality requirements," "We don't have time for reviews," "We don't have time to consult the development team about the requirements," "It won't work at our place anyway," or "We work differently." Such arguments, I am sorry to say, are not based on rationale and data—they are simply excuses to explain the fact that we do not follow basic good practices.

The excuse titled "We don't have time" is one of the most common. Let's turn the situation around a bit—we don't have time to develop the right requirements, we don't have time to talk to the customer, we don't have time to consult the requirements with the team, we don't have time to do a review. But do we have the time and resources to fix the defects resulting from these problems? Do we have time to explain to the customer why the results of our work are of poor quality? Do we have the time and resources to repeatedly revise requirements, re-consult stakeholders as a result of defects in requirements discovered during the implementation and testing phases? We have time for all this—but we don't have time to implement mechanisms to prevent these problems.

I would ask a different question: For what reason do we not have time to do our work well, correctly, to get results with a minimum acceptable level of quality? My practice indicates that most often we don't have time because we haven't planned for it—or we haven't planned for it because there was no planning stage at all.

We threw ourselves into the project without thinking about what we actually have to deliver in the project, what we need to do to deliver it at the right level of quality.

So I would start by learning from our own mistakes and the mistakes of others. Since we find that in previous projects we ran out of time for stakeholder analysis, requirements validation, or whatever, let's draw a conclusion. Were these activities planned? Were they at least estimated in any way? If not, let's start planning.

If the quality of our work products is rated low, at least by the project team, let's draw conclusions. For what reason do they rate our work products as low quality? Is it because the information contained in the requirements specification is not sufficient for implementation and testing, or is it because the information is sufficient, but is provided in an unreadable form, requiring increased effort for understanding and interpretation? If so, let's change the approach to the work. Instead of simply creating work products, let's first get information from the teams on what these work products should contain, what information content should be included, and in what form they should be delivered.

Are stakeholders changing requirements late in the project? Let's consider for what reason they are changing requirements. Very often, stakeholders change requirements not because business needs have realistically changed, but because they see a solution design, or even a piece of a working solution, and realize that what they see is not what they really need. Again, let's ask ourselves what this is due to. Often, it stems from the fact that our requirements specification and subsequent solution design do not reflect real business needs. In other words, we have misunderstood the needs and intentions of the stakeholders. Again, let's consider what the reason for this was. Very often the reason is that we do not have validation processes in the design. If we would like to avoid similar mistakes in the future, let's plan work product validations as part of the solution design and delivery process, so that we don't forget about them when implementing future initiatives.

This is how we can improve our work practices, with relatively little effort. The most important thing, however, is to be aware of the fact that the errors and problems that occur during the project are due to something. As a rule, we only see the symptoms of a problem—we don't see the causes. It is worth learning about the concept of root cause analysis and applying it. This will give us information about what is really the source of our problems. And if we know the source, we will be able to choose the appropriate mechanisms to prevent the occurrence of similar problems in the future.

Let me cite an example.

The project follows the tenets of agile methods. A business analyst supporting the product owner is responsible for detailing user stories by developing acceptance criteria.

During the course of the project, there is a recurring situation in which the development team rejects the user stories detailed by the analyst—they do not accept them for implementation in given iterations. They argue the decision on the grounds that the user stories and their acceptance criteria are not understandable, not complete; in a word, the stories are not ready to be implemented.

The analyst's first reaction was that the development team doesn't understand the business and "everything has to be explained to them in detail," and "after all, they don't have time to describe the requirements in detail." With the objective of understanding the problem, we held a meeting at which members of the development team and the analyst were present. We gathered information from both sides—what is the point of view of the members of the development team, what information in the user story documentation they are missing, what information they need. Then, from the analyst's point of view, what information he can realistically provide and what information he cannot.

Determined:

- The acceptance criteria are not complete. This is because they do not include alternative and exception scenarios. The business analyst described the behavior of the system from the point of view of positive scenarios ("happy path"). Those preparing for and executing system tests needed this information to cover not only positive scenarios, but also negative ones. In the current situation, test preparation was greatly hampered by the lack of input information for testing.
- The documentation of user stories did not mention data specifications in any way. For example, if a user story was about the ability to add a product to a product catalog, the development team had no information about the mandatory and optional attributes of the product, or what information the user adding the product must enter in order for the product to be saved to the product catalog.
- Acceptance criteria are described in a form that is difficult to understand. They were documented in list form, often as sentence equivalents. People who were the recipients of this documentation were unable to guess what the author meant and what behavior was expected of the system.
- The acceptance criteria focused exclusively on functional aspects, completely ignoring the qualitative features of the system. As a result, the team had information about the functionality of the solution, but no information about the quality requirements, which is an important input for designing the solution architecture.

  During the discussion we learned that:
- According to the business analyst, his job is to develop business acceptance criteria; the rest is up to the team. The analyst was not aware that aspects such as data specification (in the sense of what data is processed by the system, what are the logical constraints on this data) are not "technology" and "system implementation," but business rules that need to be obtained from business stakeholders—programmers will not invent them.

- The business analyst believes that quality requirements should be handled by the team. His understanding was that quality requirements require a certain amount of technical knowledge, which the analyst did not have—so he did not feel competent enough to deal with the subject.
- The team, on the other hand, expected the business analyst to provide the information necessary to understand how the system is supposed to function, what the results of executing the various functions are supposed to be, what exceptions may occur, what data the system processes (both as inputs and outputs), what the quality of the system is supposed to be expressed as quality requirements.

Then, after explaining what the quality requirements are, what data specification the development team expects and at what level of detail, and why it is important to obtain and document information about alternative scenarios and exceptions in the flows, we proceeded to establish working principles. And so:

- The business analyst described the acceptance criteria in the form of a list. The acceptance criteria had to take into account the initial conditions for the requirement, the input information for the functionality, the scenario for the execution of the functionality with alternative flows, the exceptions that may occur, and the results of the function execution. Where necessary, the business analyst defined quality requirements in a constraint-like form (e.g., report presentation functionality, constraint: it is to take no more than 5 s from the start of the "report generation" command to prepare and display data to the user).
- Those involved in testing supported the business analyst in assessing the completeness of the acceptance criteria, particularly in terms of alternative scenarios and exceptions. This not only helped catch potential glitches while the criteria were still being created, but also gave the testers a chance to more quickly understand the essence of the functionality they would be testing.
- The business analyst agreed with business stakeholders and documented the specification of the data processed by the system. This data specification included data name, format, and constraints.

For example, the "product" specification includes product name (text up to 50 characters), product description (text up to 200 characters), and product type (selected from a list of possible product types, also agreed with the business). An example of a restriction on the "product" object was that no two products with the same names can exist in the product catalog.

- The development team is responsible for mapping this logical data structure into the system design.
  The above working method was implemented as a pilot.

After the first two iterations, we held a retrospective to look at how the new working method improved the process and eliminated the problems identified earlier.

A peculiar side effect of the above exercise was the team's increased awareness of their roles and responsibilities AND the possibility of cooperation in different areas. With this knowledge, in subsequent projects, it was possible to plan work in a slightly different way from the beginning.

If we really want to improve processes, to learn, to improve our workbench, the first step is to understand what is currently a problem.

Implementing the practice of retrospectives and continuous learning brings a number of benefits:

1. *Continuous improvement*: Constant learning—an obvious benefit. In this industry, given the ever-changing business and technological context, failure to expand competence leads to a decline in value in the market. Over time, we can deliver less business value to customers when we are not up to date with technology or possible solutions to improve work. Lack of knowledge about new solutions and approach techniques can lead to a loss of competitiveness. An additional side effect is that customers and stakeholders learn more easily—getting information faster, combining facts faster, which allows you to effectively deliver valuable results.
2. You gain *humility*: It's a controversial thought, but I observe that people in the role of a business analyst often lack humility to some extent. They often don't realize their own limitations, they don't have full knowledge of methods and tools, and their perspective is limited. They focus on their own directions, not always accepting that the ideas of others may be just as good, or perhaps better. Opinions, especially those that contradict their own, are not infrequently treated as an attack and an attempt to undermine competence. The practice of retrospection and continuous learning helps you identify areas for improvement, accept the need to improve your practices, and change the way you view reality and approach your work.
3. You are *open to asking questions*: Realizing our own fallibility and cognitive limitations makes us more open to asking questions of stakeholders or the team. We learn to consult others about our suggestions and learn from the feedback given.

3.1.11 Monitor the Progress and Results of Work

If you don't monitor the progress of your work, you may find that the time allotted for the task has run out—and you haven't had time to deliver a worthwhile result. As a result, you either fail to complete the task you are responsible for, or you complete it in a hurry, under time pressure—most likely poorly.

Although the concepts of retrospectives, inspections, adaptation, and continuous learning have become quite widespread with the proliferation of agile approaches, unfortunately in many projects and organizations these practices are not performed or are performed inadequately.

Let's start with the objective of retrospectives, monitoring project status, and performance. The objective is not to point the finger of blame if the work does not go as planned. The objective is not to unreflectively complete a task, because this is enforced by the accepted method of work (colloquially speaking, ticking a task off the list is a done deal). The objective is not to complain about ineffective leaders, lack of communication in the team, customer problems, and so on.

The aim of monitoring the status and results of the work is to get information about what condition the project is in, whether it is realistic to complete the project as planned, and whether there are any obstacles or risks that could negatively affect the workflow. It is simply to provide information so that we can take appropriate corrective action, that is, apply mechanisms that allow us to continue and complete the initiative in such a way as to achieve the objectives.

Unfortunately, quite often the concept of monitoring and retrospectives is associated with control, drawing consequences when problems arise. People are wary of monitoring results because they may indicate delays in the work, poorer quality results, and other "negative" symptoms. In itself, the information that there is a delay in the project with poor-quality results does no harm to anyone—it is simply information that we will use in a way to improve the work or in other ways. For example, the objective may be to look for solutions to problems, not to find fault.

So how do we monitor and how do we use information from monitoring work status in a way that actually improves rather than harms?

Determine what values/parameters you want to monitor. In this section we discussed the concept of metrics and their applications. Let's remember to draw the right conclusions from the acquired information; the information should be meaningful and provide a certain value.

Let's consider an example. Let's assume that in a given project we are monitoring the progress status of tasks. We assume that it takes half a day on average to complete a particular task. If it takes longer than that, we escalate the problem—we start asking the person assigned to the task why it is taking so long to complete it, what the problems are, when he will complete the task. What could be the consequences of this approach? One of the more obvious consequences will be that team members will be discouraged and frustrated by the fact that instead of focusing on their work, they have to explain from time to time why they are taking longer than expected to complete the work. They also have to make declarations about when they will complete particular tasks.

There are several sources of the problem. One may be the assumption that tasks take half a day on average. We have not determined the types of tasks, their complexity, and how that complexity might affect labor intensity. We treat all tasks equally—this in itself can lead to absurd situations in which we expect a task titled "detailing user stories" to take the same amount of time as a task titled "performing market research in a specific area."

Determine the right ways to monitor the right parameters. I remember holidays in which the project manager would make a kind of rounds almost every day, and ask each member of the team what they were doing, how much longer they were going to work on it, and what percentage of the work they had done. I'm already leaving aside the fact that this task was monotonous and the resulting consequence. The problem was that this way of monitoring was quite effective in knocking team members out of the project rhythm—before focusing on the work, we were pulled away from it in order to provide information that, dare I say, contributed little. What valuable information comes from what percentage of the requirements specification I have completed? Who needs the information presented in this form? If monitoring yields the information that today I estimate the completeness of a requirements specification at 45% and tomorrow at 50%, what does that tell us? Before starting to monitor randomly selected values, in a random way, it is worth asking myself what I really want to know, the answers to what questions to get. I am interested in the percentage of completion of the requirements specification: will this specification be ready for acceptance by the date specified in the project plan?

Leaving aside the question of the parameter we are monitoring, let's consider the method of monitoring itself. Indeed, is an effective way of monitoring the progress of the work a direct conversation between the interested parties and tearing them away from their work? It is possible that in certain projects this may be legitimate—because, for example, in addition to just asking about the parameter, we can get additional contextual information necessary to understand the current situation of the resulting consequences. In most cases, however, project management tools, of which there is an abundance on the market, are entirely sufficient for gathering basic information. With such tools, there is no need to ask questions—because we can monitor the values of certain parameters in real time. With the assumption, of course, that team members will provide this information, which leads to the next practice.

Ensure that information is provided as needed. No monitoring will be effective if it is based on outdated data. For example, if for some reason we would like to check the progress of a job every day, and the team updates the status of the job once a week, our daily monitoring practices will not only be ineffective in themselves, but will also lead to inappropriate conclusions. This is because in such a case, we may presume that there are some real obstacles to task completion—since the status of task completion has not changed for 3 days, this indicates that there is a problem. In reality, there is no problem, with team members simply adopting the practice of updating task statuses once a week.

To make sure that the monitoring process goes hand in hand with the process of providing information, explain to the team the reason why you need certain metrics, what they are for, the reason why it is important for the team—at certain intervals—to provide information that will feed certain metrics. Communication is good practice—if we, as managers, need certain information from the team, the team needs to know why providing that information is important. We, in turn, need to know whether providing this information at the frequency we want is achievable within the specified project realities. Discussion with the team may make us aware of factors we were not aware of, such as the fact that daily reporting of task status information is without objective, since most tasks are relatively time-consuming and no change in status will occur on a daily basis.

Interpret information wisely. Information obtained without a reference point and context is just information. No meaningful conclusions and decisions can be made based on it. For example, if monitoring revealed that certain tasks are taking longer than you planned, what decision can we make as a result? None—until we understand what the cause of the delay is, and what impact this delay has on the final completion date of the task. We can neither understand the magnitude of the problem (insofar as it is relevant), nor make a decision about the potential need to interfere with the process. My opinion is that the information obtained from monitoring is the input to the information analysis process. Depending on the result of the analysis, we will decide whether or not appropriate measures are needed. Numbers alone do not tell anything yet. What is crucial is how we interpret these numbers in a given context.

It is the process of interpreting the information that is crucial for planning any improvements. From analyzing the information collected, we can conclude that:

- Delays are due to lack of competence—team members need more time to complete tasks because they are just acquiring the necessary skills.
- Delays are due to over-optimistic estimation of work, which in turn is the result of incorrect assumptions made during planning.
- Poor quality results from lack of knowledge—team members lack information about quality criteria, quality gates, quality assurance, and quality control mechanisms.
- Low quality results from an inadequate way of working—reviews of work products are not provided for, the concept of definition of readiness (DoR) is not implemented, and defects are not prevented; only the consequences of their occurrence are reacted to.
- Poor quality and delays result from the replication of bad practices—which can be the result of a lack of verification of the correctness of the work methods adopted (retrospective). Lack of retrospectives means that we can continue to implement ineffective practices for a long time because we are not even aware that they are ineffective. The project lacks checkpoints that would allow us to stop for a moment and think about whether what we are doing makes sense, whether it was done in the right way, what should be improved.

Other conclusions can be drawn from the analysis of the collected information. In the most general terms, regarding process improvement and competence, I would classify them as follows:

- Competency deficiencies, especially lack of knowledge
- Communication problems
- Lack of coordination of tasks
- Inadequate planning
- Inadequate selection of processes, methods, and tools
- Lack of retrospective mechanisms
- Unclear roles and responsibilities

3.2 Stakeholder Engagement Planning

Success in stakeholder management—as in leading an orchestra—lies not only in technical skills, but above all in understanding and responding to human nature and social dynamics. Project stakeholders can be compared to an orchestra and the leader to its conductor. Each musician (stakeholder) brings his unique personality, playing style and emotions, often shaped by stress and pressure. Just as in an orchestra, where violins, trumpets, flutes and other instruments have different sounds and roles, the stakeholders in a project have different perspectives, motivations and ways of responding. A good conductor must go beyond the ability to read notes, he must learn to 'read' his musicians—understanding their emotions, responding to their uncertainties, and adjusting his approach so that each can play to the best of his ability. Like a project leader, he or she must develop personal relationships with stakeholders, listen to them, build trust, and use different communication styles to effectively manage the socio-political complexities of the project.

Małgorzata Kusyk, AgilePMO Founder

3.2.1 Communication Shall Be Planned

Many project failures do not come from the complexity of the issue. They stem from our inability to communicate. And we can't because we haven't planned for communication, taking it for granted as an aspect so obvious that it doesn't need to be planned.

One of the most important parts of planning any way of working on a project or initiative is to establish communication rules. This topic is very important, and unfortunately, extremely often ignored. It seems to us that communication is a skill we have from birth, that we don't need to perfect it or work on it, that it is enough to simply get along somehow and the cooperation will work itself out. Nothing could be further from the truth. Communication skills, like any other, can and should be developed. This is especially important in the work of a business analyst, who, by virtue of his profession, should be able to communicate efficiently with people of different experience, motivations and backgrounds, with different knowledge and different communication styles. It is also worth considering that communication is not just verbal communication or conversation. We communicate in different ways, one of which is verbal; another, for example, is the documentation that the analyst creates and shares with stakeholders.

In order to choose the right approach to communication, it is first necessary to understand what the objective of the communication is, to whom this communication is to be directed, who are the participants in the communication, and what are the information requirements of each person. Wanting to ensure the effectiveness of communication, we should be able to provide the information needed by the recipient—in the way the recipient expects it, in a form that is convenient for him. This sounds like the obvious, while in practice I have repeatedly encountered a complete lack of any communication planning. As a result, problems arise, such as lack of understanding of the communicated information by stakeholders or reluctance to communicate. If there are any communication problems, it is important to remember that problems do not come out of nowhere; they can be a symptom of another phenomenon, such as problems with stakeholder relationship management.

When considering communications planning for a project, it is worth considering a few key elements that form the foundation for effective information sharing.

- *Objective*. As with any other task, communication planning involves precisely defining the objective of the communication. We will direct a different message if the objective is to obtain information on a set objective, for example, to obtain information on stakeholder requirements. We will use a different message if the objective is to communicate information to specific people. For example, if our objective is to obtain information, the communication will be question-oriented, which will often include trying to understand the context in order to determine the right questions to ask. If, on the other hand, our objective is to communicate information, we should determine exactly what we want to communicate and to whom, and what the most effective form and channel of communication will be. We should also get information on potential risks and problems that may occur and affect the effectiveness of the communication, for example, the risk of our target group not understanding certain vocabulary.
- *Target group*. Another important element of communication planning is to determine the target group. Projects or other ventures involve a variety of stakeholder groups, both so-called business and technical. An important factor for success is to tailor the message to the individual needs of each of these groups. A properly tailored and delivered message can effectively reach and be understood by the audience, which is the objective of communication. Understanding the target group, its expectations and limitations, is a prerequisite for clear and lucid communication.
- *Communication plan*. If you already know the objective of the communication and its participants, it is worth developing a communication plan, which will define when and how the information will be communicated, who will be the recipients, who is responsible for conveying the information, and what methods, tools, and techniques will be used. Part of the communication plan can be to determine the channels of communication—the choice of appropriate tools, such as face-to-face meetings, emails, or other form of documentation, as well as modern platforms for online communication, directly affects the quality of information exchange. The communication plan should also specifically provide for obtaining feedback—this can be done, for example, through document review and approval sessions, and design validation at product increment demos. Without the provision of feedback mechanisms, unfortunately, we will never be quite sure whether the recipients have properly understood the content being communicated and whether we have properly understood the content being communicated to us.
- *Monitoring the effectiveness* of communication. Planned communication methods and techniques can change in effectiveness over the course of a project. This is due to

various factors, such as the increasing complexity of the project and new participants in communication with the emergence of new forms of information. Therefore, it is worth monitoring the effectiveness of communication and evaluating its effectiveness regularly. For example, over time we may notice that face-to-face meetings are becoming less effective. We spend a lot of time on discussions from which little results; we involve a lot of people who are not necessarily essential for this type of meeting. As a result, a sense of frustration and fatigue begins to set in, often manifested by statements such as "We have too many meetings; there is no time to work because we are constantly sitting in meetings." At such a point, we should anticipate a change in the form of communication, since the existing one has apparently ceased to fulfill its objective.

3.2.2 Determine Roles and Responsibilities

IF YOU HAVEN'T DETERMINED WHO DOES WHAT AND IS RESPONSIBLE FOR WHAT, HOW CAN YOU EXPECT THE WORK TO BE DONE?

Very often during planning we focus on defining tasks and their expected results, connections, and dependencies. Sometimes, in doing so, we forget to define responsibilities and roles. Of course, a business analyst is not responsible for all planning in a project—but he is responsible for planning his area. In this area, many people have a specific role. Part of planning, therefore, is to determine the involvement of each role in specific tasks and activities. A simple assignment of a person or role to a task can be used for this purpose, but this method is quite imprecise, as it only defines the assignment of a person to an activity, not the level of involvement in performing that activity.

An example of a simple tool for determining selected properties of stakeholders is the power/interest matrix (Figs. 3.9 and 3.10).

A more complete method of defining responsibility is the RACI matrix, including variants such as RASCI (Fig. 3.11). With the RACI matrix, we can define how a position is involved in the execution of specific tasks. This ensures transparency and reduces the risk of later misunderstandings.

In some circles, there is quite strong criticism of the RACI matrix and tools in general for defining roles and responsibilities. Arguments against such tools include:

- The creation of an RACI matrix ends up with a rigid and artificial assignment of responsibility to individual roles, with the result that some people may lose their sense of responsibility for all the work carried out within the project. The effect of "I am responsible only for this and that, the rest are not my tasks" appears.
- RACI matrices are not needed if the team knows its objective. Instead of wasting energy on establishing roles and responsibilities, it is better for the team to define its objectives and work together to achieve these goals.

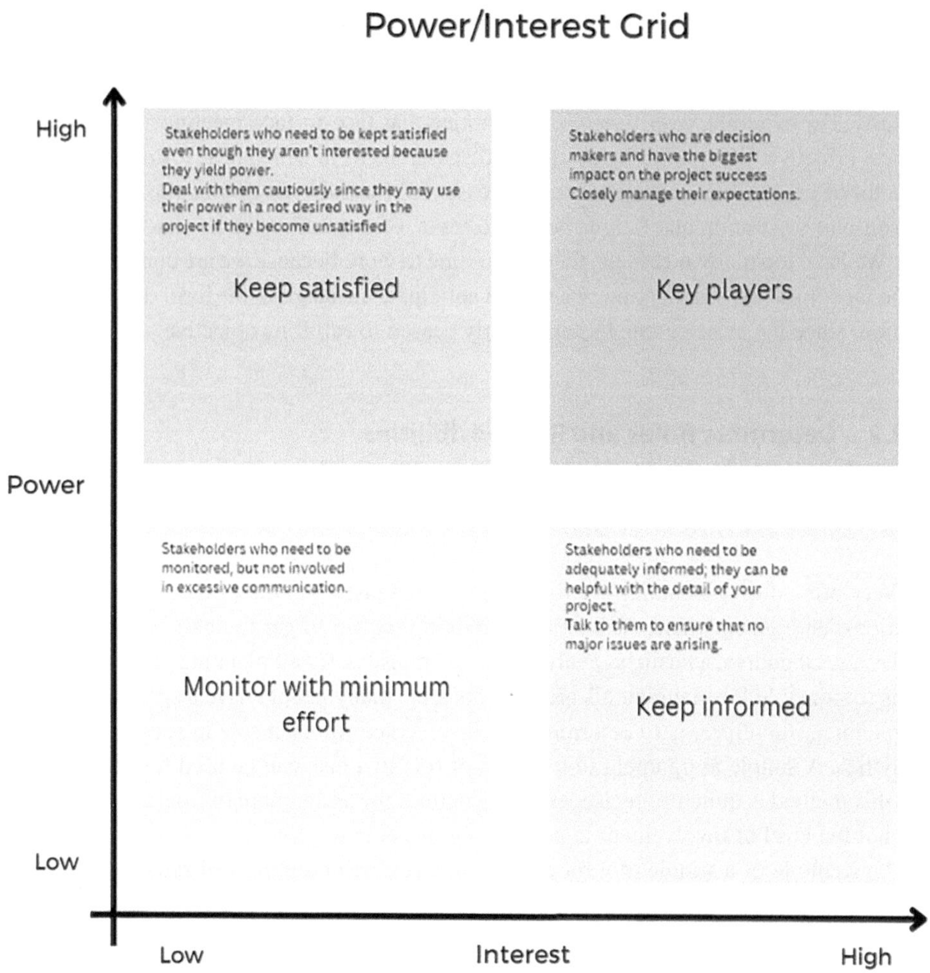

Fig. 3.9 Power/interest grid—template

There is some truth in these arguments. Indeed, defining responsibilities assigned to roles can cause some people to feel no responsibility for tasks not assigned to them. As a result, we may lose a sense of common objective and the responsibility of all team members to achieve that objective. However, the RACI matrix or other ways of defining roles and responsibilities are just tools—they do not generate any side effects on their own, if used correctly. These tools do not serve to rigidly define the responsibilities of individuals and, at the same time, indicate that since a person is not responsible for a given task, he or she may completely not care about its implementation and outcome.

The objective of tools that help define responsibilities is to organize knowledge, to think about what competencies are required to complete certain tasks, what role should be involved, in what way, in the implementation of the task. It does not necessarily have to be

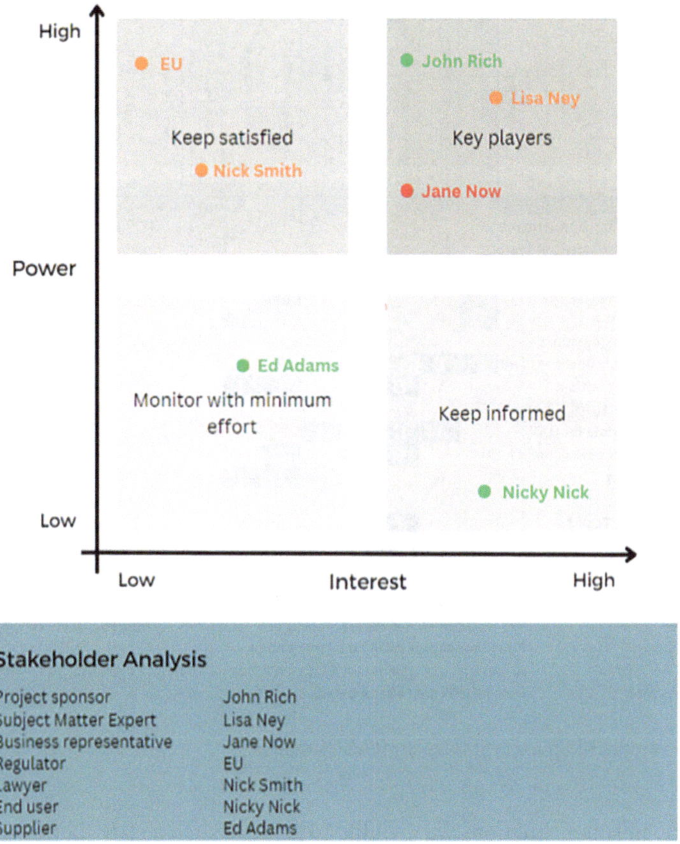

Fig. 3.10 Example of a completed power/interest grid

a commitment to the task—it can be a commitment understood as informing the role about the work results obtained.

The second argument is valid for specific initiatives or projects for which a specific objective can be defined and the team is fairly constant. However, let's imagine a situation in which we are conducting a strategy analysis for a customer's company and our task is to determine a change that carries value for a specific business process. We are working with stakeholders on the customer side. Under such conditions, it is quite difficult to imagine a situation in which we can afford to define only the objective of our task and assume that all people involved in achieving this objective will be equally motivated to achieve it. The reason may be simple—some of the stakeholders may be mainly involved in carrying out their work and achieving the objectives set before them (which do not necessarily coincide with the objectives of our initiative). Do we have enough empowerment in the organization to bring these stakeholders to a situation where they feel that they care about the objective of our initiative, that they will benefit from it, that it is worth it for them to be actively involved?

ROLES	Owner	Business ower	Business analyst / SME	Technical SME	User representative	Business analyst	Project manager	QA lead	QA / tester	Dev	Infrastructure	Legislations	Producers	Name or Role	Name or Role	Name or Role
Deliverable or Task	Business stakeholders					Project team						Other stakeholders				
Area 1 Business analysis																
Stage A Strategy analysis																
Business goal definition	A	R				I	I									
AS IS analysis	C	A	R			I										
TO BE analysis	C	A	R			R	I									
Stage B Elicitation																
Requirements sources ident	C	C	R			R	A									
SPOC identification		A	C			I	I									
Area 2 Testing																
Prepare scripts for UAT		I	C		I	S	A	R	R							
Prepare test environment for UAT			C	C		C	A				R	C				
Execute UAT		A	S		R	I	I									
Phase 4																
Deliverable/Task 1			I			A	R						R		S	
Deliverable/Task 2			I			A		R								

R	Responsible	Assigned to complete the task or deliverable.
A	Accountable	Has final decision-making authority and accountability for completion. Only 1 per task.
S	Support	Provides support during implementation.
C	Consulted	An adviser, stakeholder, or SME who is consulted before a decision or action.
I	Informed	Must be informed after a decision or action.

Fig. 3.11 Example of an excerpt from an RASCI matrix

Arguably, in some situations we are able to achieve such a state, but in very many situations we are not. Unfortunately, we often do not stand in a position to bring about such a situation. Since we have no influence on the motivation of stakeholders, or this influence is very small at the beginning, and on the other hand we have specific objectives to achieve and we know that to achieve these objectives we need input from specific stakeholders, the only thing left is to get information on who is able to provide us with data, who is able to help us with our tasks, who is the decision-maker, who—for various reasons—should be informed about the status of the work. Tools such as the RACI matrix will help us organize our knowledge and determine how we can involve individual stakeholders in analytical and non-analytical processes.

However, it is worth paying attention to ensure that such matrices are not overloaded with information. Unfortunately, as a rule, the larger the matrix, the more roles and tasks we establish, the lower the readability, and the less practical application of such a matrix. We create it because it is the right thing to do at the beginning of a project, and then we do not use it because it is—due to its complexity—difficult to use. So how do we define roles and responsibilities in such a way that it actually brings benefit?

- Identify *key tasks*. By key, I mean those that are necessary to realize intermediate and final work products. If the project consists of phases, you can divide the RACI matrix into matrices for each phase.
- Identify the *roles* that will be involved in any way in the execution of the work. If the project involves a supplier, any third-party company, identify the roles occurring on that company's side.
- Determine what *competencies* each role has. This is important because depending on the organization and the project, the definition of roles may vary—meaning that specific roles may have different competencies and be able to perform different tasks. If at this stage we are not able to determine what competencies each role has, bravo, we have just identified one of the most important gaps. If we want to make sure that the project work goes fairly smoothly, one of the first things we should do is determine who should do this project work and what competencies are needed to do it. Deficiencies in competence should be filled before the work begins, or treated as a design risk that we will face at later stages.
- Identify which *role* in what way is *involved* in the task. Remember that there is only one person who makes the decision to start the implementation of the task, only one "business owner of the topic." If for any task you identify two decision-makers, it may mean that the task should be decomposed into smaller parts. It is worth being aware that determining the level of involvement is a very good test of understanding stakeholder responsibility. If for a given task we are not able to identify a responsible person, a decision-maker informed about the implementation of the task, it may mean that the structure of the organization or project lacks such a role or competence. Another example could be the definition of a stakeholder's role and the inability to identify a task in which this stakeholder is involved in any way—again, this could indicate a lack of understanding of the stakeholder's role. It could also indicate that the stakeholder is a so-called statistic—so his importance is not high enough to specifically deal with the management of his involvement at a given stage.
- Remember that creating an RACI matrix should not be done by one person. Let's treat it as a team effort—let's gather key stakeholders who have the necessary knowledge, and together develop a preliminary version of the RACI matrix. This proposal is worth discussing and confirming with the other stakeholders to make sure everyone understands their roles and responsibilities.

The definition of roles and responsibilities can change, just as project risks or product scope change. Therefore, it is worth checking systematically whether our definition of roles and responsibilities is still up to date. If any changes are required, let's make them on an ongoing basis—otherwise the RACI matrix will simply become another document that is not necessary to anyone, whose provisions can at best create confusion.

3.2.3 Determine Single Point of Contact

IF YOU CAN REDUCE THE NUMBER OF COMMUNICATION PATHS IN THE PROJECT, DO IT. YOU'LL MAKE YOUR JOB EASIER WHILE ELIMINATING MANY RISK FACTORS.

In most cases, we are dealing with a large number of stakeholders. Collaborating, especially communicating, with a large number of stakeholders can pose many challenges. The more people in communication, the more communication channels we have to define and maintain.

Let me give an example of a real project situation here. In one project for the insurance industry, more than 40 stakeholders representing the business were identified. These stakeholders were quite selectively involved in the work of requirements elicitation and their analysis, validation, and acceptance. The selectivity was that due to limitations in stakeholder availability, different stakeholders attended the requirements elicitation workshops, depending on availability. As a result, many times we had to return to topics already discussed, rehashing agreed decisions, because often the stakeholders had a different opinion than the people with whom discussions were held earlier. This was frustrating and enormously time-consuming. The apogee of the problem, however, came only when the requirements were accepted.

After drafting the initial version of the requirements specification for the solution being designed, the business analyst circulated the developed document to all 40 stakeholders. They were asked to review the document and provide any comments or suggestions for changes. After an agreed time, the results of the review began to flow in. The document, which is several hundred pages long, was reviewed by 40 people, receiving some 3000 comments and feedback. The wording of this seems quite intimidating. An additional problem was that many of the comments were contradictory, covering the same area, but phrased in slightly different ways. It took the analyst about 2 weeks to pre-process the review comments.

After 2 weeks of analyzing the comments, the analyst came to the conclusion that further work on improving the documents in this way would miss the objective. A decision was made to hold a workshop to discuss the key comments and observations and decide on next steps. This time the work was organized in a slightly more efficient way. Instead of inviting all 40 stakeholders to the workshop, the business analyst asked for representatives from each area. Workshops were held with these stakeholders, which made it possible to handle the comments and improve the document fairly efficiently and quickly.

What is the result of this design situation? That involving everyone in the implementation of the work is very often ineffective and leads to chaos. As a rule, it is possible to reduce the number of stakeholders with whom we need to communicate directly.

Imagine that we have identified 30 people representing the so-called business. We don't necessarily need to communicate with each person to establish, discuss, or accept requirements. To make our job easier, we can apply the concept of Single Point of Contact (SPoC), that is, from a specific group of stakeholders, identify one person who will be a kind of spokesperson or representative of the group. In this way, we will not have to communicate with three people, but with one.

Of course, this does not mean that this one person will make decisions independently of the rest of the group, that the opinions of the other business stakeholders do not interest us, and that all decisions and arrangements will be made by one person. The SPoC concept assumes that from our side, the business analysts, we communicate with one person, and this person represents the interests of the entire group. This means that the role of this person is to gather opinions from the entire group, discuss options, and agree on needs. This person will be a kind of coordinator of the work carried out by the group. This, of course, requires the consent of the interested party and making sure that the representative of the group is the right person to perform such a role.

A person in the role of SPoC should:

- Have some leadership skills necessary to coordinate work within their group.
- Communicate efficiently—both within the group and externally, i.e., to the business analyst.
- Have substantive competence, i.e., knowledge of the area in question. Otherwise, this person will not be able to assess the reliability of information obtained from group members.

Individuals acting as a point of contact do not necessarily have to be high up in the organizational hierarchy. In order to represent a particular group and be an ambassador for the needs and expectations of that group, it is theoretically sufficient to possess the above-mentioned skills and to have the appropriate authority within the organization. Quite often, those designated as SPoCs are leaders, area managers, people with a certain function in the hierarchy. This is not necessarily due to the need to mark one's place in the organization, but to the fact that people holding a certain position usually have the appropriate competence and decision-making power, and can—without the need to implement specific organizational arrangements—represent the entire area.

If no SPoC has been identified in our project, let's take steps to identify such people for the sake of smooth workflow. After identifying the stakeholders, we can make some classification, and determine what area they belong to, what interests they represent—examples of stakeholder groups are end users, and business, marketing, or sales department representatives. After making such a classification, let's determine or ask decision-makers who could represent each group. If an organization on a project does not have a practice of identifying SPoCs, explain the benefits of such a practice.

Those designated as SPoCs should be clear about their role and the resulting responsibilities and authority. It is good practice to hold a short familiarization meeting to explain the objectives of the initiative and expectations for each group, and explain what the role of the SPoC is and the benefits of the concept.

In this way, we can significantly reduce the number of communication paths in our project.

3.2.4 Determine Sources of Resistance

Often reluctance is the default attitude of many people toward the coming changes. However, it is much easier to accept change if you feel you are a co-author of it.

Radosław Grębski, Business Analyst, Coach, ITability

The natural human reaction to change is resistance—we are afraid of what is unknown because we don't know how it will affect us and our environment. Any change—whether it is a change in the way we work, organizational changes, or a change in attitude—hits our comfort zone. If the reason for the introduction of change is known and its consequences for us do not affect our surroundings, it is easier for us to come to terms with the changes and adapt to them. It is worse if the changes are introduced top-down, and we don't know the rationale behind them, and the potential impact. Your role as a business analyst is to support the introduction of change. This includes not only the definition of process or technology changes—it also includes properly preparing the change for implementation. And it involves properly preparing stakeholders to embrace such a change.

Have we ever noticed the following signals?

- Stakeholders see no reason to make any changes. The status quo is desirable.
- Certain stakeholders are overtly against driving the solution you are working on, to the point of sabotaging the project.
- Some stakeholders refuse to provide information, or deliberately provide information that is not entirely truthful. As a result, they delay the work, which leads to the need to redo certain tasks because your work products and decision-making were based on false or incomplete information.
- During the implementation of project work, stakeholders refuse to cooperate, often explaining that they lack time and are overwhelmed by their responsibilities, despite the fact that they realize that the designed solution will directly affect them.
- Once the solution is implemented, stakeholders refuse to use it, arguing that "it doesn't work as it should."

These types of symptoms indicate resistance of certain stakeholders to the designed change. Resistance is completely natural—change causes a violation of the comfort zone, and this causes uncertainty, fear, and resistance. It is up to us to decide what we will do with this resistance—ignore it and continue our work without considering the consequences of the decision, or try to turn the resistance into support.

The first step in eliminating resistance is to understand its source—because there is always a source and there are always reasons for certain attitudes. The source of resistance can be, for example:

- Lack of knowledge about the reasons for change, and its scope.
- Information chaos—information about the change comes from many different sources, is partially contradictory, and may be incomplete.

- Lack of awareness of how change can positively affect certain processes or methods of operation.
- Fear of change due to fear of losing a job or revealing a lack of certain competencies.

In many cases, the first step in solving problems is understanding their source. And so, for example, in order to level out resistance, it is sometimes enough to simply explain to stakeholders the reason for the changes, what their impact will be on the work of individual people and entire departments. Even better results can be achieved by involving stakeholders in the process of defining changes. By doing so, we bring about a change that does not become imposed, but worked out by the people who will be affected by it. Of course, we are not always in a position to agree on every change, especially a major process change at an organizational level, with stakeholders at lower hierarchical, less decision-making levels. But we are always in a position to communicate—to inform stakeholders of the plans, to identify their concerns and doubts, to record the ideas and insights they raise. Even if we can't turn their ideas and suggestions into concrete decisions, we can communicate them to the right decision-makers. It is not uncommon for people lower in the hierarchy of an organization to have more up-to-date knowledge of the ills and problems associated with the execution of work than people at managerial levels.

3.2.5 Build Relationships and Engagement

Engagement does not arise on its own. Relationships don't build themselves. They have to be built.

Or we can consider building relationships—but business is about people; it is for people that services and products are created; it is people who design and deliver these services and products. At every level of business we communicate, we cooperate with people. We could skip the issue of relationships, engagement, emotions if we were machines. But we are not.

We are starting to work on a particular initiative. We will certainly be working with many people, communicating with stakeholders and other team members. We will need to obtain information from various sources—including people. We will need to agree on certain issues and make decisions—most likely among different people. How do we get stakeholders to want to work with us, to be committed to the project, to be really motivated to achieve certain objectives? The answers to these questions are not simple. Building stakeholder engagement is a very broad issue.

The starting point, in my opinion, is to understand what factors will motivate stakeholders to cooperate. To answer this question, I first need to know who the stakeholders are, what their role in the initiative is, what their attitude toward the initiative is. I need to know what their objectives are, what they care about, how the initiative and its results align or conflict with those objectives.

I should know what the context of the stakeholders is—because very often the lack of involvement is not due to bad will, but to the fact that the person is overloaded with responsibilities. Finally, I should know how to communicate with the person, build relationships, and as a result, build engagement. This, of course, in a sense requires getting to know the stakeholder as a person, a flesh-and-blood human being, not a record in a table.

Let's start at the beginning. How do we build engagement?

Let's imagine that we are members of a team of business analysts who have been tasked by a manufacturing company to analyze the feasibility of making improvements in various processes. Our task is to make changes to the production process so that production efficiency can be increased. In order to understand what kinds of changes need to be made, we would first like to understand what the production process currently looks like. The people who know this process and can explain to us how it works are probably the production manager and the production operator.

How can we approach building engagement with these stakeholders? We can, of course, hold a meeting, a teleconference, invite stakeholders to it, and ask what changes in the production process they propose. If we take such an action without understanding the mode of operation of these people and adjusting to it, without explaining the objective of the potential meeting and agreeing on the optimal form of communication, we are likely to fail at the outset. Why? Because these people most likely have their own work schedule, are not as available as we might expect, and are not necessarily familiar with the teleconference mode. In addition, we plan to invite them to the meeting with the idea that they should be the ones to offer us suggestions for changes.

Trying to identify suggestions for changes in the process without understanding what factors are currently causing the process not to be as efficient as expected is definitely a false start. Even if these people have some thoughts about possible changes, they are unlikely to express those thoughts. For a simple reason: we are a representative of a foreign company, inviting them to a meeting whose objective they don't know—because we haven't explained it. Instead of first building trust and rapport, we expect stakeholders to come up with ideas for changes in a process that, from their point of view, is crucial because it relates to their jobs.

They don't know how the changes they are going to propose will affect their future in the company, how the change the way work is accomplished—Or whether they can cause stakeholders to have to do additional work. They have none of this information. And the lack of information makes us feel insecure.

In the situation described above, there is no question of any attempt to build relationships or commitment. We go straight to completing tasks in a bad way, without taking the trouble to get to know the people we have come to work with, to learn their expectations, their concerns, their perspectives. We didn't take the trouble to build any relationships through which we would establish any understanding.

If we haven't done that, what reason do stakeholders have to help us accomplish our work? Why would they give us their time if we can't even define what we expect from them and for what objective we engage them in certain tasks? What reason would they have to actually think honestly about the possibilities of making changes in the process, when they don't know how those changes will affect them?

The above method is, unfortunately, an effective way of discouraging stakeholders from working with us, rather than building commitment.

Building engagement requires understanding the motivations and needs of stakeholders and addressing them appropriately during project work. For example, if we would like to involve business representatives in requirements work, we need to consider what might be an appropriate motivation for them to participate fully and satisfactorily in this work. We cannot assume that sufficient motivation is merely the fact that someone, perhaps a decision-maker, has delegated these stakeholders to support our project. Unfortunately, very often we do not know the exact circumstances of this "delegation," and we cannot assume whether the stakeholders joined the project of their own free will, or whether they were merely given business orders. Depending on how stakeholders joined to work on a particular initiative, we can expect different results:

- They may be actively involved, willing to participate in the work because they understand how the results of the work will affect the operation of the organization, especially in their areas of interest.
- Alternatively, they may be "forced" to participate in a project whose objectives they do not understand, see no reason to engage in the project, and do not see the benefits of the project work or the results obtained.

I suggest the following approach to the subject. If we care about building commitment, let's build it consciously and without haste.

Assessment of *stakeholder relevance*. First, let's determine which stakeholders will be key to us. Let's use the results of the stakeholder analysis, which will provide information about how this is the stakeholders' area of expertise, their role, level of decision-making, and attitude toward the project. If the stakeholder analysis makes it possible to identify stakeholders whose attitudes are negative or indifferent, and they are key to our tasks, it is worth applying appropriate measures to change this negative attitude to a positive one (Thomas et al. 2012).

Determining which stakeholders are "key ones" does not at all mean that no relationships are worth building with "less important" stakeholders. The characteristics of stakeholders often change during the course of a project (one who is irrelevant today may be one of the decision-makers tomorrow). This means so much that we will know who to focus on first.

It's also worth remembering that we don't always work on an initiative from the very beginning, nor are we always introduced to a project in a mature way. Sometimes we don't know the results of the stakeholder analysis; instead, we are put in front of it and are presented with a list of people we will work with. In such a case, it becomes all the more important to start by determining who the people we will be working with are, what

Role	Sponsor	Business owner of area X	cBusiness owner of area Y	Business owner of area Z	SME of area X	SME of area Y	SME of area Z	Business architect	Project manager	Business analyst	Solution architect	Developer	QA	Legal department		Name or Role	Name or Role	Name or Role
Task	**Business stakeholdersl**								**Project team**					**Other stakeholders**				
Stage 1 - processes																		
List of business processes	A	C	C	C				C		R								
Selection of processes for analysis	A	R	R	R	C	C	C	C		R								
Analysis of process X	I	A			C			S		R								
Modeling of the target state of the process X		A	I	I				S		R	C, I			C				
Specification of process changes X		A								R	I			C				

Fig. 3.12 Example of an excerpt from an RASCI matrix

attitudes they have toward the project, and whether there is anything we can do to make these attitudes positive and conducive to effective and pleasant cooperation.

Determine the *needs* and *expectations* of the stakeholders. Let's determine what tasks we will need certain stakeholders for, what information we will need them for, what results we will need them for. This will help us avoid awkward situations, such as when we would like to say hello to stakeholders, explain our role in the project, and let them know what our expectations of their role are, and we are unable to, because we don't know ourselves what we will need them for. It can be useful here to develop the RASCI matrix mentioned earlier, so that we can organize information about what tasks are to be performed at a given stage and what roles should be involved in their implementation (Fig. 3.12).

Introduce yourself. Let's introduce ourselves. This is so obvious; it is one of the rules of good manners, and yet we often forget it. We approach stakeholders without taking the trouble to introduce ourselves. It is important to realize that we are probably one of many people who stakeholders contact. They don't necessarily know who they are dealing with, what our role is, what we expect of them, what they should expect of us. Instead of making them guess, we explain it.

A practice I highly recommend is to hold a familiarization meeting—a short "kickoff" meeting—during which we introduce ourselves, get to know the rest of the team, explain what the project is about, what its objectives are, who will be involved in the project and how. During this relatively short meeting, I usually ask stakeholders to introduce themselves, say a few words about themselves, what they do in the organization, whether there is something special they expect from the project and its results. This will help stakeholders understand the context of the project, their role in the overall initiative, the results of the project, and ideally, the effects of the project results on their work, their position in the company.

Keep in mind that such a meeting should not be long—its objective is to allow people to get to know each other, to make first contact. Under no circumstances should it turn into a long and tiring meeting, which is likely to be counterproductive—stakeholders may be alienated and discouraged from the beginning.

It is worth realizing that there may be people among the stakeholders who, for whatever reason, feel resistance to change. In order to achieve the established objectives of the initiative, it will probably be necessary to level out this resistance and bring about a situation in which we work as a cohesive team. The fact that a few or dozens of people have been working together on a topic for a certain period of time does not yet prove that it is an effective team. A team needs to be built. At the very beginning, we are simply a group of people, each with their own objectives, experiences, and motivations, and probably don't know the other members of the group.

A kickoff can be one step in turning resistance into curiosity and then commitment.

Agree on a plan of action. People generally feel more confident if they know what's going on, what the work plan is, what we're aiming for. Let's not surprise them with unplanned meetings or tasks they haven't heard about before and aren't prepared to handle. Let's develop a plan that specifies what tasks you have to do, what the time frame is, what the results of the tasks are. Discuss this plan with the stakeholders and make sure they feel comfortable with it. Let's make it clear what we expect from them in the implementation of each task.

One of the very common mistakes that disrupts relationships between people is putting them in front of things—we simply inform them that they should do something, without explaining how, what we expect, without making sure that they are able to do the task or need help in doing it. Don't. Treat stakeholders as members of your team and make sure that as a team you are able to work efficiently.

Instead of communicating the plan, develop a draft plan; present it as an initial proposal for discussion and modification. Explain the assumptions of the plan—don't make assumptions that are obvious. Let's explain what our proposal for implementing the plan is and ask for feedback. If any concerns or doubts from stakeholders surface during the discussion, handle those concerns. Remember that these are very preliminary stages of relationship building, and we can't afford to ignore signals that might say that stakeholders don't feel confident, aren't fully aware of their role in the project, aren't sure of their competence.

Build new competencies. A very valuable side-effect of implementing a business project can be to increase stakeholders' competencies in other areas, such as business modeling, requirements development, identifying business needs and distinguishing them from solutions, and the ability to analyze and synthesize information. So let's treat this as an opportunity to build additional skills in the people you will be working with. We will get the opportunity to further strengthen relationships, as people are generally grateful for the opportunity to learn new competencies that can help them grow professionally or simply perform their daily duties more efficiently.

Get to know stakeholders as people. In the process of building engagement, it is extremely useful to get to know individual stakeholders more deeply. Of course, in project realities, we usually don't have the time to establish deep social relationships, but to some extent we are able to get to know people, their personality traits, communication styles, etc., with the analysis work we do. For example, if the first specific analytical task in a project is to determine the business processes to be recognized, we will most likely conduct several interviews or simply conversations with stakeholders to get a list of potential processes. We will then hold a meeting to discuss this list and select processes for analysis and modeling. This meeting, like the earlier interviews, gives us an opportunity to interact with stakeholders, learn about their ways of communicating, their approach to the project, and identify potential risks associated with working with them. It is worth remembering that a substantive meeting is not only an opportunity to gain domain knowledge, but also information about the stakeholders themselves. With this information, we will be able to plan the work and the means of implementation in such a way that the stakeholders feel that they have an impact on the change, that their opinion counts, and that they themselves want to participate in the definition and implementation of the change.

Communicate effectively. Effective communication is not about talking to people—it is about both parties understanding each other. Relationships are built largely through communication. If you ignore this fact and fail to ensure proper communication, you will find it immensely difficult to build positive relationships and stakeholder engagement. Effective communication should be matched to the audience, to their state of knowledge, in their communication style, their learning style, to the situation—we will communicate differently in a noisy production hall from how we communicate when conducting a phone call from the office. Let's learn to listen actively. Let's learn to ask for feedback.

Build ownership. One of the best ways to build commitment is to give people some authority, decision-making power, to build a sense of ownership for a topic or area. Even if it's the power of having stakeholders in a meeting to make a list of requirements on their own, to decide on their priorities on their own, to change that decision on their own—this will already build commitment.

We want to determine what changes are required in a particular process. Let's gather information from stakeholders with expertise in the topic. Let's develop initial proposals for change and discuss them and agree on a target solution with the stakeholders involved. Let them be aware of their influence on decisions made in the company—even if the scope of those decisions is very small.

During workshops or other meetings, or any other task involving stakeholders, remember to really involve them. Unfortunately, there are times when, for various reasons, we take over the reins and dominate the entire meeting. Instead of working as a team, we do the tasks and make the decisions ourselves. We ask questions and answer them ourselves. We ask stakeholders to explain a topic, then we try to figure out how the process works, we explain it to ourselves, we model it ourselves, we validate it ourselves.

This approach is a very effective way of destroying a team before it has time to build. This is, by the way, a perfectly natural reaction—if we ourselves invite people to a meeting where we supposedly expect these people to give us information, work something out together, make a decision together, and then do the exact opposite, let's not be surprised that stakeholders will not be engaged, will not be interested in the progress of the work or the change itself. We can inadvertently create a situation where we make opponents out of stakeholders whose attitude was positive, who really wanted to help bring change to the organization.

Use tools to build engagement. There are many tools through which even boring meetings can be turned into a form of fun. There are techniques that will get weary stakeholders fired up. Let's learn about these techniques; thanks to them you will be able to do your job professionally, but also in a way that engages participants.

For example, a workshop whose objective is to learn about business processes and establish a new way of working can be organized as follows: use a whiteboard, physical or virtual. Ask stakeholders familiar with a particular business process to write on small pieces of paper the name of the activities they can identify within the process. Ask them to simply focus on identifying the activities in the first step. Then, when the slips of paper with the names of the activities are ready, ask the stakeholders to help you arrange them in order according to the flow of the process. Let them do this task on their own—focus on moderation, in asking questions to clarify the activities and how the processes are carried out.

When the process flow is ready, summarize it to make sure all stakeholders have the same interpretation of the process flow. Then ask stakeholders to think about what in the current process can be improved, what can be changed, added, removed. Provide an example so they know what you expect from them. Give them a few minutes to do this. Then ask them to write down their observations on slips of paper and place the slips in the appropriate place on the process diagram. You may find that several stakeholders have the same idea, which may indicate that this is one potential sensible proposal.

Then move on to discuss the suggestions for change. Read the content of a particular piece of paper and ask the author to explain. Encourage stakeholders to comment on a given idea, pointing out the risks, potential problems associated with implementing a given change, but also the benefits of a given idea. Discuss each change proposal in this way—let each stakeholder feel that his or her suggestions are being taken seriously—even if, in the course of discussion, you come to the conclusion that a particular proposal is not feasible in a particular context.

As you approach the end of such a session, you can summarize the topic by creating a target process diagram based on the current process diagram you have already created and the suggestions for change. In this way, you will summarize the findings and stakeholders will understand how the new process could work and what benefits can be achieved through the change.

Don't be afraid to ask for feedback. One effective way to build engagement is to ask people for feedback on the results of the work done, how it was implemented, opinions and thoughts on the topic. Imagine that we are modeling a business process and we are not sure we understand it well. What can we do in this situation? Let's present the results of our work so far to the stakeholder and ask for feedback. Let's ask if our interpretation is correct, if we should put something else on the model, or if we left out something important. In this way, we will not only avoid the problems associated with delivering an erroneous work product, but we will also value the stakeholder's expertise. Our questions will make it clear that we value their opinion, and see them as experts in the field, whom we trust and with whom we count.

It is worth asking for opinions and feedback even when we are absolutely certain that what we are doing is correct. Let's keep in mind that our confidence is not necessarily based on sound reasons. The results of our work represent our state of knowledge and our understanding of a given reality from your perspective. We cannot be sure that this perspective is correct and that the results of the work correctly reflect the object of interest. So even if we are sure that what we have done is done well, let's ask for feedback. At best, we'll make sure we've done the work correctly, and at worst, we'll get a chance to improve its results before it's passed on to someone else.

Remember that we are human beings. People feel emotions. People usually have families and private lives that you know little about. If, in an interaction with a particular person, you notice that emotions rather than substantive arguments are coming into play, stop the discussion and let both sides "cool off." Let's not take it personally. It's probably not at all about the masses and the fact that the stakeholder doesn't feel like talking to us at the moment. What we can do without violating a person's private sphere is to ask, "Is this the right time to talk about this topic?" "Wouldn't you like to postpone this meeting until later?" If we have a closer relationship with the person, we can ask, "Is there anything I can do to help?" but don't try to force confidences.

In the role of an analyst, we work with people, discuss various topics, ask various questions. Often these are questions on sensitive topics, evoking a lot of emotion. If during an interaction with a person we notice that emotions, rather than substantive arguments, begin to take over, let's stop the discussion—even just for a few minutes. We don't have to make it clear that according to us the person is reacting nervously—in most cases it is enough to say: "I would like to think about it. Can we take a 10-min break and come back to this discussion?" "I have the impression that the discussion of this topic requires analyzing many threads. I suggest that we postpone this topic for a later time. In the meantime think about possible solutions. Would there be such a possibility?"

Continuing the discussion when emotions come into play is, in many cases, completely pointless—because where emotions prevail, merit ends. There is nothing wrong with that—people are emotional beings. Both risks and opportunities arise from this. For example, you can use emotions in a very positive way, using smiles and humor to build friendly relationships with the people you work with. Of course, each of us would like to be seen as a professional at work. In my opinion, however, smiling, asking others how they are feeling, a small joke, will not make those around us stop perceiving us as professionals—they will start perceiving us as other people who feel, who can joke, who can ask others about their health, who are worth trusting because they function just like us. Being professional doesn't mean having to be deadly serious and drained of emotion. Being professional also means being able to build relationships—to be able to build relationships, in my opinion, you need to skillfully combine professional, substantive communication and behavior with an encouraging and open manner.

What else can we do to build engagement?

- Change the rhetoric. Let's not impose a way of working, but present a proposal. People will react differently if they know that the way of working is not imposed, and that our proposal is only a suggestion, a point from which we start the discussion.
- Don't impose solutions. If we are working on a solution project, and the starting point is requirements, try not to suggest solutions. Instead, let's ask questions that will make stakeholders realize that there are many solutions, that they have different advantages and disadvantages. Let them come to their own conclusions about what the solution options might be, how to analyze and evaluate them. In this way, stakeholders will have a sense of ownership—they are the ones who defined the solution, they are the authors of change.
- Don't change the findings without communication. If we have previously made a decision, and now, for various reasons, this decision needs to be changed, let's involve stakeholders in the process. Let's not make the decision alone, especially if other people were involved in the decision-making process earlier. We can explain the situation—that new circumstances have arisen that make it worthwhile to revisit the topic and make sure that the previously made decision is justified. With this approach, we will avoid a situation in which stakeholders spend time and energy analyzing the topic and coming to certain conclusions, and we then cross that out, making the decision ourselves.
- Respect people. Just like that—let's respect the people we work with. This respect is expressed, among other things, by giving feedback. If we have asked stakeholders to provide information, present a work product or anything that requires them to provide information, let's give them feedback. Let's thank them and explain how and for what we used the information we obtained. If the situation involves a sensitive topic, such as quality control, let's make sure the feedback is complete. For example, let's imagine that stakeholders are giving us feedback on the process model and have made several comments and suggestions for changes. After analyzing the comments, we incorporate some of them into the model, while rejecting others as unfounded in our opinion.

What happens if we do not provide feedback on what we have done with the results of the review? Most likely, stakeholders will feel that they have done their job and we have underestimated, perhaps even ignored, their efforts. If at some point they find out that the process we modified did not address some of their comments, there is a good chance they will feel they wasted their time unnecessarily. After all, they conducted the review at our request, they provided the results at our request, and we didn't take their comments into account, didn't even take the time to explain why. This is another effective way to destroy motivation and commitment in advance. In addition, there is a high risk that we will discourage stakeholders from participating in the review process at all.

3.2.6 The Importance of Direct Communication

If you want to discuss an issue, make a decision, you can write an email or two. For complex topics, you can write 15 of them, generating hundreds of communication noises in the process. Or you can arrange a meeting, communicate directly, and solve the issue in half an hour.

In today's world, technology dominates business interactions. The Internet, teleconferencing, virtual whiteboards—all of these means perfectly facilitate work, and allow for reduction of operational costs in the case of initiatives carried out by distributed teams. Remote work is becoming the standard. And indeed, with proper motivation, setting certain rules, remote work with efficiency does not differ from the traditional way of performing tasks. Many tasks, especially ahead of business analysis, can be successfully performed without personal contact with the people involved. If we want to conduct an interview, a remote communication tool can work perfectly. If we want to conduct a workshop with a wider group of stakeholders ensuring their involvement, we can use a number of tools, such as a virtual whiteboard.

So in the age of today's technology it is not a problem to accomplish tasks; the problem is building relationships. Relationships are built through personal contact, conversation, including not necessarily on strictly business topics, but also body language.

Limiting communication with stakeholders only to remote means may result in us completing tasks, but not building trust, commitment, and stakeholder motivation. For a simple reason—we will not get to know one another as people; we will not establish a relationship or build understanding. This is unfortunately a subject that is very often neglected. We focus on the implementation of tasks, choose the right tools, completely neglecting the human aspect. As a result, we often fail to communicate, because we speak the same language, but about different things; we don't know in what context individuals function, and hence various misunderstandings arise. Added to this is very often the problem of managing expectations. We don't have a chance to build relationships, which unfortunately affects the effectiveness of people's work. People function better if they have a sense of common objective, understand each other, feel affection or at least respect for each other. Neglecting direct communication can result in very tangible consequences for the project—delays, wrong decisions, financial losses.

Every business is based on people. Every business involves people. In every project we work with people and for people. You cannot overlook this aspect and pretend it is not important.

If we work with people, relationships are important. Face-to-face communication is important.

The initiatives I participate in usually start with a kickoff meeting. If possible, these meetings are held stationary, so as to give team members a chance to get to know each other, to establish any thread of understanding, to talk not only about the project we are doing, but also about ourselves, our interests, expectations, plans. If we get to know the team members as people, and not simply roles in the team, it will be easier for us to determine what state of knowledge they may have, experiences that may affect their judgment. It will be easier to understand and react appropriately in crisis situations that arise from non-professional factors.

On-site meetings give us this opportunity. Of course, it is not always possible. Sometimes we are half a world away; sometimes other factors make it impossible to meet face to face. However, this does not mean that we irretrievably lose the opportunity to establish relationships and cooperate effectively. Such meetings can be successfully organized in remote conditions. However, it is important that they do not focus solely on discussing the project, but also give people a chance to get to know each other. And this involves a number of challenges. Usually we are able to perfectly control the course of the on-site meeting, we can see people, see their reactions, behavior, and on this basis we can assess whether the participants are bored, whether the meeting is engaging for them and really provides an opportunity to build a foundation for effective cooperation.

In the case of remote meetings, there are no such opportunities, unless we ask for them in advance. And so, for example, meeting participants should have their cameras on. Everyone should be able to see each other. The role of the meeting organizer or facilitator is to prepare such an agenda so that it is not tedious, to present basic information about the project on the one hand, and to give the team an opportunity to get to know each other on the other.

During one of the more interesting kickoff meetings I attended, the moderator asked participants to write a few words about themselves on virtual cards presented on the screen at the introduction. He asked specific people to write the three most interesting things I have done in my life, three things I would like to do in the near future, the title of a book I have recently read. Each person had to present this information about himself, and the moderator made sure to keep the discussion going. It turned out that several people had read the same book, and the meeting turned into a brief exchange of opinions about the reading.

At another meeting to initiate the project, the facilitator organized a short team-building game. Solutions for breaking the first ice are many—the challenge remains choosing the right tools for members of a particular team. Not everyone may feel like talking about their private lives, and this should also be respected. Not everyone is comfortable with team games—and this should also be taken into account. The initiation meeting should help break the first ice, not build more ice. In my opinion, this is one of the more critical responsibilities in the role of a project manager or other person coordinating an initiative.

The first meeting of team members sometimes determines later relationships. If we don't do such a get-to-know-you meeting and get into work mode right away, we will most likely not work effectively because we will find it difficult to communicate with others. If we don't begin to systematically build these relationships through face-to-face communication (whether physical face-to-face meetings, phone calls, or teleconferences), we may find that problems arise during the implementation of the initiative that could easily be avoided. Let me cite an example of one project situation.

I started working on a particular project at a time when it was already underway. My role was, most generally, to introduce a quality management process. Among the project problems identified were poor requirements quality and problems in test coordination. When I start working on a project or any initiative, I begin with a kind of inventory—gathering information about the objectives, deliverables, the way of working, the tools used, the people and their responsibilities.

During this inventory, it became apparent that the poor quality of the requirements was due to the fact that the author of the requirements, i.e., the product owner, was not competent in this area and was not properly trained. The product owner was simply a business person, an expert in the field, who by virtue of his subject matter expertise was assigned to the product in the role of owner. The typical responsibilities of a product owner were explained to this person, but no care was taken to check who this person was, what experience he or she had, or whether the competencies he or she possessed were sufficient for the project. This person was simply added to the project and expected to effectively perform the role of product owner. In my first conversation with this person, I learned that she was aware that her requirements documentation was of inadequate quality (i.e., insufficient for the needs of the project team). The problem was that she didn't know exactly what the problem was and how to solve it, because no one made the effort to discuss and clarify the topic. The project team raised concerns about the quality of the requirements, the project manager raised expectations for improvement, but there was no attempt to communicate with the stakeholder to determine the source of the problem and develop a solution. The solution turned out to be surprisingly simple—after identifying the deficiencies in the requirements documentation, explaining to the product owner the reason why it was important to fill these deficiencies and improve quality, it was enough to implement the practice of learning by example. For some time I worked with the product owner on the requirements documentation. The product owner would create an initial version of the requirement, and by asking questions, I would help him figure out the details and then specify them in a form agreed upon with the team.

We did not physically meet with the product owner even once. All communication, exercises, and validation of requirements took place via teleconference, with the camera on, with screen sharing. It was not uncommon for such teleconferences to last several hours at a time, but interestingly, they were not tiring for either party. We organized the work in such a way that when the product owner planned to work on a set of requirements, we would hold a teleconference. The product owner would provide a screen and start working on the requirements. I only asked him to say out loud what he was thinking, so I got to know his way of thinking and could react at the right moment by asking the right questions.

I joined the project about 6 months after it started, and a problem that took us a few days to solve lasted for 6 months. It was enough to talk openly, understand the other party's point of view and situation, and focus on solving the problem.

I recommend direct communication especially in the following situations:

- When we start working with *people we have not worked with before*. Through direct communication, either remotely or in person, we are able to get to know these people's way of thinking, their reactions in different situations, approaches—so it will be easier for us to understand their point of view, their expectations, and address them accordingly.
- When we *care about understanding*. Sending an email asking for confirmation of a given piece of information will probably enable us to achieve our objective—the recipient will confirm the information. The question, however, is whether we have actually achieved the objective. Do we need a statement of confirmation of the information, or do we care about real understanding? If we care about real understanding, it may be more effective to communicate directly, explain your point of view, your understanding of a certain aspect, and ask the recipient for his opinion, additional information. This will reduce the risk arising from selective interpretation of the information presented.
- When we are working on a *complex topic*, involving *many people*, practice shows that long email discussions are completely ineffective. It will be much faster to come to some findings, conclusions, or decisions by holding a workshop meeting with those involved.
- When we communicate *"unpleasant" things or issues* where misunderstandings easily occur, it is important to remember that the reception of information is affected not only by the content of the message, but also by nonverbal communication—our facial expressions, gestures, tone of voice. In such a case, in order to avoid misunderstandings that can, for example, inflame a conflict, a phone call or teleconference, or ideally a face-to-face conversation, is a better solution. In this way, we are better able to control the message we send, as we can soften it with facial expressions, gestures, other means that are simply unavailable in email communication.
- When we need to *choose between different options*, alternatives, variants, of course we can make a decision based on our knowledge and experience. However, when working on a particular initiative in a team, it is worth asking the team for opinions and suggestions. Especially considering that we represent a certain perspective, and other team members see the topic from a different point of view. Their opinions, guidance, and insights enable us to make decisions based on a much wider range of information than the information we possess alone. And since, as a rule, if we need to make a decision on an option, it involves a certain responsibility, the consequences of a wrong decision can be critical. It is therefore worth making sure we understand each other well when discussing the alternatives in question, and making a choice. Again, direct communication, the organization of a meeting involving team members, can significantly facilitate our achievement of this objective.

3.3 Information Architecture and Information Management Planning

3.3.1 Why So Many Types of Requirements?

Various sources on the area of business analysis or requirements engineering indicate that there are specific classifications of requirements. For example, the *BABOK® Guide* distinguishes between business requirements, stakeholder requirements, and solution requirements, including functional and nonfunctional requirements. A fairly similar classification is used by IREB® (IREB 2024), additionally introducing domain requirements and quality requirements in place of functional requirements.

In view of the rather elaborate classification of requirements, the question may arise whether we really need so many types of requirements, or whether it is not enough to operate on the general concept of requirements.[2]

The operating model of an organization implies the existence of a number of layers and dimensions—the dimensions of context, concept, logical, physical, etc. The organization cannot be described by a single dimension, because it touches many areas and aspects. Similarly, in the case of requirements, each level and type of requirement describes a different aspect of the issue under consideration.

If we accept the fact that we divide analysis into a business area and a solution area, this alone justifies the existence of at least two levels of requirements—business requirements and solution requirements. At the business requirements level, we define a business need, what we need in order to solve a certain business problem. At the business level, we do not yet enter the solution area in any way, we do not determine the solution, we do not talk about specific systems, for a simple reason—they are not yet known.

As we know at least from reading the *BABOK® Guide*, at some point during the analysis activity, the scope of the business problem is already known and we can move on to developing solution proposals. For these solution proposals, we establish the specific requirements associated with that particular solution. The solution requirements, or in other words the system requirements, will determine how our solution will function and the quality characteristics of our solution. Thus, they are a kind of detailing of the high-level requirements. Is it possible to abandon the level of requirements and operate only on one type of requirements?

In theory, anything is possible, but if we operate only on business-level requirements, we miss information about the expectations of the solution. This means that the manufacturing team will not have enough information to design and implement a solution in line with the specified business needs.

On the other hand, if we use only the requirements for the solution, we don't know where these requirements come from, we don't know what the business motivation was and what needs the specific system requirements are supposed to meet. Simplifying the subject,

[2] General definition of the requirement "Useful representation of a need" (IIBA® 2015).

we design a solution without knowing what business value this solution is supposed to bring, how it is supposed to enable the fulfillment of specific business needs and objectives.

Using a very trivial example, let's imagine what the consequences of not having levels of requirements would be.

We are designing a dollhouse. We can focus on specifying the dimensions of the house, the materials, the equipment, the details necessary to build such a house. So we focus on the specific requirements of the solution—our solution in this case is a house. Based on these requirements, we can produce quite a nice dollhouse. The problem arises when we ask ourselves why and for whom is this house created? The answer to this question may change our approach to the subject a little—we will probably design and build a house that is to be actively used by a small child differently; we will approach the design of the solution differently if we assume that our need is to develop a demonstration house—such a house will never be used by children; it will serve as a kind of demo. In this case, the lack of business motivation, the failure to define the needs and requirements of the stakeholders, causes us to lose sight of the objective—we do not know what problem we want to solve and what needs we want to address; we focus on the design of the solution. As a result, we may produce a solution, a pretty good working solution, that turns out to be useless.

On the other hand, if we focus only on business needs, we can approach the topic of house design in such a way that we define the need and expectations of the stakeholders (let's assume that the main stakeholders at this point are children and their parents, with the end user of the solution being the child). We will obtain information about how exactly the child wants to play using the house, roughly what size the house should be, that it should be a dollhouse or perhaps another type of toy, and so on. If we don't go down to the solution layer at the next stage, we won't be able to design the structure of the house on the basis of the high-level information acquired, because we will lack information about the details.

The example with the dollhouse is quite trivial. In the reality of design situations, we are dealing with much more complex business problems and solutions. This makes it all the more important to properly divide the information into business information and system information. It is worth noting that such a division is very simplified. In reality, there are many more levels of requirements, as explained by the concept of the Requirements Abstraction Model (RAM), which has been known for years (Gorschek and Claes 2006; Gorschek et al. 2007).

An example of the organization of requirements under the change initiative is presented in Fig. 3.13.

Dividing requirements into different levels of abstraction is just one possible aspect of requirements classification. You can also divide requirements by types—here an example is the standard division of functional requirements and quality requirements. These types of requirements usually refer to the level of the solution. When describing a solution, it is necessary to indicate what behavior and what properties this solution is supposed to provide to users and other elements of the system environment. The behavior of the system is

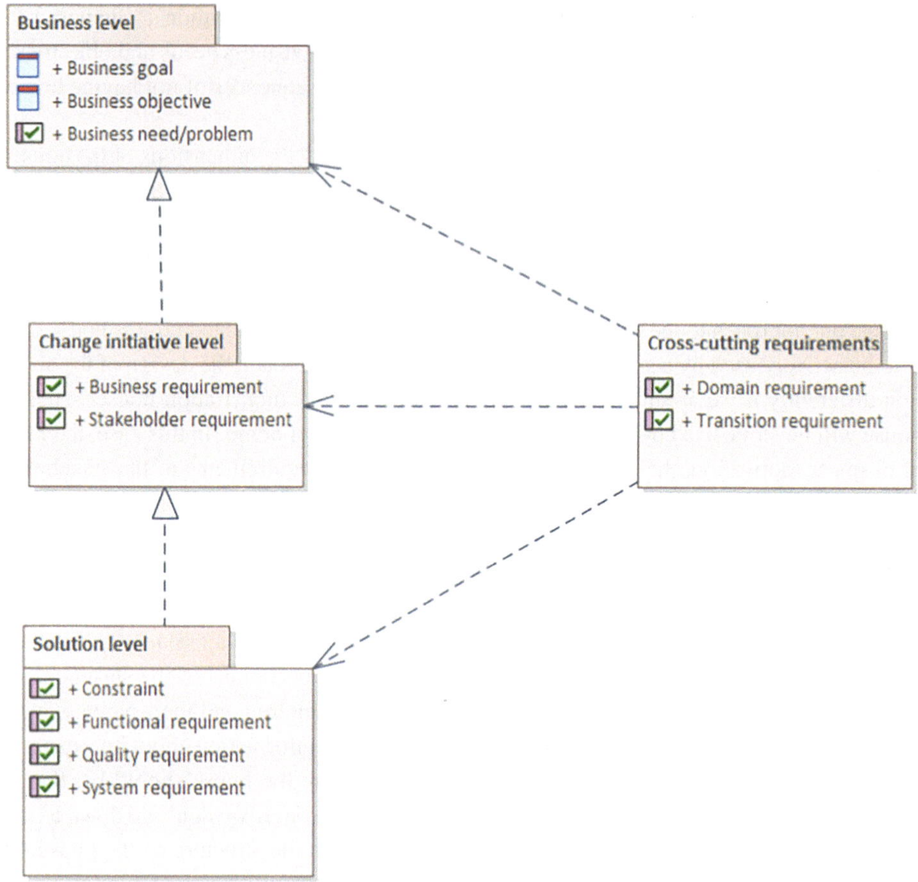

Fig. 3.13 Example of requirements structure

otherwise known as functionality, so we use functional requirements to define it. However, in addition to the behavior itself, we can also talk about certain aspects, which are kinds of constraints and properties that describe not the functionality itself, but its delivery.

Let's consider the following example of a functional requirement:

> The system allows the user to add products to the shopping cart.

The functionality described is adding products to the shopping cart. However, when analyzing this requirement, additional questions are bound to arise, such as: Are there any limits to the capacity of the shopping cart? In other words, what is the maximum number of products that can be in the shopping cart? Can the same product be added to the cart several times? If so, what happens in such a case? The number of products in the cart is increased?

In addition, there may be questions about the response time of the system to trigger the functionality of adding products to the cart. For example, how long after triggering the "Add to Cart" action will the system actually update the status of the cart?

There may be questions about the very method of triggering the Add to Cart functionality, the location of this function in the system—in other words, usability issues. These aspects are beyond the scope of the definition of the functional requirements themselves. Of course, you can consider detailing the functional requirement with additional acceptance criteria and constraints, so that you record the information related to quality aspects. Or you can treat them as quality requirements related to specific functional requirements.

Regardless of the approach taken, there is no denying the statement that the aspects described relate to different properties of the system. Not every solution requirement is a requirement describing functionality. Not every system requirement is a functional requirement. This is worth noting, if only because, as a rule, the implementation of quality requirements is associated with specific challenges—something we will return to later.

CHOOSE THE RIGHT REQUIREMENTS CLASSIFICATION.

THE IMPORTANCE OF REQUIREMENTS CLASSIFICATION IS NOT SIMPLY TO DETERMINE THE TYPE OF REQUIREMENT. IT'S PART OF BUILDING INFORMATION ARCHITECTURE.

If a requirements classification has been established in a given project or organization, let's either adhere to it correctly or adjust it according to the needs of the project. Otherwise, this will lead to a situation in which we theoretically apply a certain classification of requirements, but do not use the benefit that this classification gives—we only introduce information chaos.

For example, many times I have seen "business" requirements, defined in the methodology for the implementation of business analysis according to the *BABOK® Guide*, and which in reality had nothing to do with the level of business requirements. These requirements read "the system is to allow the generation of reports," "the administrator can create a new user account," "system integration with CRM." These requirements do not relate to the business layer, but to a specific solution. Therefore, they should be treated as requirements of the solution. In this particular example, if we considered reclassifying these requirements as solution requirements, we would have no information about either the relevant business requirements or stakeholder requirements, which could be sources of expectations from the designed solution.

Assuming that at the level of business needs we only need one level of requirements—either business requirements or stakeholder requirements—we still lack information about these requirements. What should we do as a result? If we would like to follow the rules of art (and logic), we need to define the right business or stakeholder requirements and map them to the already defined requirements of the solution. Since this is a kind of reverse engineering, I would make sure that the business requirements identified in this way are really a reflection of the right objectives and aspirations, or simply an artificial hole to justify the existence of the solution requirements.

The second approach, which I've observed in many projects, is that you leave the "business" requirements as they are, and the solution requirements are simply an exact copy of them. I am already leaving aside the fact of duplication of work when following such a practice. It seems more important to answer the question: If the business requirements are the same as the solution requirements, what is really the justification for the initiative? For what reason, to solve what problem, are we creating a solution? With the approach of duplicating requirements theoretically representing different levels of abstraction, we completely lose this information; there is already more risk of delivering a system that can function quite efficiently, but will not bring any business value.

So what do I recommend? Probably the simplest possible approach—let's choose a requirements classification structure that is appropriate to the needs of the project and the stakeholders.

If we are responsible for the solution area, to put it in simple terms, designing the system based on stakeholder and business requirements, for our purposes, solution requirements, probably broken down into functional and quality requirements, will suffice. We will not specify business requirements or stakeholder requirements, as these have already been developed by the party ordering the solution. The only thing we should provide is tracking of the relationship between your requirements and the higher-level requirements.

If we are responsible for identifying a business need, developing a solution concept, and then supporting the implementation of that solution, we will need requirements representing these "stages" of work. It is likely, then, that we need business requirements, stakeholder requirements that will serve as input to the development of the solution concept. The scope of the solution will be defined by the solution-level requirements—and this is the requirements structure we need.

If in our solution implementation project, for various reasons we need precise information about the type of system requirements, such as security requirements, performance requirements, or reliability requirements, we can use a software quality model that defines a whole range of quality characteristics and sub-characteristics, such as SQuaRE (ISO 2014).

If at some point we find that the adopted requirements classification no longer meets its objectives, in consultation with stakeholders, modify it as appropriate.

If we are not sure what kind of requirements classification we need, we should ask ourselves the following questions:

- What area should the requirements describe—the business area or the solution layer?
- Does the requirement address the organization's strategic objectives? Does it represent the expectations of different stakeholder groups?
- Does the requirement relate to a specific solution, or is it abstract and can be met by many different possible solutions?
- Is the source of the requirement the organization's external environment, such as standards or regulations?
- Is the requirement supposed to describe the behavior expected from the planned solution?

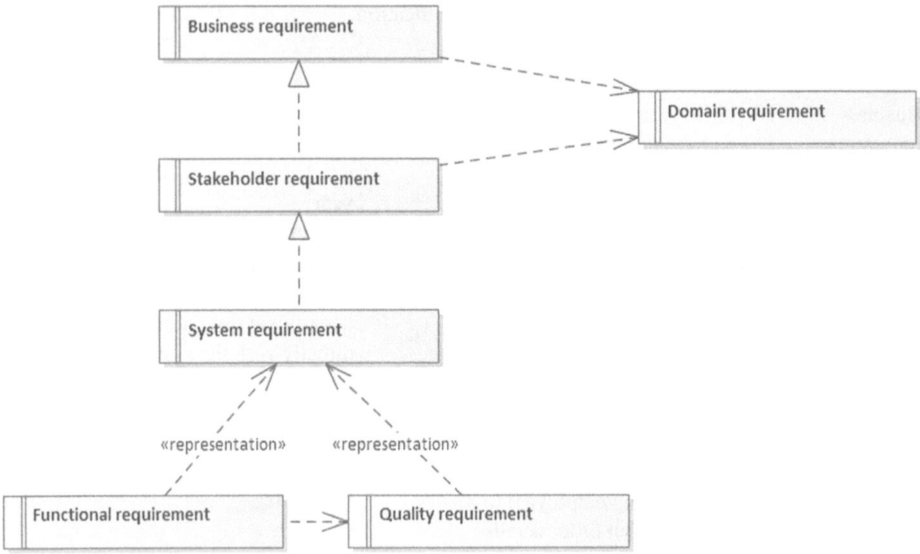

Fig. 3.14 Example of requirements classification with dependencies

- Is the requirement supposed to define quality characteristics, such as usability, performance, or security features of the planned solution?
  An example of requirements classification is shown in Fig. 3.14.
  An example of the requirements representing each type is shown in Table 3.1.

3.3.2 Requirements Big or Small: Determine the Level of Granularity of Requirements

REQUIREMENTS CAN BE VERY DETAILED OR GENERAL, DEPENDING ON THE OBJECTIVE THEY SERVE. THE GRANULARITY OF REQUIREMENTS SHOULD NOT BE THE RESULT OF CHANCE, BUT OF CONSCIOUS PLANNING.

The term granularity generally refers to the degree of detail or "fineness" of the elements that make up a given system, process, or product. In the context of requirements, granularity refers to the degree of detail at which we describe individual requirements. The higher the granularity, the more detailed and accurate the requirements specifications. The lower the granularity, the more general and abstract the specifications.

In practice, the decision on the level of granularity depends on many factors, such as the specifics of the project, the expectations of the project team, the needs of the stakeholders, the availability of resources, and other project constraints.

Requirements can be described in great detail or at a general level of detail. Choosing the right level of granularity depends on a number of factors, such as:

Table 3.1 Example of the use of requirements classification

Type of requirement	Example	Dependency
Business requirement	BREQ 1 Ensure secure shipping of orders placed by customers	Business objective: Achieve customer satisfaction of at least 4 on a 5-degree scale by the end of the year
Stakeholder requirement	UREQ 1 [Order Processing Department] needs information on the type of products included in the order [standard, fragile, hazardous material]. Rationale: information on the type of product is necessary to determine the correct method of securing the product so that it is not damaged in transit	BREQ 1 Technical limitation: the system used in the order processing department does not communicate directly with the system used in the production department
Functional requirement	The system allows a user in the role of [order processing employee] to access information about order details Acceptance criteria: • Order details information includes a list of products that are part of the order • For each product included in the order, information is available: product type [standard, fragile, hazardous materials], quantity, size [s, m, l]	UREQ 1 DREQ 1 PREQ 1
Quality requirement	PREQ 1 System response time to user action Scale: second Measurement: from the time the user initiates the command to the display of the system response understood as [expected function result] or [delay handling] Wish: max. 2 s Minimum acceptable quality level: max 5 s	UREQ 1
Domain requirement	DREQ 1 Transportation of dangerous goods Source: Directive 2008/68/EC of the European Parliament and of the Council of September 24, 2008, on the inland transport of dangerous goods (*Official Journal of the EU* L 260 of 30.09.2008) Law on transportation of dangerous goods (*Journal of Laws* 2022, item 2147)	

- The characteristics of the project, especially the requirements arising from industry standards or regulations
- Contractual issues—provisions of the contract between customer and supplier
- Stakeholder needs, especially the project team's expectations regarding information content
- Process requirements, especially requirements for the level of traceability

Of course, when determining the level of requirements granularity in a given project, project and organizational constraints, such as time or budget limitations, must be taken into account. Selecting the right level of granularity is key to ensuring that stakeholders understand the requirements and that the requirements specification provides them with the necessary information. On the other hand, proper requirements granularity is one of the prerequisites for effective requirements management during the project process.

What exactly does this mean?

Let's consider an example.

Let's imagine the following requirement description.

> The system should allow the user to manage the product database.

This requirement is very general. It most likely includes at least some specific functionality, such as adding a product, deleting a product, or editing a product. As it stands, the requirement can be understood in many ways. You can understand it to mean that the user is able to add, delete, or edit a product. One can also develop one's interpretation and assume that product base management also includes the creation of product classifications, special categories, assigning specific tags for searching the product base. As part of product database management, we can also think about importing and exporting data in specific formats.

The requirement in such a general form is therefore probably not precise enough for the development team to understand how it is to design and execute the system. Of course, it can be assumed that the team has an excellent understanding of the customer's business and is able to guess what the requirement entails. However, this does not change the fact that requirements so general—if they were the basis for system implementation—generate unnecessary risks.

Let's imagine that under this requirement, the team designed functionality for adding, deleting, and editing a product. The system has been given to the customer for evaluation. The customer denies the correctness of the implementation, stating that it lacks functionality it would like to have as part of its product database management, such as the ability to import a product specification file.

At this point we have created a problem for ourselves, because in its current form the requirement is not detailed enough to create a kind of contract—accepting such a requirement and accepting it for implementation means that we agree to implement something whose scope we do not really understand.

A solution could be to add acceptance criteria to this requirement, which would clarify what specific "management" activities we have in mind.

Requirement: The system should allow the user to manage the product database.
Acceptance Criteria:

1. The system allows a user with administrator privileges to add a new product to the database. In order to add a product, it is necessary to enter its data, such as:

   (a) Name
   (b) Detailed description (up to 150 characters)
   (c) Color (select from list, optional parameter)
   (d) Price
   (e) Manufacturer.

2. The system allows the user of administrator rights to edit all product data, except ID (order number).
3. The system allows the user of administrator rights to delete a product from the database if the product does not appear in any current customer order. Otherwise, deleting the product is not possible, and the system displays an error message "Cannot delete this product," indicating that there is an existing link to the current customer order.

Another solution is to use a different level of requirement granularity. In this case, instead of documenting the requirement as "The system should enable the user to manage the product database," we can break it down into more atomic requirements:

1. The system allows the user to add a new product to the product database.
2. The system allows the user to edit product data.
3. The system allows the user to delete a product from the database.

So instead of one requirement, we have three. If, for some reason, we don't want to lose track of the fact that all these requirements belong to the "product base management" group, we can use mechanisms for grouping information, such as hierarchical structure of

Table 3.2 Hierarchical structure of requirements

	Requirements group	Requirement
ID 1.0	Product database management	
ID 1.1		Adding a product to the product database
ID 1.2		Editing product data
ID 1.3		Deleting a product from the database

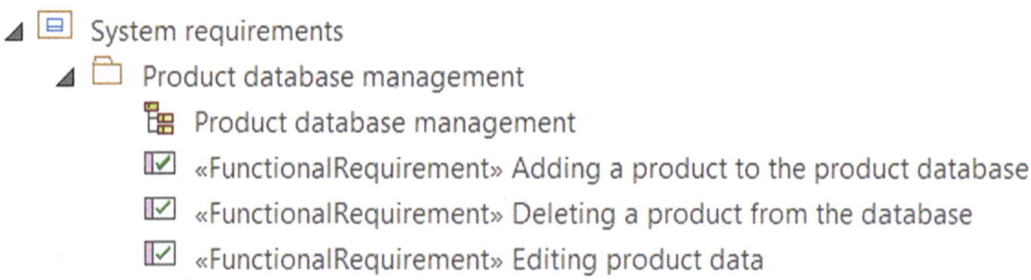

Fig. 3.15 Organization of requirements into folders

requirements (Table 3.2) placing requirements under specific categories, using the concept of epics (epics), organizing requirements within folders (Fig. 3.15), etc.

There are many ways to organize information, depending on the level of granularity chosen. The level of detail in the documentation also affects the type of information we would like to manage. We already know that there are different types of requirements, such as functional requirements, quality requirements, constraints, business requirements, stakeholders, and so on. Is it possible to describe some of these requirements together, within a single document or specification? Theoretically you can, but this generates certain consequences.

Let's use the example considered earlier regarding requirements for adding products to the shopping cart.

> The system allows the user to add products to the shopping cart.

For this functional requirement, we can identify several constraints and quality requirements.

How can the remaining information be documented?

Let's look at the options.

Variant 1

REQ 01

Title: Adding to shopping cart

Description: The system allows the user to add products to the shopping cart.

Requirement type: Functional

Restrictions:

There can be a maximum of 50 items in the shopping cart.

If the user tries to add a product to the shopping cart that is already in the cart, the system displays an error message.

Acceptance criteria:

The user must be able to find the Add to Cart function within no more than 2 s after the product details screen is displayed.

After selecting the Add to Cart function, the system updates the status of the cart in no more than 2 s.

After adding a product to the cart, the number of products in the cart is increased by 1.

Variant 2

REQ 01

Title: Adding to shopping cart

Description: The system allows the user to add products to the shopping cart.

Requirement type: Functional

REQ 02

Title: Maximum shopping cart volume

Description: The system limits the number of products in the shopping cart to 50. If the user tries to add more than 50 items, the system displays an error message.

Requirement type: Limitation

REQ 03

Title: Location of Add to Cart function

Description: The user must be able to find the Add to Cart function in no more than 2 s after the product details screen is displayed.

Type of requirement: Usability

REQ 04

Title: Update shopping cart status

Description: the system updates the cart status in no more than 2 s after the user starts the add function.

Requirement type: Performance

In principle, both options, the first and second, are acceptable. The main difference is the use of different granularity of requirements—and the resulting consequences for the information management process. In variant one, we have a single requirement with acceptance criteria and constraints. In variant two, each aspect is described as a single requirement. If we are concerned with ensuring accurate tracking of the links between atomic requirements, variant two may be preferable. If our objective is simply to describe the behavior of the system and possible constraints, and we have no specific requirements for the requirements management process, variant one may be acceptable.

From the point of view of traceability and analysis of test coverage of requirements, variant one may result in the fact that for a single requirement several tests are sublinked—in order to check both the basic functionality of adding a product to the shopping cart, as well as individual constraints and acceptance criteria. Tracking links exist between the requirement and individual test cases (Fig. 3.16). This solution, unfortunately, does not overtly provide information about which specific test case checks which specific constraint or acceptance criterion.

One solution may be to link individual test cases to specific constraints (Fig. 3.17). However, this requires that these constraints are identifiable (in the simplest terms of the subject, labeled with specific, unique sequence numbers)—otherwise defining explicit traceability will not be possible.

Variant two makes it possible to keep traceability more precisely. The requirements are atomic, one might say very detailed. Thus, it is easier to create relationships between the various elements and thus ensure that we are able to provide precise information about exactly what test cases are to verify specific requirements and features (Fig. 3.18).

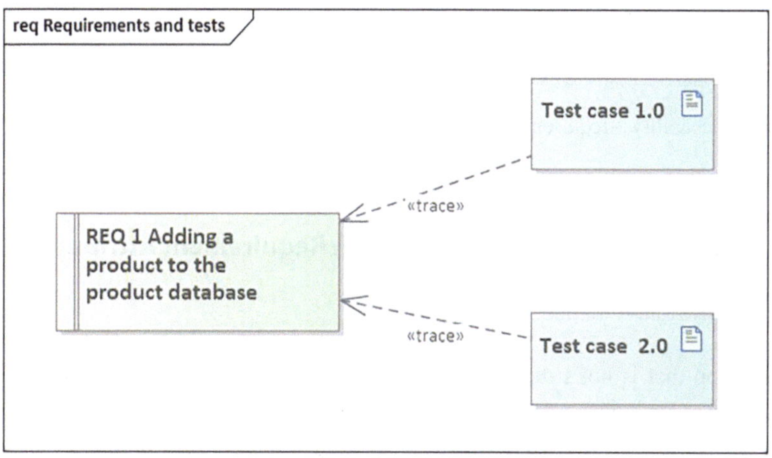

Fig. 3.16 Traceability between requirement and test cases

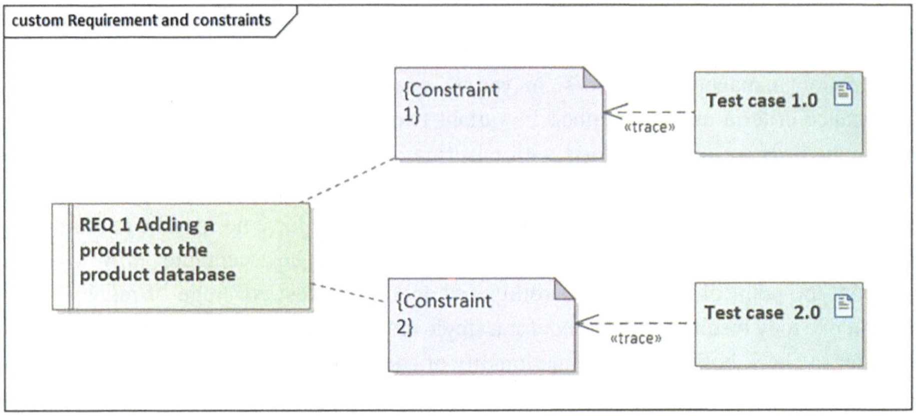

Fig. 3.17 Traceability—requirement and the constraints vs. test cases

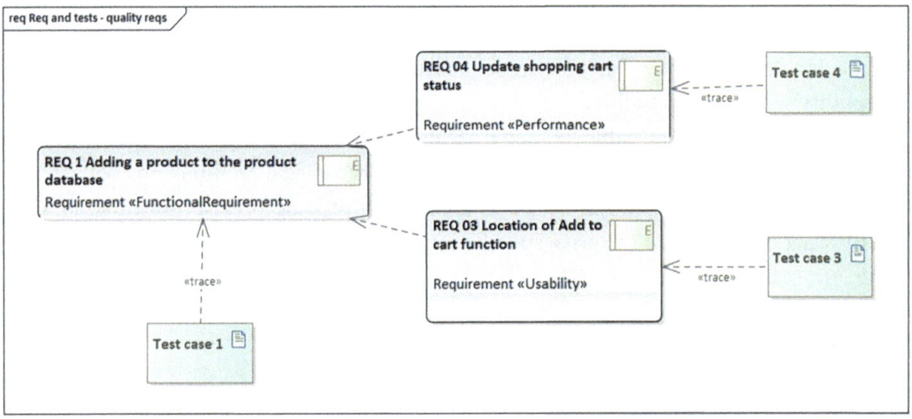

Fig. 3.18 Traceability—requirements of different types and test cases

3.3.3 To Manage Information: Establish Requirement Attributes

Chaos cannot be managed.

Information that is not structured cannot be managed. Information describing requirements and other analytical artifacts, regardless of how they are represented, should be properly structured and prioritized, and what type of requirements we are talking about should be identified. The source and the people responsible for the work product at a given stage of development should also be identified. Attributes provide a mechanism for such structuring.

Requirements without attributes would likely be documented as a string of text or graphics. Such a form tells us little about the context of the requirements, nor does it usually provide classification information so that we can view the information selectively—without having to look at the entire dataset.

When planning the management of information in a project, it is necessary to determine what artifacts will be created in this project, what information they should contain, and how to organize this information. We will therefore develop a so-called attribute schema, which can be individual for each work product.

For example, a business requirement may have the following set of attributes defined:

1. Unique number identifying the requirement
2. Priority
3. Source (business need)
4. Justification
5. Impact on business areas
6. Submitter
7. Status

A test case, in turn, can have the following set of attributes:

1. Unique identifier
2. Priority
3. The number of the requirement to which the test case applies
4. Version
5. Execution status
6. Execution result
7. Author
8. Tester assigned to the test case execution
9. The number of the defect detected during test case execution

Determining the attribute schema for a specific work product is not at all a trivial task. It requires obtaining data from various sources—data that will allow us to understand what information should be included in the work product specification. Then it is necessary to decide how to present and organize the information about work products.

When determining the attribute schema for a particular artifact, it is important to consider:

- What information should be included in the work product specification
- Who is the recipient of the work product—now and in the future
- What are the requirements for tracking links between artifacts

- Organizational standards and guidelines or those derived from external sources (some regulations and industry standards may dictate the need for a specific set of attributes for a particular work product)

Lessons learned from observing many projects and policies in various organizations indicate that establishing an attribute schema is another basic task in business analysis and requirements engineering that is very often not done correctly.

In many projects, there is no practice of establishing an attribute schema at all. When developing a requirements specification, the analyst simply uses the set of attributes defined by the tool. He doesn't consider which of these attributes are actually needed in a given project context, or whether the available attributes are sufficient for the stakeholders' information needs. It falls into a routine and uses the available solution without reflecting on whether the solution covers the actual project needs. As a result, it may turn out that the standard set of attributes defined within the tool does not include an attribute that turns out to be crucial to the team's needs.

To give an example, in a certain project it was established that root cause failure analysis would be performed as part of manufacturing process improvement initiatives. At the end of each test cycle, the QA person was to analyze information about reported defects and draw conclusions about possible improvements based on the results of the root cause analysis. The problem was that at no stage of the defect analysis was information about the root cause entered. This was not because these causes could not be determined by the team, but because the tool used to handle defects simply did not define a field for entering such information.

As a result, testers entered information about the defect in the way it was reproduced, the priority; developers added comments explaining how they fixed the defect and informing testers that the fix was ready for testing. However, information about the cause of the problem was missing. As a result, the person in charge of root cause analysis had to supplement the data recorded in the defect tracking system by interviewing team members. The problem was fortunately detected relatively early, after the first test cycle was completed.

Unfortunately, in many cases it turns out that such problems are revealed much later—it happens that only at the stage of product maintenance, when the maintenance team tries to analyze the impact of changes on a production-functioning system and is unable to, because the information available in the repository about requirements, projects, source CODE, or architecture does not contain information about the relationships between different artifacts.

When planning to establish an attribute structure, one should also be aware that attributes are a means to quantify requirements. This is especially important in the case of quality requirements, but it is relevant for "ordinary" functional requirements as well. After all, it is necessary to specify the expected result of the function's execution, and we can do just that with an attribute called "result." In addition, each functional requirement may have its own qualitative constraints, such as the expected execution time of the function.

Id FR 01
Name: Generation of XYZ report

Report data specification: Sales values of each product group in the period {from} {to}
Constraint: Unable to present sales values for {product group 12}
Desired result: Presentation of data in no more than 5 s
Minimum acceptable quality level: Presentation of data in no more than 15 s

An example of using attributes to quantify requirements is shown below:

Adopting the convention of organizing information through an attribute schema not only increases the readability of the specification, since each piece of information is separated from each other, but reduces the risk of omitting important data. Because if a specific attribute is defined in our attribute schema, we know during requirements specification that it should be filled with information. If we are unable to determine the value of a particular attribute, we have just discovered a gap in the information we have that needs to be filled.

3.3.4 Selecting an Analysis Repository

TOOLS CAN HELP US GET THE JOB DONE OR HINDER IT. TOOLS WILL HINDER IF THEY ARE NOT SELECTED FOR SPECIFIC NEEDS.

One of the biggest challenges in analytical projects is the configuration of the information repository. Creating an analysis repository is not just about selecting a tool in which to "hold" requirements. Planning an analytical repository that will actually allow us to meet specific process objectives and facilitate the work requires analyzing a number of factors.

Objective. Let's consider the objective for which we will use the repository. Do we need a place where we can store textual requirements specifications? If this is our only objective, we probably don't need an advanced repository, CASE tools, etc. A standard office tool such as a word processor or spreadsheet will probably suffice.

If, on the other hand, we need a tool where we can store requirements specifications, define and maintain relationships between requirements, and between requirements and other artifacts such as test cases, if we need a tool that will help us perform impact analysis, then a simple text editor will prove insufficient.

Users. So we know what the repository will be needed for—what objective it will be used for. Next, we need to determine by whom it will be used and what those people need. If the only user of the repository will be us, let's choose a tool that realizes our needs. If the users of the repository will be the project team, choose a tool that will also meet their needs, will be relatively easy to use for the team and will match the tools used by the team. If the users of the repository will be stakeholders on the customer side, let's make sure what their needs are. As a rule, these stakeholders do not need access to very detailed information; instead, they need status information as a basis for decision-making.

Time of use. Another aspect, often overlooked, is to determine how long the repository is to be used—whether it will be used solely for project implementation, or whether it will also be used by the maintenance team. If, in turn, the maintenance team (whether on the solution provider's side or on the customer's side) uses a different knowledge repository, let's make sure that it is possible to export data from our repository to the maintenance team's repository. Otherwise, there may be a risk that all the information we gather during the implementation phase of the project will simply be inaccessible from the maintenance team's point of view.

Costs. Let's think about costs, not only the cost of the eventual purchase of a tool that acts as a repository, but also the cost of maintaining the tool, the costs associated with learning how to use it and other indirect costs. It happens that, enthralled by the technological possibilities, at first impulse we would like to implement a repository with very advanced functionalities. A tool with high maintenance costs. Using such a tool may be beneficial from the point of view of developing our skills, but from the point of view of the project and its objectives, the situation may be quite different. The costs associated with purchasing, implementing, and learning to use the tool should pay off—on what time scale, of course. The return on investment can be expressed, for example, by the fact that the tool significantly reduces work time, eliminates the risk of human error, and allows access to information to a wide range of stakeholders. Another benefit can be the ability to automatically or semi-automatically generate information of a certain type. If the tool does not provide us with real benefits, then at the very least we should consider whether it is the right tool for us.

Once we have determined whose and what specific needs the analytical repository is supposed to meet, let's plan the way it will be used. Specifically, you should plan:

- The artifacts that will be stored in it. Will they be individual requirements or entire specifications and other documents? An example of a fragment of the artifact structure is shown in Fig. 3.19.
- Attributes of individual artifacts. What attributes of individual artifacts will you need? For example, in addition to name and content, you may need information about unique identifiers, artifact type, author, editing history, individual versions.
- Hierarchical structure—the division of information into levels of detail, for example, according to the approach adopted for the implementation of analysis work. An example of the repository structure is shown in Fig. 3.20.

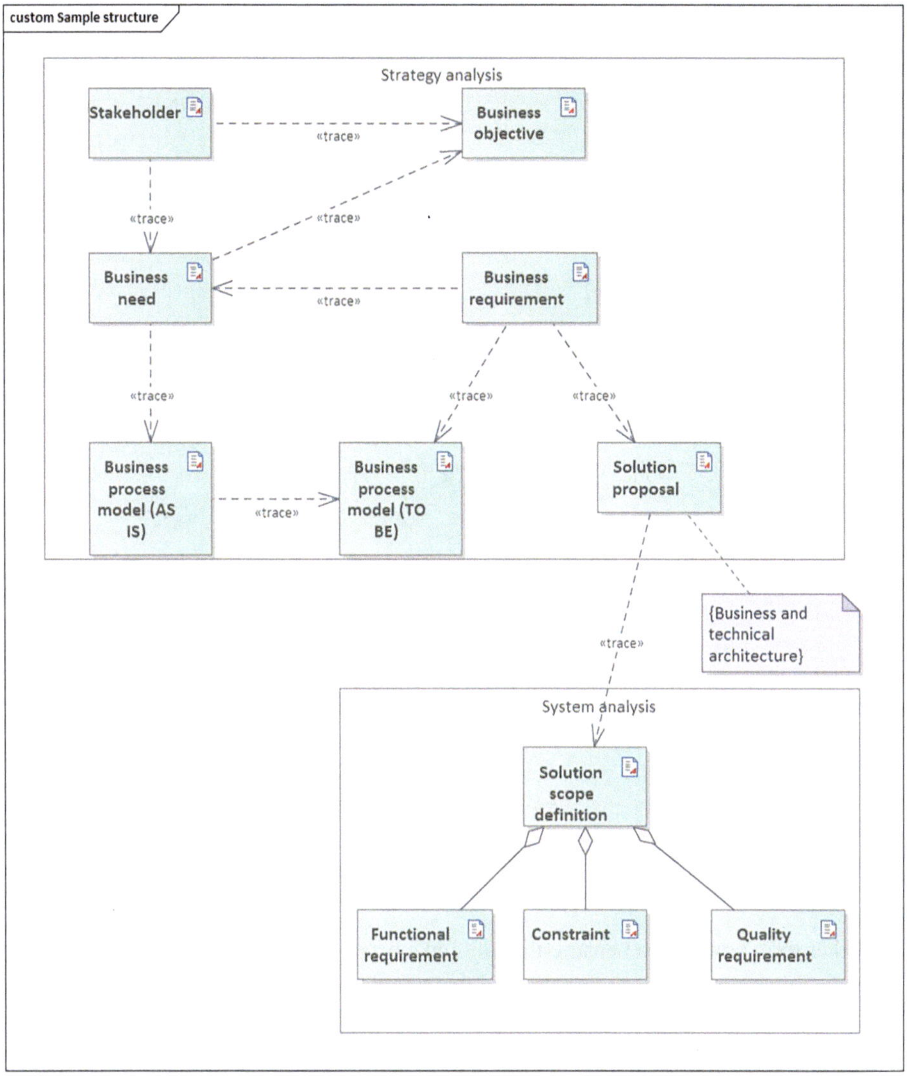

Fig. 3.19 Excerpt from the structure of artifacts with traceability information

- Links between individual artifacts and how they are implemented. For example, the links between high-level requirements and low-level requirements, expressed in the form of links between artifacts. In particular, you may need links between specific versions of specific artifacts.
- Access to the repository—who should be able to access and edit the data, who should only be able to view the information. Example access rules are shown in Fig. 3.21.
- Integration issues with other tools, if needed. For example, if you store information about requirements in an analytics repository and information about test cases in

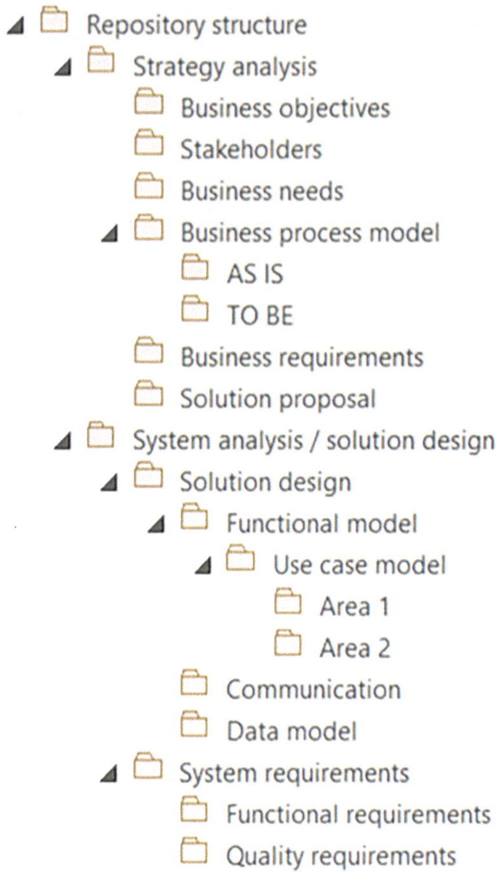

Fig. 3.20 Example of analysis repository structure

another tool, how do you ensure that the links between one and the other are tracked? This is important because you may find that a tool has capabilities to integrate tools, in which case your solution to the linkage tracking problem may be to develop a linkage tracking matrix. An example of a plan for using tools to handle individual artifacts is shown in Fig. 3.22.

3.4 Case Study

3.4.1 Example of a Plan for the Requirements Elicitation Process Carried Out Under Project Discovery

A project for a customer in the domain of property security systems.

Planning for information acquisition began with establishing the expected results of the project. For this purpose, a map was created, showing the final artifacts to be delivered to

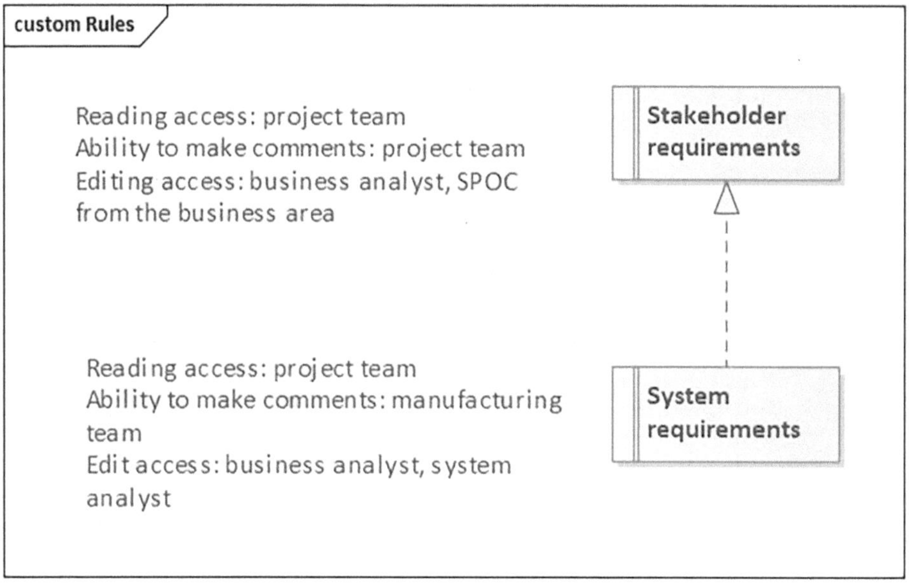

Fig. 3.21 Excerpt of rules for access rights to view and edit information

the customer and the intermediate artifacts to achieve these objectives. The artifacts were related to each other according to their relationship.

For example, an artifact labeled product backlog was linked to individual requirements and technical elements. Requirements, in turn, were linked to an artifact named business processes and system actors. In order to extract specific requirements, it was necessary to understand the essence of the business processes supported by the designed solution, i.e., the specific activities and resources involved in these processes.

From the artifact map, it was clear what needed to be achieved, and what steps needed to be taken to obtain a particular artifact. Each work product resulted from performing a specific activity. For each work product, a specific task was identified that needed to be performed to obtain the information necessary to develop that work product. In addition, the input information for the task was identified.

For example, the following activities had to be performed to identify specific requirements:

1. Analyze the customer's existing solution.
2. Analyze competing solutions.
3. Discuss requirements proposals with stakeholders representing the business.

Inherent in the planning of requirements elicitation activities was the identification and analysis of stakeholders and the identification of requirements sources. Due to the relatively low availability of stakeholders, the initial requirements elicitation plan was to focus first on requirements sources in the form of documentation and systems.

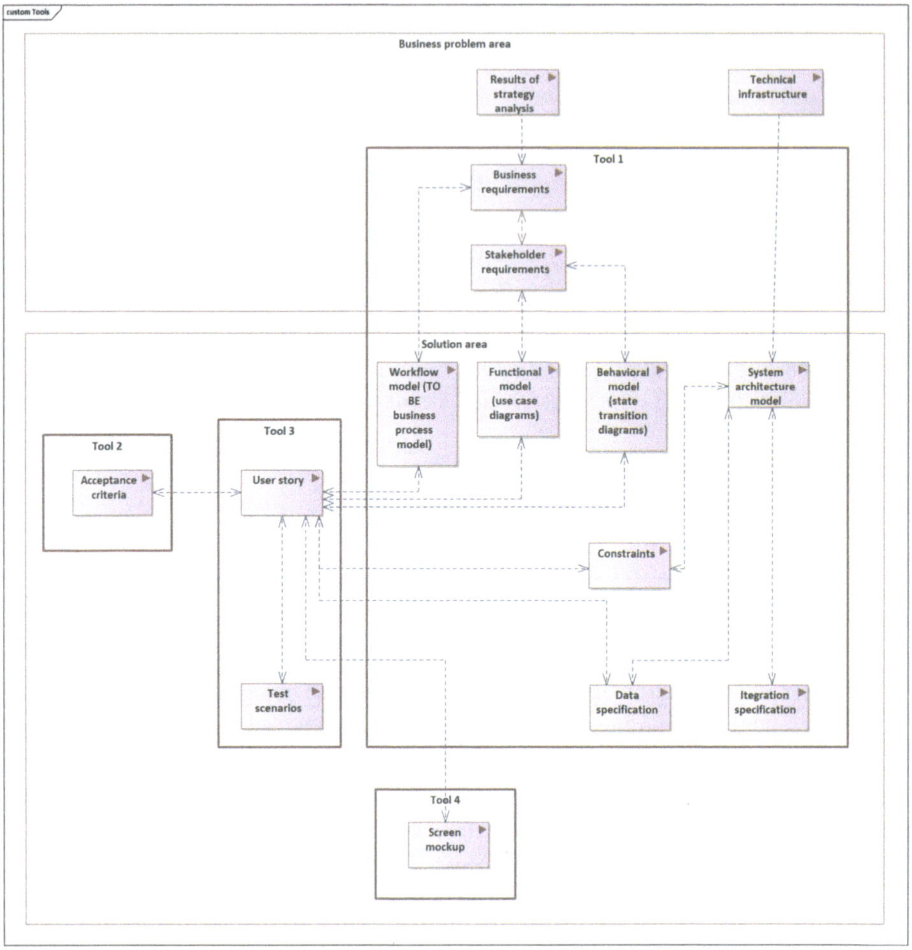

Fig. 3.22 Sample of tool application plan with respect to artifact structure

With these sources, initial requirements could be obtained, which could then be discussed and confirmed with stakeholders. The objective was to relieve the customer's staff as much as possible.

The initial long-term plan for requirements acquisition activities assumed the following stages:

1. Stage One: Recognizing the current state
2. Stage Two: Determination of the target state
3. Stage Three: Development of a solution concept

Three weeks were allocated for the first stage. Within these 3 weeks, it was necessary to determine:

- Who the customers of our client are, and what their characteristics and main needs
- What the competitors' offerings are
- How these needs are currently being met
- The functionality of the existing customer portal
- How customer service processes are implemented
- How the alarm system works

  The information acquisition objectives for this stage were identified as:
- Definition of end users (groups of users: owner of the premises, person authorized to operate the alarm system, passive user of the alarm system, e.g., family member with authority only to arm the system, operator on the side of the company providing the solution)
- A list of end user needs, divided into addressed and unaddressed
- Description of the functionality of the existing portal
- AS IS business process model (list of main business processes: arming and disarming the system, activating the alarm, monitoring the facility, installing a new peripheral device, installing the control panel, managing roles and permissions, on-site intervention)
- Model of alarm system operation (component model, data flow model, and functional model expressed as a high-level use case model, with linkage to individual business processes)
- Competitor analysis results (analysis of three companies providing similar services)

The second stage was planned for 4 weeks. As part of this stage, the plan was to obtain information:

- Which business processes will be carried out by the contracting company, and which can be carried out by end users?
- What functionality will the end user solution have (I deliberately do not refer to it as a portal, as it was assumed that the target solution would not necessarily be an extended portal; it could also be any other solution identified as suitable for achieving the identified objectives)?
- What will be the constraints and risks associated with the target state (i.e.,what will be the limitations of the solution for end users, what they will not be able to do on their own, and what will have to be left to the contracting company)?

  The acquisition objectives for this phase were identified as:
- Business process model TO BE
- List of stakeholder requirements for the planned solution (requirements in the form of user stories, organized into epics representing modules of the solution)

- A list of domain requirements for the planned solution (these requirements were to be included in the solution scope as constraints and acceptance criteria for stakeholder requirements)
- Variants of the solution, including technical aspects such as architecture (joint work with an architect on the vendor side)
- Constraints and risks associated with the various solution concepts

The third stage was planned for 5 weeks. This stage was to develop the solution concept, both business and technical. A product backlog was to be created as a result of this stage.

The acquisition objectives for this stage were identified as:

- Acceptance criteria for the individual requirements that are part of the backlog (for each requirement, a list of acceptance criteria in Gherkin format, taking into account both positive and exceptional scenarios)
- High-level mock-ups of the planned solution (for the end user module of the application)
- Use case model of the planned solution (use cases mapped to individual user stories)
- A model of the high-level business processes supported by the planned solution (used TO BE process model developed at the previous stage, with a focus on how the solution supports individual processes and activities)
- Solution architecture model (responsibility: vendor-side architect)

A preliminary work plan was prepared in cooperation with the architect and the business owner on the customer side. The developed plan was presented and discussed with the other stakeholders on the customer side and with the consulting provider's team. The plan in draft form was prepared using the Miro tool, and once the plan was approved, the resulting tasks and activities were registered in the JIRA tool. The progress of the work was tracked in this tool. The results of the work, such as specific models and requirements, were registered in Confluence, DrawIO, and Figma (screen mock-ups).

3.4.2 Appendix: An Example of a Checklist for Planning the Business Analysis Process

Dictionary

BA—business analyst
UXD—user experience designer, UX designer
PM—project manager
HL—high level
SME—subject matter expert, domain expert
SA—system analyst
AC—acceptance criteria
US—user story

Planning stage of business analysis activities

Planning the analysis approach

Activity	Who participates	Work product/ outcome	Example
□ Identify the purpose of the analysis work	BA, stakeholders (decision-makers), e.g., business, sponsor	Description of the scope of analysis work	Development of the basis for XXX platform implementation
□ Specify work product/result/ artifact/document	BA, business, design/ production team	List of work products (to be delivered under the project)	Final (e.g., system, functional documentation, architecture design)
			Indirect (e.g., requirements specification) • Functional requirements • Mock-ups • Business and technical constraints • Specification • Data model
□ Determination of responsibility for the creation of work products	BA, business, design/ production team	List of work products with specific responsibilities	• Functional requirements (responsibility: system analyst) • Mock-ups (responsibility: UXD) • Business and technical constraints (responsibility: business analyst, system analyst and architect) • Integration specification (responsibility: architect) • Data model (responsibility: business analyst, systems analyst, architect, data quality expert)
□ Specify the form/ level of detail of work products	BA, business, design/ manufacturing team, standard issuing body/ legislation	Template for requirements documents, requirements specifications, etc.	Functional requirements: user story (US)
□ Identify what you need to do to get work products	BA, business, design/ production team	List of tasks to be performed Whoever is involved in this work What input (e.g., analysis of regulations)	Functional requirements—requirements elicitation session (interview + prototyping) Validation of requirements

(continued)

Activity	Who participates	Work product/ outcome	Example
□ Identify the relationship between work products and tasks	Business Analyst (BA), business, design/ production team	Sequence of work	Functional requirements and mock-ups Data model and functional requirements
□ Estimation of works	BA, business, design/ production team	Assessment of works	2 man-day (MD)—HL functional model
□ Define the work schedule	BA	Timetable, analytical work plan	
□ Agree/confirm work schedule with stakeholders	Business, design/ production team	Confirmed schedule, analytical work plan	

Business analysis—strategy analysis phase

Stage of identifying business needs, defining change in services, processes, systems

Activity	Who participates	Work product/outcome	Example
□ Identify/confirm the business need	BA, stakeholders (decision-makers), e.g., business, sponsor	Business need	ERP—eliminating paper-based workflows
□ Identify the stakeholders of change—the people involved	BA, sponsor, stakeholders	List of stakeholders	Sponsor Business owner Administration department (SME)
□ Determine the scope of the change required	BA, sponsor, stakeholders (business and technical)		
• AS IS analysis	BA, SME	Model AS IS	Paperless workflow
• TO BE analysis	BA, SME, *Market Research Department*	Model TO BE	Process supported by a workflow system
• Gap definition—scope of change	BA, technical expert	Scope of change	Digitization of documents Change in documentation handling procedures
□ Definition of high-level requirements	BA, technical expert	Business requirements	Improving access to information
□ Development of a solution concept	BA, technical expert	Proposal for a solution	Workflow system (Commercial-Off-The-Shelf (COTS))
□ Risk analysis	BA, sponsor, stakeholders,	Risk register	Effort to digitize paper documents

(continued)

Activity	Who participates	Work product/outcome	Example
□ Development of a business case	BA, sponsor, stakeholders, *controlling, finance*	Business case	
□ Selection of solution to be implemented, project launch, selection of teams	Steering committee, sponsor, PM	Project charter, decision to accept the undertaking of the project	

Detailed analysis phase—system analysis and solution design

Solution design and implementation phase, detailing business requirements into system requirements

Activity	Who participates	Work product/ outcome	Example
□ Kickoff	Project participants, stakeholders	Note	Agenda: Presentation of the project objective, participants, work plan
□ Establishing the WoW (way of working)	Project participants, stakeholders	Communication plan Principles of cooperation	Established way of working—division into teams, iterations Establishing a contract e.g., • If BA creates a US and starts working on it, he creates a task for UXD so that UXD knows which story to link the mock-up to • Change of requirement is communicated to team members via messenger + email notification (title: change of requirement {number})
□ Planning the work	BA, System Analyst (SA), Project Manager (PM)	Work plan	
□ Analysis of high-level requirements, determination of details to be clarified, preparation for development of system requirements	BA, SA	Initial system requirements, questions, concerns, preliminary mock-ups/concepts	HL requirements analysis (Excel), initial breakdown into user stories and registration in the repository

(continued)

Activity	Who participates	Work product/ outcome	Example
□ Obtaining additional/ missing information	BA, SA, stakeholders	Specification to the initial system requirements Input to the system requirements specification	Acceptance criteria (KA) for user stories in the form of scenarios Completing the requirements specification Mock-up concept
□ Development of mock-ups	UX designer/SA	Mock-ups linked to relevant requirements	
□ Submission of requirements for review	SA, manufacturing team, *business*	System requirements (US from KA) submitted for review	US being candidates for the next iteration communicated to team members 5 days before the iteration starts
□ Analysis of review comments, improvement/addition of requirements	BA, SA	System requirements (US with KA) checked/met DoR	A meeting in which team members provide comments on the requirements, the analyst makes corrections on the fly, agreeing on the content of the requirements with the team members
□ Acceptance of requirements	BA, SA, manufacturing team, *business*	System requirements (US with KA) planned for implementation	
□ Development support	BA, SA	Feedback, explanatory information	Consultation on how to implement the requirements.
□ Support for internal testing	BA, SA	Feedback	Verification of test cases, assessment of coverage, suggestions for test data
□ Support initial testing with business/demo/ presentation of development results	BA, business	Changes, new requirements	Assessing how requirements are implemented, providing suggestions for design options
□ Analysis of changes/ new requirements, impact analysis, effort estimation, prioritization	BA, SA, PM, dev, architect, testers	Implementation plan for change	
□ Support for acceptance tests	BA, business	Changes, new requirements	Evaluation of change proposals from acceptance test participants
□ Delivery of training to users/preparation of user documentation	BA	User manuals	

Support/maintenance phase

Solution operation stage in production, support for change and further development

Activity	Who participates	Work product/outcome
□ Solution evaluation (planned, systematic)	BA, SA, architect	Evaluation results: changes, new requirements, technical improvements
□ Identification of business needs	BA, stakeholders representing the business.	New needs

4 Requirements Engineering

> Software requirements engineering is the discipline that deals with developing a complete, consistent, unambiguous specification to be understood by all stakeholders, describing what the software will do, for whom and why.
> *Barry Boehm* (Yourdon 1997)

> Requirements engineering is an approach in systems engineering that starts with all critical stakeholders and their values. Requirements engineering analyzes the entire set of requirements at once, prioritizes them based on quantitative value/cost, and finds a reasonable balance in their satisfaction architecture.

> Engineering is about solving problems upstream, rather than suffering the consequences of unsystematic thinking downstream, at a cost of 10 times or more.
> *Tom Gilb*

Requirements engineering. Requirements gathering. Requirements analysis. Requirements stage. Documentation of requirements. Unfortunately, very often these terms are completely confused, including in the business analyst community, especially painful because requirements are one of the basic work products in business analysis.

Requirements gathering, or rather requirements elicitation, requirements analysis, requirements specification—these are individual practices within the discipline of requirements engineering, a discipline whose name is not fashionable enough to arouse particular interest in the market, not catchy enough to become a buzzword, not enigmatic enough to arouse interest and expectations.

Requirements engineering is often associated with something technical, closer to solution design and architecture than to business. It is confused with software engineering.

Requirements engineering is associated with requirements gathering and documentation—yet beyond these two practices, requirements engineering is a whole huge branch of knowledge (ISO/IEC/IEEE 2018; Wiegers and Joy 2014; Wiegers and Candase 2023).

K. Zmitrowicz, *Business Analysis Done Right*,
https://doi.org/10.1007/978-3-031-62194-9_4

Business analysts tend to use a small slice of this area, focusing mainly on requirements elicitation and analysis activities to develop solution concepts. Topics such as requirements management, including managing the information architecture, tracing relationships to control the scope of the project, and providing evidence of implementation, are often outside the focus of business analysts. Of course, it can be argued that a true business analyst deals with the business layer, not solutions, so there is no need to get involved in details such as requirements engineering. But requirements engineering is not just about solution requirements—the same principles that apply to developing and managing solution requirements should be applied to managing business requirements, stakeholder requirements, and other artifacts that can be viewed as "requirements" (business objectives, business needs).

> REQUIREMENTS ENGINEERING SKILLS ARE A KEY QUALIFICATION FOR ALL PROFESSIONAL BUSINESS ANALYSTS.
> *Stan Bühne, Managing director at IREB® GmbH*

After all, to develop and manage valuable requirements, it's not enough to source requirements and document them—there are a whole host of other practices and processes that must be learned and applied to be able to effectively manage information.

Requirements engineering encompasses a whole set of practices aimed at developing a solution that meets stakeholder needs and delivers value. To be effective, these practices should be structured—meaning that just as we plan business analysis activities, we should also plan requirements engineering activities. These activities should be selected according to the project context, stakeholder expectations, and overarching requirements such as regulatory or domain requirements.

One of the primary objectives of requirements engineering is to develop a solution concept that meets specific business needs. This solution concept can be expressed in the form of models, requirements specifications, or other artifacts to understand the essence of the solution being developed. In order to achieve this objective, it is not enough just to obtain requirements and document them—we need a whole range of practices, among which are:

- Requirements elicitation
- Requirements analysis and negotiation
- Specification of solution requirements
- Requirements validation
- Requirements management

Requirements elicitation. As part of this practice, the sources of requirements should be identified and information should be extracted from these sources. There are a number of different sources of requirements (not just stakeholders), which has implications for developing an approach to extracting information and choosing the right techniques. Information acquisition techniques are plentiful—interviews or workshops, so often abused by business analysts, are just two of the possible options. These techniques can be classified in various ways, one of which is the division into techniques that support obtaining information from available sources and techniques for generating ideas. Idea generation techniques are classified as creative techniques and have the objective of creatively solving a problem, developing innovative concepts, and generally providing solutions that increase competitive advantage.

Requirements analysis and negotiation. The information obtained is often incomplete, contradictory, and requires further analysis. These issues are addressed by requirements analysis, which makes it possible to organize information, classify it, understand the connections between information, and identify potential conflicts. Requirements analysis is one of the key aspects of requirements engineering—because we cannot assume that the acquired information is complete, consistent, or understood in the same way by the stakeholders. The results of requirements analysis are often negotiated, that is, agreeing on the scope and content of requirements with stakeholders. As part of requirements negotiation, we can handle requirements conflicts, often arising from different objectives and expectations of stakeholders. A prerequisite for developing a coherent solution concept is a consistent set of requirements—obtaining such a set is one of the objectives of requirements analysis.

Specification of requirements and solutions. The agreed-upon information should be documented. In requirements engineering, the term "specification" is often used to mean a precise description of an object. We specify requirements; we specify solutions. As with requirements elicitation techniques, here too we can speak of a range of techniques, tools, and notations for requirements specification—both in purely textual form and in the form of models. Developing a valuable requirements specification requires an understanding of the objective of the documentation, the needs of its audience—current and future—and project considerations. The documentation can be general or very detailed; it can be textual or in the form of an information model—the choice of the right form is dictated by an understanding of the objective the documentation is intended to achieve.

It is worth noting that the value of documentation is often underestimated—it is relatively common to think that documentation is an almost superfluous product from the point of view of providing a solution—for the objective is to provide a solution, not to create documentation. However, in order to understand and appreciate the value of documentation, one must understand its entire life cycle. The documentation life cycle includes not only the design stage—from the start of the project to its completion, but also the time after the solution is deployed to production. Sometimes we forget that the solution we are working on will function for many years—and during this time it may change, develop, integrate with other solutions. With the right specification, we are able to understand what impact the proposed changes may have on the functioning of the system—and thus mitigate the risk of introducing changes in an uncontrolled manner. Documentation is a tool for consolidating knowledge in a permanent way—so it is worth thinking about it in the long term, and not just through the prism of the current project.

Requirements validation. The quality of requirements is critical to the decisions made based on them. These can be decisions about the solution, implementation priorities, changes. Requirements documentation often contains errors. This is because the source of requirements is largely people, the authors also. People make mistakes. One of the key principles applicable to requirements engineering according to the IREB® organization is that unvalidated requirements are useless. Requirements are in a way objectives. If we don't validate their correctness, measurability, clarity, we can never be sure that we understand them as the authors intended. And since key decisions are made on the basis of requirements, it is necessary to do everything possible to ensure that these decisions are based on reliable and complete information.

Based on the business requirements, a solution concept is developed. If the business requirements are untested, contain errors, we will replicate these errors by making assumptions about the solution. Based on the system requirements, the solution is implemented and tested. If these requirements are not complete, precise, we cannot expect the system to be of good quality. Poor-quality requirements mean increased costs due to the need for repairs and rework, increased design risk because we base decisions on incomplete or erroneous information, and business risk—we invest resources in implementing an initiative based on faulty premises.

So let's avoid these risks by ensuring that requirements and other work products are of sound quality. We can apply reviews, we can ensure that requirements, specifications, models meet certain quality criteria, we can implement validation sessions with stakeholders to make sure we understand their expectations correctly and the work products we create properly reflect the information.

Requirements management. Another practice of requirements engineering is requirements management. Requirements management is usually associated simply with the creation of a requirements repository, which is just one of many areas of this practice.

To understand the essence of requirements management, one must understand the essence of information management. In order for information to be managed, you need to define it, that is, determine what the structure and objective of the information is, understand its life cycle—the process of evolution it undergoes. Information management helps to properly classify and structure information, among other things, with the help of requirements attributes, a kind of content classifier. Having the right set of requirements attributes is a prerequisite for enabling proper configuration management—in simpler terms, version control. Version control, in turn, is important for being able to manage the changes that occur in almost every solution implementation effort.

Another key practice in requirements management is linkage tracking. Linkage tracking is not just a representation of dependencies between requirements, it is a mechanism to manage the scope of the solution, allowing requirements to be linked to the strategic layer of the organization (e.g., to business objectives). This makes it possible to understand how requirements implement the company's strategies. Tracing also makes it possible to link requirements to the artifacts that arise from them—such as to test cases or source code. This gains the ability to analyze coverage. Tracing linkages is also a mechanism that allows us to analyze the impact of changes, which is a pain point for many projects, especially IT projects. Introducing changes to requirements without understanding the impact of those changes on other requirements and the system in general generates a huge project risk. By making a minor change, we can destabilize the entire system. By making changes, we can cause the project to no longer meet the agreed-upon business needs. It is therefore necessary to have mechanisms by which we can assess the impact of a proposed change on various aspects: the system, the business, and the stakeholders and their needs.

Requirements engineering is a broad comprehensive field that encompasses a wide range of practices to ensure that the solution being developed actually meets the expectations of the business and stakeholders, and can be effectively developed and optimized at the production work stage. Successful implementation of requirements engineering practices requires a number of specific competencies, such as systems engineering, modeling, risk management, and knowledge of requirements specification standards and their application, including context-specific customization. Having these competencies significantly increases the chances of successfully executing a business case, i.e., delivering real business value to stakeholders, without undue risk resulting from the need for fixes, rework of underdeveloped requirements, or a solution implemented on the basis of poor-quality requirements.

Requirements engineering is important. Lack of proper skills in this area can generate a number of negative consequences. Some of these are discussed by Howard Podeswa in his publication (Podeswa 2023):

> Organizations that do not pay sufficient attention to developing requirements engineering competencies suffer from the following symptoms:
>
> - Disrupted user experience
> - Unnecessary errors and rework
> - Soft skills deficit
> - Delays
> - Real value is still not being delivered faster to the customer

4.1 Requirements Elicitation

> The concept of a single requirements owner is a myth. It may work when a product is created for a hypothetical customer.... But what about those endless organizational projects that modify business processes, optimize resource management or address ESG (Environment, Social and Corporate Governance) issues?
>
> They will always have multiple stakeholders and multiple requirement owners.
>
> The role of the business analyst is to understand their needs and issues, understand them, and develop a consistent set of business requirements.
>
> *Yulia Kosarenko, BA Mindset Mentor*

4.1.1 Establish an Approach to Requirements Elicitation

ELICITING REQUIREMENTS IS NOT SIMPLY THE EXECUTION OF INTERVIEWS. IT IS MUCH MORE THAN THAT. AND THE KEY SUCCESS FACTOR IS PROPER PLANNING.

Requirements elicitation is not simply about asking questions of stakeholders. To effectively elicit the right information from the right sources, the requirements elicitation process should be properly prepared.

Here is a sample preparation procedure for requirements elicitation.

Prerequisites:

- Defined initial scope of the solution
- Defined business objective of the initiative
- Defined artifact structure of the project
- Defined stakeholder roles and responsibilities for requirements acquisition

Requirements elicitation procedure:

- Based on the business objective, the initial scope of the solution, and the structure of the artifacts, determine the extent of information that will need to be extracted.
- Identify the sources of requirements and other information affecting the designed solution.
- Prioritize the sources of requirements. Which sources will be primary, which secondary, which alternate?
- Identify which requirements source can provide specific information.
- Identify techniques by which information can be obtained from the identified requirements sources.
- Identify constraints and risks relevant to the requirements elicitation process.
- Based on the risk analysis, plan the use of specific techniques.
- Based on the structure of the artifacts to be created as part of the initiative, determine the optimal order in which to obtain information.
- Determine the plan for individual requirements elicitation sessions. Take into account stakeholder availability and communication preferences.
- Agree on the plan of requirements elicitation activities with stakeholders and get their approval.

4.1.2 Knowledge of Context Is Essential

USING THE OBJECTIVE AS A TOP-LEVEL REQUIREMENT HELPS US FOCUS ON WHAT WE NEED TO DO AND WHAT WE DON'T NEED TO DO. A BETTER UNDERSTANDING OF WHAT WE SHOULD AND SHOULD NOT DO IS ONE OF THE FACTORS THAT ALLOWS US TO DO LESS WHILE DELIVERING

MORE. CONTINUOUS REQUIREMENTS ENGINEERING AND MANAGEMENT ARE ESSENTIAL TO OPTIMIZE PROJECT DURATION.

NIELS MALOTAUX, PROJECT COACH, N R MALOTAUX, CONSULTANCY

Imagine that you are embarking on a new project. The objective of the project is to develop a certain solution, for example, an information system. The customer has provided a list of high-level requirements that need to be detailed to a level that allows implementation and testing. Where do you start your work? From choosing the right technique for requirements composition, or from interviewing customer representatives?

Can you start by trying to understand the business context, that is, why the customer decided to design this solution in the first place? In some cases, the customer provides a business case as part of the documentation describing the scope and motivation for the project. In other situations, such a justification is absent, or not presented to the team working on the system design. We can, of course, proceed on the assumption that the customer knows what it is doing, and its requirements correctly and completely describe the scope necessary to implement the business change. In other words, we consciously or subconsciously place the risk of an incomplete or incorrect analysis on the customer. In the worst-case scenario, if it turns out that the system we designed does not meet the business needs, we can claim that we designed the system according to the customer's requirements, and if it is poorly designed, the reason is the customer's faulty requirements. However, this is an unprofessional approach and not very effective in either building the right products or customer relationships.

The role of a business analyst is not just to accept information unreflectively and rely on it, but also to ask the right questions, try to understand reality, emerging problems, and possible solutions. In fulfilling the role of a business analyst, we must remember that our task is to support stakeholders in reaching certain conclusions, enabling the development of the best solution in a given situation. And here we return to the heart of the problem. Without knowing the business context, how would we propose the optimal solution? Since we don't know what was the motivation for starting the project, what business problems the solution is supposed to solve, what are the needs of the stakeholders, and what business processes are affected by certain business problems, I dare to put forward the thesis that we can't propose a solution. At best we can guess.

If in our role, in a given project, in a given business relationship, the expectation is that we will help customers and select the right solutions, we must start by understanding and assessing the business context. To put it in very simple terms, even if the customer has provided you with a list of requirements, don't assume that the list is full and complete, don't assume that the requirements are sourced and documented correctly, don't assume that the customer has done the analysis work in a fully professional manner. What to do about it?

First of all, we can always ask questions—this is, among other things, our role: questions about why the project was launched, what business problems need to be solved, what is the scope of these business problems, what divisions, departments, processes, stakeholders are affected? What activities have been done to prepare the initial list of requirements, have any other documents been created in addition to this already from the initial list of requirements that can explain the reason for starting work on a particular change initiative?

Obtaining answers to these questions will help us one way or another. Either we will find out that yes, all the requirements have been confirmed and constitute a complete list on which to base the detailed analysis, or we will find out that certain activities have not been performed and this will be a space for us and the team to act. Of course, it is possible to foresee situations, in my opinion extremely unlikely, in which the customer will say that the answers to these questions are not relevant, the correct analysis has been done, "The customer knows what he is doing." I consider this situation extremely unlikely, because with proper argumentation and explanation of the reason for asking the above questions, a customer aware of the financial and business consequences of wrong decisions will not avoid answering. Most likely, he will also not shy away from saying that he does not know the answers to these questions and this is an area that will need to be addressed. However, if for some reason the customer recognizes that a list of requirements is all we need to make decisions, without knowing the context, without analyzing the business case, it is our job to at least communicate the potential consequences, the consequences of basing important and expensive decisions on hypothetically anecdotal information, the consequences of choosing the wrong solution, resulting in a loss of resources and potentially business risk.

In this situation, it will be very important to explain the potential consequences and risks to the customer honestly, based on facts. If the customer decides with full knowledge that he accepts these risks, of course it is his right and his decision.

4.1.3 Don't Collect Requirements. Elicit Them

YOU CAN COLLECT MUSHROOMS IN THE FOREST. REQUIREMENTS ARE BEING ELICITED.
RADOSŁAW GRĘBSKI, BUSINESS ANALYST, COACH, ITABILITY

The discussion of requirements elicitation should begin with semantic issues. In many sources—I will deliberately not mention which ones—one can encounter the notion of "gathering" requirements. This notion implies that requirements are "collected." The semantics of the word "collecting" suggests that requirements are simply gathered, taken up—and the requirements themselves are waiting for the fruit of collection. This interpretation causes us to proceed to requirements elicitation with the expectation that these requirements are practically ready to be collected; all we have to do is ask for them, and they will simply be communicated to us. Nothing could be further from the truth.

In most cases, requirements are not ready to be collected; stakeholders are often not fully aware of them and are not ready to express them in the form we would expect from the process of "gathering" information. Hence, a more appropriate term to express the essence of the process we are talking about is "requirements elicitation." The use of the term "elicitation" implies that information must be obtained from somewhere, consolidated, acquired. And this is exactly how these activities take place in practice. We do not collect information ready to be taken; we are not a scribe waiting for stakeholders to provide information about requirements. We have to acquire the information ourselves, starting by identifying the right sources of information, determining the right techniques for acquiring the information, and further analyzing that information.

Gathering vs. eliciting—some may consider it purely a matter of semantics, a matter of one word. What could be the meaning of using one word or another to describe the activities involved? Perhaps in some industries words don't matter; however, in the business analysis and requirements engineering industry, precision and clarity of communication depend on the words used, and we need to be aware of this. By using this vocabulary and not others, we are communicating with the team, business stakeholders, and creating certain expectations. So let's use this vocabulary consciously.

4.1.4 Eliciting: But Eliciting What?

Within the framework of requirements engineering we distinguish many activities, among which is requirements elicitation. However, it is worth realizing that in the elicitation process we aim to obtain information not only about the requirements, but also about other aspects relating to the planned system.

One of the typical mistakes of business analysts is that during the elicitation activity they focus only on asking questions about requirements. And because, unfortunately, they often don't plan the elicitation process or specify what types of information they want to obtain, they ask questions about requirements—without acceptance criteria, expected results, exceptions, metrics, input and output parameters. They overlook requirements risks, business and technical constraints, and other aspects that can significantly affect the shape and scope of the planned solution.

It is important to remember that requirements elicitation is intended to elicit all the information necessary for proper requirements specification and solution development. Such information includes, in particular:

- Information about the requirement itself, functional, qualitative, other according to the accepted classification. By information about the requirement itself, I mean capturing information about the essence of the requirement—the capability of the system, the property desired by the stakeholder. Information about the requirement should explain the essence of the requirement and the results we want to achieve through its implementation.
- The business case, the value derived from the implementation of the requirement. This will allow us to assess the legitimacy of the requirement and decide whether the requirement will enter the scope of the planned system, be rejected, or perhaps planned for future stages of development.

- Constraints and assumptions on the requirement. This information will allow us to consciously shape the scope of the solution and inform customers that certain options will not be available in the system.
- Risks associated with specific requirements, so we are able to make decisions about design options based not only on the desired characteristics of the system, but also on risk analysis.
- Relationships between requirements and between requirements and other aspects of the system, or other systems. With this information, we are able to perform an impact analysis and determine what the consequences of the implementation of the requirement may be for particular areas of the system or other systems operating in the organization or its environment.

In the process of requirements elicitation, we must obtain the information necessary for subsequent requirements specification. Therefore, this information should also enable us to define the attributes of the requirements, according to the attribute scheme we have adopted. This does not mean, of course, that we must obtain all the information of interest in a single requirements elicitation session. It does mean, however, that when planning the requirements elicitation process, we must also plan what information we want to obtain at what stage and from whom.

For example, if we plan to acquire information about the expected behavior of the system, let it be, for example, the functionality to "sign up" an attendee for a conference, we need to obtain the following information.

Determine what services should be provided by the system. In our case, the system should probably offer the ability to register a participant for a specific event (defined by its title, time, and other parameters), select a conference package, and pay for participation. Each of these features should be detailed.

And so, for example, exploring the topic of registering a participant for a specific event, we need to obtain information:

- What are the initial conditions? For example, can a user register for a conference if the entire pool of tickets has already been sold out? Can he sign up for the reserve list? In such a case, is it not possible to register at all?
- What input information does the registration process require? For example, participant details, company details, etc.
- What is the result of the requirement and output information? For example, a confirmation of registration and payment sent to the participant's email.
- What are the constraints? For example, can a user register for a conference on the opening day of that conference? Can the user register only himself or also other people? What is the maximum number of people that can be registered with one registration transaction?
- Additional requirements, such as data security requirements. In the registration process, sensitive user data is processed, so this data should be properly secured. So a

functional requirement for user registration for a conference will be linked to a data security requirement.

- Risks associated with the functionality. For example, is it possible to register for a conference without paying? What risks might be associated with this? What if many users register for a conference without paying in advance and then cancel their participation at the last minute? By identifying the risks at this stage, we are able to analyze the requirements more efficiently and determine the final content and solution concept.

The more targeted[1] information we obtain during the requirements elicitation process, the more efficiently we will perform the subsequent requirements analysis and be able to determine the optimal solution. Omission of relevant information runs the risk of returning to discussions about the requirements in question and re-engaging stakeholders in the process of setting expectations for the planned system. Respecting your time and the time of others involved in the project, let's provide mechanisms by which we increase the chances of getting the right information at the right stage.

4.1.5 Determine the Sources of Requirements

THE SOURCE OF REQUIREMENTS IS THE CONTEXT OF THE SYSTEM. STAKEHOLDERS ARE ONLY ONE ELEMENT OF THE CONTEXT.

The first question that should arise before eliciting requirements elicitation is the question of sources—where to get requirements from. Of course, the first thought that comes up will be: from stakeholders. This is a fairly obvious statement, repeated by many sources on business analysis, with the *BABOK® Guide* at the forefront. In many cases, stakeholders are the key source of requirements for a planned solution. We can elicit requirements from stakeholders using a variety of techniques, such as interviewing, observation, or collaborative techniques, among which the workshop play a leading role.

However, sources of requirements are not limited to stakeholders. In addition to them, there is a whole range of other possible sources of information, which we happen to forget or even not be so aware of. It is just as good as from stakeholders, and in many cases much better, to derive requirements from documentation analysis or analysis of the operation or architecture of existing systems.

Most generally, we look for the source of requirements in the context, otherwise known as the system environment. This concept is for some reason often unknown among business analysts, which I consider to be one of the cardinal mistakes. Without knowing the

[1] By "targeted" information, I mean information that is valuable in a particular context, serving a specific objective. In the process of requirements elicitation, it is very important to ensure that we know what information we want to obtain and what purpose it serves. Otherwise, we may end up in a situation where we collect massive amounts of information that is irrelevant from the perspective of the established objective.

context of the system, we cannot source the right requirements or design the right solution. For what reason? Well, the reason is that the system context is the source of requirements. Elements of the system context are stakeholders, systems with which our system integrates, regulations, laws, standards, or business processes that our system is supposed to support.

Depending on the type of system, certain sources may be crucial. And, counterintuitively, it is not necessarily the end user or what are enigmatically called customer type stakeholders that must be the primary source of requirements. For some systems, operating in highly regulated environments, the primary source of requirements may be standards and regulations, that is, documentation. In this case, requirements elicitation relies on artifact-based techniques, by systematically extracting requirements from relevant documents. Attempting to extract requirements from end users or the contracting authority may be virtually doomed to failure in advance, since in a given project context these stakeholders may not be affected by many of the requirements derived from domain rules and constraints.

Other documents from which requirements can be extracted are:

- Documents describing the business processes that our system is intended to support
- Documentation of the company's business objectives and strategy
- Requirements specifications of similar systems
- Generally accepted standards and regulations for the business area
- Market research reports through which we can obtain information about business needs

It's also worth bearing in mind that the elicitation process includes not only requirements elicitation, but also the identification of constraints and other relevant information necessary to determine the final scope of our solution. This is something we forget just as often, focusing on establishing requirements and ignoring other relevant information, including quality requirements.

Documentation is one source of requirements; another is systems, systems that our project integrates with, as well as competitor systems that may inspire our solution. We don't necessarily have to create all the requirements from scratch; existing systems on the market very often solve the problems that our system is supposed to solve. In such a case, reinventing the wheel from scratch may be a waste of time, to say the least.

It is also worth noting that analysis of competing solutions can provide valuable insights into the potential features our system should have. These additional properties can complement those that were originally defined. Of course, the minimum prerequisite for this approach is market knowledge and knowledge of similar solutions. Thus, it is worthwhile not to limit ourselves only to your own project and project context.

In conclusion, requirements elicitation is not just about asking the customer questions. There are many other sources to consider when planning our requirements elicitation activities.

4.1.6 Select the Right Techniques

There are many different techniques for requirements elicitation. Depending on the source, we can divide these techniques into information elicitation techniques and creative techniques, which are more about creating requirements or creative problem-solving (IREB 2024).

The classification presented in the *BABOK® Guide*, on the other hand, divides requirements elicitation techniques into collaborative, research, and experimental techniques (IIBA® 2015). Regardless of the classification adopted, it is worth bearing in mind that not every technique can be used effectively in a given project context. Hence the importance of proper preparation for requirements elicitation, since without preliminary analysis we are practically unable to select the right techniques. For example, in a project where stakeholders are scarce, the use of large-scale interviews may not be feasible due to the inability to engage stakeholders sufficiently to implement an effective interview and to process and confirm the results obtained.

So, we start the selection of requirements elicitation techniques again by analyzing the impact factors and project considerations. Depending on the specific source of requirements, the objective, and the scope of the requirements elicitation activity, we select the right techniques, and then consider which of them realistically have a chance of success. Not necessarily all techniques that could theoretically be applicable in a given context will prove successful in practice. For example, even if we have available stakeholders willing to participate in interviews or workshops, the characteristics, communication skills, and attitudes of these stakeholders may almost eliminate these techniques of use.

Imagine a situation where stakeholders are invited to a requirements elicitation workshop—competent and decisive, ready to provide information; however, they are in open conflict with each other. Instead of an effective requirements elicitation session, an inadequately prepared and executed workshop may end in a clash. As a result, instead of eliciting requirements and building relationships with stakeholders, we may achieve the opposite effect.

We also need to remember that the effectiveness of requirements elicitation techniques varies depending on the source of requirements, needs, and constraints. A technique that produces excellent results in one project may be completely ineffective in another initiative.

The choice of requirements elicitation technique can be improved as follows.

Start by asking questions:

- What is my objective, and what information do I want to acquire?
- What is the source of the requirements?
- In the case of multiple sources, which of these sources will be the most reliable and effective?
- Are there any limitations that may affect the requirements elicitation process?

Based on the answers to the above questions, let's make a selection of techniques.

If, among the techniques that may be applicable, there are some that we have never used in practice, consider using these techniques on a limited basis, for example, only with stakeholders with whom you have a trusting and friendly relationship. Use a form of piloting to test the effectiveness of new approaches and techniques.

4.1.7 Tailor the Technique to Your Needs

Techniques are a type of tool to achieve a specific objective. The tools are selected according to the needs, taking into account the limitations and other considerations from the context.

Even if we decide to use a standard requirements elicitation technique, nothing prevents us from modifying it according to current requirements. Rigid adherence to the rules of a given technique may be advisable in some situations, but just as often it can significantly limit the effectiveness of our work. For example, when conducting an interview with a stakeholder, we do not necessarily have to limit ourselves to just asking questions. We can just as well demonstrate to the stakeholder examples of solutions, competitor offers, consequences of certain decisions, in order to facilitate his understanding or formulation of his requirements by referring to actual solutions and specific information. Alternatively, nothing prevents us from extending the interview to prototyping and sketching solution concepts on the fly, models imagining business processes, functionality or other aspects of the planned system. It is worth remembering that the classification of requirements elicitation techniques is conventional and based on certain assumptions. These assumptions are not necessarily true in our context, so we should constantly analyze the reality of the resulting constraints and adapt the technique to current needs in the best possible way.

The following is an example of modifying a standard requirements elicitation technique.

You plan to conduct an interview to understand the process of installing a new peripheral (e.g., a camera) in an alarm system. You plan to conduct the interview with a stakeholder representing an alarm system service technician. You have developed a basic list of interview questions:

- What peripheral devices can be included in an alarm system?
- Are there restrictions on the maximum number of peripherals in an alarm system?
- What is the step-by-step procedure for installing a new peripheral device?
- Can any emergencies occur and how should they be responded to?

As you prepare for the interview, you notice some risks. The process of installing a new peripheral recounted by a stakeholder may not be complete due to the fact that for this particular stakeholder, peripheral installation activities are performed on a daily basis. Consequently, some of the activities may not be seen as an important part of the process.

Due to the fact that you yourself do not have deep enough domain knowledge, you may not even be aware that some important steps of the process have been omitted by the stakeholder and will not inquire about them.

To mitigate this risk, you decide to expand the interview to include contextual inquiry. The first part of the session will be done as a standard interview, while the part on discussing the equipment installation process will be done as a contextual inquiry session. You will close the entire requirements elicitation session with a final interview summarizing the most important steps in the process, possible limitations, risks, and contingencies.

Supplementing the interview with a contextual study will allow you to observe the user as he or she performs the task of interest, and to conduct the interview in the context of real situations in which the system is used. This will enable a deeper understanding of users' needs, objectives, context, and challenges. A requirements elicitation session structured in this way will allow us not only to ask relevant questions, but also to get a more complete picture of the environment and processes of interest.

4.1.8 Quality Requirements Are Also Requirements

> Functions define what the system does. Quality requirements define "how" a system performs functions. It is the qualitative requirements that determine the suitability of the solution in a given context—it is through them that a huge part of the business value is delivered.

I have repeatedly encountered the belief that quality requirements (called nonfunctional requirements in some sources, such as the *BABOK® Guide*), such as security or performance, are the domain of architects and technical people. The business analyst has nothing to do with them. It's hard to figure out what the source of this belief is, but it's extremely damaging, leading the business analyst to deliberately overlook the qualitative aspects of the planned solution during requirements elicitation and analysis, and focus solely on functionality. What about the quality aspects, which often determine the quality of the product?

Well, it sometimes varies. Either the business analyst assumes that quality requirements will be obtained by someone else at some unspecified time and in some unspecified circumstance, or he is not aware at all that such requirements exist, can be very important for the success of the planned solution, and should be developed in the same way as functionality requirements.

Quality requirements are simply another type of requirements. They can be successfully elicited and analyzed by a business analyst. I will agree wholeheartedly that in the case of quality requirements dealing with more technical aspects, such as performance, the evaluation and specification of these requirements can (and should) be done with the support of the technical team, especially the architect, designer, and programmer. However, nothing prevents the business analyst from initiating the activities of eliciting these requirements. After all, analysis activities are not performed in a vacuum—we are part of the project team and it is necessary to cooperate with other members of this team.

For example, obtaining information about what the expected response time of the system is to be to indicate user actions or external signals, and under what maximum load the system is to operate and how it is to behave, can be done by people without technical knowledge. Obtaining information on which platforms the solution is to operate on, on which browsers in which version to operate as expected, also does not require technical knowledge. Note that the requirements do not describe the technical solution. So nothing prevents eliciting both functional and quality requirements as part of business analysis and requirements engineering.

The elicitation of quality requirements should not be an exception; it should be a standard of the analyst's work. Simply setting expectations for the quality aspects of a solution is not necessarily difficult. A significant difficulty in sourcing quality requirements specifications is the issue of measurability.

Quality requirements, in order to meet the quality criteria for requirements and properly represent stakeholder expectations and constraints of the planned solution, must be expressed on a specific scale—they must be measurable. Of course, all other types of requirements, such as functional ones, should also be measurable. However, in the case of functional requirements, the situation is relatively simple—either the system performs a certain function or it does not; this can be measured on a true/false scale.

When it comes to qualitative requirements, on the other hand, evaluating these requirements on a true/false scale is rather impractical, as it would lead to a situation where qualitative requirements, such as "the system is to be intuitive," are evaluated as "the system is intuitive or not." Requirements declared in this way and the way it is evaluated are completely unmeasurable, and therefore impossible to implement and test.

So I recommend using a different approach, assuming that we define a specific scale expressing the expected quality attributes and a process for measuring those attributes. Such an approach can be based, for example, on Tom Gilb's Planguage (Gilb 2015), according to which, in order to accurately express requirements, we need to quantify those requirements in a specific way.

Thus, for example, the requirement "System response time" can be supplemented by the following attributes:

Name: System response time
Scale: Seconds
Measurement: From the moment the user initiates an action to the moment the system displays a response. Response types can be information about the processing of the user's request (i.e., simply a status message).
Wish: In a minimum of 95% of cases under 2 s
Tolerance level: In a minimum of 80% of cases under 3 s
Best case scenario (aspiration): In 100% of cases under 1 s

By expressing requirements in this way, we know what is expected, how to measure it. We also know what the worst-case acceptable scenario is and the scenario we ideally aim for. Not only do we have a ready-made requirement specification, business acceptance criteria, and input information for planning acceptance tests, but we also have the information to design the appropriate solution architecture in advance. And all of this is still at the requirements elicitation stage.

A business analyst is competent enough to do this—he or she has communication skills, knows information acquisition techniques, and should be aware of various quality characteristics. Personally, I recommend using tools such as a quality model-based checklist to support elicitation and analysis of quality requirements. Software quality models, such as the SQuaRE proposed by the ISO 25,000 series, not only provide a classification of characteristics under specific characteristics (Figs. 4.1 and 4.2), but also provide guidelines and examples of measures that can be used to express particular types of characteristics.

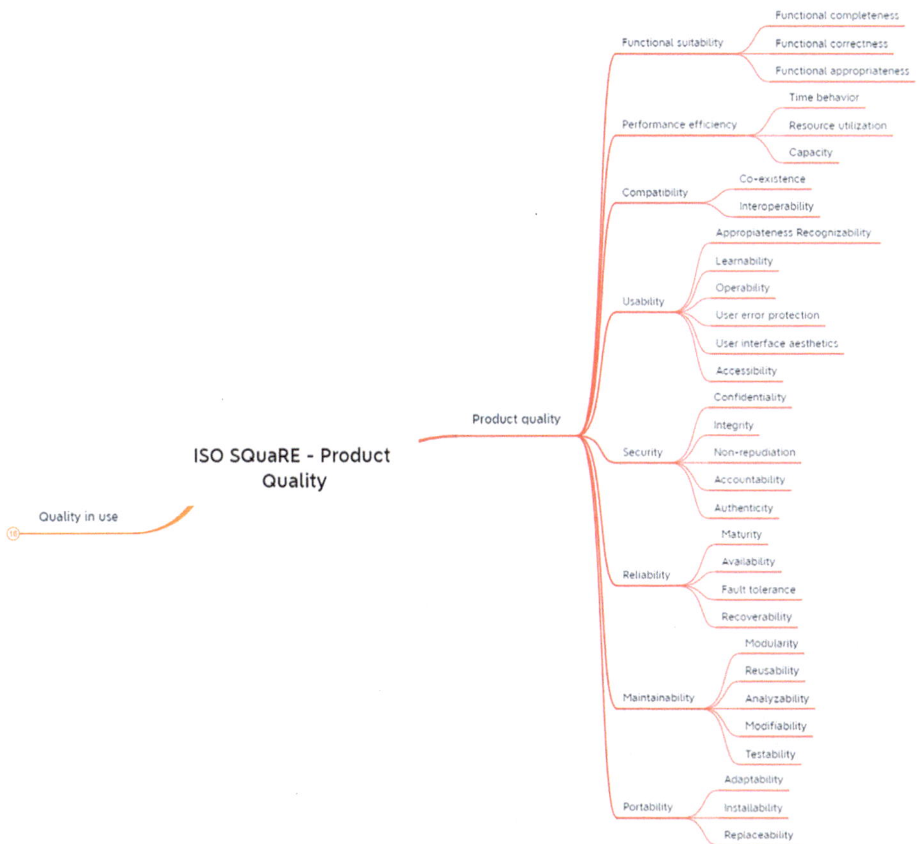

Fig. 4.1 Simplified model of software quality (developed by the author on the basis of the standard (ISO 2014))

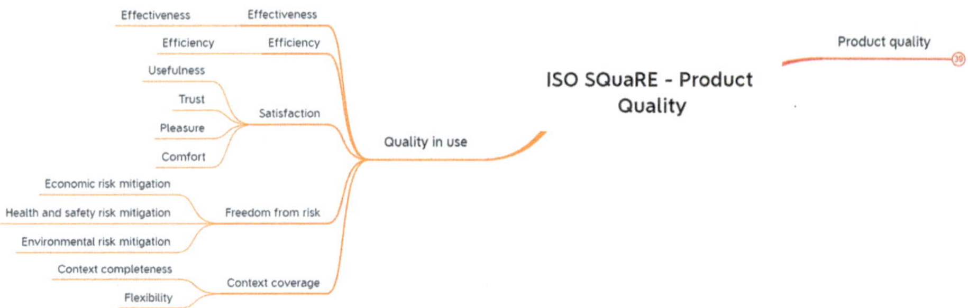

Fig. 4.2 Quality in use (developed by the author on the basis of the standard (ISO 2014))

4.1.9 The Difficult Art of Active Listening

LISTEN FIRST, REALLY LISTEN. STOP THINKING ABOUT SOLUTIONS AND START REALLY LISTENING TO YOUR STAKEHOLDERS.

FILIP HENDRICKS, INNOVATING BA, AUTHOR, COACH, CONFERENCE ORGANIZER, PRESIDENT @ IIBA BRUSSELS CHAPTER

One of the key areas in business analysis is eliciting information from a variety of sources, with stakeholders leading the way. Effective cooperation with stakeholders means skillfully built relationships and the ability to communicate properly. One is very strongly related to the other—it is difficult to build relationships without the ability to communicate effectively, and vice versa. We mentioned the importance of communication in the work of a business analyst in Sect. 3.2.1, Communication Shall Be Planned.

Let's now focus on a specific key skill within communication, namely the ability to actively listen. There is a difference between listening and hearing the other person—unfortunately, we are not always aware of this difference, and we do not always know the resulting consequences. It is not enough to listen to hear. It is not enough to talk to communicate. In order to really actively hear the other person, we should first of all give the interlocutor the opportunity to speak freely on the issue at hand, without judging, without homing in on specific tracks and solutions, without trying to convince us of our own rationale.

In the process of requirements elicitation, we are not the "star"; we are not the ones who should shine and surprise the interlocutors with our eloquence. Our role is to ask questions in such a way as to gather and present information to stakeholders so that we get answers to questions that are relevant to the business problem at hand. Of course, as part of the conversation, we can present some similar solutions, cite existing systems or processes as a point of reference for discussion—but this is to provide a basis for discussing needs and requirements, not a topic of discussion in itself.

It is desirable to use a variety of means and tools to support communication, but keep in mind the primary objective of the information-gathering process, which is to get information from the interlocutors, not to convince them of your right or preferred solution.

In my professional work, I have encountered several times when a business analyst conducting an interview or workshop focused not on what the other party wants to convey, not on the concerns or doubts of the respondent, but on discussing his suggested solution in order to gain acceptance from the stakeholder. In my opinion, this is not the right course of action. A business analyst is not a canvasser selling ready-made solutions, but a person who is supposed to help identify business needs and propose the right solutions (per the definition provided in the *BABOK® Guide*). To identify business needs, you need to gather information and analyze it properly. Proper analysis does not mean accepting only the information that is at our fingertips. It means accepting information from a variety of sources, often conflicting, often inconsistent with our own reasoning or preferences. We should keep in mind that the solution is supposed to bring value not so much to us, but to the business and its stakeholders—so with all due respect to ourselves, our personal preferences and sympathies should not be dominant here. And this is where the skill of active listening comes in handy, among other things, to overcome the urge to suggest solutions before knowing the facts, to avoid the temptation to manipulate information or stakeholder attitudes to push through a solution that is convenient for us. Finally, active listening is an excellent support for effective conflict resolution—because conflict resolution requires gathering information from a variety of sources, from different stakeholders representing different attitudes, motivations, and perspectives. Coming up with a solution that meets the interests of the various parties requires first and foremost knowing the motivations of these parties.

Here are some tips that can be useful in building active listening skills:

1. Refrain from *long monologues*. There are times when we are tempted to explain to the respondent all our thoughts, solution proposals, and suggestions on a particular business problem. We feel obliged to let the stakeholder know how we would approach the topic, what our opinion is. Unfortunately, the requirements elicitation process is not the right time for such declarations. Focus on asking simple questions that you need to get answers to in order to be able to understand the business problem, and the needs and expectations of the parties.
2. *Don't judge* either the respondent or the information they present. Accept that every stakeholder has the right to present his or her perspective, even if it is inconsistent with your way of thinking and your beliefs. Don't overly judge or comment on a stakeholder's concerns, perceived problems, opinions, or thoughts—simply acknowledge them as input to the requirements-setting process and limitation.
3. *Don't interrupt*. Have you ever witnessed a conversation in which one party notoriously interrupted another party's statements? It's sad to listen to, isn't it? At such moments the question arises: If the questioner knows so precisely what his respondent wants to say that he goes so far as to get into his words and supplement his statements, then what is the conversation needed for at all? What is missing here is the basic element of effective communication—respect for the other party. Let's remember that in the requirements elicitation process, stakeholders are a kind of customer from whom

we need to get information. Let's respect this customer—since we are engaging their time, asking them to help us get information, let's patiently listen to what they have to say.

4. Don't try to *prove anything* to anyone. The mistake of a novice analyst—trying to demonstrate your professionalism and very broad knowledge by proving others right. If in a conversation with a stakeholder information is given that is inconsistent with your state of knowledge, do not try to convince the stakeholder that he is wrong, do not barrage him with arguments aimed at making him change his mind and admit you are right. Why?
   First, counterintuitively, you may not necessarily be right—you may have some information that is true in a certain context and in certain situations, but in relation to the situation or conditions your respondent is dealing with, that information may not be correct. Instead of demonstrating your professionalism and deep knowledge, at most you will show ignorance and lack of knowledge of the business context.
   Second, even if indeed the stakeholder is in error, a requirements elicitation session is not necessarily the right time to lead them out of their mistake. It may be worthwhile to first consult other stakeholders about the acquired information, to verify whether indeed the information is wrong, or whether it is simply the result of some oversimplification. Sometimes it is worthwhile to hold off on trying to correct information as soon as it is obtained; instead it is worthwhile to mark such information as information to be checked with other stakeholders and, if this proves to be valid, to return to our interlocutor after some time with feedback.
5. Pay attention to the fact of *filtering information*. Very often during a conversation with stakeholders we learn a lot of different information—some of which may seem to us to be off topic, irrelevant to the conversation at hand. As a result, we are tempted to cut off these discussions and move on to the next relevant topic. In such a situation, I recommend far-reaching caution.
   Let's remind ourselves of the moment we are in—we are at the moment of acquiring information, we don't yet have a set of data, we don't yet know which information is relevant, which is not. It may turn out that we have deliberately interrupted the discussion of a particular topic, deeming that topic irrelevant to the business problem at hand, and then at a later date it turns out that the topic is critical to understanding the overall issue. In what light do we put ourselves in such a situation?
   We interrupt a conversation with a stakeholder who wants to inform us of certain facts. We consider these facts irrelevant—thus, in a way, indirectly, we reject the stakeholder's help. After some time, we return to that stakeholder with a request to discuss the same topic again.... Sounds quite unprofessional. How to remedy this? Let's accept that at the beginning of the requirements elicitation process we do not have the full picture, we are not able to accurately assess which information is important, which is not. If we have doubts about whether the issue being discussed is relevant to the theme of the discussion, let's not be afraid to ask the stakeholder a question: "Why do you think this

is relevant to a particular process, business problem, solution?" or "How can this information affect the planned solution, designed process, etc.?"
Maybe instead of judging on your own which information is relevant and which is not, ask the stakeholder for what reason he or she thinks the topic is worth discussing at that particular moment. In the worst-case scenario, it will turn out that the stakeholder himself admits that the topic has nothing to do with the main theme of the discussion, but is merely a side thread that he found appropriate to discuss at that moment.

Active listening is also a psychological element. If we want to get a sense that the respondent really feels heard, let's make sure that both our communication and behavior, including body language, are consistent and really say that we want to hear the other side. What does this mean? If we're talking to someone, let's look at that person, let's not run away with our eyes, let's not respond with half words. Let's not be afraid to smile and encourage with a gesture.

4.1.10 Discussions with "Difficult Customers"

THERE ARE NO DIFFICULT CUSTOMERS. INSTEAD, THERE ARE PEOPLE WHO LACK THE COMPETENCE TO PERFORM CERTAIN TASKS AND INEFFECTIVE PROCESSES THAT BLOCK OPPORTUNITIES FOR EFFECTIVE COLLABORATION INSTEAD OF BUILDING THEM. THERE ARE CONSTRAINTS THAT MAKE CERTAIN OPTIONS IMPOSSIBLE—AND FACTORS THAT WILL ALLOW US TO CIRCUMVENT THOSE CONSTRAINTS.

More than once in various situations I have encountered the statements: "The customer doesn't understand us," "The customer doesn't know what he wants," "The customer keeps changing requirements." Sound familiar? Have you ever had situations where customer stakeholders have changed previously agreed requirements, decisions, decided on a different course of action than before? Have you found yourself returning repeatedly to the same discussions and topics because previous conclusions turned out to be wrong? Have you ever been put in a situation where you had to make changes to requirements specifications, designs, models, even those accepted by the customer, because it turned out that the information presented in these work products did not fully meet the customer's needs?

In response to the above situations, did the thought occur to you, "This is a difficult customer; it's hard to work with him"? A difficult customer because he changes requirements. A difficult customer because he changes his decision. A difficult customer because he demands changes in the documentation so that this documentation reflects real and current business needs. Is this really a difficult customer?

I dare say that this is a perfectly normal attitude of a customer whose business operates in a changing environment. It is natural that when undertaking an initiative or project, we would want the results of that initiative to be relevant and in line with current business needs. This often means that changes need to be made at the project implementation stage.

This is how business works—in a changing business environment, often under time pressure and pressure from the market. Does this mean that the customer is difficult, or that our processes are not tailored to adequately support such an environment?

When undertaking a project, we should be aware that the result—from a business point of view business point of view—is business value, and not necessarily an IT system or other solution in itself. If we would like to help the customer actually solve business problems and bring in the value, our processes and our approach to work should be modified to:

- Be able to identify what brings real business value.
- Propose solutions that bring optimal business value.
- Design our processes in such a way that it is relatively easy, or at least feasible, to make any changes.
- Accept the fact that every business operates in a changing environment beyond its control. Changes arise not from the malice of the customer, but from the fact that the customer wants a solution that addresses not only predefined and stated business needs, but also constraints and other factors arising from this changing context.

Here are some tips.

- Consider whether the stated requirements might *change significantly* if something in the context from the planned system changes. If so, engage in a discussion with stakeholders about what those changes might be, what implications they might have for the system concept, and other aspects that might affect the customer's business. As a result, the entire team will have a minimal understanding of how the changes may affect the business.
- Verify that the way the requirements were stated actually allows the *business needs to be reflected*. Unfortunately, in many cases requirements do not describe business needs, but aspects of solutions. In other words, we quite often confuse requirements with solutions. As a result, we are not defining needs, but solutions, systems, projects. Apply root cause analysis techniques, particularly the "5 x Why," to understand what real need a requirement addresses. Once you have identified a business need, go deeper with the objective of understanding the factors that affect that business need and the aspects that will be affected by implementing a solution for that business need. In this way, you will perform an impact analysis that will help you identify possible changes, both within the ongoing project and in other business areas. This can help stakeholders identify changes that will need to be made in other areas, and processes performed in the organization.
- Systematically apply *validation* of requirements and solutions. Make sure that the work products you develop properly address stakeholder requirements and identified constraints. Avoid validation attempts reduced to asking the question: "Is my documentation, my model, these requirements understood? Is this what you had in mind?" These questions accomplish nothing and validate nothing.

Why? Because if stakeholders don't understand the document you are presenting to them, there can be basically three scenarios of events. The first scenario boils down to stakeholders being aware that they don't understand the content and openly expressing their lack of understanding. This is a comfortable situation—you will get feedback from stakeholders who state that they do not understand the document. It is quite another to have such feedback so that you can understand what is not understood in the document.

The second scenario is that the stakeholders, not understanding the content of the document, will be apprehensive to admit their ignorance, and will claim exaggeratedly that they have understood the content and the resulting consequences. Such a scenario leads to very serious consequences—you will assume that your document is understandable and properly reflects business needs; stakeholders may hold the belief that the author (i.e., you) knows what he is doing. As a result, your document will become the basis for designing, building, and implementing a solution. In the darkest scenario, the fact that the solution is based on wrong assumptions, wrong requirements, will only be revealed when the product is accepted. The end result? The manufacturing team has done a "piece of good work unnecessary for anyone," because the solution created does not meet expectations.

The third scenario assumes ignorance on both sides. You ask the stakeholders the question, "Is this what you wanted?" The stakeholders, in good faith, confirm that yes, this is what we meant. This is not because they consciously agree with the document presented with its contents, but because they do not fully understand it and are not even aware of it. From the picture of a defined business problem, defined by a set of requirements, they create a certain visualization in their minds, and try to fill in the gaps and interpret the requirements in such a way as to justify their value and correctness. In other words, they unconsciously add interpretations to the requirements and assume that these requirements actually describe their needs. In effect, they conclude that this is what they had in mind; you assume that your document correctly describes the scope of the solution. The consequences will be very similar to those described in scenario two.

How do we prevent such situations?

First, don't assume that everyone understands the document the same way we do. That's what we have validation sessions for—to gather feedback to help us identify potential areas for addition or improvement.

Second, let's not ask questions such as "Do you understand?" or "Is this clear?" Instead, we can go through the document or model in question, explaining the assumptions we made—let's talk about our understanding of the system, the business process, how we designed the aspect, what assumptions and constraints we made. Let's ask for feedback on specific topics. For example, if we are modeling the process of making purchases in an online system and have assumed that the maximum purchase value is 50,000, let's ask stakeholders whether this assumption is appropriate.

Third, let's acknowledge that many people absorb information and connect facts better if they have something tangible, visual, in front of them, something they can relate to. Natural language and text have their limitations, mainly related to the fact that every sentence, every statement, can be interpreted in several different ways. Therefore, it is helpful to use other media.

Are you documenting a business process? Describe it in text and present it in diagram form. Consult with your stakeholders on both forms—using two different forms of content communication should trigger slightly different courses of thought and allow you to discover potential errors, inaccuracies in the process description, or simply topics for discussion.

Are you documenting the functionality of the system? Describe the function, for example, in the form of scenarios or use cases. Additionally, even make illustrative screen mock-ups. In most cases, your audience will find it easier to understand how you see the system functionality if they can look at the visual concept.

Keep in mind that in most cases it's not the customer who is difficult; it's our ways of working and our approach that are inadequate for the situation. As a result, we try to do our job to the best of our ability, yet we get mediocre results. We fall into frustration and discouragement, and often, quite naturally, we try to explain the problems with the attitude and actions of the "difficult" customer.

4.2 Requirements Analysis and Specification

4.2.1 Determine the Approach to Requirements Analysis

Requirements elicitation is the first step in developing a solution. Requirements analysis is the next step, which allows us to select the most relevant from the vast amount of collected information, organize it, and agree on its final content. Out of the chaos, a coherent model of the solution must emerge.

Requirements analysis, as the name implies, involves a structured, systematic evaluation and synthesis of the information gathered. As part of this evaluation, we can make sure that:

- The data obtained during the acquisition of information is complete and sufficient for analysis for the development of a solution concept. The assessment of the completeness of the requirements should be supported by tracing the links to the business needs.
- Relationships and linkages between requirements are identified and the implications of these relationships are known.
- Similarly, the dependencies between the designed solution and elements of its environment are known.
- For each identified requirement, the information necessary to develop the required set of attributes has been obtained. With these attributes, further classification and grouping of requirements will be possible.
- Requirements are classified according to the method of requirements classification adopted in the project.

A sample procedure to analyze and specify requirements may be as follows (developed by the author on the basis of the requirements specification procedure by Tom Gilb (2015)).

Prerequisites:

- Defined solution scope
- Preliminary scope of requirements defined
- Identified key stakeholders and other sources of requirements
- Defined stakeholder roles and responsibilities for requirements acceptance

Requirements analysis and specification procedure:

1. Evaluating the completeness of acquired requirements against the initial scope of requirements
2. Assessing the completeness of the acquired requirements information—in particular, making sure that a source is identified for each requirement
3. Arrangement of requirements by type—according to the adopted requirements classification scheme
4. Identification of functional requirements
5. Identification of quality requirements by category
6. Defining the traceability between the analyzed requirements and business needs or other artifacts that are the source of requirements
7. Identifying assumptions and constraints on the planned solution or individual requirements
8. Specification of requirements according to the template adopted at the planning stage
9. Quality control of the requirements
10. Acceptance of requirements by relevant stakeholders

4.2.2 Establish Relationships and Dependencies

INFORMATION IS NOT LINEAR. IT IS CONNECTED IN A NETWORK OF RELATIONSHIPS. IF YOU DO NOT ESTABLISH THESE CONNECTIONS, YOU WILL NOT UNDERSTAND THE ESSENCE OF INFORMATION.

An important part of requirements analysis is to identify and understand the relationships and dependencies between requirements. This is important because certain assumptions about the planned solution can be derived from these dependencies. Without knowledge of these dependencies, we are therefore unable to design a properly working system.

For example, let's consider a system like an online store. We assume that this online store can order products and pay for them online. To make the payment, the system is supposed to use a ready-made solution on the market and a payment integrator. At this point, the relationship between the requirements for ordering, specifically order finalization, and integration with payment systems becomes very apparent.

Without knowledge of the dependencies at the requirements level, we could incorrectly design the order handling process. For example, we could skip the payment status verification step in the final steps of order finalization. As a result, the order could be placed successfully even if the status of the payment transaction returned from the payment system was negative, i.e., payment failed. Without considering this scenario arising from the dependency between requirements, we will not be able to properly design the business logic of the designed system. This is because we do not know whether an unpaid order should be cancelled, or whether the customer should be informed of the payment error and asked to pay again.

Regardless of the business decision made, the entire discussion begins with identifying the dependencies between requirements and understanding the implications of these dependencies for the planned system.

How do you identify potential dependencies? One way, the effectiveness of which I have repeatedly confirmed in various projects and undertakings, is to try to identify and understand the business processes and operations to be supported by the planned system. If—based on the requirements and knowledge of the system's target application and context—we understand what operations the system is intended to support, it is easier to understand how the requirements will depend on each other. It is also easier to understand other influencing factors beyond the requirements.

When approaching the topic of requirements dependency analysis, I suggest starting by asking yourself the following questions:

- What is the context of the system—what systems, equipment, other elements of the system's environment does it interact with?
- What business processes is the system intended to support?
- What are the elements of the system context that may have a significant impact on the shape and development of the planned solution (e.g., regulations, laws, standards that may change in the near future and have a significant impact on the scope and forms of the solution)?
- Who or what (system, other hardware components) is the user of the system? In what operational modes will the system be used and what might be the implications?

Understanding the interrelationships and dependencies is the first step in developing a coherent solution concept that will meet the business objectives set for the project.

4.2.3 Don't Write Requirements. Start Specifying Them

You can write a letter or a book. Requirements are being specified.

Quite often I come across the statement that "The analyst writes requirements in." This statement and its implications cause me some resistance. The resistance is caused specifically by the word "writes." According to my understanding of the role of an analyst, or of a person involved in documenting information in general, requirements are not "written" but "specified." There is a fundamental difference between the terms "write" and "specify."

According to dictionaries, "write" is a general term for creating text or recording information, while "specify" refers to the more precise process of defining and describing the details, specifications, or requirements of something, such as a project, product, or task.

To specify (Cambridge University Press and Assessment 2024):

"to explain or describe something clearly and exactly"

To write (Cambridge University Press and Assessment 2024):

"to make marks that represent letters, words, or numbers on a surface, such as paper or a computer screen, using a pen, pencil, or keyboard, or to use this method to record thoughts, facts, or messages"

To write (Polskie Wydawnictwo Naukowe 2024):

1. "to draw graphic characters on paper or other material by hand or to reflect them with a machine in order to express something"
2. "to create something in writing, usually for publication"
3. "to formulate one's thoughts in writing"
4. "to communicate something in writing"

To specify (Polskie Wydawnictwo Naukowe 2024):

1. "accurately, strictly specify something, present it"
2. "make specifications of goods purchased by a customer"
3. "make specifications of production costs and commercial costs related to the turnover of the enterprise"

Understanding these two concepts is key to understanding the essence of the analyst's requirements activity. Requirements are not "written" but "specified"—because requirements should be precise, measurable, and specific enough to truly reflect stakeholder needs for the solution being designed.

"Writing" them is not enough—the word implies that the form of description can be anything, as long as it conveys some information in a fixed form. With regard to requirements, fixing some information in some form is not enough—both the form and the information content of the requirements should be at the right level of quality, appropriate to the objective. The objective of requirements is not simply to "describe a certain state of affairs"—the objective is to specify needs, to express stakeholder expectations precisely, to express the features and characteristics of a solution in a measurable, complete, unambiguous way. That's why—with regard to our activities related to the documentation of solution requirements—let's actually use the word "specify" and not "write."

In addition to the purely semantic difference, the difference between the two terms also implies differences in the activities that need to be carried out to specify requirements. Writing something is simply transferring thoughts and certain information to a medium. Specifying requires:

- Obtaining and documenting specific information about a product or service, such as expected values or input information.
- Choosing the right form of information representation—for example, requirements specification can be done in the form of natural language—but also in the form of a model. Forms combining different approaches are also popular.
- Representing information according to a specific template, syntax. To specify requirements, it is not enough to simply write them in some form; this form should have a proper structure.

So let's stop talking about writing requirements. Let's start specifying them.

4.2.4 Start with Information Planning

Requirements specification is one of the most important tasks of a typical analyst. While it may seem simple at first, in practice it can be quite a challenge. This challenge is important because requirements specification is, contrary to appearances, not just creating "some" documentation; it is laying the groundwork for system development.

Many analysts begin the specification using a ready-made, battle-tested template. We assume that a solution that has worked in the past will be simple and effective. Unfortunately, it is usually not very effective. Why? Because even a perfect template, if not properly applied and adapted to the context, does not guarantee success. That's why template selection should be one of the last steps in specification planning, not the starting point.

Information content of requirements is the basis for decision-making and input for other processes in developing a solution. Therefore, it should not be a coincidence, but the result of planning that takes into account the key factors and information needs of stakeholders.

So where should we start? It's best to start at the beginning, that is, by planning the information we intend to document. The information content of the requirements is influenced by several key factors: the objective of the requirements, the type of requirements, the target group and its information needs, and any constraints or standards that need to be followed.

Let's discuss these one by one.

1. *Defining the objective*

Why do we document requirements? The objective of the requirements specification may vary depending on the project stage and objectives. For example:

For the objective of design and implementation: requirements usually should be comprehensive and detailed enough for designers and developers to be able to do their job, that is, for example, to develop the architecture and source code of the system.

For the objective of knowledge documentation: requirements are not only the basis for creating a system, they also store information about what the system was built on. Requirements will inform future users and those maintaining and developing the system about what functions the system offers, what assumptions were made in developing the system concept.

For the purpose of demonstrating regulatory or contractual compliance: requirements should provide evidence that certain assumptions, provisions of standards, regulations, or simply the contract with the customer is met.

2. *Understanding the types of requirements*

The first step in requirements specification is to identify the type of requirements. Examples of different types of requirements include functional, nonfunctional, and domain-specific requirements. Each type may require different information content. For example, while functional requirements are relatively simple to describe (the system is supposed to perform some function, and the performance of that function can be evaluated explicitly on a true/false scale), qualitative requirements usually require more information. Moreover, they require information that is much more precise and measurable.

3. *Adapting to the audience*

Considering the audience is key to proper requirements specification. Different stakeholders, such as end users, developers, project managers, and business representatives, may have different information needs. For example, if the target audience is business representatives, the specification should focus on business value, business rules, and acceptance criteria. On the other hand, if the audience is programmers, the specification should form the basis for detailed design, implementation, sometimes testing, containing enough information for these tasks.

4. *Understanding constraints*

In regulated industries (e.g., automotive, healthcare, aviation), adherence to industry standards is key. Such requirements can affect the specification structure and requirements management mechanisms. For example, it may be necessary to ensure traceability between requirements and their sources (according to the standard) to verify compliance with standards.

There are many other influences that can significantly affect what our requirements specification should look like. The most general principle we should follow can be summarized by the statement: Before you start writing requirements, find out what information you should document and how.

4.2.5 Understand the Value of Documentation

IF YOU WRITE IT DOWN, YOU WILL BE ABLE TO SEE FLAWS IN THE WAY YOU THINK AND CORRECT THEM BEFORE THINGS GO WRONG. IF IT IS WRITTEN DOWN, OTHERS CAN HELP YOU SEE THE FLAWS.

NIELS MALOTAUX, PROJECT COACH, N R MALOTAUX, CONSULTANCY

In many communities, the concept of documentation is conveyed in a very bad way—with the need to create formal, extensive documents that never serve anyone, with spending a lot of time documenting various information.

Documentation is the capturing of information in a permanent form. What is it for? Not to add to our responsibilities and worthless work. To consolidate knowledge, to be able to return to it at any time in the future, to reduce the effects of communication noise and misunderstandings, and to have a basis for validating understanding.

In the projects and initiatives we carry out, we process massive amounts of information. Some of this information is quite irrelevant and can remain in the verbal realm. However, much of the information processed in a project is critical to understanding and establishing the scope of the project, the details of how the work will be carried out, the adversity of collaborative resources, and many other objectives. Writing down this information in the form of a document is not an unnecessary formality—it is necessary to avoid certain problems:

1. *Forgetting arrangements and decisions*: In the vastness of the information we communicate and receive, sooner or later we will forget something, some information will be distorted. If this information is not fixed in the form of a record, we have no reference point that can help us confirm the reliability of our memory.
2. *Distortion of information*: Many of us probably remember the game "Deaf telephone." This game quite faithfully reflects what can happen in projects and during any other collaboration between people, where several people are involved in interactions. At every step we can talk about communication noise. Information repeated from mouth to mouth is subject to quite natural distortions due to differences in interpretation.
3. *Providing evidence*: This aspect of creating documentation can sound quite unpleasant—we need evidence in order to be able to demonstrate that certain people actually made certain decisions as part of project implementation. The practice of maintaining evidence is most often associated with projects or organizations that have had some unpleasant experiences—experiences like stakeholders changing agreements and decisions, where it was difficult to prove that indeed decisions had been changed because the original arrangements were contained in verbal form.

However, we don't always need evidence to hedge against bad stakeholder intentions. In many cases, the reason we need evidence is that memory is fleeting. A lot of information is processed in projects; it is easy to make mistakes, misunderstandings. It is also important to remember that—despite all sympathy for customers—project implementation is a business venture. Both parties have roles and responsibilities, both parties make decisions that will result in certain competencies. All this information should be written down, just as any other contract between a contractor and a customer is written. Not necessarily because we are afraid that the contractor or customer will want to cheat us, but simply so that the rules and scope of work are clarified from the beginning.

This is also the main value of documentation: to capture findings, requirements, risks, design principles—in a word, all critical information. Of course, there may be some exceptions to this rule, for example, when the relationship between the customer and the contractor is very positive, friendly, and both parties trust each other. In that case, probably not everything should be documented; we can rely on verbal agreements. But in my opinion, for the transparency of the relationship, the resource of cooperation, key information such as the scope of the project, constraints, and financial arrangements should always be documented.

In terms of business analysis, requirements engineering, the critical information that should be documented, in my opinion, is most generally all information related to work products that are defined as project deliverables, all critical information related to project management, such as risks, project plans, and team information (roles, competencies).

To determine which information potentially needs to be documented, let's answer the following questions:

- How often will the information be used by the audience?
- Who are the recipients of the information and how will they use it?
- Will the information serve as the basis for business decisions, such as the decision to implement a new service or develop a new product?
- For what period of time will the information be used—only for the duration of the project or throughout the life cycle of the business need?
- Does the information affect the definition of the project scope and solution?
- Can misunderstandings about the information generate project risk?
- Does the information address business objectives, project goals, or organization strategy?
- Will the information be communicated or shared with others outside the current stakeholder team?
- Will the information be the basis for budgeting and scheduling?
- Will the information be the basis for solution architecture decisions?
- Will the information be needed for auditing, controlling objectives, to demonstrate compliance with standards or regulations?

4.2.6 Determine One Source of Information

If information is documented in many places, which place is a reliable source and a reference point? Information that has multiple sources is information susceptible to manipulation.

A very common mistake made by business analysts is to duplicate information in different places. For example, functional requirements can be described both in the functional requirements specification, expressed, for example, through use cases, and through detailed descriptions added as a supplement to the design of screen mock-ups.

Another case is the practice of describing functional scenarios, including not only the flows and interactions of actors with the system, but also the specification of the appearance of the system itself. If we plan to design mock-ups, sooner or later this will lead to duplication of information in several places. This is a major problem in information management, because duplicated information in many places makes maintenance difficult, especially in case of changes. It is also difficult to guarantee consistency, which can lead to a situation where one source presents information in a certain way, while another gives contradictory data.

The problem is not only the lack of consistency, but also the increased labor intensity of maintaining such an information model. Rather than changing information as needed in one place, it is important to remember that the same information is in several places, and then make changes consistently.

Duplicating information is one of the worst practices used in information creation. Unfortunately, it occurs quite often. Some believe that if the information is very important, it should be duplicated in several places to minimize the risk of not being noticed by the recipient. In other cases, duplication of information is due not to conscious decisions, but to lack of coordination of tasks and communication problems between team members.

The simplest solution will be to properly design the information architecture at the very beginning of the project. Determining which information should be created and in which artifacts it should be placed, as well as establishing tracking of the links between artifacts, is a relatively simple mechanism that will significantly reduce the risk of duplicate content and subsequent problems.

Consider an example showing the consequences of duplicate information.

We describe the functionality of adding a product to the shopping cart. This functionality is described as a scenario.

FREQ 12 Adding a product to the cart

Description: The system allows the user to add a product to the shopping cart.

Interaction scenario:

1. The user is on the product details screen. On this screen, the system displays the following:
   (a) The name of the product
   (b) Product photo. If there is more than one product photo on the product page, the photo set as the main photo is displayed, and more photos are available by clicking the icon showing an arrowhead.
   (c) Product description—text of up to 200 characters with specials.
   (d) "Add to Cart" and "Buy Now" buttons.
   (e) At the bottom of the screen icons are displayed: Home, Shopping Cart, User Profile.
2. The user clicks the "Add to Cart" button.
3. The system:
   (a) Adds the product to the shopping cart.
   (b) Displays a confirmation message "Product in Cart." The message is visible on the screen for 3 s.
   (c) Updates the number of products in the cart, increasing it by 1.
4. If the user wants to add a product that is already in the cart, the system displays the error message "Product is Already in the Cart".

In addition to the above scenario, the requirement specification includes a mock-up screen (Fig. 4.3).

The interaction scenario repeats the information already contained in the screen mock-up, such as the elements visible on the screen. The consequence of this duplication of information can be that if I make any change on the screen mock-up, such as changing the way buttons are named, it will also be necessary to make those changes in the scenario. This means that by making one change, I have to make it in two places. Not only does this involve doing the work twice, it also creates the risk of inconsistencies. By making changes in one place, there is a risk of forgetting to make them in the other. As a result, we have two sources giving conflicting information.

4.2.7 Don't Be Afraid to Use Templates

There are many sources providing good-quality templates for describing both individual requirements and entire specifications. It is worth using such templates. A well-chosen template is:

1. The ability to standardize specifications throughout the project, making such specifications easier to learn and also easier to create, since there is one consistent template to follow.

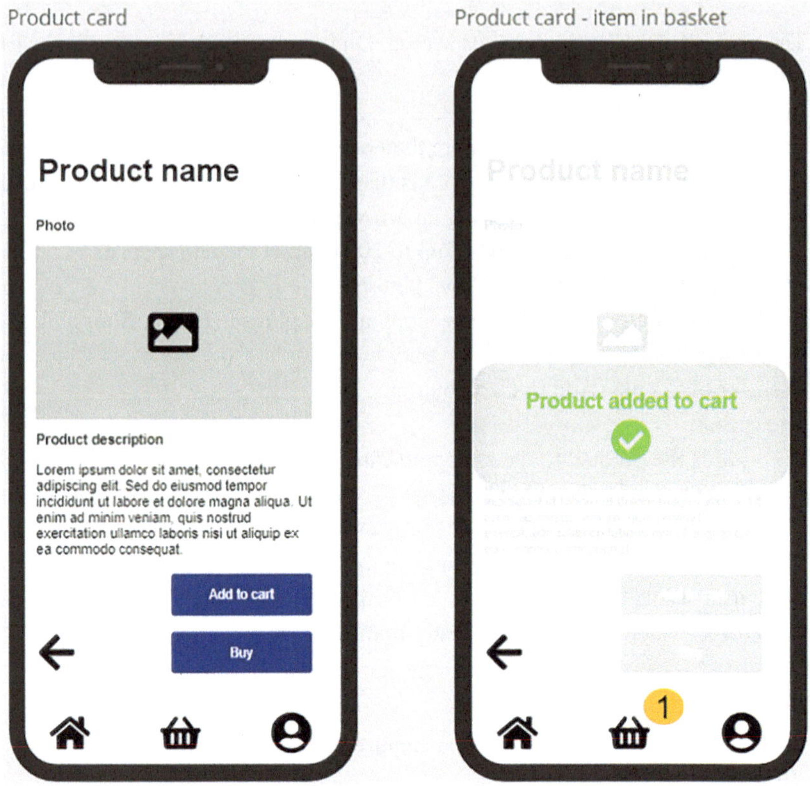

Fig. 4.3 Product card—screen mock-up

2. Reduced risk of omitting important information, since the template "forces" the entry of specific information.
3. Reduced risk of information chaos, quite common for projects and organizations that do not use any uniform template to describe requirements. Such chaos can be expressed in duplication of information by several authors, providing information at different levels of detail (one author writes in great detail, another at a high level of abstraction).

A well-chosen template will allow you to avoid basic mistakes. This is because it will provide a template of information and often a guideline of conduct, so that you will not have to remember many things—the template will be your checklist.

There are many templates, widely available on the market (Alexander 2002; Alexander and Ljerka 2009; ISO/IEC/IEEE 2018; Atlantic Systems Guild Ltd. 2019; Robertson and James 2012; Glinz et al. 2022; Wiegers 2023). Many of them are free. And yet novice analysts use them rarely. As a result, they themselves lead to fundamental mistakes, such as:

- Focusing only on the content, while ignoring the form. Of course, it can be said that the content of the requirements is crucial; the form is a secondary matter. However, let's remember that we create requirements specifications not for ourselves, but for the audience. They are the ones who should be able to easily read our documentation, easily search for the information they are interested in. A properly selected template supports these objectives.
- Omitting important information from the requirements documentation. For example, focusing only on the core content of a requirement can result in the omission of important information, such as priority attributes, the source of the requirement, or the business case. Counterintuitively, this information is just as important as the core content of the requirement, as it allows you to manage requirement information.
- Routine approach to the topic of requirements specification. Depending on the project and the characteristics of the system being designed, you may need to provide specific information in the requirements specification. Such information could be, for example, a reference to the industry standard from which the requirement is derived. Lack of a proper template may cause us to follow a routine—"We have always described requirements this way." We will proceed to the specification of requirements quite unreflectively, duplicating the method of work previously used in other projects, in other contexts, with other products. This method of work will not necessarily be appropriate in the current context. Starting work by choosing the right template, starting from an analysis of the necessary information that should be provided as part of the requirements specification, minimizes such risks.

The use of a template can thus fundamentally improve the creation of requirements specifications, especially for analysts with relatively little experience who have not yet developed their own mature working standards. For them, a template can provide a certain beginning, a starting point that will provide guidance and direction on the information content of requirements.

Of course, not every template will be appropriate in a given context. For this reason, the choice of a template, like the choice of any tool, should be preceded by some needs analysis.

- What type of requirements do we want to describe? Slightly different templates will be appropriate for describing business requirements, for system requirements, slightly different for functional or quality requirements.
- What information content should it provide to stakeholders? The starting point, of course, will be to determine who are the stakeholders of our work products.
- What information will be needed to manage the scope of the project, track the progress of the work, manage requirements in general? The answer to this question can identify the specific requirements attributes that should be provided as part of our specification.

Of course, a template is not the solution to all problems. It is not a golden mean to ensure extremely high-quality requirements—it is another tool whose effectiveness in a specific context is determined by how it is used.

Consider an example of a requirements specification template, based on ISO/IEC/IEEE 29148 (ISO/IEC/IEEE 2018):

> [<Condition>] <Subject> <Action> <Object> [<Constraint>]

The information in brackets [] is optional. Here is a sample requirement specified using this template:

> Once the payment operator confirms the payment, the system changes the status of the order to "paid" within 2 s.

In its current form, the requirement describes the functionality of changing the status of an order after payment confirmation. A condition and limitation is indicated—change of status within 2 s. We have used a template. The question, however, is whether the requirement formulated in this way is clear and understandable. There is a lack of information about how exactly we will determine that the payment is confirmed. The definition of the restriction is not clear—we do not know whether 2 s is the maximum time in which the status change is to take place, or whether the status change is to take place exactly 2 s after the payment is confirmed.

The use of a template reduces the risk of missing information, but does not guarantee that the information entered into the template will be of good quality.

In addition, the template used is quite good for formulating the content of the requirement itself; however, it does not allow us to enter additional information about the requirement, such as priority, source, or type of requirement. The template does not include an attribute schema.

However, using this ready-made template, we can expand it to get our own pattern:

> **Id**—The unique identifier of the requirement
> **Title**—The name of the requirement
> **Content**—<Subject> <Action> <Object> [<Constraint>]
> **Initial condition**—Specification of measurable initial conditions that must be true to trigger the requirement
> **Result**—Specification of the measurable result of the requirement, the state of the system after the requirement is executed
> **Constraint**—Specification of measurable constraints that affect the scope of operation or impact of the requirement

Requirement priority—Relative to importance, the requirement in relation to a set of requirements

Type of requirement—The type of requirement, according to the accepted classification

Personally, I follow an approach in which, based on the templates provided by standards and experts, I build my own templates tailored to the needs of the project, the product, and the expectations of stakeholders.

4.2.8 Watch Your Words

CONSCIOUS USE OF LANGUAGE IS AN ART. WORDS HAVE MEANINGS—DIFFERENT DEPENDING ON THE CONTEXT OF USE. IF YOU WANT TO COMMUNICATE EFFECTIVELY, FIRST LEARN TO CONTROL THE VOCABULARY YOU USE.

Requirements specification is a kind of art, requiring the ability to handle words very deliberately. There is a reason for this, since any word can be understood in many ways, depending on the context and assumptions made. Some words and phrases are particularly dangerous, as they generate ambiguity and opportunities for misunderstanding.

Consider some examples:

1. "The system is supposed to be more useful."

Question: More useful than what? In the citation, we inadvertently invoke something, comparing the performance of our system to something that, unfortunately, has not been defined. As a result, we have a statement that the system is supposed to be more useful, but we do not know what it is supposed to be more useful than.

2. "The transfer amount is to be at least EUR 1."

This wording of the transfer amount requirement suggests that EUR 1 is the minimum value that can be provided. However, it is not clear whether you can specify EUR 1 and this is the minimum amount, or a value above EUR 1. In addition, it is not clear what the maximum amount is. We have provided only the lower limit value, and moreover, in a vague manner.

3. "The system is to generate reports at the user's request. Among these reports is to include a sales summary."

With a requirement worded as such, the only thing that is clear is that the system is to generate reports. We assume that there are various reports, because among them there is one specific one: the sales statement. However, it is not clear from the requirement what reports in addition to the sales statement should be generated by the system. The lack of this knowledge introduces a very high risk regarding the scope of the system.

4. "The system is supposed to work on different browsers, for example Chrome version 120.0.6099.201."

From the example above, we know that the system is supposed to run on various browsers. However, we don't know on which ones specifically, because the body of the requirement states only one browser with a specific version.

5. "The system is to enable product management."

The word "management," like "support" or "service," generates enormous confusion. A dozen different requirements can be hidden under these words. For example, product management could mean the ability to add a new product, delete a product, edit product details, deactivate or activate, and probably a whole host of other functionalities. By phrasing the requirements as "management," we don't know what the author has in mind and what specific aspects of management the requirement is about.

6. "Ability to edit the product."

In phrasing the requirement this way, the subject is missing. We do not know who or what is to be able to edit the product, nor do we know if there are any specific initial conditions that must be met for there to be the ability to edit the product. For example, can a product that has been sold to a customer still be edited?

7. "When critical system errors occur, an error message should be displayed."

For this requirement, we don't know what a critical system error is and how to recognize that an error is critical. Therefore, we don't know what actually triggers the exception handling. We also don't know how to interpret the phrase "should be displayed." Implicitly, we could assume that it is the system that is supposed to display a message informing the user of the error. However, this is only our interpretation.

Such examples can be multiplied. They result both from the analyst's workshop deficiencies (inadequate syntax of the requirements statement) and from the use of vocabulary that we categorize as "dangerous."

To avoid ambiguity and further problems with understanding requirements, let's avoid using the following vocabulary:

Greater, smaller, faster, more efficient, more optimal—avoid comparisons. The use of comparisons generates problems because it imprecisely defines what a solution or a particular aspect of it is being compared to.

> Example of a requirement: "The system is to be faster."

A requirement formulated this way immediately generates questions. How much faster and faster than what? In addition, how do we determine whether we have achieved the desired level of "speed"? Even if we have refined the requirement, stating that the system is to be faster than the existing system, we do not eliminate the risk that our comparative value may change. The speed of the benchmark system may deteriorate over time.

Best, fastest, most intuitive, optimal—these phrases introduce a great deal of ambiguity. The author of a requirement in the body of which such words appear attempts to formulate the need to ensure the highest possible level of system quality, but fails to define this measurably, using a vague vocabulary that defines "the best level of quality." Instead, let's define specific measures—parameters expressing the expected quality of the system and the expected values of these parameters.

Example of a requirement: "The intuitiveness of the system is to be optimal."

How to define the term "optimal"? For whom is it to be optimal and how to measure it?

In order to formulate this requirement more precisely, it is necessary to provide a specific definition of "optimality" and identify the target group for whom the intuitiveness of the system is crucial. In addition, it is necessary to define methods of measurement to assess whether the system meets the stated requirement.

Covers, includes—this wording implies that the content of the requirement is not complete. Instead of using this type of vocabulary, let's describe the requirement in such a way that it encompasses the entirety of the behavior and characteristics expected of the system.

Example of a requirement: "Product management functionality includes adding and deleting a product."

In addition to adding and deleting a product, what other functionality can we talk about within product management? Editing of data? Assignment to categories?

Between, larger, smaller, later, earlier, mid, end, beginning—these words are often used to define ranges, but do not precisely define the values to which they refer. The exact limits and format of the data should be specified.

Example of a requirement: "At the end of the day, the system is to generate a summary report."

At the end of the working day, calendar day, understood as the end of the day at 23 o'clock 59?

If possible, *where necessary*, *where appropriate*, "*if applicable*—these phrases are often used when specifying optional features of the system or specific conditions under which some situation may occur.

Example of a requirement: "If there is a need, the system should handle exceptions".

We do not know when the "necessity" occurs—what could cause an exception, what specific situations or events generate exceptions, and how exactly to handle them. The use of the phrase "if there is a necessity" is vague and generates questions about who or what evaluates when a necessity occurs, and what to do if it occurs.

In addition, keep in mind the general principles of requirements documentation:

- The requirement must describe what who is doing, on what object, and with what result.
- When specifying requirements, it is useful to ask the questions: Who? What? How? When? With what result?
- Requirements should state what the system does, not what it does not do.
- We define requirements in an active form, not a passive one.
- If a requirement is in a certain range, boundary values and data format should be defined.
- Requirements should define significant emergencies and how they are handled.

Very good guidance on requirements specification is provided in Wiegers and Joy (2014), Gilb (2015), Glinz et al. (2022), and ISO/IEC/IEEE (2018).

4.2.9 Measurability, Measurability...

YOU CAN AMBIGUOUSLY SPECIFY THE PRODUCT.

BUT YOU CAN'T AMBIGUOUSLY BUILD IT.

JUSSI MÄKELÄ, OWNER, CHIEF VALUE OFFICER, FLOWCUS AB

Good-quality requirements are those that are measurable. Measurability means that we are able to say unequivocally whether a specific requirement has been implemented as expected. Why is this important? Imagine that we consider the following examples of requirements:

1. The system allows the user to quickly search for a product.
2. The user has the ability to perform a bank transfer.
3. The system is expected to run on the current version of the Chrome browser.

Referring to the first requirement, how will we determine that the system will indeed enable “fast” product search? What will be the measure of speed? What do we expect as a result of this requirement? We expect a contractual speed of product search. Does this mean the ability to quickly enter search criteria, or to quickly obtain results consistent with those criteria? The declaration of this requirement does not contain a measure or indication of the parameter that will define the expected speed. Nor does it contain measurability in the sense of defining the expected result. As a result, we do not know what the intention of this requirement is, what result we expect, which makes it impossible to properly implement and understand this requirement.

The second requirement relates to the ability to perform a transfer, which is a fairly typical functional requirement describing the behavior of the system. However, through the wording used, the requirement becomes unmeasurable—we do not know what result we expect. For example, we don’t know whether the result is an executed transfer or only the ability to execute it, i.e., the availability of the “Execute transfer” option in the system. The unmeasurability of this requirement is due, among other things, to its ambiguity. The consequence of the lack of measurability is that we do not know what is supposed to be the result of the implementation of the requirement. We may therefore adopt our own interpretation, which will turn out to be inconsistent with the author’s intention.

The third requirement is a fairly typical example of a misspecified quality requirement, specifically a portability requirement. At first glance, this requirement looks quite measurable, but there is no clear way to specify that the system is to run on the “current” version of the Chrome browser. The unmeasurability is that we don’t know how to measure the timeliness of the version. Should it be the current version as of today, the date this requirement is documented, or the date the system is received? The term “up-to-date” used in this context means that there is no point of reference—no specific version of the browser that would represent the value of the specified parameter.

Another aspect of the lack of measurability of this requirement is the use of the word “work.” What is the expected result of the system “working”? On a specific Chrome browser, is the system simply supposed to be able to run, to achieve the specified performance parameters? This is not clear. All we know is that it is supposed to work.

If there is no benchmark and no definition of how we will measure whether it works as expected, the consequence of accepting this requirement in its current unmeasured form could be that we create a system that “works” on the version of Chrome current as of the date of implementation of the source code. However, this system may not be accepted by the recipient, since the browser version may have changed as of the implementation date—and as a result, the way the system works may not be in line with the recipients’ expectations. Even if the browser version has not changed, or the change has not had a major impact on the operation of the system, there is still a risk that the system does not “work” as expected by the recipients, because the requirement has not defined a specific measure of performance, nor has it specified references to other requirements, such as performance requirements, that could complete the specification.

The consequence of the lack of measurability is that we are unable to create a precise contract that describes in an unambiguous way whether the system has been implemented as expected. As a result, the solution we create is unquantifiable, just as the requirements are unquantifiable.

We could use the analogy here of a situation in which we expect a hairdresser to give us a "good" haircut, but without providing any clues that can specify what the term "good" haircut means to us. Interestingly, a professional hairdresser would probably never agree to perform a service having only this information from the customer.

In the field of software engineering, the habit of documenting vague, unmeasurable requirements is so entrenched that very often we do not even pay attention to this fact and accept unmeasurable requirements for implementation. This, of course, generates a whole series of problems, such as:

- The need to clarify with stakeholders the details of requirements that have theoretically already been accepted
- Problems with delivering the agreed scope of requirements if, while detailing imprecise and unmeasurable requirements, it turns out that stakeholder expectations for certain system parameters are at an unfeasible level, given the project circumstances
- Making assumptions about requirements that turn out to be wrong when, for example, during acceptance testing or production operation of the system, it comes to light that the stakeholders' needs were different from what the implemented solution provides
- Delivering a solution that offers a certain functionality, but does not meet quality features that were not sized in the project at all

A good requirements specification is one in which every aspect of the requirement can be unambiguously stated in the implementation. Several strategies can be used to ensure that requirements are measurable. Consider the following example of a simple functional requirement:

> The system allows a user to generate a report of the user's daily work time.

In the most straightforward view of the subject, functional requirements are measurable in a zero-one manner—either the function is delivered or it is not, as stated by Tom Gilb (Gilb 2015): "A function is an action of a system or system component. Basic functions are 'binary' in nature: They are either present, or not, in specifications or in actual testable systems."

In the case of our requirement, the measurability of a report generation function can be tested by determining whether or not a report was generated. The problem is that because the term "generation" is ambiguous, we are unable to achieve measurability for this requirement. This is because we do not know what will demonstrate that a report has been "generated." Generating can mean creating a PDF file that the user can save to disk, but generating can also mean simply preparing data that will be made available to the user on the screen. Until we specify precisely the expected behavior of the result of the function's execution, we cannot ensure measurability.

So let's make some assumption about functionality and modify this requirement as follows:

> The system allows the user to view information about the user's daily working time.

The result of the function, therefore, is the provision of information on daily working hours. However, we still do not know what this information should contain. We don't know whether the statement should contain only the number of full hours worked per day, the number of hours and the number of minutes, or more detailed information, such as the start time, the end time, the working time in minutes, etc.

In addition, the requirement statement assumes that we will provide the user with information about the user's daily work time. The question arises, however, as to which user. The one who started the given function? Or any other user, an employee of the company? What would it mean if employee A has access to view employee B's time information? This statement would also need to be clarified, as the ambiguity affects the ability to determine the achievement of this requirement.

The statement "the system allows the user to view information about the user's daily working time" also does not clarify what period we are talking about. For example, does the user have access to information about hours worked on a given day? Does he have access to information about hours worked on a selected day, for example, during the last month?

So let's make some assumptions about the business logic and complete the requirement as follows:

> The system allows the logged-in user to view information about the number of full hours and minutes worked on a given day.

In a similar way, we can iteratively build measurability into our requirements. Of course, in many cases, the amount of information that accurately describes a requirement is relatively large. However, this does not mean that we need to create an elaborate requirement statement. We can use mechanisms such as acceptance criteria or other attributes that allow us to organize the information in a readable way.

Below is an example of another requirement expressed in the form of a template that includes a set of attributes:

Requirement name: System response time to user action
Scale: Seconds
Measurement: The interval of time counted from the moment the user triggers an action, operation until the system response (result of operation execution) or (processing information) or (exception information) is displayed on the screen
Objective: 3 s
Worst-case scenario: 5 s (exception information)

We interpret the requirement specified in this way as follows. We measure the system response time in seconds. When we talk about the response area of the system, we mean the response of the system to a user action expressed as a response to a command (e.g., a user initiates a product search). The system response in this case will be:

A response to a command (e.g., a user initiates a search for a product; the response of the system in this case will be to display the search results on the screen)

Information about the processing of the result (e.g., displayed on the screen information about the search for a product in the database)

Exception information (e.g., an error message displayed on the screen in the case of an inability to search for a product due to a database connection failure)

The objective defines our aspiration—the parameter value we want to achieve. The worst-case scenario is the minimum quality, the "worst" value of the parameter that stakeholders are able to accept. The above approach to requirements specification can, of course, be extended as needed. An excellent reference is Planguage (Gilb 2015), which provides a series of tags with which we can dimension requirements very precisely.

Table 4.1 contains definitions and descriptions of some elements of Planguage.

Here is an example of a requirement built using Planguage elements:

GIST:
Users should be able to quickly order a product of their choice from an online store.
SCALE:
Time in seconds
METER [time]:
Measurement of the time from when a product is selected to when the store receives an order confirmation
MINIMUM (minimum acceptable quality level, worst case):
Ordering the product within 2 min
STRETCH:
Ordering the product within 1 min
RECORD:
The best known result is ordering a product within 30 s.

STAKEHOLDERS:
End- Users who purchase from the store and the customer service team.
AUTHORITY:
Product Manager and UI/UX Leader
DEFINITION OF CHARACTERISTICS:
Usability, in this context, is defined as the ease and efficiency with which users can order selected products using the ordering function in the app interface.

It is worth noting that the use of a similar method of requirements specification implies the need for quite a lot of data—and this is undoubtedly an advantage of this method. Instead of specifying unmeasurable, incomplete, ambiguous requirements, it is worth the effort to obtain the information necessary for proper requirements specification, thus minimizing the risk of later problems resulting from poor-quality requirements.

The use of Planguage in its full glory certainly requires a lot of effort, but in many cases it is not necessary to dimension requirements so precisely. You can use a variety of conventions and methods, and develop your own way of specifying requirements, through which you will provide information critical to understanding the essence of the requirement, ensuring that the design and implementation will be based on precise and validated information.

Table 4.1 Selected elements of Tom Gilb's Planguage (© Tom Gilb)

Tag	Explanation
GIST	Rough, informal, brief description or summary
PLAN	The level at which success can be claimed
SCALE	The scale of measurement used to quantify the declaration
METER	The process or instrument used to measure using the SCALE
MUST	The minimum level required to avoid failure
STRETCH	The best result if everything goes perfectly
WISH	Desired level of outcome
RECORD	Previous result, which is the best known result
PAST	Previous results that can be used for comparison
TREND	Extrapolation of past data, trends, and new technologies to specific conditions (time, place, event)
STAKEHOLDER	Any person or organizational group with an interest or ability to influence the system or its environment
AUTHORITY	The stakeholder or role responsible for determining status and enforcing usage
DEFINED	A definition, usually expressing a relationship to other user-defined terms (user Planguage)
QUALIFIER: [. . .]	A qualifier adds more detail to the specification in terms of time, place and event conditions (when, where, if)

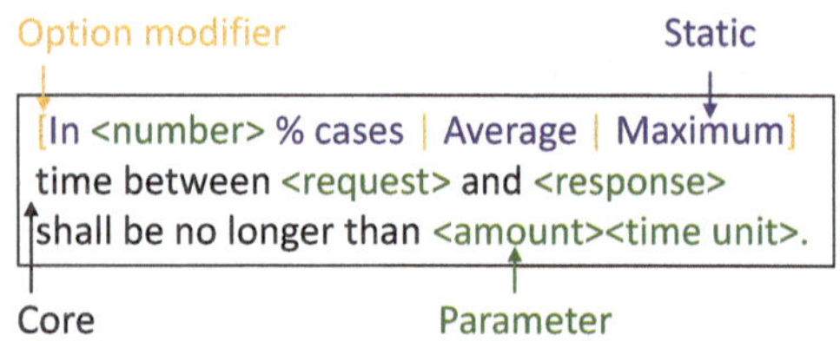

Fig. 4.4 Quality requirement description template (IREB 2023) (© 2018, Kopczyńska, Nawrocki i Ochodek)

An interesting quality requirement specification template (Fig. 4.4) is proposed by Sylwia Kopczyńska et al. (2018).

With relatively little effort, we are able to ensure the measurability of requirements at a minimum level. To do this, in most cases it is enough to ask ourselves the following questions:

- What is the outcome of the requirement? What measurable result do we expect?
- How do I determine that the requirement has been delivered correctly? What indicator do I need to use, and what value should it have?
- Is there any value tolerance? Can this indicator change over time?

A very good way to evaluate the measurability of a requirement is to verify the requirement from the tester's point of view. When developing a requirement, let's try to state how we would like to test this requirement, and what is the expected result. What test data should we use, and what should be the state of the system after the test? If we are not able to answer these questions, the requirement is most likely unmeasurable.

4.2.10 Obviousness...

WE ASSUME THAT CERTAIN THINGS ARE OBVIOUS. IN DOING SO, WE FORGET THAT ASSUMPTIONS ARE WHAT WE BELIEVE TO BE TRUE AT A GIVEN POINT IN TIME, BUT WE ARE UNABLE TO PROVE IT.

One of the more interesting challenges regarding requirements specifications and solutions is the issue of so-called obviousness. This is information that can be seen as commonly known and understood facts that do not need to be explained or documented. This are also information that we take for granted because it arises from the context of the solution we are designing.

Consider the example of an online store requirement.

"The system allows adding a product to the product catalog."

If we are talking about the functionality of adding a product to the catalog, then the fact is somewhat obvious that the result of this requirement will be the addition of information related to the new product to the product catalog. For example, if we had 40 products in the product catalog, after adding a new product we will have 41. This is a fairly obvious implication from the content of the requirement. What remains less obvious is whether the newly added product becomes immediately visible in the online store's offer (let me remind you that we are discussing the requirements for an online store), or whether it is given the status of unpublished, pending administrator approval, etc. after being added. This is no longer clear and obvious.

The example with adding a product is quite trivial, but it already reveals the consequences of making assumptions about requirements. Let's consider another example, this time for a hotel room reservation system.

"The system allows the user to book an overnight stay at a hotel."
Acceptance criteria:

1. The user can make a reservation of accommodation for a maximum of 14 nights.
2. The user can make a reservation up to 3 months in advance from today's date.
3. To make a reservation, the user must enter the details of the person who is the guest of the hotel, and the email address to which the confirmation of the reservation will come, and pay for the night in advance by the selected payment methods (reference to the relevant requirement).
4. After the reservation is made, the system displays the reservation confirmation on the screen, and the reservation confirmation is also sent to the user's email indicated during the reservation.

The acceptance criteria describe with relative precision the expectations for the results of the requirement. However, there is at least one important acceptance criterion missing that says from when the booking is possible. We can assume, since this is fairly obvious, that the user can make a reservation starting from the current day, no longer than 14 days—as indicated in one of the acceptance criteria. In other words, we assume that it is obvious that a reservation starting in the past cannot be made. This is logical, but the question is whether it is obvious to everyone involved in the product. If the requirement is not sufficiently specified, an example of the consequences could be that the programmer does not implement the constraints on the start date of the reservation, because there is no such requirement. As a result, the system may allow the execution of a reservation starting, for example, 3 days earlier, which will likely lead to an unhandled exception.

Consider another example of a requirement omitting "obvious" information.

"The system allows the execution of bank transfers."

Acceptance criteria:

1. The user can execute a transfer from a designated bank account to another designated bank account.
2. To request a transfer, the user selects a source account from the list of his accounts—if he has more than one account. If the user has one bank account, the system automatically supplements the source account number with the data of the account held by the user.
3. To request a transfer, the user must enter the data of the destination account: account number, name or surname of the account owner.
4. To request a transfer, the user must enter the title of the transfer and specify the date of the transfer—the transfer date is set to the current day by default; the user has the option to change the transfer date to a future date. The transfer can be ordered up to 30 days in advance.
5. Authorization of the transfer is made by a digital code sent by the bank to the user's phone number (link to the relevant requirement).
6. If the user does not authorize the transfer within 60 s, the transfer transaction is cancelled.
7. If the user authorizes the transfer, the transfer is ordered for execution, and the system displays confirmation of the transfer on the application screen.

The above criteria describe the behavior expected from the transfer execution functionality. The author has described what input information should be entered to order a transfer, what should be done to authorize the transfer, and what the results of the transfer execution are. However, some key information is missing:

1. To perform a transfer, you need to specify the transfer amount—this is completely omitted from the description of the requirement. The value of the transfer amount has some limitations—there is a minimum amount set, for example, Polish zloty (PLN) 1, and a maximum amount, which can be, for example, the value of the balance of the source account.
2. The requirement mentions the execution of a transfer, but there is no information about what kind of transfers the author has in mind. We can indicate many types of transfer, for example, tax transfers, loan repayments, and so on. Depending on the type of transfer, there may be other conditions for the execution of the transfer—for example, tax transfers require the entry of additional information, such as the tax return number and the tax period. This is not mentioned in the requirement. It was probably assumed that it is obvious that the described requirement talks about "normal transfers." The problem is that based on the information provided, we don't know what these normal transfers are.

3. There is no information about the currency of the transfer—yet either the source account or the destination account or both can have different currencies. It is probably assumed that the transfers are for the currency of the country.
4. There is no information about the format of the destination account, yet the transfer can be ordered to a foreign account. In this case, providing the account number without the country code and additional information will be insufficient to complete the transfer.

So we can see that the above requirement lacks a great deal of information necessary to properly understand the implementation of this requirement. Some of these deficiencies are most likely due to the fact that the author assumed that some of the information is obvious because it is obvious from the context. However, even if we assume that we are designing a system to provide banking services to individual customers, the requirement still does not provide enough information.

The above examples are just a few possible examples of making assumptions about the information we introduce as part of the requirements specification. It is important to keep in mind that information that seems "obvious" to us is not obvious to everyone—members of the manufacturing team and other stakeholders will evaluate information that is documented. They are not able to address the undocumented assumptions that the author made when creating the requirements specification because they are not aware of them.

What is obvious to the author—for example, that when we talk about transfers we mean transfers from current accounts, domestic, within acceptable limits—will not be obvious to the programmer, the tester, the user of the system. Of course, we can assume that not all the information needs to be included in the requirements specification, because the details will be clarified in face-to-face communication, when agreeing on the details of requirements implementation. However, in this case, the results of these agreements should at least be documented in a general form. Otherwise, we lose some of the knowledge of what the designed behavior and limitations of the system are—the production team may get the information necessary to implement the solution, but the test team and the people receiving the system will no longer have this knowledge. We may end up with a situation where team members make comments on the system based on their interpretation, without knowledge of the findings made verbally.

Let's remember that the requirements specification is a contract between the contractor and the ordering party—if the contract is not precise, this is grounds for undermining the contract itself and the results of the work. For this reason, let's be especially sensitive to issues of "obvious" assumptions. I suggest documenting all information that pertains to the following:

- Constraints of the system or process
- Permissions to perform particular functions or operations
- Specifications of input and output data
- Quality attributes of the system or process, such as performance or security
- Business rules

If we are interested in minimizing the need to document information, we can refer the requirements specification to overarching documents, such as organization policies, general guidelines for the appearance or behavior of the system, relevant regulations, etc. In this case, we may find that not everything needs to be documented within the requirements specification, as we can refer to a specific source.

For example, for a requirement for the execution of transfers, the acceptance criteria may say that the requirement is for the execution of transfers with types defined in a specific document.

When deciding what information should be included in the requirements specification, consider the following:

- Who is the audience of the documentation now and in the future?
  - Identifying the recipients of information will help us understand their expectations and information needs.
- What knowledge does the documentation recipient have? Does he or she know the business area? Does he or she have knowledge of business rules?
  - If the recipient is not a domain expert, he or she probably does not have knowledge of many specific business rules. This knowledge should therefore be included in the documentation.
- Does the recipient have knowledge of the context of the planned solution?
  - If the recipient does not have full knowledge of the context of the solution, a lot of information that is obvious to us may be unknown to him.
- How important is the specified information?
  - If the information is critical to defining the scope of the solution, how it will function, and its limitations, it should be documented openly.

The above considerations will help us tailor the scope of information and the way we document requirements to the needs of specific audiences. Above all, it is worth remembering that the requirements specification is not only documentation for the development team, but also for other stakeholders, such as business representatives or the solution maintenance team.

4.2.11 Not Always a User Story...

User stories are a good way to document stakeholder requirements. One of many good ways.

A user story is a very common tool in agile methods. By definition, a user story is "a short, simple description of a feature told from the perspective of the person who desires the new capability, usually a user or customer of the system" (Cohn 2004).

This is a method commonly used to capture mainly functional requirements expressed from the perspective of a specific role or user profile. The user story works well for expressing stakeholder or system requirements, as long as it is supplemented with acceptance criteria informing the desired behavior and properties of the system.

However, it is worth remembering that the user story is neither the only method of describing requirements, nor the most effective method. Another myth, unfortunately quite often reproduced, is that in agile projects the user story is virtually the only way to capture requirements. No source, no standard or recognized expert in the community, has ever claimed that the user story is the only way to describe requirements that can be used in agile methods. Also, don't assume that user history is a one-size-fits-all method that fits every possible context. So the origin of the myth that says agile projects equals user stories will remain a mystery.

So what are user stories good for? Obviously, for expressing requirements from the perspective of a specific customer or user, which is explained in the very definition of this method. User stories are very suitable for expressing the functions and behavior of a system, but nothing prevents you from using them to express quality requirements as well. In doing so, it is important to keep in mind the basic principle of formulating quality requirements, namely, to ensure that they are precise and measurable.

As mentioned above, the user story is a good example of a stakeholder requirement. Stakeholder requirements describe business needs; they do not yet define the solution. For this reason, you can successfully use stories like user stories to describe not only requirements for IT systems, but also expectations for processes, services, or any product.

Examples of user stories can vary, as follows:

1. As a trainer, I want to have information about the list of participants in my upcoming training so that I can plan accordingly to customize the program to the specifics of the participants.
2. As a customer of an online store, I want to be able to add a product to watch in order to be informed when the price of that product changes.
3. As a warehouse manager, I want to be informed of the production department's plans so that I can properly plan my warehouse space.

In contrast, the following examples are typical anti-patterns for using the user story method:

1. As a system, I want to update to have the best protection available.
2. As a programmer, I want to add a table to the database.
3. As a tester, I need acceptance criteria to develop test cases.

All of the above examples are from real projects in which I have participated. The first example regarding system updates is a consequence of using user stories in a project where this method does not fit. An embedded system where there is a great deal of interaction between system components and the system itself has virtually no direct interaction with the end user. So for what reason were user stories used? For the reason that the aforementioned organization, enthralled with agile methods, tried to implement them in all projects and departments, partly by force, without understanding the basics and assumptions of the whole agile philosophy. It assumed that it was enough to work in iterations, using user stories and certain tools to ensure agile software development.

The next two examples exemplify the use of user stories not to describe business features and needs, but to describe tasks that should be performed by project team members. This approach was not the result of consciously using requirements classification and the user story method to capture stakeholder-level requirements. It was the result of routine—the organization's projects used user stories to express all kinds of requirements and so-called stuff. In this project, the actual stakeholder requirements were documented in the form of a sheet. These requirements were decomposed not into lower-level requirements, but into individual tasks for the team.

One might ask, well, what's wrong with that? If the approach works and the team knows what to do, what's the problem? The problem is that, decomposed into tasks, stakeholder requirements are virtually impossible to monitor. Sure, we can track information on which tasks have been completed, which are in progress, which are yet to be planned. But we won't be able to straightforwardly answer the question of which stakeholder requirements have already been implemented and how. We will miss the level of system requirements and system design, as these artifacts have been replaced by tasks to be completed. Thus, we lose not only the ability to track relationships, but also the ability to track the progress and results of the work.

4.2.12 Use Cases in Requirements Specification

> Use cases are a powerful requirements elicitation tool for discovering and exploring the important user transactions that a solution must deliver (Wiegers 2024).
>
> *Karl Wiegers, Author of "Software Requirements Essentials" and numerous other books, Principal Consultant at Process Impact*

Use cases are a fairly common method for capturing and specifying requirements. The concept of use cases is not new and has been around since at least 1992 (Jacobson 1992).

Despite its well-established position in the market, the term "use case" is often misused in the IT business analyst community, deviating from its original meaning (Jacobson 1992; Jacobson et al. 1998). Some confuse use cases with business process descriptions, others combine them with user stories. Still others use them to describe the user's interaction with the system in great detail, along with descriptions of screen elements, data specifications, and all other more or less relevant information.

The concept of use cases itself is nothing more than a description of the interaction between a system and an actor, a specification of a functional requirement from the user's point of view (Cockburn 2000). A use case defines a specific user objective (Fowler 2003).

The implemented functionality allows users to execute a use case to achieve a given objective. It is worth paying attention to this aspect, as one of the most significant mistakes related to use case specification is related to this.

- A use case is not a description of the data specification—for this purpose there are more suitable methods, such as entity relationship diagrams, class diagrams, data structure specification, etc.
- A use case is not a description of the appearance of the system interface—for this purpose, more appropriate methods, such as prototyping, are worth using.
- A use case is not a description of a business process—if you want to describe business processes, use business modeling tools such as BPMN, workflow diagrams, SIPOC, or similar tools.
- A use case is a scenario-expressed description of a system's behavior in interaction with a user. Use case documentation usually includes a so-called specification, a description of the basic scenario, alternative scenarios, and exceptions. (Some sources do not. The use case method is also complemented by diagrams, using the Unified Modeling Language (UML) and depicting the relationships between actors and use cases and between the use cases themselves.)

An example use case description for the Add to Cart functionality might be as follows:

UC 01 Add to cart
Actor: System user
Prerequisite: Product information exists in the system
Basic (main) scenario:

1. The user views the product information and adds the product to the shopping cart.
2. The system adds and updates the list of products in the shopping cart.
3. The system displays a confirmation of the operation.

Alternative scenario:
2a. The product has already been added to the cart—the system displays an error message.
Success guarantee: Product added to the cart—updated cart status

Note that a use case description describes the general interaction between the system and the user; it is not a detailed step-by-step description of how to perform a particular operation. According to the concept of use cases, they should be abstract to some extent, focusing on the flow and interaction rather than implementation details.

So much for theory. The practice presents itself in different ways. Many times I have seen use cases written out in the following form:

UC 01 Add to cart
Actor: System user
Prerequisite: The user is on the "product details" screen.
Basic scenario:

1. The user clicks the "Add to Basket" button at the bottom of the "product details" screen.
2. The system runs the "addToBasket" method.
3. The system updates the view of the cart—the product added to the cart is visible in the cart.
4. The system updates the view of the home screen—the number of products available in the basket is displayed next to the basket icon. The number is increased by 1.
5. The system displays a pop-up with the message "Product added to the cart" and an ok icon.

Alternative scenario:
2a. The product has already been added to the cart—the system displays a pop-up with the message "The product is already in the cart."

The above description is a significant departure from the concept of use cases—it focuses not on the interaction, but on how to perform this interaction exactly. We get into details that can be considered system design, such as the application screen elements and the specification of the "addToBasket" method. Of course, it can be argued that the above description is appropriate because a given team needs such details to be able to properly design and implement a system. However, the approach to the basic concept of use cases can be questioned.

Let's consider whether it is definitely the right approach. First, the specification of use cases in such a detailed form requires the author to have knowledge of the screen design and the software itself. At the functionality analysis stage, we don't necessarily have this information. What then? Should the analyst design the screen and the methods invoked by the software? The answer depends on the morality and competence of the person writing the use case scenario. However, it is worth considering this aspect before undertaking requirements specification in such a detailed form.

A second potential problem arising from such a detailed description of requirements could be the question of the maintainability of the specification. If we specify use cases in such detail, any change to the screen interface will result in the need to change the use case scenarios. Is this what we want to achieve?

The only argument for creating such a detailed specification of use cases, in my opinion, is that the specification is the only source of information about the system's behavior, its graphic design, and, to some extent, its architecture. If we don't have screen mock-ups in addition to the scenario specification, and no other supporting documentation, this may justify the need for such a detailed specification. In this particular case, however, I would recommend that not only the analyst work on this specification, but also the rest of the team, especially the developers and testers.

Another myth related to the concept of use cases is that many teams believe that use cases do not fit into projects implemented according to the tenets of agile methods. According to some, use cases are one of the tools used only in cascading approaches to development; in general the concept is outdated and has no validity. In my opinion, these are completely unsupported statements.

To quote the words of Karl Wiegers in a private communication:

> Use cases are a powerful tool for requirements elicitation and analysis that have unfortunately gone out of fashion in recent years. I say unfortunately, because they work perfectly well in many types of projects. Adopting a use case approach is much more effective than simply asking people what they need or what features they would like to see in a product, and then trying to create a solution from many such bits of information.

When working on agile projects, it's not necessarily essential to use use case diagrams and write a complete use case specification—we can use the concept to supplement other, "lighter," documentation. Nothing prevents us from using the concept of scenarios to supplement user stories. In many projects, user stories are supplemented with acceptance criteria—because without them, the user story statement alone does not provide the information necessary to design a solution. Acceptance criteria can be in the form of points, narrative descriptions, as well as scenario descriptions.

I will show the result of combining the user story method and use cases in the following example.

User story

As a customer, I want to be able to cancel an appointment to inform the clinic that the appointment will not take place

For this user story, we can propose the following acceptance criteria, expressed in the form of natural language.

Acceptance criteria:

1. There is a possibility to cancel a booked appointment not later than 5 h before the scheduled time of the visit.
2. The cancelled appointment should be restored to the pool of available appointments.
3. If the customer has made an advance payment for the cancelled appointment, it will be returned to the customer.
4. If the visit has been booked for more than one service, it is possible to cancel only the indicated services.

At the time of designing the solution, we can detail the above acceptance criteria into the following:

Acceptance criteria/system behavior design:
The system allows a logged-in customer to cancel a booked appointment a maximum of 5 h before the booking time:

- The system displays a list of booked appointments to the customer.
- The customer has the ability to trigger the appointment cancellation action using the 'Cancel appointment' button.
- The system displays a pop-up with details of the visit, including a list of booked services.
- If the visit has been booked for more than one service, the system allows for selecting the selected service.
- The customer must confirm the visit cancellation with the "Confirm" button.

After the cancellation is confirmed:

- The system restores the cancelled appointment to the pool of available appointments in case of cancellation of all services booked within the visit.
- The system reduces the appointment time by adjusting to the services in case of cancellation of selected services.

The system returns the advance payment to the customer's account if it was collected in connection with the reservation.

In scenario form, based on the use case concept, the acceptance criteria can take the following form:

Acceptance criteria/system behavior design:
Access to function: my account -> visit list
Scenarios:
Cancellation of the entire visit

1. The customer is on the visit list screen.
2. For visits in the status "accepted," the option *Cancel visit* is displayed.
3. The customer selects *Cancel visit* for a specific visit.
4. The system displays a screen with information about the visit—details of the visit and a list of services (link is a draft of the screen).

5. The customer confirms the visit cancellation with the “Confirm” button.
6. The system:

   (a) Changes the status of the reservation to ‘cancelled’
   (b) Restores the cancelled appointment to the pool of available appointments in case of cancellation of all services booked within the visit
   (c) Returns the advance payment to the customer’s account, if it was charged in connection with the reservation (link to the “Return of advance payment” requirement)
   (d) Displays the confirmation message ‘appointment cancelled’
   (e) Notifies the user of the clinic’s application about the cancellation of the appointment (pop-up)

Partial cancellation
Precondition: there >1 service within a visit

5. The customer selects which services he/she wants to cancel.
6. The system recalculates the visit duration/price.
7. The customer confirms cancellation of visit with “Confirm” button.
8. The system

   (a) Returns the advance payment to the system account in proportion to the cancelled customer services (business rule 1), if it was collected in connection with the reservation (link to the requirement “Return of advance payment’”)
   (b) Restores the time resulting from cancelled services to the pool of available appointments if the “saved” time ≥30 min
   (c) Displays a confirmation message “part of the appointment was cancelled”
   (d) Notifies the user of the outpatient clinic application of the change in the scope of the visit (pop-up)

Resignation of cancellation
At any time the customer can cancel the cancellation of the visit. In this case, the system does not save any changes.

No possibility of cancellation
In step 3, the customer selects *Cancel visit* for a visit to which less than 5 h are left. The system displays the message “unable to cancel the appointment.”

System error
In the case of a system failure at any stage of cancellation, a message is displayed telling the customer to contact the clinic (by phone or in person) (link to screen design).

Additional requirements:
Business rule: Advance refund policy

At first glance, both forms—the list form and the scenario form—cover the same information. On the surface, it seems that the use case-based form requires more effort and will take more time. The benefit of this method, however, is that using the scenario-based form allows the analyst to trace the operation of a specific functionality step by step. Thus, it is easier to discover potential shortcomings in the business logic, with exception scenarios so far not included in the acceptance criteria.

The scenario-based form is similar to business process modeling. In order to model a business process correctly, it is necessary to define its start and result, the required resources, and the order in which the various activities should be carried out. Without this, the process description would be incomplete. The same is true for the description of functional requirements—input and output specifications must be provided, as well as rules for the function. Scenario forms make our task easier here, forcing a certain way of thinking.

Another use of use cases, or more specifically, use case diagrams, can be to organize the scope of a product described in the form of user stories. A use case diagram will show the overall design of the system's functionality (Fig. 4.5). Use case scenarios will provide

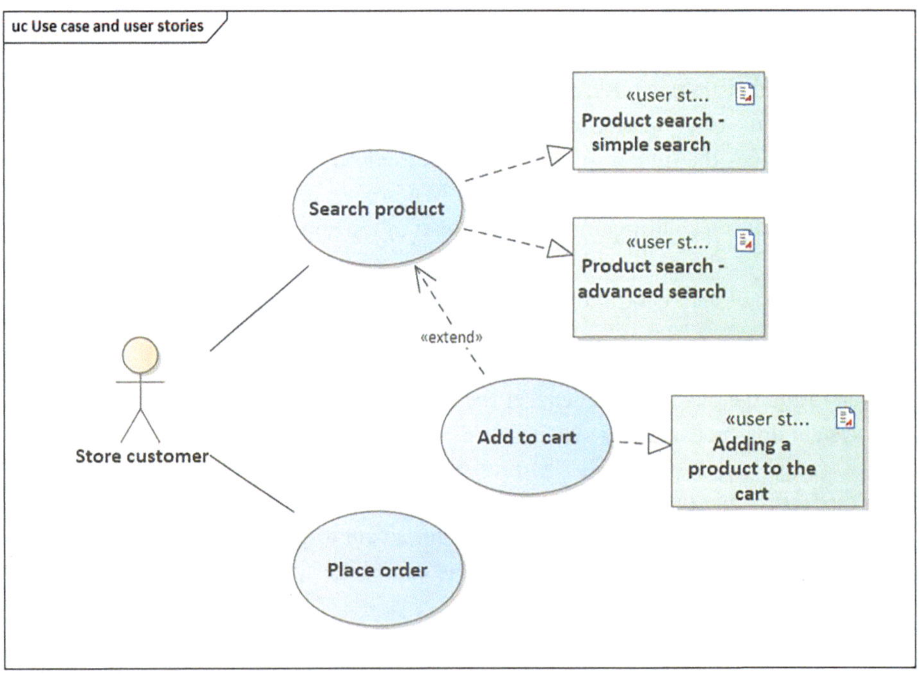

Fig. 4.5 Application of use cases and user stories

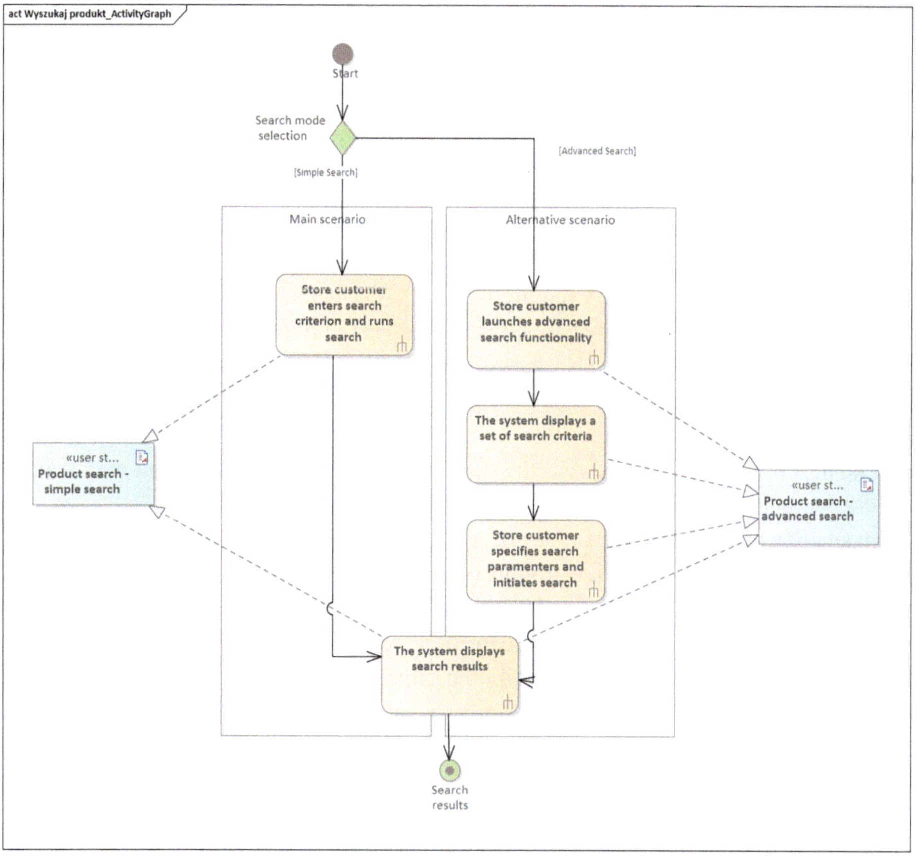

Fig. 4.6 Covering user stories with use case scenario elements—a simplified model

behavioral specifications. The user stories, in turn, will help plan the implementation of the product and their acceptance criteria can cover specific use case scenarios (Fig. 4.6).

In conclusion, the concept of use cases itself is quite old. However, this in no way affects its relevance and usefulness in requirements analysis and system specification.[2] Even if you find the original form of use cases inapplicable in a given context, it is worth considering using some principles of use case documentation to supplement and enhance the quality of your specification.

[2] Moreover, renewed interest in the method has been evident for some time. The authors themselves, Ivar Jacobson, Alistair Cockburn, along with other experts on the subject, including Karl Wiegers, are working to develop a fundamental understanding of use cases and how they can coexist with other methods of describing requirements, such as user stories (as of February 16, 2024).

4.2.13 A Picture Worth More Than 1000 Words

EVERY WORD CAN BE INTERPRETED IN MANY WAYS.

A WORD IS AN ABSTRACTION; AN IMAGE IS TANGIBLE—IT IS EASIER TO COMMUNICATE IF WE CAN REFER TO TANGIBLE INFORMATION.

IF YOU WANT TO AVOID AMBIGUITY, REPLACE WORDS WITH IMAGES.

The traditional way to specify requirements is to use natural language. However, this is not the only option, and in many cases it is not the best option either. Many aspects of the planned solution can be effectively expressed using a model. Examples of such models are mock-ups representing the appearance of a screen in an application, diagrams representing functionality, and changes in the states of system objects or task flows. With the help of such models it is possible to express the same thing that could be described with text, but in a clearer and more readable way.

An analogy can be made here to the design of a house. Information about the structure, the square footage of the layout of rooms on each floor of the building, elements such as windows and doors can be presented in natural language, in the form of detailed descriptions. They can also be expressed by means of a model—a building design. The information presented in both forms is essentially the same, but the forms differ in the method of conveying the information. These differences result not only in the understanding of the information and ease of assimilation by the recipient, but also in a reduced risk of misunderstandings and incorrect assumptions.

The same is true for software production and the design of various service systems. Functionality, system behavior, or architecture can be represented by both text and model. It depends on the preferences of the target audience, the objective of creating the information, and the risk of misunderstanding whether we use only textual form or enrich our information with diagrams or other forms of visual representation of information.

In what specific ways can modeling be used in designing information solutions?

- If you want to describe the business processes performed within an organization and supported by a solution, use business process models, flowcharts, or activity diagrams.
- If you want to describe system functionality, user interactions with the system, and system responses, use use case diagrams, activity diagrams, or sequence diagrams.
- If you want to describe the state changes of objects in the system, use state transition diagrams or other forms based on the state machine concept.
- If you want to depict the logical architecture of the system, such as the division into modules and functional components, you can use a package diagram.

- If you want to depict data and its structure and the relationships between data, use data modeling, such as class diagrams or entity relationship diagrams.

It is important to understand which information can and should be presented in text, and which is better expressed in visual form. As I mentioned earlier, this may depend on your target audience and preferences, as well as your plans for further development of the system depending on the decisions you have made and the aspect you want to express. You can choose the right type of model, keeping in mind that models are not just diagrams or other types of "drawings." A model can also be decision tables, with which you can express business rules and the resulting actions. Models are data dictionaries, by means of which the structure of information can be defined. The text itself, if created in a certain way, with a certain syntax, is also a form of model representing a certain aspect of the planned solution.

The use of models does not at all mean abandoning the traditional textual form of description. Models also contain textual elements, defining, for example, individual elements of the model, relationships between them, or simply additional supplementary information. It is also worth knowing that even if we decide to model, not everything has to be presented on the model—complex business rules, explanations, specific exceptions do not necessarily have to be modeled; they can be described using textual comments to the model.

Thus, on the one hand, we will ensure that communication is streamlined by providing a visual expression of information; on the other hand, this will not lead to overly complex models requiring excessive cognitive effort from the audience.

What if you would like to use modeling, but the customer or stakeholders do not feel the need to do so? Of course, you can attempt to explain the benefits of modeling and make the team aware of the rationale for communicating in this form. However, you may be met with refusal. Does this mean you should abandon modeling altogether? Not necessarily. Personally, I use modeling regardless of whether the customer has expressed a desire to have documentation in this form or not. For a simple reason: creating models allows me to understand the information and combine it accordingly. So it's part of my requirements and solution analysis, helping me develop a coherent and complete solution concept. I need models to understand how to design the logic, functionality, high-level architecture of the solution; how to design a new or streamlined process, how to organize the information. This is my way of arriving at a business analysis result. Whether the customer uses these results or not remains his decision. Either way, the models are an intermediate product of my work, allowing me to arrive at the final products.

Let's consider the use of modeling and its benefits on a simple example.

Variant I Specification in text form
REQ 01
The system allows the user to add a product to the shopping cart.
Detailed description:
The functionality is available from the product details. The user can add a product to the shopping cart by selecting "Add to Cart." The system adds the product to the shopping cart, increases the number of products in the shopping cart by 1, and displays a confirmation of the operation of adding to the cart (message "Product added to the cart").
After adding a product to the cart, the "Add to Cart" option is still active, but it is not possible to add the same product again. If a specific product is already in the shopping cart, the system will display the message "Product already added to cart."

Variant II Specification in the form of a model with text elements
REQ 01
The system allows a user to add a product to a shopping cart.
Functional scenario: Fig. 4.7
Screen design: Fig. 4.8

Essentially, the test form and models express the same thing—they differ only in the way the information is conveyed. For the audience, it remains a matter of judging which form of communication is more clear and unambiguous to them, which requires less cognitive effort to assimilate the information. In many cases, visual forms are a better way to describe complex flows and rules than forms based solely on natural language. As a rule, models are also easier to verify for completeness and unambiguity. Nothing prevents models from complementing textual specifications—but make sure that both forms of content delivery are consistent.

4.2.14 Don't Try to Be Perfect

THE SOLUTIONS WE CREATE ARE NOT MEANT TO BE PERFECT. THEY ARE MEANT TO BE GOOD ENOUGH TO DELIVER BUSINESS VALUE THAT MATTERS.

Sometimes we attempt to make the results of our analysis and requirements specifications perfect, to make our specifications anticipate all possible and impossible situations, exceptions, alternative paths. We want our specification and models to be as complete as

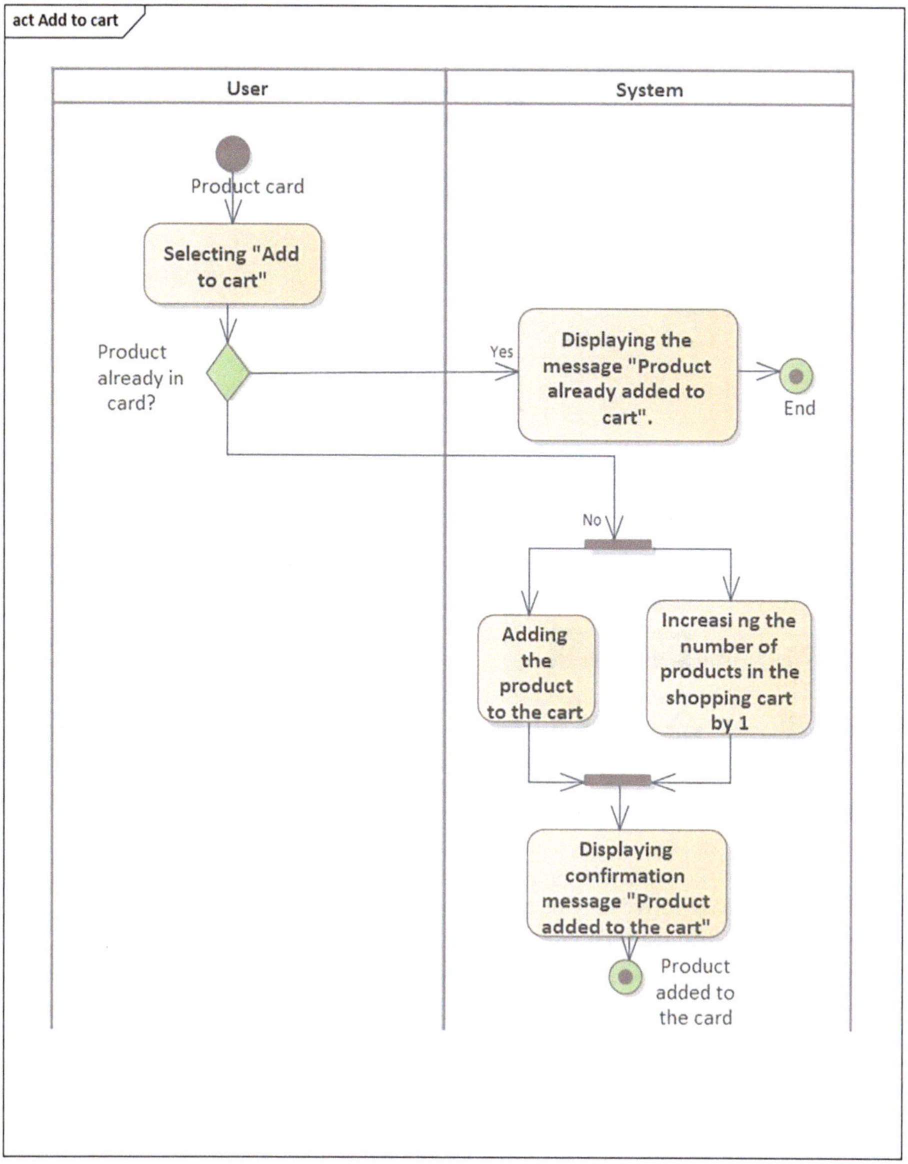

Fig. 4.7 Activity diagram with definition of responsibility

possible, a contender with as much detail and additional information as possible. Contrary to appearances, this is not necessarily a good practice. In requirements engineering, the principle of "the more, the better" rarely works. Instead, the principle of "good enough" works. Specifications and other work products are not meant to be perfect—they are meant to be a good enough basis for achieving specific objectives. As we have already

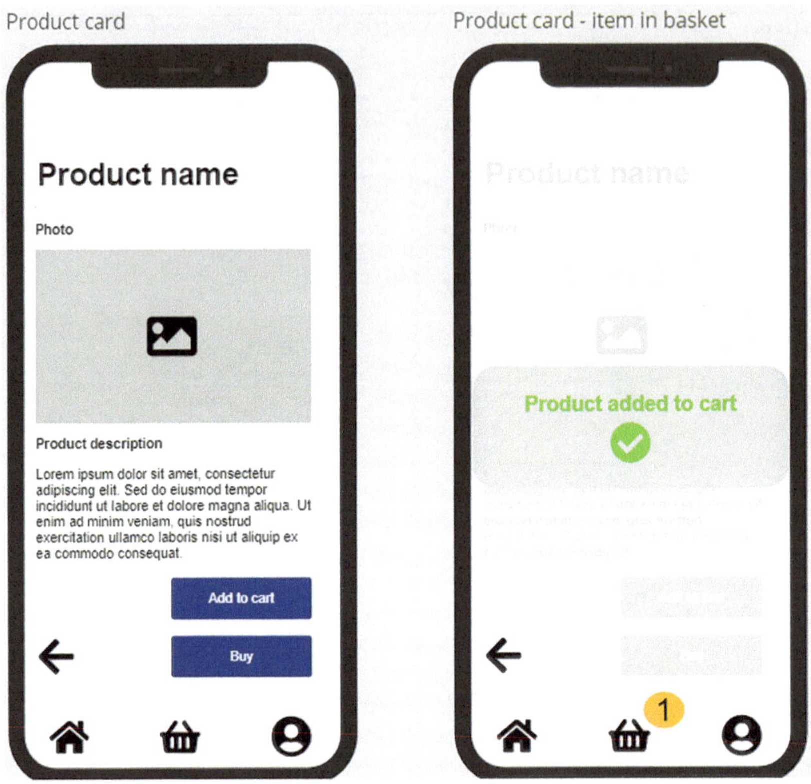

Fig. 4.8 Model representing the design of the application screen

mentioned, such an objective may be to provide design input for implementation, to create a contract between the customer and the contractor.

Attempts to develop a perfect document completely describing all possible situations and input and output conditions will, at most, end up in such a way that we use the time allotted for analysis activity exclusively for requirements analysis and specification, leaving ourselves no space for validation or requirements management practices, including change management.

In many cases, striving for perfection is a completely unnecessary endeavor because:

- Requirements and models are meant to describe what is relevant to the system being designed, what brings value, what generates risks that need to be addressed.
- Requirements, models, specifications, and other work products serve specific objectives—and it is these objectives that they are supposed to realize well enough.
- Work products are dedicated to specific audiences. These audiences do not necessarily need every possible piece of information that only comes our way. Before developing

any documents and models, it is worth taking the trouble to know the information expectations of the audience and to provide only the information that will be of value to them.

- Providing an excess of information causes difficulties in understanding and assimilating that information. Thus, we increase the cognitive effort required to understand the essence of the designed system, its behavior, or, on another note, our expectations of the manufacturing team.

Let me cite an example of the consequences of overly "perfect" requirements specification. In one organization where I worked, I was asked to perform an audit of analytical processes. The request stemmed from the project manager's concerns about the effectiveness of the analytical processes—in the project manager's interpretation, the business analyst was "not doing his job and not delivering to the team the results expected by the team." The audit was conducted on the basis of analysis of documentation (requirements, models developed by the analyst, work products created from these) and interviews with individual team members.

During these interviews and a review of the documentation, it appeared that:

- The requirements specification developed by the business analyst included functional scenarios with detailed descriptions of the appearance and behavior of each screen, input and output data specifications with database structure, and integration specifications between systems.
- The requirements specification, the project team felt, was not complete, as the data specification did not properly reflect the database structure, and the integration specification did not include all the details necessary for implementation.
- The requirements specification, the team feels, is an inadequate basis for the development of test cases because, despite extensive descriptions of functionality, all foreseeable contingencies are not specified.

Based on these results, one might conclude that the business analyst's performance did not meet the quality expectations of the team members. Nothing could be further from the truth.

In fact, the business analyst did his work, the work of the screen designer, the work of the system designer, and some of the work of the tester. He tried to do his job to the best of his ability; however, due to time constraints, frequent changes in requirements and design concepts, and a constantly growing production team, he was unable to maintain a satisfactory level of quality.

Once again, I will reiterate the fact that the business analyst tried to include everything in his specification—functional specification, data specification, integration specification, application design specification.

Why the decision to take this approach? The problem was that the project team expected the analyst to provide the full basics necessary for implementation and testing, including method and integration specifications, which are not exactly the business analyst's job. He was also expected to provide very specific test scenarios that would allow testing to be performed without special preparation.

What was the source of this problem? At the very beginning, the scope of the project was relatively small, with the project team consisting of an analyst, a part-time project manager, and three developers. At this stage, the business analyst successfully performed the tasks of many people and excelled in controlling both the progress and quality of the work. Over time, the project began to grow, the customer added more and more modules and functionalities for implementation, and new people joined the team. At one point, the team consisted of one analyst, two testers, and eight developers. There was a boiling frog situation—the business analyst, the project manager, and the rest of the team did not notice the moment when the scope of work exceeded the analyst's capabilities. The team continued to assume that the business analyst should provide all the necessary input, and project realities prevented the analyst from working to such an extent. As a result, the business analyst was still trying to provide an ideal, complete set of inputs for implementation and testing, and was often working overtime, with meager results.

The solution to this state of affairs was the decision for a kind of design reset. The result of my audit indicated potential problems and their consequences—in response to the audit report, we scheduled a project meeting to explain the current situation, the consequences, and how to solve the problem. The solution to the problem, on the other hand, was to develop a new way of working at a meeting where all team members were invited, and rules were worked out together:

- What work products are generated by the project?
- Who is responsible for creating and completing the work products?
- How is communication to take place between team members and team members and business stakeholders?
- How to implement reviews to eliminate the risk of omitting important information?
- What should the work products contain, so as not to duplicate information, not to provide information unnecessary to anyone, and not to provide information that should be in another work product?

It was important that the new work model was developed together as a team, which not only ensured that the new way of working was accepted and understood by all members of the team, but also provided team members with the necessary contact required to understand the reason for the change in the previous method of working. As a result, instead of "complaining" about the analyst's poor performance and setting unrealistic expectations, the team members divided the work among themselves, in accordance with their competencies and project limitations.

4.2.15 Appendix: Step-by-Step Requirement Specification

Step-by-step requirement specification instructions:

1. Identify the features of the function, and the property you want to describe.
2. Specify the result obtained by implementing the requirement.
3. Specify the initial conditions for the requirement.
4. Specify the input information.
5. Specify the output information and measurable results.
6. Specify constraints.
7. Identify special requirements/quality characteristics.

Example (Table 4.2):

Table 4.2 Example of the application of the procedure for the specification of a requirement-defining behavior

Step	Example result
1. Identify the features of the function, the property you want to describe	Booking a doctor's appointment
2. Specify the result obtained by implementing the requirement	Booked doctor's appointment for a specific day and time
3. Specify the initial conditions for the requirement.	The booking calendar contains at least one date available for booking
4. Specify the input information	• Patient data: name, surname, contact phone • Doctor's data: first name, last name, specialty • Date and time of the visit • Details of the clinic: name, address
5. Specify the output information, measurable results	• Booked appointment for a specific day and time with a selected doctor at a selected clinic • Confirmation of the appointment reservation in the form of an SMS • Marking the selected visit date and time as unavailable in the calendar of visits available for booking with the selected doctor
6. Specify constraints	• The user can book a maximum of three visits at a time • The user can book a maximum of five visits per month • It is not possible to book more than one visit on a given day if the intervals between visits are less than 1 h
7. Identify special requirements/quality characteristics	• The average time to book a visit from the moment of selecting an appointment in the calendar to the moment of receiving a confirmation of the visit booking does not exceed 60 s in 90% of cases for users of the new user type • The average time to book a visit from the moment of selecting an appointment in the calendar to the moment of receiving a booking confirmation does not exceed 30 s for a user of the regular service user type

Table 4.3 Example of the application of the procedure for the specification of a requirement defining a quality feature

Step	Example result
1. The scale in which the requirement will be expressed	(A) System response time in seconds (B) Number of browsers including browser version
2. The method of measuring the parameter	(A) The time from when a user launches a function until the system responds in a way that is visible to the user (B) Functional and performance tests covering key business scenarios executed on a specific browser version
3. The minimum acceptable level of quality for the expected result	(A) System response time to user action does not exceed 5 s (B) Test scenarios performed successfully on browsers: Chrome versions XX.YY and ZZ.II, Edge version XYZ
4. The desired level of quality for the expected result	(A) System response time to user action does not exceed 2 s in 95% of cases (B) Test scenarios performed successfully on browsers: Chrome versions XX.Y, X.IZ, and ZZ.II, Safari from version XYZ to the current version as of the start date of system integration, Edge version XYZ
5. Benchmark	(A) The average response time of the system to user response in similar systems is 3 s in 80% of cases (B) Test scenarios performed successfully on browsers: Chrome versions XX.Y, X.IZ, and ZZ.II, Safari version XYZ to the current version as of the date of the start of system integration, Opera version CC.DD to version XX. DX, Edge version XYZ

For descriptions of quality requirements, additionally specify:

1. The scale in which the requirement will be expressed
2. The method of measuring the parameter
3. The minimum acceptable level of quality for the expected result
4. The desired level of quality for the expected result
5. Benchmark

Example (Table 4.3):

4.3 Requirements Management

4.3.1 To Avoid Chaos: Structure the Information

Requirements, specifications, models, and other artifacts produced and used in the business analysis process are information. This information needs to be properly managed to achieve the expected results, such as the ability to prioritize, manage scope, track relationships, or effectively manage change. To properly manage information, it should be properly structured. What exactly does this mean?

Let's consider it with an example. The following excerpt is a description of the requirements specification:

> "The user is to be able to search for a product using specific criteria. To enable the search, at least three characters must be entered into the search field. As a result of the search, the system will display products according to the guided criteria. The results should be displayed in no more than 3 s. Otherwise, the system should communicate an error. The list of products will include: thumbnail photo, product name, price, vendor name."

The above excerpt is a description of the functionality of the system, expressed in the form of natural language, describing the user's interaction with the online store type system. Information presented in this way is practically impossible to manage. Starting from the very beginning, we do not know how many requirements there are in this excerpt, what is a requirement, and what is a detailing of a requirement. What is the importance of each requirement, the types of requirements? If our requirements specification looked like the above, then:

- We are not able to answer the question of what is the scope of the project and how many requirements we have, because in the example above, the requirements are not atomic.
- We are not able to compare requirements in terms of urgency, business value, or other criteria because we do not have requirement attributes such as priority.
- We are not able to tell at what stage of analysis, design, or manufacturing a requirement is, because we lack a status attribute.
- We can't tell which requirement is being tested and how it is being tested, because since requirements are not atomic, it will be very difficult to define and maintain proper tracking of the relationship between requirements and test cases.

Consequently, we will not be able to answer the questions:

- How many requirements are currently in analysis, in implementation, in testing?
- What is the test coverage of the requirements?
- How are the requirements dependent on each other, and which requirement affects which?

Thus, we cannot properly manage the scope or the evolution of requirements, or monitor the progress of the work.

Requirements written in such a way cannot be managed. This is because there is a lack of means by which we can properly classify and organize information related to requirements.

How can this situation be remedied?

First: Ensure that requirements are atomic, one at a time. A basic principle in requirements engineering is that each requirement is to be described one at a time. In the example above, the given piece of text would need to be broken down into individual requirements:

Requirement #1: Search for a product using criteria.
Requirement #2: Display the search results.

Second: Separate the essence of the requirement from the details. In its basic form, a requirement defines the following elements: subject, result, object on which the action takes place. The details that talk about how the result is achieved, the specifics of the subject or object, are not necessarily in the essence of the requirement itself.

The rest of the information, such as the need to write at least three characters in the search field or the method of displaying the results list, is not the essence of the requirement itself, but the detail—so we can include it in the acceptance criteria when describing the requirement in detail.

Thus, for example, requirement #1 could be specified as follows:

Title: Product search using criteria
Acceptance criterion: To search for a product, the user must enter at least three characters in the search field. Otherwise, the search function cannot be run. Only numbers and letters can be entered in the search field; special characters are not allowed.

Third: Classify the requirement with attributes. Such attributes can be the priority, type of requirement, source, or other information that you will need to manage the requirement in a given project. This will not only define the requirement itself, but also provide additional information to understand the requirement in context.

Priority: High
Source: End user
Type of requirement: Functionality
Related requirements: Voice search

This is how we can transform a simple textual specification into a structured set of information that provides the minimum data necessary for basic requirements management.

Remember that without proper information structure, you don't know where to look for certain information, you don't know how to interpret information, you don't know what the connections between information are. Without information structure, it may also be that the information exists, but you can't find it, that is, it's as if it doesn't exist.

4.3.2 Define the Requirements Life Cycle

Every object has a life cycle. Requirements also. Their life cycle does not end with acceptance and handover for implementation.

An important part of requirements management is understanding their life cycle. The concept of life cycle is nothing new—it is nothing more than a defined sequence of stages or phases that a specific object (project, process, organism) goes through, starting from inception or initiation, until termination, usually through successive stages such as development, maturity, and sometimes fading or termination.

There is a rather serious misunderstanding of this issue—many people confuse life cycle management with requirements management, i.e., repository creation, attribution, requirements acceptance. However, the difference between these concepts is quite significant. The life cycle allows us to monitor at what stage of development a particular requirement is, which is an elementary part of information management. For example, a requirement that has just been acquired can be marked with the status "new." The same requirement taken for detailed analysis may take the status "in analysis." This way we know at what stage of evolution the requirement is. We can therefore track the progress of the work and control the progress of the analysis. We also have baseline information for possible escalation, for example, if a particular requirement has been in the "in analysis" status for too long (too long compared to the defined schedule of activities).

It is worth noting that the concept of the requirements life cycle in a business analysis environment is sometimes misunderstood. I will refer here to the well-known source *BABOK® Guide* and the interpretation of its provisions. Analyzing this source, one gets the impression that the requirements life cycle boils down to relationship tracking, keeping requirements current, prioritization, change assessment, and acceptance. These issues are the subject of the "requirements life cycle management" knowledge area. However, this is not the full requirements life cycle. Why? Because the life cycle generally describes all the stages an object can go through, from its inception to its terminal state, or contractual death.

As defined in the *BABOK® Guide* itself, a life cycle is a series of changes that an object undergoes from beginning to end. Completion—let's pay attention to that. Analyzing the *BABOK® Guide*, it can be deduced that the requirements life cycle boils down to states: proposed, accepted, verified, postponed, cancelled, or implemented (Knowledge Area:

Business Analysis Planning and Monitoring, Task: 3.4 Plan Business Analysis Information Management). It is worth noting that this is neither a complete list of possible states nor a complete life cycle, since the terminal state is missing. The "implemented" state does not necessarily mean the end of the life of the requirements, since even implemented requirements can undergo changes, and they can also be withdrawn from a running system if, for example, they expire. Even if the requirements are not subject to change, at some point (sometimes after a very long time) they will cease to be valid and will be archived, because the life cycle of the product itself will come to an end—the product will be retired, and with it the requirements that formed its basis (Fig. 4.9). Of course, from the perspective of a specific product development project, we rarely see terminal states. These states usually occur when a product containing certain implemented requirements reaches its "death" state.

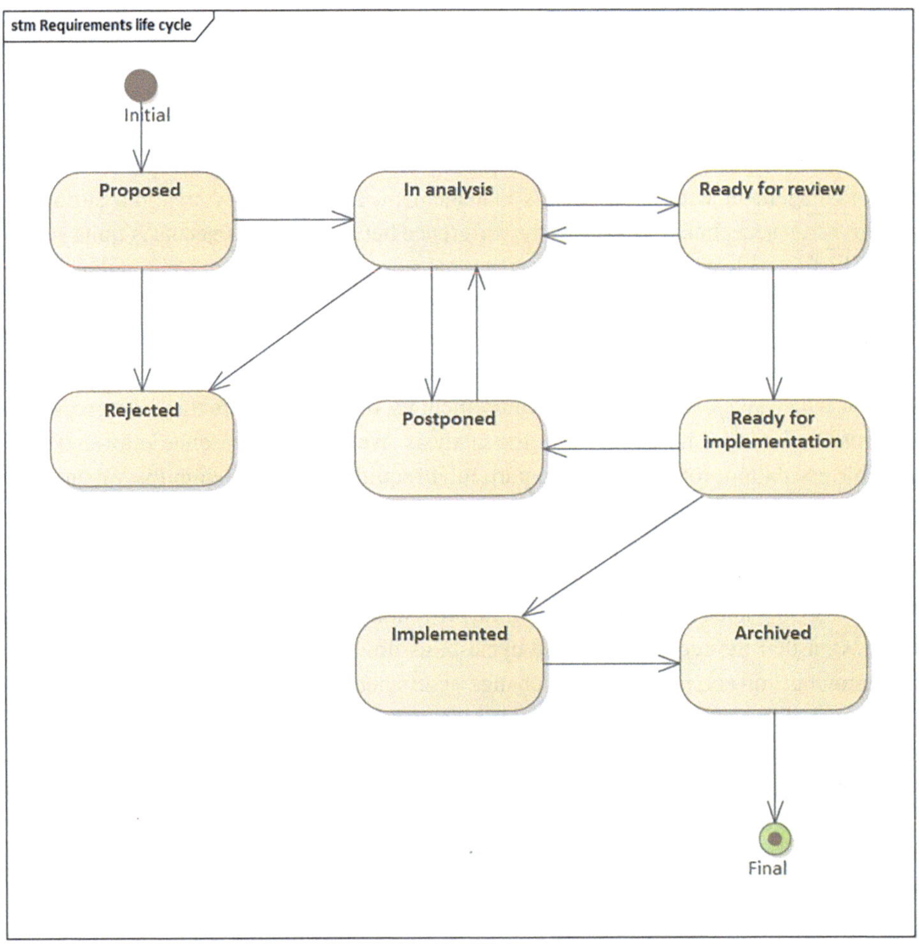

Fig. 4.9 Example of a requirement life cycle model

A reasonable complement to the BABOK® *Guide* may be the approach presented by IREB® (IREB 2024). IREB®, in addition to paying attention to the end states of requirements, points to a very important element of life cycle management, namely version control. Requirements evolve, change, move from one stage to another. This usually involves changes: changes in attributes or changes in content. The mechanism to monitor these changes is precisely version control.

Why is knowledge of the full life cycle so important? Because in many cases we focus on acquiring, documenting, and implementing requirements. In other words, we focus on the initial area of the life cycle. We often overlook what happens to the requirements after they are implemented in the system and while it is running in production. We focus on creating the solution, but unfortunately we very often neglect maintenance and development issues.

The result can be that from the point of view of the implementation of a manufacturing project, the requirements seem to be adequately specified and managed with sufficient mechanisms. For example, in a project, we can handle the requirements with a backlog and simple user stories—from the point of view of the needs of the project, this approach may be sufficient for the production and implementation of the system. It is sufficient for understanding the scope of work, and provides a sufficient basis for communication within the team. However, from a product life cycle perspective, it can generate significant negative consequences.

Why? Because this approach to requirements documentation and the creation of a system information model may be effective from a project implementation perspective, but not necessarily for maintaining an already implemented system. For example, if the only source of requirements is the backlog, then we will most likely lack information on tracking the links between requirements. This means that any changes to already implemented requirements may be difficult to implement. We won't have the ability to analyze the impact of changes, which results in the risk of destabilizing the system. We also can't assume that the maintenance team has knowledge of the system architecture and interrelationships, because usually the maintenance team is not the same people who took part in producing the system. And even if we were to assume that it is the same team, it is difficult to expect that the people who have knowledge of the system's construction today will have the same reliable and complete knowledge some time from now when maintenance work is needed.

Thinking in a way that is focused on the current project, its needs, its current objectives, is certainly important. But not sufficient. Thinking ahead, with a long-term time horizon, including a plan for the entire requirements life cycle, is crucial. Thinking in terms of future development. Understanding and recognizing that the mere production of a system is only the beginning of its life cycle. The operation of a system in production tends to be much longer than the manufacturing project. Making decisions that are convenient from the point of view of the manufacturing project, but will have negative consequences for the ability to efficiently maintain and develop the system, is therefore at least responsible.

However, this kind of thinking, forward-looking and oriented toward facilitating work in the future, is only possible if we understand the essence of the entire life cycle (both of individual requirements and of the entire product). The life cycle is all stages of existence, including the terminal state, the conventional "death" of a requirement or system. This should be our focus even if our task is only to design and implement the system, not to maintain it afterwards. It may seem that maintenance is not our concern—the contract with the customer is only about producing the solution. But sooner or later it will become our customer's concern. By definition, our role is to deliver value—value understood not only as the product and the resulting benefits to stakeholders and the business. Value also includes other work products, enabling further efficient development of the system, and the processes and mechanisms developed.

4.3.3 To Manage Scope and Coverage: Maintain Traceability

Tracing is one of the key practices that provide the ability to manage the evolution of requirements, manage scope, or analyze the impact of changes. Yet, in many projects and organizations, traceability is not maintained. There are many reasons for this, among which are the following:

- We don't have time to do linkages.
- We have no need to track linkages between requirements and other artifacts.
- The customer does not require traceability.
- Maintaining traceability causes us additional work, and there is no benefit from it.
- Our requirements cannot be tracked because they are not atomic.

Arguments for not maintaining traceability can usually be found in abundance, and some of them may even be valid. However, by consciously managing the practice of traceability, we accept the following consequences:

- It will be difficult for us to manage the scope of the solution because we don't know which system requirements are derived from which higher-level requirements. We also don't know which higher-order requirements have been properly addressed at the system level and which have not.
- We don't know what the test coverage of requirements is, because there is no way to simply link individual test cases to requirements. Consequently, to the question of "What is the coverage of requirements, and what percentage of requirements are currently covered by test?" we are unable to provide specific information. At most we can guess.
- We cannot reliably predict the impact of requirements changes on other artifacts, such as design, source code, or testing. When we make a change, we rely on our hatching,

intuition, and competence, estimating the impact of the change made on the basis of discretion rather than concrete data. As a further consequence, it very often happens that by introducing a relatively small change, we destabilize a significant part of the system.
- We are unable to demonstrate compliance with requirements. We are unable to easily trace from the requirement, through the design to the source code level. We are not able to show how the requirements are implemented, how they are covered by design elements, such as screens. We are not able to show how individual requirements implement business needs and other high-level artifacts, because we lack the links between the requirements and the business layer.

These can be the consequences of failing to keep traceability. Consequences resulting essentially from the failure to apply one of the basic practices in requirements management, enabling—let me remind you—management with the scope and evolution of requirements. And yet, defining traceability and maintaining it requires no special effort, as long as it is planned in the right way.

Without traceability, you don't know which requirement covers which business need, you don't know how the system design covers those requirements, you don't know which requirements were tested and what the test results were. Without traceability, you don't know the impact of changes submitted to one artifact on other artifacts in the system. Without traceability, you have no control over the information.

What can be done to optimally define traceability?

- *Atomicity of artifacts*. One of the factors that is a prerequisite for enabling traceability is ensuring that requirements and other artifacts are atomic (single). Without proper structuring of information, traceability is virtually impossible.
- *Traceability structure of artifacts*. In most projects, there is no need to define tracking relationships between all work products. For example, it may be sufficient to trace business requirements to system requirements, system requirements to test cases. Traceability requirements may be driven by the customer contract, project specifics, or simply requirements for how the product should be implemented. Note that even if the customer does not require traceability, it can significantly help the manufacturing team to track the progress of the work.
- *How to define traceability*. Defining traceability is, in the simplest terms, creating relationships between artifacts. This can be done, for example, by linking artifacts between each other using the functionality provided by the tools. Tracing can also be defined using attributes. For example, a system requirement specification may contain an attribute "Business requirement ID," which stores information about the requirement that is the source of the system requirement.

- *Responsibility*. Traceability in most cases[3] will not happen on its own. It needs to be determined who is responsible for defining and maintaining traceability. Linking requirements to each other may be the responsibility of the business analyst. Linking test cases to requirements, on the other hand, may be the tester's responsibility. Note that not everything must and should be done by the business analyst—this realization can eliminate one of the typical arguments against defining traceability, namely the "I don't have time for that" argument arising from the fact that we happen to take on too many tasks, some of which are not at all crucial to the success of the project, while some can be successfully delegated to other team members.
- *Tracking as part of the process*. Let's implement the practice of defining links as a work routine. In other words, every time we develop a system requirement based on a higher-level requirement, let's remember to create a trace. Let's not postpone this task, and let's not follow the practice of first developing the entire set of requirements, and only after that task is completed plan to tackle defining traceability. Such a practice will lead to a situation where even if we find the time to complete the traceability, it will very often be incomplete, because with the circulation of time we forget some aspects, which makes it difficult to reproduce our way of working. Therefore, in my opinion, the best way to work is to perform the necessary practices on an ongoing basis. At some point, this will become a work routine to the point that we won't even have to think and remember to define the tracking, because it will become a habit.

Let's consider an example. Figure 4.10 depicts a simplified, general model expressing the stages of activity execution and the main artifacts (labeled <<information>>). For requirements elicitation activities, additional sources of requirements, such as stakeholders and documentation, are also marked.

Work products are the result of specific activities. There are specific links between them; for example, the requirements elicited in the requirements elicitation process should be related to the business need they address. The elements that make up the solution concept should be linked to specific requirements. An example of how to implement the traceability between artifacts is shown in Fig. 4.11. This figure also includes information on responsibility—which role is responsible for defining the traceability between artifacts.

The above visualizations show what artifacts will be created in a given project and how they are related to each other. They also include information on who is responsible for developing specific artifacts and defining traceability.

To ensure that the creation of traceability is a work standard, it would still be necessary to define at what point in the process a specific role should define the linkage between work products. Thus, for example, a business analyst, after having completed

[3] It is possible to automatically create tracking relationships between artifacts. Such capabilities are provided by some CASE tools—but they do not provide full coverage of artifacts. With current technological capabilities, much of the tracking relationships must be defined manually.

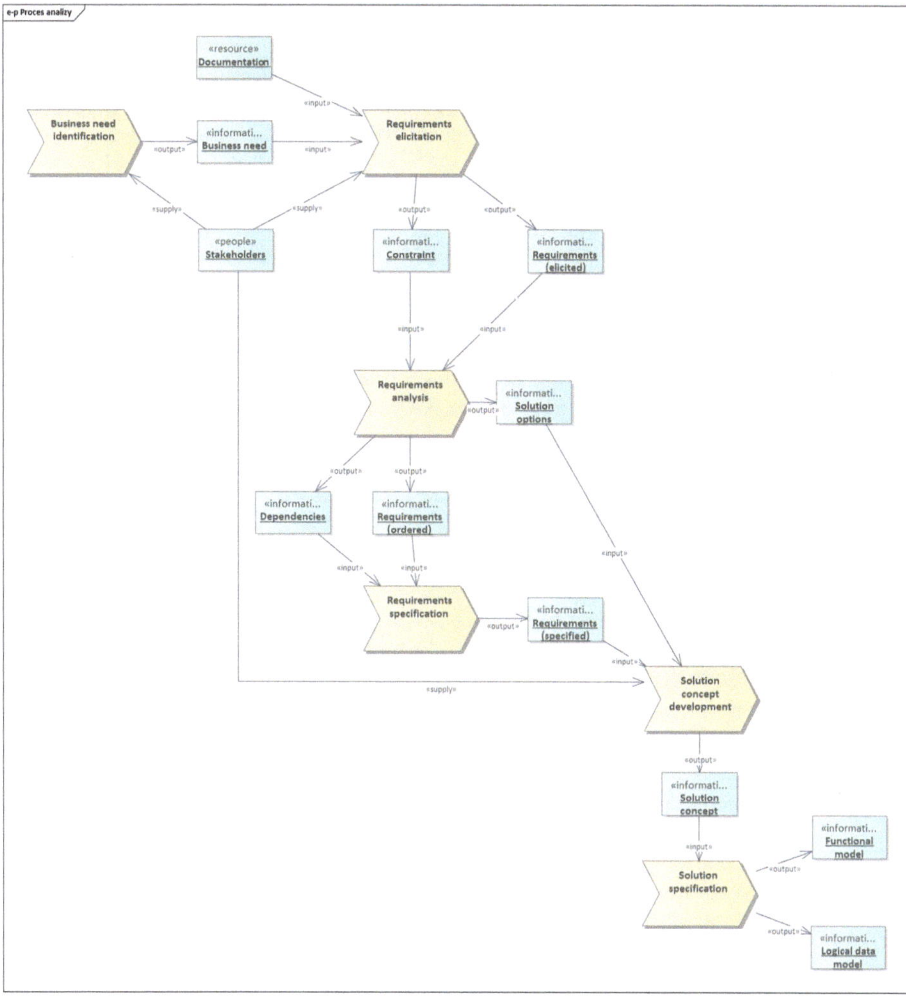

Fig. 4.10 Simplified model of main analysis activities and products of analysis work

requirements elicitation for a specific scope, should immediately link the requirements to the relevant business need. A tester, after developing test scenarios, should immediately relate the scenarios to the right requirements that the scenarios address.

- *Checking the completeness of the traceability.* It may happen that we omit linking between some elements for various reasons. Quality control mechanisms, such as reviews, and verification of the requirements traceability matrix, should catch these omissions (Fig. 4.12). Just as defining traceability should be part of the process, quality control practices should become a process routine.

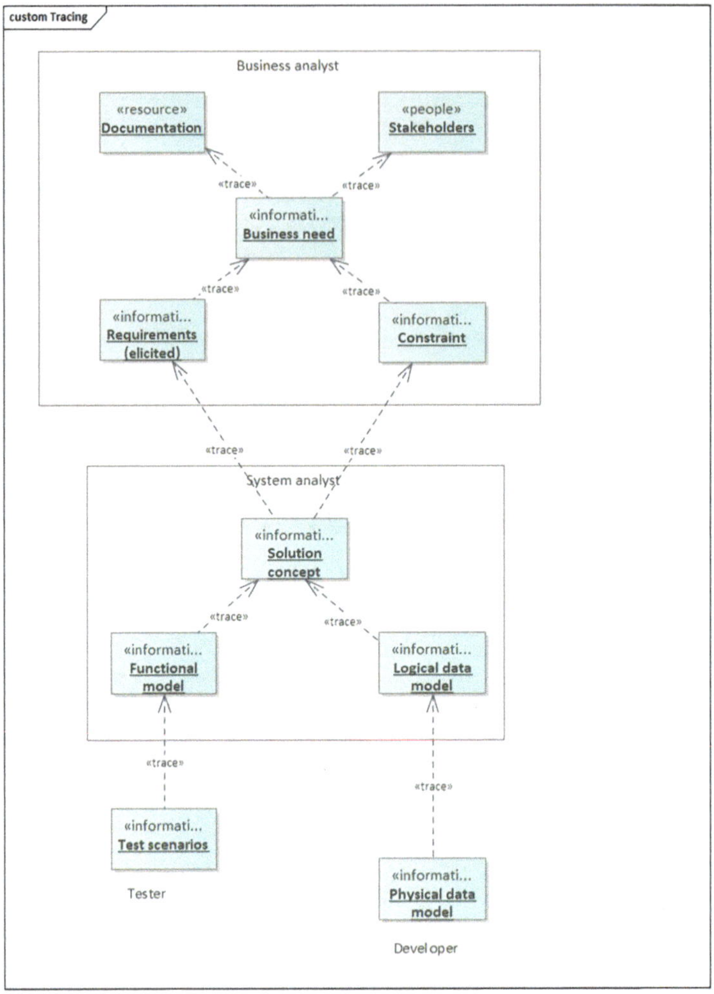

Fig. 4.11 Example structure for the implementation of traceability between artifacts

The above set of rules is not particularly complicated and does not require special effort to implement. In my opinion, even if we implement traceability with minimal scope, for example, at the level of requirements and testing, in most cases we will still achieve quite significant benefits. So it's worth a try—if only to see for yourself the convenience of systematic information management.

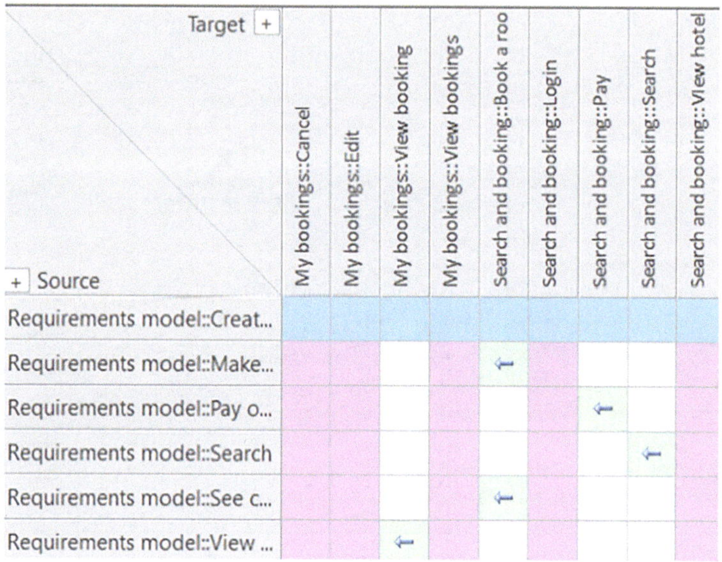

Fig. 4.12 Example of a traceability matrix indicating gaps in coverage of requirements (rows) by use cases (columns)

4.3.4 Develop a Structure for Traceability

The traceability structure allows you to determine what artifacts are being developed as part of an initiative and the relationships between them. This supports the planning of analysis activities—because it allows you to understand the time dependencies between the activities of developing individual artifacts.

In the previous section, I mentioned that it is important to establish a structure for traceability. This is quite logical—in order to maintain traceability, it must first be defined. The tracking structure allows us to define what artifacts should be linked to other artifacts. We can use the artifact structure developed as part of the project's analysis activity planning for this purpose.

The structure for traceability is determined on a project-by-project or initiative basis, as each project or initiative has different process requirements, different stakeholder characteristics, and different information expectations. Different industry standards and regulations may also apply.

Thus, for example, automotive projects implemented under the Automotive Spice standard require mandatory tracking between:

- stakeholder requirements
- system requirements
- software requirements

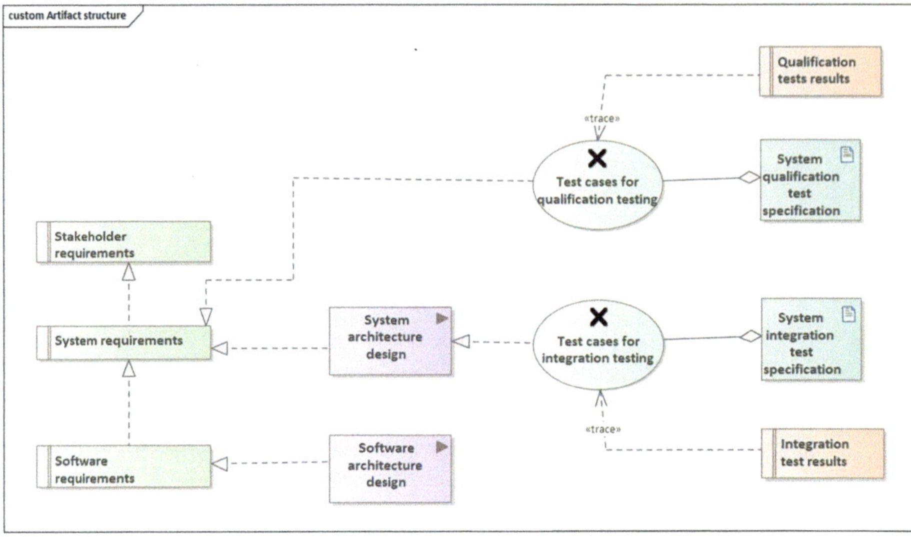

Fig. 4.13 Excerpt from structure for traceability—Automotive Spice

In addition, it is necessary to ensure traceability between requirements and relevant test cases to verify the fulfillment of requirements at each level. For projects implemented in accordance with Automotive Spice guidelines, traceability is not a matter of choice, but an obligation under the provisions of the standard.

The result of implementing the standard in a project can be seen in an example of a traceability structure (excerpt), shown in Fig. 4.13.

Similarly, if an organization would like to ensure compliance with the *BABOK® Guide* and IREB® CPRE in terms of requirements classification, this would mean establishing the following requirements classification:

- Business requirements
- Stakeholder requirements
- Solution (system) requirements broken down into functional requirements and quality requirements
- Transition requirements
- Domain requirements
- Constraints

Between all these types of artifacts there must be defined relationships. An example of a visual representation of a fragment of a tracking structure is shown in Fig. 4.14.

Developing a structure for traceability will allow us not only to plan the relationships between individual artifacts, but also to indicate what artifacts will be created in the project in general. This is, of course, part of planning the approach to analysis work—establishing the expected results of the work and the links between them. It is worth noting that

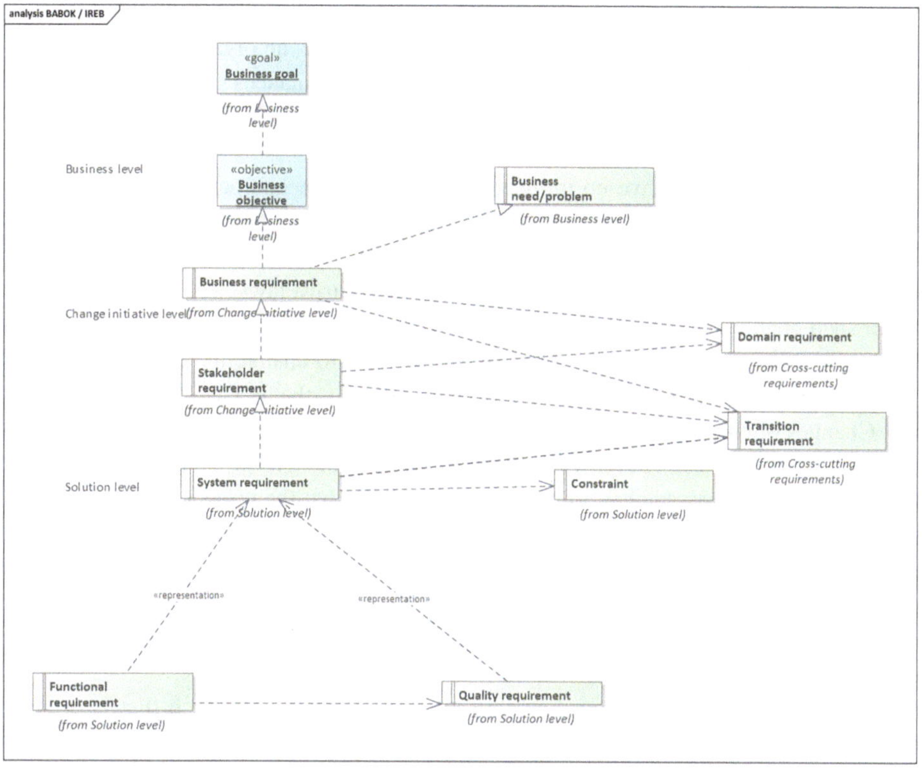

Fig. 4.14 Excerpt from the structure for traceability—based on the requirements classification according to the *BABOK® Guide* and IREB® CPRE

in many projects there is no need to ensure full traceability. When I say full traceability, I mean traceability from business objectives, through business requirements, down to the level of artifacts created as part of solution development. The extent of traceability is one of the factors that should be discussed with stakeholders at the planning stage of analysis activities.

4.3.5 Changes, Changes...

THE ONLY CONSTANT THING IN LIFE IS CHANGE.
HERAKLIT

Changes in scope are a fairly natural turn of events. This even constitutes one of the principles of requirements engineering according to the IREB® organization and their IREB® CPRE certification programs (IREB 2024).

Changes in requirements can and do happen sooner or later. For a very simple reason—the source of requirements is the context of a given system, solution. The context is constantly changing, which as an organization we have no control over. We only have control over how we respond to these changes. For example, an organization has no control over whether there will be changes in regulations or ordinances specific to a particular business area, but it does have control over how to incorporate those ordinances into its day-to-day business operations.

Likewise, we usually have no influence on what kind of competition emerges in the market. A scenario in which we communicate with competitors and set mutually acceptable rules for market sharing is an unlikely scenario. What would be likely instead would be that such an action could qualify as a violation of antitrust laws.

All such changes in the organization's environment, when analyzed more specifically in the context of a given project, can result in the need to change the existing course of action. The result is often changes in requirements, that is, the de facto scope of the solution. Changes often cause quite negative reactions from the project team, who are anxious to implement the project smoothly and deliver results as soon as possible. However, from a business perspective, changes are necessary to ensure that the project outcome actually delivers business value with respect to the changing business need. It would be difficult to justify continuing a project with the objective of delivering a specific solution, at a time when we know that this solution was proposed on the basis of assumptions that are no longer valid. Continuing the project unchanged would at most result in the delivery of a result that was already outdated at the time of its creation.

Therefore, it is worth shifting your thinking a bit from an approach that is oriented toward achieving predetermined objectives, to a mindset whereby we are able to deliver a business result in a changing environment. The first rather difficult step will be to accept that changes can, and will, occur. As a result, these changes, if they do occur, will not cause us negative emotions, frustrations, and defensive reflexes. We won't perceive them as stemming from bad intentions on the part of stakeholders, in particular from inconsistent decision-making. The next step, which is not at all easier, will be to try to estimate what coefficient of variation we can face in the context of a specific project. There are projects implemented in environments that are relatively stable—requirements are set, accepted, the company is not subject to particular market turbulence, there are no internal or external factors that would cause a high risk of change during the project. On the other hand, there are projects where almost at the very beginning of the initiative, we know that what is true today may be outdated in a month. These types of projects are planned in slightly different ways. Projects where we anticipate a relatively high coefficient of variability generally follow the tenets of agile methods, whereby we are able to adapt to change in a certain way.

For example, since we know that there is a risk that the requirements will change, we stop the practice of describing the requirements in great detail in the early stages of the project. We document requirements quite generally, just to have information about what features should be implemented in the planned solution, what scope is defined at a given point in time. The details of the requirements, information on how to implement them, are established when it is decided that the requirements will be implemented in the near future.

When discussing the topic of change, it is worth noting that we very often focus on changes that relate to the project implementation stage. And yet, the life cycle of an entire business need is not only the stage of realization of a solution for that business need—it is also the operation in production, maintenance, and further development. When setting assumptions for the planned solution, it is worth noting what can change at the implementation stage of that solution, and what needs to change in the second phase of time. In this way, we are able to make the right decisions about the architecture of the solution, the business logic, and even decisions about business issues, such as the contract with the solution provider versus maintenance and further development issues, at the early stages of designing the solution. For example, if an organization outsources the development of a solution to a single contractor, and the responsibility for maintaining that solution is not yet established, this can have a significant impact on decisions about how to implement the project and the results of the work (in particular, the documentation of the solution). If there are changes to the requirements during the solution phase, these changes should be properly incorporated into the system documentation, so that the team maintaining the solution—whatever company will be responsible for it—will be able to efficiently take over the work of the contractor's team, focus on maintaining and developing the solution, and not on reproducing information about the functioning and architecture of the solution.

4.3.6 Handling the Change: Don't Rush to Take Action

Every change carries the risk of destabilizing the system. Every change poses a threat to the established business change strategy. Therefore, the decision to implement change is not made hastily, suggesting only the opinions of selected stakeholders. The decision to implement a change should be largely determined by the results of the change impact analysis.

The first reaction to a change requested by a customer may be to accept the change for service. This is not surprising—it is the customer's wish, which in the first instinct we want to implement. If his wish is to make a change, we make the change. However, it is advisable not to rush into decisions and concrete actions, and to start by assessing the validity of the change.

It happens that stakeholders come up with changes, inspired by the solutions of the competition, enthralled by the technology and its possibilities, or simply unreflectively—at some point they come to the conclusion that since we are building a solution, it might as well still be this and that in this solution. There is nothing wrong with such a course of action in principle—stakeholders can theoretically put forward their ideas, whatever they are. However, the role of the person in the position of business analyst is to evaluate these ideas, especially their business value, and help decide whether we definitely need to make certain changes.

An excellent help here can be to refer to the original business need, the business case, which explained what the assumptions were for implementing a particular initiative. If the proposed change, after initial analysis, does not seem to bring any real business value to the designed solution, the question becomes: For what reason would we implement it? Again, we can use questions here to assess the validity of the requirements:

- Who or what needs the change?
- Who will use it, and how often?
- What business problem does the change solve?

If the answers to the above questions do not clearly explain the validity of the change, I would suggest discussing the change proposal with the submitting stakeholder, voicing our concerns. Not infrequently, in the course of such a discussion, the author himself will already come to the conclusion that his change is basically unnecessary; it is what we call a "water feature" in software production.

The initial assessment of a change is important because many organizations and projects have a fairly formal change management process in place. According to this process, a submitted change goes to the analysis stage, in which we estimate the impact of the change on processes, systems, and specific system components, estimate the implementation of the change and related activities, and plan this implementation. Such analysis requires considerable effort. Before we undertake to devote such an amount of time and resources to analyzing a change request, let's make sure that this change request is legitimate.

Assessing the validity of a change request can, of course, be accomplished through a conversation between the business analyst and the stakeholder making the change request. However, this is a rather inefficient solution. It requires involvement on both sides. One can make the task easier and modify the work procedures as follows:

The stakeholder reporting the change must fill out a kind of change form. In this form it is necessary to provide:

- The rationale for the change
- The scope of the areas affected by the change
- Priority of the change
- A description of the current solution or process, the one we want to change
- A description of the target state (i.e., a proper description of the change)

With this exercise, it very often turns out that the stakeholder is not able to provide the required information, because he simply does not have it. He is unable to explain how the process currently works, but demands a change. It is quite risky to accept such a request for change, because on the basis of the information provided, we are unable to assess whether the change is desirable at all.... Because if we don't know how the process works at the moment, on what basis do we want to change it?

Analogously with the rationale for change, if a stakeholder is unable to rationally and measurably explain why he wants to make a change to the system at the process, it may mean that either he himself does not understand the motivation for the change he is requesting, i.e., de facto he does not know what effect he wants to achieve, or that the change request is formulated inadequately. Introducing a simple template can provide a kind of qualitative gateway to reject at the outset a change proposal that is not well thought out, does not generate value, or—from a formal point of view—is not completely formulated and is not good starting information for further analysis.

4.4 Requirements Quality Assurance

> IF THE REQUIREMENTS ARE UNCLEAR OR WRONG, WE WILL SPEND TIME DOING THE WRONG THINGS, WASTING TIME AND MONEY. THIS IS CONTRARY TO THE OBJECTIVE OF THE PROJECT.
> *NIELS MALOTAUX, PROJECT COACH, N R MALOTAUX, CONSULTANCY*

4.4.1 Requirements Shall Be Tested

Testing is usually associated with quality control of a finished or intermediate product in the context of software development. We mainly equate testing with the process of checking that the software works according to requirements. Quite a few people involved in software production are aware that there are different types and levels of testing. There are also different testing techniques, among which, to quote the ISTQB certification program, we can distinguish between static and dynamic techniques (ISTQB® 2023). Static techniques involve checking source code, requirements documents, and models, specifications. The object of testing here is not the application or the running system, but the work products that result from the software development process.

What does this have to do with the requirements of their quality?

Testing is quality control. Quality control can apply to any work product, as well as requirements. Given the importance of requirements quality to the success of an initiative, quality control should address the requirements and artifacts underlying the development of a solution first and foremost.

Using static testing techniques, requirements, models, designs, and specifications can be tested. Unfortunately, quite often business analysts lack awareness that requirements can and should be tested. We conclude that:

- At such an early stage, when requirements are being developed, there is nothing to test yet. As a result, any testing activity is out of the question.
- Requirements are not tested. Lack of knowledge often causes us to assume that testing applies only to end products, not to specification documents or plans.
- There is nothing to test in requirements. After all, requirements are information—information is not tested, it just is. Nothing could be further from the truth. Both the information itself and its structure contained in requirements and specifications may simply

be wrong, incomplete, contradictory compared to other requirements. Without testing, these errors will not be caught and will move on to the next stage in the design and production of the solution.

It is a myth that requirements do not have errors. They do, and, as a rule, quite a few. In turn, faults in the requirements result in faults in the software, or any other type of solution. Industry statistics have shown for years that some of the defects in software are not implementation errors (improperly developed code), but errors resulting from problems with requirements. What conclusions can be drawn from this? Such that in order to minimize the number of defects detected in running software, it makes sense to focus on testing, not software, but requirements. By doing so, we prevent defects from occurring—we prevent the solution from being defective, because we make sure that the basis for designing and producing the solution is of good quality.

How can requirements be tested? Probably the most popular methods of testing requirements are review techniques and evaluation of meeting quality criteria. If the requirements are modeled in the form of a model, and the model is based on a standardized syntax (such as the UML), testing the model can be supported by tools. Professional CASE tools make it possible to validate the syntax of the model, and thus we can make sure that the model is built according to the rules of a given notation or modeling language.

Of course, syntactic correctness does not ensure that the model is substantively correct and correctly reflects reality—this can be checked using review techniques—but it does ensure that minimum quality criteria are met.

An analogous approach can be applied to testing requirements documented in natural language form. If we assume that our requirements documentation is based on some defined syntax, we can use algorithms to check whether the requirements actually implement this syntax.

An example of such syntax could be the adoption of a requirements description standard:

The system enables [user role] to perform [action] on [object].

Testing the requirements specification would check that all requirements are written according to this syntax, that is, that the specification contains information about the action, the objects on which the action is performed, and who, which user role, is able to perform the action.

A slightly more sophisticated quality testing mechanism could be based not only on the syntax of a single expression, but also on the syntax of the entire requirements specification. Such a mechanism could check whether each requirement has a completed set of attributes according to the defined requirements specification template. Attempts are being made (successfully) to train machine learning algorithms to control the quality of requirements and improve the requirements specification according to the objectives defined.

These attempts may not yet be perfect, but it is hoped that with time and the level of sophistication and accuracy of the learning algorithms, the results will become more and more satisfactory.

Even without the use of advanced artificial intelligence mechanisms and professional CASE tools, we are able to test requirements at a minimal level:

- Verify that the requirements documentation is developed according to a specific template.
- Verify that the content of the requirement conforms to the specified quality criteria.
- Verify that the requirements are understood by the production team and stakeholders.
- Check that the requirements specification does not contain duplicate information, gaps, contradictions, and omissions.

Possible planning of requirements testing activities should start with an understanding of what requirements quality is and how it can be tested. This is interesting because relatively rarely do we ask ourselves "What is a good requirement?" Unfortunately, falling into a project routine, we thus focus on completing specific tasks without reflecting on how to do these tasks best. Let's try to get away from this pattern and at the very beginning of the analysis work, even before developing the requirements, ask ourselves: What should the requirements be so that we can say that they are of good quality?

4.4.2 How to Define the Quality of Requirements?

> QUALITY IS THE DEGREE TO WHICH A SET OF INHERENT CHARACTERISTICS OF AN OBJECT FULFILS REQUIREMENTS.
>
> ISO 9000:2015

> QUALITY IS A CERTAIN DEGREE OF EXCELLENCE.
>
> *PLATON*

> QUALITY IS COMPLIANCE WITH REQUIREMENTS.
>
> *PHILIP CROSBY*

There are a number of different definitions of quality, defining different aspects—from product quality to process quality to quality of life. My perception of the concept is quite strongly related to business value—quality is the usable business value delivered to the recipient of an entity, which can be a product, service, or process. We can also talk about the quality of requirements. The quality of requirements can most simply be defined as a certain level of goodness of requirements, that is, how requirements serve their recipients and enable them to meet their objectives. The objectives of requirements can be to provide information for proper implementation and testing, to clarify the contract between the principal and the contractor, or to provide information that specifies what properties and features should be provided in the product so that it complies with the specified standards and guidelines.

Good-quality requirements are requirements whose content makes it possible to meet such objectives. Let's start with the simplest objective, namely to provide output information for the manufacturing team. For a requirement to be considered a good-quality requirement, its content should be sufficient for proper design, implementation, and testing. What does this mean in practice? It can mean a number of different things depending on the project and the specifics of the manufacturing team. For some teams, a very high-level requirements statement is sufficient, because they know the business context and can "predict" how the solution should behave. In other projects, on the other hand, it is necessary to provide very precise requirements, if only because of formal or contractual issues. Thus, the quality of requirements defines their objective and their usefulness in achieving that objective.

To be considered "good," requirements should first and foremost be understandable and precise. This is especially important for the objective of establishing a kind of contract between the ordering party and the supplier—an imprecise contract is a ready recipe for spectacular failure. Imagine the following example. A customer orders a system to enable electronic documentation workflow. Among the various requirements, we can highlight the following: "The system response time should not exceed two seconds." At first glance, this requirement is understandable; the customer's expectation is to provide a certain system response time. However, upon closer examination, we realize that the content of the requirement in no way explains what the system is supposed to respond to. Response time to what? To a user action? To a signal coming from the context of the system? It is not clear, because this information is not included in the content of the requirement. Consequently, we have no idea how to implement this requirement, because we don't know how it should work. What is the expected result of the system's behavior. Requirements specified in this way can at best be a prelude to further discussion, and are in no way precise or clear enough to be a comprehensive description of the system behavior expected by the customer and the conditions that the solution provider must provide to be sure that the customer will accept its solution. In a word, this requirement is an example of a very poor-quality requirement, failing to meet its primary objective of providing sufficient information to accomplish the task at hand (recall that the task in this case is to create a contract between customer and supplier).

4.4.3 Quality Criteria: Ensure Quality of Requirements

THE DEFINITION OF QUALITY CAN VARY FROM ORGANIZATION TO ORGANIZATION AND TEAM TO TEAM. IN ORDER TO ENSURE THAT OUR WORK PRODUCTS ARE OF HIGH QUALITY, WE MUST FIRST DEFINE THAT QUALITY.

Good-quality requirements are characterized by certain quality criteria. These criteria are nothing more than certain characteristics of the properties that a requirement should exhibit in order to be judged as "good"—appropriate for the achievement of a specific objective in an established context. There are many sources of quality criteria, among

Table 4.4 Examples of quality criteria for a single requirement according to the Guide to the Systems Engineering Body of Knowledge (SEBoK) (Incose 2023)

Characteristic	Description
Necessity	A requirement defines an essential capability, feature, constraint, and/or quality factor. If it is not included in the set of requirements, there may be a lack of capability or feature that cannot be met by implementing other requirements
Relevance	The specific objective and level of detail of the requirement is appropriate for the level of entity to which it relates (level of abstraction). This includes avoiding unnecessary constraints in the architecture or design to ensure implementation independence as much as possible
Unambiguity	The requirement is formulated in such a way that it can be interpreted in only one way
Completeness	A requirement sufficiently describes a necessary ability, characteristic, limitation, or quality factor to satisfy a need for being without using other information to understand the requirement
Atomicity/ singularity	The requirement should specify a single capability, feature, limitation, or quality factor
Feasibility	The requirement can be implemented within the constraints of being (e.g., cost, schedule, technical, legal, regulatory) with acceptable risk
Verifiability	The requirement is structured and formulated in such a way that its implementation can be proven (verified) with customer satisfaction at the level at which the requirement occurs
Correctness	The requirement must be an accurate reflection of the need or intent of the stakeholder
Compliance	Individual requirements should follow the approved standard template and requirements writing style when applicable

which we can distinguish industry standards (Incose 2023; IREB 2024; IEEE 1998;[4] ISO/IEC/IEEE 2018).

With quality criteria, you can assess the quality of requirements. You can also use quality criteria to support the requirements development process. If the analyst has an idea of the existence of quality criteria and understands their importance, then already at the requirements specification stage he will make sure that the requirements he creates meet the quality criteria.

Several times I have encountered the opinion of analysts and other project team members that quality criteria are not practical. They don't really help improve the quality of requirements; they only introduce the need to do additional work. My opinion is that any tool, if used improperly, will not bring real benefits and will not enable us to achieve our objective. Quality criteria are tools with which we can ensure that requirements are of the right quality. It is only necessary to know how to use them.

We'll get to how to use quality criteria in a moment. Let's first explore a list of typical quality criteria (Table 4.4).

[4] IEEE 830 has been replaced by ISO/IEC/IEEE 29148:2018.

I would add one more very important qualitative criterion to the above list, namely measurability. Every requirement not be expressed in such a way that it is clear whether the requirement is met or not. In the case of quality requirements, measurability is particularly important because, unlike functional requirements, for quality requirements a specific scale of measurement, method of measurement, and expected values should be indicated. Other sources provide even more quality criteria for requirements. In a given project, we don't necessarily have to apply all of these quality criteria—on the contrary, I would advise against such a practice, because it leads to a situation in which, in a strenuous effort to meet all quality criteria, we waste a great deal of time and energy developing requirements at a level of quality that is not appropriate to the needs of the project and the people involved (in other words, we create requirements that are "too good").

It may sound absurd to say that requirements are "too good," but consider the fact that requirements development is a job with certain costs. These costs must be recouped in some form. One of the benefits of high-quality requirements is that they provide a clear basis for solution design, implementation, and verification. On the other hand, however, there is not always a need to provide such a high-quality basis—as we can work with a team that has an excellent understanding of the business context of the change, understands the rationale behind the change, and is able to select the right solutions for specific business needs. In simple words, this particular team doesn't need a very detailed requirements specification, because it knows perfectly well what it should deliver, and replaces extensive documentation with direct communication. Of course, we are not always in such a comfortable situation, and instead of relying on guesswork and communication, one of our tasks is to provide very precise requirements records. This means that, depending on the characteristics of the project, the solution being developed, and the team, we may find that we get specific values by applying only a few quality criteria.

As a rule, regardless of the project circumstances, the quality criteria that I consider absolutely mandatory for requirements are:

- Unambiguity
- Measurability
- Necessity
- Atomicity/singularity

I consider unambiguity to be a mandatory quality criterion, because in the absence of unambiguity, a requirement can be interpreted in different ways—as a result, we don't know which interpretation is the "correct" one, the one the requirement author had in mind.

Let's consider an example of a stakeholder requirement:

> UREQ1 As the recipient of a package, I want to be able to track the package to know where it is.

At first glance, the above requirement looks pretty good. However, after a brief analysis, we may come to the conclusion that we do not know what the stakeholder's real need is—what he really wants to track. Does he realistically want to track the shipment, to see it, to have a preview of what it looks like at each stage of its journey, come to provide information about the location of the shipment at any given time. The requirement is not explicit, so we don't know what the stakeholder's real need is and how to understand the requirement.

A solution could be to reformulate the requirement, for example as follows:

UREQ1.1 As the recipient of a package, I want to have access to information about which branch of the carrier the package shipped to me is currently in, so that I know how far away from the destination point the package is.

Of course, the above example is just an assumption about the intent of the stakeholder requesting this requirement. The stakeholder's intention could just as well be the following requirement:

UREQ1.2 As the recipient of the package, I want to have access to information about the current location of the package (geographic location to the nearest 100 m) in order to know how far the shipment is from the destination point.

And that's the problem with the lack of clarity of the requirement—the UREQ1 requirement is so ambiguous that we don't know which option to choose, 1.1 or 1.2, or some other option.

As a result, in order to be able to properly evaluate this requirement, the effort required to implement it, to identify possible solutions, we need to obtain a whole lot of additional information, not currently included in the specification of this requirement. Another solution to avoid the unambiguity of the requirement is to add detailed information, such as acceptance criteria. Thus, for example, for our requirement

UREQ1 As the recipient of the package, I want to be able to track the package to know where it is

we could develop the following acceptance criteria:

The package recipient has access to status information on the parcel given to him.

The status defined for a courier shipment is:

Shipment created—the sender has generated a shipping label.

Shipment transferred to courier—the sender has transferred the package to the courier.

Accepted at branch (city)—the package was accepted at a specific branch of the shipping company.

Sent from branch (city)—the package was sent from a specific branch.

Issued for delivery—the package was handed over to the recipient for delivery.

Delivered—the package was delivered to the recipient.

Recipient absent—the courier attempted to deliver the package, but the recipient was not present at the specified location. The courier will make another attempt to deliver the package. The maximum number of attempts is three, after which the package is returned to the sender.

Returned to sender—the package was not received by the recipient and is returned to the sender.

Another quality criterion I have identified as a key criterion is necessity. Necessity most simply determines whether a requirement actually delivers business value. Requirements that are not necessary do not deliver business value. The question then becomes: For what reason would we implement this requirement? To quote the words of one of the experts in the field of management and trainer of looking at quality over time, Niels Malotaux (2011): "Who is waiting for this?". In developing this question, we can ask additional questions: "Who's going to pay for it, how will we know we've done the work properly, how will we know when we're ready?"

To these questions I would add a few more, so that ultimately the following questions are answered:

- Who is waiting for this requirement?
- Who will use it?
- How often will this person use it?
- What problem will this requirement solve?
- How will we know that the problem has been solved?

Atomicity of requirements, or the right level of granularity, is another important quality criterion and one of the aspects that not only constitutes comprehensibility of requirements, but also significantly affects the project's ability to manage information. Atomicity in the context of requirements means, more or less, whether a particular statement contains only one requirement or more.

Let's consider the following example of a system requirement:

REQ 01
Title: Adding and editing a product
Description: The system allows the user to add a product and subsequently edit its data.

This requirement is actually two separate requirements—one relates to the ability to add a product, the other relates to editing. We should not include these two features in the description of one requirement. There are many reasons for this, some of which are mentioned in Sect. 4.3.1, To Avoid Chaos: Structure the Information.

One of the arguments for breaking a requirement into two, at least, is that there are different preconditions and restrictions for these requirements. For example, for the ability to add a product, we can imagine the following precondition: only a logged-in user with appropriate permissions can add a product. Restriction: a product with a name identical to the name of a product already existing in the product database cannot be added.

For the requirement to edit the product data, we can indicate the precondition: only a logged-in user with appropriate permissions has the ability to edit the product. Editing product data is possible only under the condition that the product has been added to the product database. Restriction: you can change all product data except the identification number, and you cannot change the product name to a name that already exists in the product database. If we treated these requirements as one, we would probably lose information about the very specific prerequisites and constraints specific to each requirement.

We discussed the importance of measurability in detail in Sect. 4.2.9, Measurability, Measurability…

One could talk about quality criteria and their application for a long time. Equally, one could talk about their benefits. In some circles, one can encounter quite far-reaching criticism of qualitative criteria and their benefits. The leading argument against qualitative criteria is usually that the application of qualitative criteria takes a lot of time and brings little benefit. In a sense, I can agree with this—if we choose quality criteria badly and apply them even worse to the creation of good-quality specifications and subsequent evaluation, then indeed the costs incurred may be disproportionate to the benefits gained.

Many times in organizations and projects I have encountered a situation where elaborate checklists have been developed to evaluate requirements and entire specifications, based on a long list of quality criteria. The development of such checklists took a lot of time in itself, and the average use of such checklists in projects to evaluate requirements specifications consumed another huge amount of time.

If only this investment would pay off in the form of concrete improvements, the costs incurred would be defensible. Unfortunately, one of the problems with using these checklists was that specifications were being evaluated. Lots of comments were made on the requirements, comments that were sometimes significant, but in most cases quite trivial, not really affecting the value in use of the requirements. Processing these comments and making corrections again required spending a lot of time, and that was the end of the process. What was missing? Drawing conclusions.

Since we are already applying, as it were, a quality control process (testing specifications to meet quality criteria), we have a process for fixing defects, and the logical continuation of the steps taken would be to implement an improvement process. This process would first require analyzing what errors occur most often—and not allowing them to occur on subsequent projects, subsequent specifications. This was lacking. As a result, those involved in developing requirements and specifications, with admirable consistency, made the same mistakes. Reviewers of work products consistently used the same checklists, reported almost the same problems. The authors then corrected the specifications. There was a lack of learning lessons, learning from mistakes, improving work practices. In such a context, the aversion to checklists, and quality criteria, is completely understandable. But the problem is not these quality criteria, or the checklists, or the review process itself; the root of the problem is that the organization is not learning.

I propose a slightly different approach. To successfully apply quality criteria, make sure that:

- You have determined *what aspects* and *characteristics* determine the quality of the requirements and other work products you create. Sometimes measurability is key, sometimes compliance with a specific requirements description template. If you haven't established this, you don't really know what quality criterion and aspect of quality to focus on.
- You have chosen a *small set of quality criteria* that will apply. Usually it's three to four quality criteria for non-critical projects that are not encumbered by regulations and overarching requirements. This number of quality criteria is quite enough to start with. As needed, this list will be supplemented with more quality criteria.
- You have *planned* how these quality criteria will be used. And here is where we most often make the mistake of assuming that we use quality criteria only to evaluate the quality of the specification requirements. Nothing could be further from the truth. Quality criteria are, as the name implies, a kind of criteria that can be at the same time acceptance criteria for the requirements themselves—not their content, not their substantive content, but the very form and completeness of the information content. What follows from this? The fact that already during the development of requirements and specifications we should be aware of what quality criteria these work products should meet. If we have determined that our requirements are to be measurable, then already while creating these requirements let's ask ourselves: What is the measure? How to measure how well the requirement is met? How to test them—in what way? In what environment? Using what data?

- You use quality criteria as *quality goals*. Requirements that clearly do not meet the quality criteria should not be passed on to the next stage—which could be, for example, submitting the specification for review. Requirements that still do not meet the quality criteria after review should not be forwarded for implementation—unless you consciously make a different decision and accept the resulting risk (such a risk could be, e.g., the inaccuracy of assumptions made at the implementation stage and resulting from the lack of precision of the requirement).
- You apply the agile principle of *inspect and adapt*. Quality criteria are a kind of tool—the effectiveness of the tool can change depending on different conditions. In such a condition may be, for example, the changing business awareness of the team. At the very beginning of a project, for example, a key quality criterion could be the completeness of requirements, understood as compliance with a certain method of specification. The criterion of completeness of description may have been a way to mitigate the risks associated with the team's lack of business knowledge. Over time, as team members continue to learn, learn the context, and communicate directly with business stakeholders, completeness of description may paradoxically lose its importance as documentation is largely replaced by direct communication. In such a situation, forcing every requirement to be developed according to a template established at the outset can become an unnecessary practice, generating only frustration on the part of the specification writers, the team, overwhelmed by information overload.
- *You draw conclusions*. If the application of quality criteria has revealed that the author is making specific mistakes during the development of the specification, this provides an opportunity to improve practices and work methods in such a way as to avoid or at least minimize these mistakes. In my case, quality checks based on quality criteria at one time revealed that I notoriously use so-called mental shortcuts. Because in developing a specification I am stuck with my thoughts in a given context that is familiar to me, I subconsciously make the assumption that what is familiar to me will also be familiar to the recipient. This assumption was obviously wrong, as the reviews clearly showed. The results of the reviews made me realize that there was a problem with my way of working and the results I was getting. Consequently, I decided to use a specific requirements specification template, which greatly reduced the risk of omitting information—the inclusion of this information was enforced by the template. In addition, after developing a set of requirements, I verified their quality by simulating an attempt to explain their content to stakeholders outside the manufacturing team.

4.4.4 Use Reviews: A Basic Quality Control Tool

THE MAIN OBJECTIVE OF TESTING IS TO PROVIDE INFORMATION FOR DEFECT PREVENTION PROCESSES. DEFECT REPAIR IS A SIDE PRODUCT.

NIELS MALOTAUX, PROJECT COACH, N R MALOTAUX, CONSULTANCY

The simplest and most intuitive method of quality control is reviews, also known as peer review, which, in a nutshell, involves reading a given document or other work product and evaluating its contents against certain criteria. These criteria can be both formal, such as compliance with a specific template and content formatting, and substantive—consistency of content, correctness in terms of business logic or preconceived assumptions. There are at least several types of review—a detailed specification and comparison of the different types of review is contained, for example, in the ISO/IEC standard 20246:2017 (ISO/IEC 2017).

How do we ensure that the reviews we implement are effective?

First, let's determine what the objective of the review is. Depending on the objective, we will choose a different review technique. For example, if the objective is to detect non-compliance with specific requirements, with criteria, we may use inspection. If the objective is mainly to present the work product in order to inform stakeholders about our approach and collect possible feedback, we can choose a review technique.

Another important element is to think about who should participate in the review. Depending on the objective of the review, we will select other participants. Keep in mind that the review participants should be active and not play the role of extras. This means that each person participating in the review should have a role and responsibility. Contrary to appearances, the principle of involving as many people as possible in reviews does not always come true—in many cases, less is better, more effective, more motivated.

If you are concerned with a meticulous inspection of the work product, you can schedule several review sessions. The first may involve a relatively small group of stakeholders whose objective will be to check the work product for obvious problems, errors, etc. This group will conduct a kind of smoke test, making sure that the work product is ready for review by a wider audience. In a design context, a smoke test can simply be a review of the specification by a fellow team analyst. If you don't find any significant problems as a result of this review, you can expand the circle of reviewers to include more participants.

Why such an approach? Wouldn't it be better to transfer the work product to as many people as possible right away? It can be done, but in this case we accept the risk that the work product will turn out not to be ready for review, which consequently only wastes the time of many people. In addition to the undoubted cost resulting from the loss of time, we must also reckon with the damaged trust of stakeholders, who, seeing the meager quality of the reviewed work product, will acquire serious doubts about the quality of the final product. It is worth asking ourselves whether we are willing to take such a risk and what the consequences will be. Personally, I recommend the principle of small steps, especially for large work products, complex projects, or high product risk.

I suggest the following approach to implementing reviews:

- Determine the *objective* and *scope* of the review. This seems like an obvious step, but is often overlooked. As a result, we organize a document review, select reviewers, hand them the document to be reviewed, and fail to explain what to focus on during the review. The objectives can be manifold—the objective can be to formally check the document for compliance with a specific template; the objective can be to assess the correctness of business logic, validate requirements, or check compliance with established quality criteria. Without defining the objective, you don't know who should be involved in the review and what type of review to choose.

- Identify the *review participants*. The review should involve people who will realistically bring value to the review. This means that they should be able to review the document under review, verify its content against the specified review criteria, and provide valuable feedback. Unfortunately, we sometimes make the mistake of fairly randomly selecting review participants. As a result, the document is reviewed by people who are not competent or skilled. It is worth remembering that review participants should not be surprised by the fact of their participation in any quality control activities. Personally, I recommend placing reviews as part of the communication plan developed for an initiative. This way, stakeholders are aware from the outset of their participation and their role in the process of reviewing designated work products.
- Decide what *type of review* is best to use. There are many different types of reviews; depending on the objective set for the review, the right type of review is chosen. If necessary, modifications can be made to the standard form of review. Thus, for example, a walkthrough can be used to clarify the requirements to the project team, with a slight modification to add a checklist to the review procedure so that the review focuses on clarifying specific areas.
- *Communicate the documents* to be reviewed. It is good practice to clarify the objective of the review, what the reviewers should focus on, what you expect from them, and in what form you would like to receive feedback. Failure to do so can result in a review that is far from what we expected—we will receive feedback on aspects that are not what we wanted them to evaluate, or in a format that will not be practical for us. Be sure to give reviewers adequate time to review the documents and evaluate them fairly. Unfortunately, project realities indicate that a critical mistake often occurs at this stage—we hand over the documents for review and schedule a meeting for the next day to discuss the results of the review. Just reading the document will take a certain amount of time, reading it with understanding, analyzing the relationship between the information in the document and other documents will take even more time, and documenting comments and observations will also take time. Even if we assume that stakeholders are fully available and able to focus solely on the review, adequate time should be allowed for all document review work. If there are a large number of stakeholders representing a specific group, I recommend following the SPoC practice.
- Evaluate the *review results*. After the reviewers have reviewed the document and provided feedback, the author should analyze the results of the review for possible corrections and changes. If the document is significant and has a large volume, if the comments are numerous, I recommend holding a review meeting, where you as a team (the author and the reviewers) will discuss the most significant of the defects, gaps, and ambiguities detected, and determine what actions should be taken to eliminate these problems. I suggest that you establish clear criteria for evaluating the criticality of comments, so

that you first focus on comments and defects that are truly relevant to the integrity of the document under review, and leave the handling of comments with a lower level of criticality for a later time. The same principles can be applied here as in the process of reporting and resolving defects in software testing—each defect reported by the tester (in our case, the document reviewer) should have a specific priority or criticality, which allows proper prioritization of the defect repair process.

If the number of comments submitted is negligible and they are not critical, a review meeting may not be required. In such a case, email communication may be sufficient, in which we, as the author, inform stakeholders of what we intend to do with the reported issues, and when submitters can expect corrections to the document.

- *Fix defects.* Comments submitted by reviewers that are confirmed as actual problems and defects should be corrected within the agreed time frame. In doing so, it is worth noting that correcting one defect may require changes in multiple areas of the document (traceability can be used to analyze the impact of the changes). This, in turn, means that one change may result in another change to the document, so it is recommended to recheck the consistency and completeness of the document after corrections. Sometimes, after analyzing a submission, the author decides to reject a change suggestion made by a reviewer. It is good practice to explain the reason for rejecting the suggestion—this way the submitter knows that his suggestion has been analyzed, and an informed decision has been made that it is not valid or will not be included in the document for other reasons. Provide feedback—just as feedback on our document has been provided by reviewers. As authors, we wouldn't want to be put in a situation where we ask others to review documents, some people give us comments, some don't come back with any information—so we don't know if the document is good, and the reviewers don't have any comments, or maybe they didn't have time to look at it at all. Since its authors wouldn't want to be put in such a situation, let's not put reviewers in such a situation—and the lack of feedback regarding the resolution or rejection of comments would be exactly the same situation, only in terms of our communication with reviewers.
- *Draw conclusions.* As a result of the review, we get a lot of valuable feedback on the quality of our work product. We can use this feedback to identify areas for improvement in our work practices. For example, feedback from a requirements specification review may indicate that we do not fully understand the business area for which we are specifying requirements. This suggests a very significant problem and also a project risk that needs to be managed. Otherwise, we agree to accept the risk of providing a solution to a problem we do not understand. How can this problem be addressed? The simplest solution would be to ask for the transfer of business knowledge, which can be done at least in the form of a meeting in consultation with stakeholders representing the business. All areas for which factual errors have been identified should most likely be discussed during such consultations. Do not be afraid of lack of knowledge—the stakeholders representing business areas (domain experts) have knowledge of business. We business analysts possess competence in analytical practices and tools; we have communication and information elicitation skills—having a general knowledge of a particular business is generally sufficient to achieve our objectives. Let's not be afraid to

ask questions, and let's not be afraid to admit that we don't have deep knowledge of an area. Among other things, this is why we work in projects as a team, to complement each other's expertise and knowledge.

4.4.5 Appendix: Checklist for Requirements Development

• Activity	Result
Requirements elicitation	
Identification of sources of requirements	
1. Identify sources of requirements	Sources of requirements [proposed]
• Stakeholders	
• Documents	
• Systems	
2. For each stakeholder, indicate:	List of stakeholders who are the source of requirements [proposed]
• What scope of information can he or she help obtain	
• What is his/her level of decision-making	
• Availability according to the information provided in the communication plan	
3. For each document, indicate:	List of documents that are the source of requirements [proposed]
• What scope of information it relates to	
• Whether the information it contains is up to date	
4. For each system indicate:	List of systems that are the source of requirements [proposed]
• To what extent it can assist in requirements elicitation activities	
5. Determine the order in which the sources of requirements are used	A structured list of sources of requirements
6. Determine the risks associated with the use of each source of requirements	List of risks
7. Select requirements elicitation techniques that can be used for specific sources of requirements, for example: • Stakeholders: collaborative techniques, conversational techniques, observational techniques, creative techniques • Systems and documents: artifact analysis techniques, perspective-based reading, system archaeology	List of techniques [proposed]

(continued)

• Activity	Result
8. Plan your requirements elicitation sessions by determining:	Requirements elicitation plan [proposed]
• What the source of requirements will be	
• What results you plan to get	
• In what form the results will be delivered	
• What technique you will use	
9. Determine how to document the results obtained	Requirements elicitation plan [proposed]
10. Obtain stakeholder approval of the requirements elicitation plan. Make adjustments if necessary	Requirements elicitation plan [accepted]
Realization of requirements elicitation sessions	
1. Conduct the requirements elicitation session according to the plan	
• Obtain information about the requirements and their attributes, according to the requirements documentation approach adopted	Requirements [elicited]
• Obtain information on constraints and assumptions on the require-ments, identifiable at this stage	Attributes of requirements [elicited]
• Identify risks associated with the requirements	Constraints [elicited]
• Identify stakeholder doubts and concerns	
2. Document the results obtained	Note from session
3. Consult the obtained results with decision-making stakeholders in the area	Requirements [confirmed] Attributes of requirements [confirmed] Constraints [confirmed] Assumptions [confirmed]
4. If necessary, repeat requirements elicitation sessions in areas where the information obtained was not complete	
Requirement analysis	
1. Organize the set of requirements	
• Define traceability between elicited requirements and higher-level requirements	Requirements [traced]
• Remove duplicate requirements	
• Identify conflicts	Conflicts in requirements [identified]
• Use traceability to identify missing requirements and complete them with appropriate information retrieval techniques	Requirements [proposed]

(continued)

• Activity	Result
• Confirm constraints and assumptions	Limitations [confirmed] Assumptions [confirmed]
• Confirm priorities	
2. Organize the set of requirements	
• Determine the relationships between requirements	Requirements [relations]
• Organize the requirements according to the adopted criteria, for example, into functional modules	Modules Epics
• Organize the organized requirements according to the adopted prioritization criteria.	Requirements [ordered]
3. Resolve conflicts of requirements	
• Identify the people involved in the conflict	
• Determine the source of the conflict	
• Develop proposals to resolve the conflict	
• Agree on a solution to the conflict with the stakeholders	
• Obtain acceptance of the developed solution	Conflicts in requirements [resolved]
• Document the way of solving the conflict	Conflicts in requirements [documented] Requirement [updated]
Requirements specification	
Preparation for specification	
1. Determine what information will be included in the requirements specification, what in other artifacts, for example those developed by the test team, UX, designers.	Information structure
2. Confirm the validity of the template selected at the planning stage for the specification Dependency: Business analysis approach	Specification template [confirmed]
3. Determine what information will be specified in the form of natural language, and what information will be specified in the form of a model Dependency: Business analysis approach	Form of specification Information structure
4. Confirm/verify the requirements for the quality level of the requirements specification (set of mandatory quality criteria) Dependency: Business analysis approach	Quality criteria [confirmed]
5. Assess the completeness of the requirements information	Assessment of completeness
6. Determine what information can be reusable (appear in multiple places in the requirements specification)	List of usable information
7. Determine how and where reusable information will be specified	Information structure

(continued)

• Activity	Result
8. Establish a requirements specification plan, determining the order of specification of individual requirements, modules Dependency: Solution implementation plan, completeness of documentation	Requirements specification plan [proposed]
9. Estimate necessary support from team members, business stakeholders Dependency: Requirements specification plan [proposed]	Engagement plan [proposed]
10. Identify the risks associated with the requirements specification	List of risks
11. Get approval from the project team regarding the requirements specification plan	Requirements specification plan [accepted]
Specification	
1. Incrementally specify requirements	
• For functional requirements, ensure that the specification includes at least the following information: input specification (input information), subject of the requirement, output specification (results and output information), constraints, business rules	Requirement specification [stable version]
• For qualitative requirements, ensure that the specification includes at least the following information: definition of the qualitative characteristic, scale of measurement, method of measurement, desired value of the characteristic, minimum acceptable value of the characteristic	Requirement specification [stable version]
2. Define/verify the correctness of links between requirements and other artifacts	Requirement [linked] Traceability structure
3. When in doubt, mark a specific requirement so that you can return to it later	Requirement [to be reviewed]
4. In case the requirements specification cannot be completed due to missing information, it is recommended to mark a specific requirement. Add a comment or information about the problem to it. If possible and necessary, create a task related to this requirement, which can be closed when the missing information is completed	Requirement [to be reviewed]
5. When the specification of a particular module is completed, perform quality control from the set of requirements, in particular consistency and completeness	Requirement specification [version ready for review]
6. If you are using modeling according to a specific notation/language for requirements specification, select a finite set of elements of the given notation/language to be used in the specification Dependency: Expectations and preferences of stakeholders and the project team, project constraints, requirements of the business analysis approach used for the project	Definition of syntax elements
Requirements/model validation	
Validation planning	
1. Specify the scope of information that will be validated during each validation session Dependency: Requirement specification [version ready for review]	Scope of validation [proposed]

(continued)

• Activity	Result
2. Determine which stakeholders/project team members should be involved in validating the requirements/models	Engagement plan [proposed]
3. Confirm the availability of participants according to the information in the communication plan	Engagement plan [proposed]
4. Determine how those involved in the validations should provide feedback and how feedback will be handled; for example, information on editorial corrections can be entered into documents on the fly, during the validation session, while substantive comments will be recorded and handled at a later time	Procedure for handling comments [proposed]
5. Schedule validation sessions, with an indication of the objective of validation and expected results Dependency: Scope of validation [proposed]	Validation plan [proposed]
Get stakeholder/project team approval on the validation plan	Validation plan [accepted]
Prepare for validation	
1. Specify a limited set of information to be validated during each validation session Dependency: Requirement specification [version ready for review] Validation plan [accepted]	Scope of validation session [proposed]
2. Inform the people involved what topic will be discussed at the next validation session	
3. Prepare the information for validation; for example, from the set of requirements, select it and organize the ones to be validated	Scope of validation session [ordered]
4. If necessary, make sure that the validation support tools are ready and properly configured	Tools [ready]
Execution of validation sessions	
1. Briefly explain to stakeholders what set of information is being validated, e.g., what is the responsibility of the system module whose requirements will be validated	
2. Explain to those involved the objective of the validation, the process, and the expected results	
3. Remind participants what validation they should focus on, what quality criteria to pay attention to Dependency: validation plan [accepted]	
4. Handle stakeholder feedback according to the convention adopted during validation planning	List of comments [submitted]
5. At the end of the validation session, summarize the session, the extent of the information discussed and the results obtained, explain to the participants of the validation session what they can expect next, e.g., correction of defects feedback on the revised version of the requirements	Summary of comments—list of comments [submitted] Validation plan [updated]
6. If the validation is performed by stakeholders on their own, through individual reading of the information being validated, make sure to provide clear information on how to make comments before the validation session	

(continued)

• Activity	Result
7. After the implementation of the validation session, handle the feedback	
• Make changes where reasonable	Change suggestion [accepted]
• If a change suggestion is rejected, inform the submitter of the reason	Change suggestion [rejected]
8. Update the version of the documentation after making changes	Requirement specification [updated]

4.5 Case Study

4.5.1 Example of Application of Contextual Survey Technique

The technique applied in the context of a business owner's observation, simulating the work of a real user operating a control panel, with a business analyst as an expert and an architect on the consulting service provider's side as an observer.

Plan for the Execution of the Contextual Survey Technique

The implementation of the contextual survey technique was developed jointly with the stakeholders involved. The results are shown in Table 4.5.

The context survey session was conducted remotely as follows: The person assisting the product owner launched a remote teleconference. The monitor screen showed an area

Table 4.5 Realization plan for the contextual survey technique

Attribute	Value
Objective	• Understanding how the control panel works, especially integration with peripherals and available functionality through the control panel • Defining personas • Defining typical usage scenarios
Results	• Personas (list) • Business processes/operations (list)
Source of information	Stakeholder: business owner System: control panel
Session length	2 h
Participants	• Business analyst • Product owner, domain expert (device operator) • Solution architect
Organization of sessions	The product owner operated the actual control panel at the premises The observer attended the on-site, on-premises session, while the expert (business analyst) attended the session remotely

where the premises' control panel and the person operating it could be seen. In addition, the product owner was connected to the teleconference via his mobile device, a smartphone. The smartphone showed details from the device itself, as well as the exact operations being performed.

Execution of the Session

Shortly after the start of the teleconference, the business analyst summarized the objectives of the session and the expected results. Then, according to a pre-prepared agenda, which included the areas and functionalities to be discussed, the context study session began. The domain expert configured the control panel, then armed and disarmed it. Each operation was shown both on the laptop and on the smartphone camera, so observers could see both the entire device and the details relevant to each functionality.

Since the business analyst was responsible for proposing a solution that supports current processes and meets the needs of stakeholders, special attention was paid during the session to understand how the control panel works and the entire context of the alarm system. To this end, not only was the operation of basic functionality demonstrated, but also scenarios were used to simulate real-life examples of the use of such a system. We used a simplified technique of personas and scenarios aimed at presenting typical ways in which users interact with the control panel.

During the session, while the business analyst dealt with the functional and process aspects, the architect paid attention to the technical aspects, such as how the control panel communicates with peripheral devices.

Session Results

- Recording of the session
- High-level diagrams showing the main business processes
- The main personae (indicating which business processes are appropriate for them)

Deviations From Standard Contextual Survey Technique

The business analyst participated in the session remotely. This was the most significant deviation from the standard way of conducting this technique. This deviation was due to project constraints and external conditions. The implementation of the project fell during the COVID-19 pandemic, business travel was severely restricted, and we also wanted to reduce the associated potential health risks as much as possible.

We therefore made the decision that people from outside the customer's premises would not travel, and would join the session remotely. Those on-site attended the session at the test facility, with a sanitary regimen in place. Another slight deviation from the standard technique was that the notes and business process models I created were presented to the domain expert and architect already during the session, for validation and confirmation of the information. This was a way of mitigating the risks associated with the relatively low availability of customer-side stakeholders, as well as making the most of the session time.

5 Solution Implementation

The implementation of a solution requires the involvement of people with different competencies. If we are talking about solutions like an information system, as a rule we need an architect, programmers, testers—we need the competencies necessary to turn the solution concept into a working system. For other solutions, other competencies will be needed.

Is there a place for a business analyst in this process? He or she has already done his or her job—identified business needs, requirements, supported the development of the solution concept. However, the practice of business analysis is not limited to providing the basis for solution implementation; business analysis deals with the entire life cycle of a business need—from the moment it is identified, through the implementation of the solution, until it expires. And this can also be the responsibility of a business analyst—to develop the basis for the implementation of a solution, and then to support the delivery and implementation of that solution.

At the solution implementation stage, the business analyst can support the project team in various ways—from providing expertise, through design validation, to demonstrating the solution and explaining its suitability to stakeholders. The scope of a business analyst's responsibilities is, of course, dependent on the definition of the role within a given organization or initiative, but it is worth realizing that the business analyst's work does not end when the requirements are handed over to the manufacturing team. Just as the work of implementing a solution does not end when the system is produced—in many cases, producing a system and deploying it to production is only the beginning of change.

Note that the vast majority of business analysis practices, not just business analysis, address purely abstract aspects—we work on concepts, abstract entities that do not actually exist. We work on models, which are ideas we have about reality. We work on requirements, which are abstract representations of stakeholder needs. We create nothing more than mental models. We rely on assumptions; we thus base decisions on incomplete information.

K. Zmitrowicz, *Business Analysis Done Right*,
https://doi.org/10.1007/978-3-031-62194-9_5

The solution implementation stage will help us verify many of these assumptions and assess their correctness. It is at the solution realization stage that we have a chance to see the tangible results of our earlier thought process, and we can verify how our mental model reflects reality and assumptions about that reality. For this reason, it is the norm that during the solution implementation stage, we change assumptions, make new decisions about the direction of the system, notice new opportunities. These changes are not a mistake in the art of analysis—it is a natural process of forming conclusions based on the acquisition of new information and perspectives. Therefore, during the implementation of the solution, the presence of an analyst or people with business analyst competencies is crucial. We cannot assume that the results developed at earlier stages are complete, up-to-date, correctly reflecting the intentions—the result of such an assumption can be at most that we implement the solution according to the concept, requirements specification; we do not validate it in terms of delivered business value. As a result, we deliver a system that is simply not usable. Not because it doesn't work—it can work brilliantly—the problem is that it doesn't deliver the expected business value, doesn't serve stakeholders' needs as it should. This can, of course, be due to a poorly stated business need, problems in the requirements specification, but very often it is due to the fact that during the implementation of the solution there were changes in the business context, but there was a lack of business analysis to capture these changes and address them appropriately. Such changes can be changes in the market environment, new consumer needs, but also simply changes in the organization's strategy resulting from planned growth. If we don't monitor the organization as a system that is constantly evolving, we don't know whether the initiatives we implement, including solution implementation initiatives, are based on current assumptions, or whether they still have a chance to deliver valuable results. As a result, we carry out projects whose results are worthless and waste organizational resources on carrying out unnecessary activities—we focus our efforts on areas that are not central to the organization's strategy and waste resources that should be allocated to completely different objectives.

The role of the business analyst at the solution implementation stage is not simply reduced to detailing requirements, consulting with the project team. The role of the business analyst is primarily to monitor the validity of the business need and the compatibility of the chosen strategy for implementing the change with the organization's business objectives.

5.1 Solution Design

5.1.1 Does the Analyst Design Solutions?

Let's start with a philosophical discussion: Is a business analyst involved in designing a solution? The definition of business analytics implies that a business analyst focuses more on proposing solutions to bring value than on actually designing them and then producing them. Does this mean that the involvement of a business analyst at the solution design stage is not necessary?

In theory, the business analyst deals with the needs and business layer, and is not responsible for the design and implementation of solutions that are supposed to deliver value. On the other hand, within business analysis we distinguish the practice of evaluating the solution, meaning that we should verify to what extent the delivered solution delivers value, and meets the specified needs and other assumptions of the business case.

To be able to evaluate solutions, we don't necessarily have to wait until the solution is fully implemented—concepts, solution designs, prototypes, and models can also be the subject of evaluation. This is a fairly good way to mitigate the risk of producing a solution that differs significantly from expectations and does not deliver the desired business value. Instead of waiting for the manufacturing team to deliver the solution, try designing it at the conceptual level to:

- Organize information about requirements, constraints, and other aspects of the planned solution and turn it into a tangible solution design. By doing so, we can spot errors in our own thinking, gaps in the requirements, and possible changes that will bring more business value before we even get to the solution implementation stage.
- Evaluate different options for solving the same business problem—for each requirement, there are a number of potential solutions. The manufacturing team will not decide which solution is best from the perspective of the business audience and business value—this decision will have to be made by people with business knowledge and the appropriate level of decision-making.
- Facilitate the evaluation of the feasibility of certain design concepts. As I mentioned earlier, each requirement can be implemented in a number of ways—some are more difficult to implement, some are easier; some involve a higher cost, while others are relatively inexpensive. A solution design, understood as a kind of conceptual model, is an excellent input for the manufacturing team to assess what solution options would be recommended in a given situation.
- Get a chance to validate assumptions very early on. Developing a solution concept in a form that can be understood by business stakeholders can create opportunities to engage them in validating those concepts. In other words, stakeholders are able to assess how the solution design proposal meets their needs and expectations, what is worth improving, what is worth changing, which solution option is not an option at all. I point out that this happens at the conceptual stage—implementation as such is not yet in place. This practice, therefore, gives us the opportunity to avoid potential problems in the future, such as the situation in which the project team implemented the solution, and spent a certain amount of time and energy, after which the business stakeholders found that this is not the right way to fulfill their needs.

Let's also note that a solution does not necessarily consist of a single component. After all, a solution, understood as some means of achieving a business objective, does not consist solely of an IT system or process change. A solution can consist of both the development of a new system and a change in the business process that the system is intended to support, training of users and other stakeholders in the new procedures and use of the systems, and a change in work culture.

Solution design should not be equated with the design of a high-level solution architecture—solution design is the totality of the activities that need to be performed to conceptualize the changes planned in various areas of the organization's operation in order to achieve specific business results.

5.1.2 Solution Concept Design vs. Technical Design: At What Point Does the Business Analyst's Responsibility End?

THE REQUIREMENTS SPECIFY WHAT WE NEED. THE DESIGN SPECIFIES HOW TO DO IT.

Solution design is a fairly broad topic that can include functional logic design, data modeling, visual design of the solution, as well as solution architecture design or integration design between systems. Which of these aspects are typical responsibilities of a business analyst, and which are beyond the standard responsibilities?

The answer, of course, depends on the context and how the analyst's responsibilities are defined in a particular project. As a rule, however, the business analyst is responsible for the business, needs, and requirements, and designs the solution at the conceptual level, but not at the level of how it is implemented. Considering the typical competencies of business analysts, it can be said that a business analyst can be responsible for:

1. Developing the functional logic of the designed solution, which can be expressed in the form of use case diagrams and workflow diagrams.
2. Determining the structure of the data processed by the system at the logical level, which means identifying the data that is fed into the solution and generated by the solution.
3. Design of the communication in the solution, understood as the communication between the various elements of the solution, expressed as the specification of the data transferred between the elements, possibly defining quality requirements such as performance (expected response times of the solution to certain external events).
4. Design of the visual layer, in the case of software, these can be screen mock-ups, scenarios showing the implementation of individual operations in a visual way. It is worth noting that in many organizations there is a role of a graphical user interface (GUI) designer or UX specialist, who, in addition to his responsibilities for user experience design, often deals with the design of the visual layer. In this case, this task can be carried out by this role, with support from a business analyst.

If there is a systems analyst or solution designer role in an organization or project, part of the solution design activity can be performed by this role. In this case, the business analyst may be limited to providing requirements (to different levels of abstraction depending on the needs of the project), while the design of the solution itself, which will enable the fulfillment of the specified requirements, is the task of the system analyst.

There is a reason for this—system analysts have more knowledge of systems engineering, and usually have the competence necessary to create models that represent the operation of the solution from different points of view (e.g., from the user's point of view—use case model, logic—data logic model, communication—activity or workflow models, and so on). A system analyst may have quite deep technical knowledge, so he may have competencies similar to those of a solution architect and be able, for example, to design the integration of the system with other elements of the environment.

Here we come to a level to which the business analyst usually does not descend. In most cases, as defined by the responsibilities of the business analyst's role, he does not design the implementation; he focuses on what we want to achieve, not how to achieve it, what technical means to use to meet the requirements. Of course, there may be exceptions to this rule, but it is worth realizing that in such cases, the work performed by the business analyst goes beyond the standard defined for this role.

An example of a responsibility allocation matrix explaining the division of tasks between the business analyst, system analyst, and architects is shown in Table 5.1.

Table 5.1 Example of an excerpt from the definition of responsibility by role

	Business analyst	Enterprise architect	Systems analyst	Solution architect
Identification of business need	X			
Identification of stakeholders	X			
Development of a list of stakeholder requirements	X			
Specification of stakeholder requirements	X			
Identification of business constraints	X			
Identification of technical constraints		X		
Development of solution concept	X	X		
Decomposition of stakeholder requirements into solution requirements			X	
Specification of solution requirements			X	
Development of a logical data model			X	
Solution architecture design—components, integration, etc.				X

5.2 Analyst in Development Team

5.2.1 Role of the Analyst in the Development Process

Prior to the start of the project, the person involved in the business analysis activities identified the business needs, determined the requirements, and helped develop the solution concept. Does this mean that the implementation of the solution itself no longer requires the involvement of the business analyst, or will the team manage on its own?

In simple terms, the manufacturing team is responsible for producing the solution based on the established requirements. The delivered solution, or a piece of it, needs to be evaluated to meet the defined business needs—and this is where the need for the analyst's involvement arises again.

A waterfall approach to project execution would be that the business analyst provides input to the solution design and implementation process, and evaluates the results received from the team. As a result of this evaluation, we may conclude that the solution correctly addresses the business need, is the right way to deliver value, or provides the executive team with a suggestion for changes and improvements.

Sounds like an area for improvement—since we know that the result of the solution evaluation may be suggestions for changes requiring further work on the part of the executive team, the suggestion is to reduce the risk of delivering a solution that is not the optimal way to meet business needs by involving the analyst in the solution design and production processes. In other words, instead of finding faults in the solution, prevent those faults by actively participating in the solution development process. This doesn't mean, of course, that the business analyst must now become a designer, architect, and developer in one person—it means that we can use our knowledge and expertise to support the project team in making the right decisions for the business. In particular, a business analyst can:

- Provide feedback on the developed projects, how to implement the requirements—before these projects are handed over for implementation.
- Can, even earlier, explain the business context of a project to the team, so that the team is aware of what they are doing and why. In many cases, changing perspectives helps select the right solution.
- Serve as a consultant when there are doubts about a project or implementation. The business analyst probably won't answer the question of which system interface we should implement, but he or she can provide information about expectations for communication between systems, data structure at the logical level, performance expectations, or transaction security. This is input for the implementation team, so they will be able to choose the right implementation methods.

It works well to work together as one team. This means that the business analyst should be part of the executive team—which is not always as obvious as it might seem. Many times I have dealt with organizations and projects where the business analyst, after "completing" his work, i.e., delivering the requirements, ended up working on the project. The executive team was practically left to its own devices. The evaluation of the solution was carried out by business representatives during acceptance testing. And, as one might expect, the results of the acceptance tests were far from acceptable—a number of changes and improvements had to be made before the solution could be implemented in production, due in large part to an inadequate approach to meeting business needs, lack of knowledge of the business context, and misunderstanding of business assumptions.

In my opinion, based on observations and discussions with many analysts, business representatives and project management, the business analyst should be involved in the change initiative from the moment the business need arises until it expires, which means both the executive design and implementation of the solution, as well as its maintenance and further development. Otherwise, we end up with a situation where an individual or a team of business analysts defines business needs, creates a business solution concept, and passes the results of the work to another team—losing vital information necessary to understand the context and motivation for the change. Then the executive team creates a solution and hands this over to another team to maintain that solution, to further develop it—and again we lose knowledge and context. As a result, it happens that the concept of the solution at the business needs analysis stage was different, and the delivered solution no longer meets a given business need, but its interpretation. The solution running in production is evaluated and developed by a team that lacks knowledge about the motivation of the entire change—as a result, decisions are made to implement new functionality with the properties of the solution, which de facto does not bring any business value.

Assuming that in our organization in projects we have the ability to ensure that the business analyst or analysis competence is on the team from the moment the need arises until it expires, let's summarize what the business analyst can serve the executive team in the design and production stages of the solution.

- *Context of the change.* Unfortunately, quite often the executive team starts working on a solution without having any idea of what the motivation for the change was. What business objectives the solution is supposed to help achieve, in what business environment it will operate, who will use it—just directly and indirectly. This is where I see the role of the analyst—to explain to the team at the very beginning of the work what they are doing, why, for whom, and what value they want to get. With this context in place, the executive team will be able to make decisions of greater value to the business.
- *Knowledge transfer.* Without a business analyst on the executive team, the only knowledge of business needs is transferred in the form of requirements (I assume, of course, that they have been developed). However, even being the greatest optimist, I realize that a requirements specification does not write off everything, does not clarify all doubts, does not answer all questions. So, to avoid the risk of misunderstandings and of the team making assumptions that are not accurate when designing and implementing the

solution, we will ensure that there is a business analyst on the team who can clarify potential doubts and provide additional information on an ongoing basis.

- *Validation.* Instead of implementing projects according to a cascade approach, working in silos, let's make sure we work as a team. The tester develops assumptions for testing—nothing prevents the business analyst from identifying areas of highest business risk and thus helping to focus testing efforts in areas that need to be tested particularly carefully. The programmer is working on a complex algorithm—nothing prevents him from showing the results to the business analyst at any stage of the work to confirm the correctness of the assumptions made. The programmer has completed the implementation of some functionality—again, nothing prevents the tester, with the support of the business analyst, from checking the correctness of the function and how it delivers business value.

The above does not mean that I am advocating that a business analyst should engage in all possible manufacturing work (for a simple reason—many organizations similarly will not be able to afford to provide such analyst availability), but rather that they should engage in those marked as critical. For me personally, critical project work is:

- Confirmation of the *objective of the project.* Purpose understood not as producing a solution, but providing a tool to meet business objectives. Who better to explain the objective of the project than a business analyst who was involved in the change initiative from the very beginning, from the moment the business need was identified?
- Managing the *scope of the solution.* This is important especially for changes resulting from changes in the context of the organization. Assuming that a strategy analysis was performed before the project was launched, the business analyst has information about the context of the change, in the areas affected by the change. When the need for change arises, the business analyst will not only be able to change requirements, but also verify how these changes may affect related areas, projects, and other initiatives.
- *Eliciting information* needed to design the right solution. The rule of thumb is that there are several solution options for each requirement. The project team does not necessarily know which solution option is the most optimal, given the expectations of the target group and other stakeholders in the solution being designed. However, the business analyst should have this knowledge and can assist the team in making the right design decisions. Therefore, my personal preference is for the business analyst to be involved in the development of screen designs, target application flows, etc.—this way inefficient design options can be ruled out while still at the conceptual level.
- *Validating the correctness of the assumptions* made when designing the implementation of the solution. This is particularly important when there is no opportunity for the business analyst to take an active part in work such as detailed specification of system requirements, user interface design, data structure, or integrations. If there is no opportunity to co-create these work products, I believe that as a minimum, quality control mechanisms should be implemented. So, for example, just after detailed system

requirements have been developed, the business analyst can selectively review them to ensure that the right assumptions have been made and the right way to implement the higher-level requirements has been carried out.

- *Assessing test coverage.* We can't always expect a tester to have business expertise and be able to properly prioritize testing. Nor does he always have knowledge of business risks, and information about these risks is not always included in the requirements specification. This, in particular, justifies the need for analytical competence on the team.

Arguably, there are many more ways to involve the business analyst in the project team. The way and level of involvement may depend on the specifics of the team, especially the competencies and knowledge possessed in the team. Therefore, it is worthwhile, even at the stage of team building and project initiation, to answer the question: What kind of knowledge, what kind of analytical competencies, will we need at the stage of solution implementation and who possesses these competencies?

5.2.2 Supporting the Product Owner

With the popularity of agile software development methods, and not only software, the role of the product owner has emerged. With the emergence of this role, there has also been a lot of confusion and doubt about the role and responsibilities of the business analyst.

Some organizations felt that with the emergence of the product owner role, a dedicated business analyst role was no longer necessary, as the product owner and team had all the competencies necessary to develop and deliver the product to market.

Other organizations assumed that there was overlap between the product owner and business analyst roles, so that the business analyst could move freely into the product owner role.

Still other organizations assumed that since the Scrum framework defined only three project roles (product owner, Scrum Master, and development team), the role of the analyst is not considered at all, and the product owner should have all the competencies necessary to deliver business value.

The latter assumption has proven to be completely untrue in many cases, as many product owners represent the business area with excellent domain knowledge, but lack specific skills in the business analysis area. As a result, they may know the business and its needs brilliantly, but not be able to convert them into requirements understandable to the manufacturing team. Thus, in practice, it turned out that the implementation of agile principles alone is not enough to efficiently implement a project—competencies that are not necessarily present in the existing configuration of project teams are still needed (by way of explanation, some organizations "implemented" agile methods, changing only the way of working, but not making sure that with the change in the way of working there was a change in the way of thinking and adaptation of competencies to the new needs).

The above problems have caused some evolution of the concept of agile teams. Nowadays, it is common practice that in projects implemented according to the principles of agile methods, there is the role of the product owner and the business analyst. The product owner is responsible for the product as such—its scope, the business value that this product is supposed to deliver, the order in which the various features are implemented. In simple terms, we can say that the product owner defines the business needs and high-level requirements, decides on the implementation plan for the product, and changes the scope of implementation if necessary to increase the delivered business value. Where in all this is the role for the business analyst? There are at least a few options:

1. The business analyst acts as a kind of *intermediary* between the product owner and the project team. Among other things, his task is to detail high-level requirements into specific ones that are understandable to the project team. In many cases, the scope of his responsibility resembles more the role of a system analyst than that of a business analyst (according to some simplified division of duties and responsibilities, of course).
2. The business analyst *supports the product owner* in defining the product scope and delivering business value. He participates in stakeholder meetings, elicits requirements, and specifies those requirements for the project team. In this arrangement, the product owner can manage the overall scope of the solution, prioritize implementation, and provide guidance on new features and functions of the solution that should be analyzed.
3. The business analyst acts as a *mentor* to team members, often including the product owner himself. He or she supports the team in building competency in business analysis, so that over time they become self-sufficient and are able to efficiently handle the needs raised by the product owner. On the other hand, the product owner must have the two competencies necessary to identify the right business needs, assess the business value, and evaluate different solution options.

This third solution is interesting in that it leads to the development of new competencies in the team members, so that we can—after a certain time—eliminate the need for an intermediary like a business analyst translating business needs into specific solution requirements. The team is able to perform these activities on its own.

Now let's consider one by one examples of tasks performed by a business analyst in different configurations.

1. Analyst, as support of the product owner. Example tasks in this team configuration are:

- Assistance in defining the product vision in accordance with the assumptions—business case, definition of business needs and analysis of the organization's context.
- Assessing the completeness and validity of high-level requirements.
- Developing system requirements based on high-level requirements. Examples include acceptance scenarios or acceptance criteria for user stories.

- Collaborating with UX design, testing, and design professionals to develop sufficient requirements specifications.
- Support in product incremental testing—an example solution could be special "business acceptance tests" performed after system testing. This allows the business analyst to verify how business value has been delivered, and to explain this to stakeholders in a demo session.
- Support in organizing the backlog—it happens that the product owner is not fully aware of all the connections and dependencies between the different elements of the backlog. The business analyst, as a person who works with the backlog on a daily basis, can support him in organizing the backlog, taking into account these dependencies.
- Analyzing the impact of changes. Here is where a rather interesting topic arises, namely the issue of change. Unlike the so-called traditional development methods, in agile methods, changes are the order of the day and are treated as new requirements. From the point of view of the requirements management process, however, these are not always new requirements; they can be modifications of requirements that have probably already been implemented. According to the principles of requirements engineering, before implementing a change, we should perform an analysis of the impact of the change on various aspects of the system and business, including stakeholders. In the agile variant, we could theoretically skip the analysis of the impact of the change on business processes or stakeholders in some cases, because we would have to assume that the change (i.e., new requirements) submitted by the product owner is already confirmed with the relevant stakeholders, who are aware of the impact of the change on their processes, systems, or other aspects. Even with this assumption, however, we would have to admit that it would be worthwhile to perform at least a very cursory analysis of the impact of the change on the system under development. Otherwise, we could end up in a situation where the implementation of a new requirement, which is actually a change to an already implemented requirement, leads to unforeseen negative consequences, such as destabilization of the system, failure in areas that have worked properly up to now, or problems that may manifest themselves in the long term—problems with system maintenance resulting from inefficient source code. This is, of course, because the implementation of a requirement involves the creation of code, tests, and other artifacts. If we are now going to change an already implemented requirement, we should know in which parts of the code, tests, or other artifacts to make the necessary changes. If we don't know this, we may end up in a situation where instead of making changes, we create new artifacts, thus introducing inconsistency in the system design. The solution may be a standard change impact analysis requiring, in this particular context, defining and maintaining links between requirements, code, and tests. If a product owner asks for a new requirement that modifies an existing one, a business analyst can link this "new" requirement to the existing one and thus help the team determine what changes will be necessary to implement that requirement.

2. The business analyst supports the product owner in defining the product scope. In this variant, the business analyst performs his standard activities:

- Performs strategy analysis activities, including analysis of the current state and definition of the target state
- Identifies sources of requirements and needs
- Uses information extraction techniques to determine business needs and requirements
- Specifies requirements, often using business acceptance criteria
- Prioritizes requirements based on the business value provided by the requirements
- Explains to the team the objective of the product and the value from implementing each requirement so that they can choose the appropriate methods to implement the solution
- Plans and supports business acceptance testing, including supporting the preparation of scenarios for acceptance testing, introductory training for testers, assisting with test execution, and collecting and analyzing the resulting test results
- In consultation with the product owner, implements changes in accordance with the results of the acceptance tests

3. The business analyst acts as a mentor for the team. In this configuration, examples of the business analyst's tasks include:

- Building the product owner's competence in current and target state analysis, which may mean learning to apply specific techniques and tools, including business modeling techniques. This enables the product owner to more accurately identify areas for improvement and assist others in analyzing the impact of change on various business areas.
- Educating and building practical skills in information retrieval techniques and information consolidation.
- Learning how to model requirements or solutions to ensure consistency and completeness of the designed system. It can be particularly useful to model issues at a high level and then decompose to a lower level of abstraction, i.e., to develop a hierarchy of models that enables "big picture" understanding and insight when needed.
- Supporting business-level requirements specification, e.g., through joint requirements documentation workshops, developing measurable acceptance criteria.
- Building competency in solution evaluation, including learning testing techniques useful in implementing acceptance testing.

In a similar way, a business analyst can help build competencies on the project team side. Typical analytical competencies that will help the team communicate with the product owner are:

- The ability to ask the *right questions*—right in this context means those that will allow you to understand the essence of the requirements, the business value, and detect potential errors and gaps in the requirements.
- The ability to *decompose* business requirements into solution requirements and to specify the requirements in a measurable way (the specification does not necessarily have to be in the form of a document—the form of information representation should be well chosen to meet the needs of the specific team and the recipients of the project results).
- The ability to perform *change impact analysis*—this topic was widely discussed earlier.
- *Systems thinking*, that is, seeing information as elements that make up a system, which must be complete and consistent. For example, if a product owner submits a requirement that is in apparent conflict with other requirements, the project team should be able to catch this and communicate it to the product owner in order to solve the problem.
- The ability to *explain* technical aspects in business language—this can be useful for explaining risks arising from assumptions made about architecture or other technical aspects. The team should be able to explain to the product owner that the requirements they have submitted can be implemented through several means, and for each relevant option explain the advantages and disadvantages, in language understandable to someone without deep technological knowledge.

There are certainly many other activities and areas in which a business analyst can assist the team and the product owner. Those described above are just examples. Depending on the needs of a particular project and the specifics of the team and the responsibilities of the product owner, the business analyst and team members may vary. I encourage you to discuss the responsibilities of the various roles and the principles of cooperation in the initial stages of the project, during the establishment of the principles of project implementation and the development of the system development process.

5.2.3 You Join an Already Started Project

Imagine stepping into a new project. Not from the beginning. You don't have the comfort of understanding the context of the business change, sourcing the business needs, participating in a full stakeholder analysis. You are entering a project that is already started. A project where the scope is defined by requirements, sourced by someone else, a scope that in all likelihood is not complete and needs to be completed and clarified.

You join such a project and wonder where to start. Most likely, from the very first day of your involvement in the project, the team members have expectations about what you should deliver to them and by when. The problem is that you're not comfortable with the situation you're in—the team expects you to provide design input, implementation and testing, and you most likely don't yet have enough knowledge about the project deliverables, the solution you're designing, stakeholder expectations.

Many people who find themselves in this situation intuitively throw themselves into the work and try to meet the expectations of team members. They provide information rather hastily, realizing that it may be incomplete or even wrong, not wanting to delay the work of their colleagues. They begin to lead a discussion with business stakeholders aimed at detailing and completing the requirements, asking questions that have been asked many times before, and bypassing questions that are relevant at this stage. They respond to questions from team members about preferred solution options almost without thinking, wanting to provide the information necessary to move the work forward as quickly as possible. Sound familiar?

What could be the consequences of such an approach? The consequence could be that by starting the work without properly recognizing the project situation, the work results to date, without knowing the specifics of the solution you are designing, without understanding what the state of the art is in the team, you generate one big project risk. The risk being that you rush to provide information that may be wrong; design decisions will be made based on this wrong information.

- You waste stakeholders' time on conversations of little value to project objectives.
- You create a situation where changes will be needed at a later stage of the work to correct the effects of erroneous decisions resulting from the initial rush.
- You can effectively shake the customer's confidence in both your competence and the skills of the other team members, as it will be difficult to rationally explain to the customer the return to a topic previously discussed several times, corrections resulting from mistakes, and potential delay.
- You reduce the motivation of the team by changing the findings, inserting them in a situation where they have to redo work that has already been done.

These are consequences of the highest degree of undesirability. Therefore, let's avoid them. The approach I recommend is that before you do anything, understand the situation you are in. This includes, in particular:

- Learning the objectives and goals of the solution you are working on as a team.
- Learning the principles and methods of working on the project.
- Getting to know the team, both the manufacturing teams and the business and technical stakeholders influencing project decisions.
- Determining what has been done up to the moment you joined the team, what remains to be done, and at what stage the work is.

In a nutshell, you need to take the kind of inventory that will allow you to understand what is the current state of the project and the product you are working on. I suggest that this inventory include four dimensions (four Ps):

1. Product
2. Project
3. Process
4. People

Here is a sample checklist for completing such an inventory.

Product:

- Identify the basic features of the product.
- Identify the users and others indirectly or directly using the product.
- Identify the experience provided by the product to the user, and what business value the product delivers to the audience.
- Identify the product's advantages over competitors' products.
- Identify what processes and user operations the product supports.

Project:

- Know the project constraints, including schedule and budget.
- Understand the project's relationship to other concurrent ongoing projects.
- Determine the product implementation plan in relation to the project schedule. Prepare a roadmap if necessary.
- Identify project risks that may affect your work.
- Learn how the business analyst role is defined in the project, and what are the expectations of the role.
- Learn the team's meeting schedule and determine which meetings you should attend. If you are unable to determine from the meeting description whether you should attend, ask the meeting initiator to briefly explain the objective of the meeting and the expected results. This will help you decide whether the meeting will be valuable to you, and whether you will be a valuable participant in the meeting.

Process:

- Determine by what method or approach or according to what framework the project work is being carried out.
- Determine what considerations the solution development process imposes on the analysis activities.
- Determine the dependencies between analysis activities and other tasks. If these dependencies are not defined, start there.
- Determine what tools are used and how they support the various activities in the process. Determine whether and how the use of tools can be optimized to accomplish analytical tasks.

People:

- Know the composition of the manufacturing team, and determine who performs what roles and responsibilities.
- Identify who the project stakeholders are.
- Determine the area of expertise of specific stakeholders.
- Determine which stakeholders are decision-makers in specific areas. If responsibilities are not established, start there.
- To get to know the stakeholders as people, try to arrange short one-to-one familiarization meetings.

Completing the activities in the checklist above will help you understand what stage of the project you are at, what the state of knowledge is, what has been created, and what the plans are. You will also get to know the team members, which will facilitate cooperation and possible knowledge transfer. In the process, you will begin to build relationships. Accept the fact that if you have not been involved in an initiative from the very beginning, there are many things you will not know, many findings you will not be informed about. Don't be afraid to ask questions where necessary so that you can carry out your work effectively. You may probably be afraid that asking questions will reveal your ignorance; however, I believe that instead of making assumptions, it is a good idea to ask a question, formulating it in the following way, for example: "There is a possibility that this question has been asked before; however, I would like to make sure I understand correctly." By doing so, you will let the recipient know that you realize that similar discussions in general have already been held in the future, but you want to confirm the information or get new information.

Another practice that can help you understand the project situation is knowledge transfer, carried out through various meetings, among other things. On several occasions I have come across the recommendation that a person entering a project should attend all possible meetings to get information quickly. Personally, I think this recommendation is somewhat harmful. A person who has just entered the project spends a great deal of time attending meetings, where, as a rule, most of the information discussed at these meetings is completely incomprehensible to that person, because he or she does not yet have any project context. Instead of understanding, there is information noise and a sense of frustration resulting from the fact that such a person is receiving a great deal of information that he or she is unable to process on his or her own in a relatively short period of time. So I suggest, instead of attending all possible meetings, talk to key team members, such as the product owner, project manager, or developer leader, get the most relevant information about the project and the product from them, confront this information with the objectives and agenda of the meetings, and determine which meetings are a priority and which are not.

5.2.4 Analyst and Test Planning

THE ANALYST IS A TESTER OF BUSINESS CONCEPTS.

What does a business analyst have in common with test planning? Theoretically not much because it is a different area of responsibility, a different discipline, which of course is related to business analysis as well as other areas such as design and manufacturing. One may make the assumption that a business analyst is not a tester, does not have the necessary competencies, and his involvement in test planning or subsequent test execution will bring negligible benefit. Nothing could be further from the truth.

First of all, testing checks certain aspects of the solution we are working on. The business context determines which aspects are so crucial that they should be tested in particular depth and detail.

Scenarios and sequences of activities should be tested because these are the most common paths that users will take; they are also business information. The data used for testing should also represent actual business data. For example, if we are testing an electronic banking system for individual customers, we will need different types of test data. An example of such data is a customer who has only one bank account. Another type of test data is a customer who has several bank accounts, including foreign currency accounts. This is important because the test data determines the accuracy of testing and the reliability of the results obtained. Sometimes the test team does not necessarily have very deep business knowledge and is not able to determine the scenarios or test data that should be used for successful testing. In this area, among others, the business analyst can support the testing tasks.

The business analyst knows the assumptions about the solution, the target users, the business context, so he or she is able to provide information that will enable the test team to properly plan the tests:

1. Information about the required *test coverage*—coverage tells us about the extent to which tests cover given aspects. Such an aspect can be, for example, test coverage of requirements. One hundred percent test coverage of requirements says that there is at least one test case for each requirement. Coverage requirements are often driven by business needs—business stakeholders need proof of testing the system according to specific requirements; it can come from a kind of constraint, such as industry standard requirements. The business analyst's knowledge can therefore be an excellent input for testing.
2. *Test scope*—in the simplest view on the subject, a test scope is a list of requirements for a solution. However, there are times when we decide that not all requirements will be tested by the test team. For example, some of them may be tested by people with specific expertise. At this point, specific features may be indicated as those that are outside the scope of testing. Again, the business analyst can provide information about what

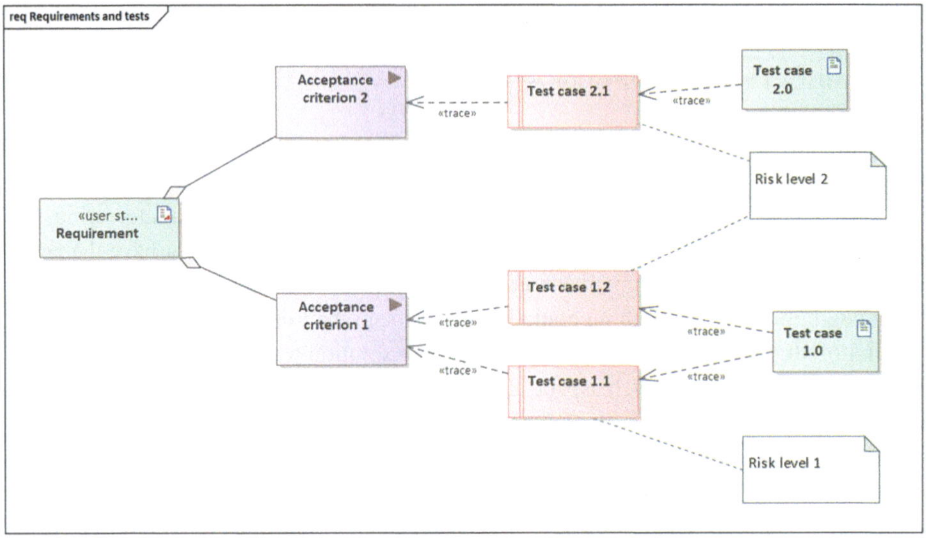

Fig. 5.1 Structure of the relationship between requirements and their acceptance criteria and test artifacts in the context of product risk

scope of the solution will need to be tested as part of the work done by our test team, and what elements will not be subject to testing.

3. Risk analysis—there is a specific product risk associated with the requirements. This risk can be an input that controls testing (Fig. 5.1). For example, the requirement "Search for a product" can be identified as a high-risk requirement, because if the implementation of this requirement does not work properly, the basic functionality of the system will be compromised—the user will not be able to search for the product he wanted to purchase. This requirement may have several acceptance criteria, among which will be criteria describing how the system should react in the event of a relatively unlikely exception, consisting, for example, of a broken connection to a database. And although in general the requirement is defined as a high-risk requirement, the specific acceptance criterion may be defined as medium risk—precisely because of the relatively low probability of occurrence (Table 5.2). The business analyst's knowledge of product risk is the baseline information for determining the priority and accuracy of testing. As a rule of thumb, high-risk requirements should be tested first, and should be tested accurately because the system must function properly within this defined range. Requirements identified as low risk have a lower priority, and it is not necessary to use as strong testing techniques to test them as for high risks (Table 5.3). This is one of the premises of the risk-based testing strategy explained, among other things, in the ISTQB certification program for testers (ISTQB® 2023).

Table 5.2 Example of risk analysis and mapping of requirements to test cases including risk level

No.	Name	Priority	Acceptance criteria	Risks	Test cases
1	Add product to cart	High	Ability to add a product to the cart	High	PT1.1 Add product to cart
			Cart status update	High	PT1.1 Add product to cart
2	Product search	High	Search using 1 criterion	High	PT2.1 Search with 1 criterion—search result
			Search using advanced criteria	Medium	PT2.3 Search using advanced criteria
			The list of results	High	PT2.1 Search with 1 criterion—search result
			Handling of no results	Medium	PT2.2 Search with 1 criterion—no search results
3	View product details	Medium	Access to detailed product information	Medium	PT3.1 View product details
			Photo gallery—main image	High	PT3.1 View product details
			Photo gallery—additional photos	Low	PT3.1 View product details
			Product review	Medium	PT3.1 View product details
			Database error handling	Medium	PT3.2 View product details—no connection to database
4	Add to favorites	Medium	Ability to add a product to the favorites list	Low	PT4.1 Add to favorites
			Update the list of favorites	Low	PT4.1 Add to favorites
5	Browsing the cart	High	Preview the contents of the shopping cart before finalizing the purchase	High	PT5.1 Browse shopping cart
			Increasing the number of products in the shopping cart	Medium	PT5.2 View shopping cart—change quantity of products
			Ability to go to detailed information about the product	Medium	PT5.1 Browse the shopping cart
6	Placing an order	High	Entering data necessary for order processing	High	PT6.1 Place an order
			Choice of payment methods	High	PT6.1 Place an order
7	Order confirmation	High	Receiving order confirmation after finalization	High	PT6.1 Place an order

Table 5.3 Example of test case prioritization based on risk analysis

Priority	Test cases
High	PT1.1 Add product to cart
High	PT2.1 Search with 1 criterion—search result
High	PT3.1 View product details
High	PT5.1 Browse the shopping cart
High	PT6.1 Place order
Medium	PT2.2 Search with 1 criterion—no search result
Medium	PT2.3 Search with advanced criteria
Medium	PT3.1 View product details
Medium	PT3.2 View product details—no database connection
Medium	PT5.1 Browse shopping cart
Medium	PT5.2 View shopping cart—change quantity of products
Low	PT3.1 View product details
Low	PT4.1 Add to favorites
Low	PT4.1 Add to favorites

4. *Process flows*—systems made with users in mind support specific operations and business processes. The functioning of these processes is not necessarily precisely known to the test team, especially at the beginning of the design work. The business analyst can explain to the test team at the planning stage what the primary objectives and operations are to support the system, how it will be used by users, and which business scenarios are critical and which are performed relatively infrequently and by a less key audience, and therefore can be tested further down the line. As a result, the testing team is able to establish a reasonable schedule for testing work, starting with the design of test scenarios and ending with the execution and reporting of tests.

The importance of the business analyst at the test planning stage can be compared to a situation where we, as testers, are asked to test a car, with little knowledge of what the car is used for, what parts of the car are critical, and it is these that we should test most thoroughly, what parts of the car are cosmetic. If someone with business knowledge does not provide us with the information with which we can properly plan and execute our car tests, we may find that we have tested very carefully the way the seats are positioned, the ergonomics of the dashboard, and the way the steering wheel is turned, we have tested forward driving in many ways, but we have not tested how the car performs when we need to reverse, and we do not know how the car functions in bad weather conditions. Lack of business knowledge can make us test the wrong aspects, leaving out the key ones, which can lead to wrong test results. This is where the support of a business analyst comes in very handy.

5.2.5 Validation of Test Scenarios

Supporting the development of effective test scenarios is one of the tasks that can be successfully performed by a business analyst. The business analyst, with his business knowledge, can verify that the test case specification:

- Covers relevant requirements or business scenarios
- Checks key features and characteristics of the solution in sufficient depth
- Is correct from a business perspective, that is, whether in designing the test cases, the testers made valid assumptions about, for example, typical use scenarios, user profiles, etc.

Consider an example simulating the validation of test cases by a business analyst.

Table 5.4 shows two requirements and the test cases designed for them. The test cases cover positive scenarios, but do not cover exception scenarios, such as a failed attempt to

Table 5.4 Example of test case design incompletely covering requirements

No.	Name	Priority		Acceptance criteria	Risk	Test cases	Expected result
1	Add product to cart	High	KA1.1	Ability to add a product to the shopping cart	High	PT1.1 Add product to shopping cart	Product added to cart
			KA1.2	Update the status of the shopping cart	High	PT1.1 Add product to shopping cart	Product added to cart, increase cart balance by 1
			KA1.3	Support for Internet failure	Low		
2	Product search	High	KA2.1	Searching using 1 criterion	High	PT2.1 Search with 1 criterion—search result	List of results
			KA2.2	Search using advanced criteria	Medium	PT2.3 Search with advanced criteria	List of results
			KA2.3	Results list	High	PT2.1 Search with 1 criterion—search result	List of results
			KA2.4	Handling of no results	Medium	PT2.2 Search with 1 criterion—no search result	No results
			KA2.5	Handling of failures	Low		

add a product to the shopping cart (resulting, e.g., from Internet problems). Acceptance criterion KA1.3 has no test coverage, and this is similar for KA2.5.

This situation may be due at least to the fact that these acceptance criteria are defined as low risk—so the tester has assumed that it is not necessarily crucial to cover them with tests. The business analyst, having knowledge of the business context, knows that handling failures of this type is important to ensure an adequate level of product quality.

Analyzing the level of test coverage achieved, the business analyst could therefore signal the need to expand testing to include exception scenarios.

Of course, at this point we could argue that, after all, the requirements for the expected level of coverage should be precisely specified in the test strategy (approach) for the project—so there is no need to involve the business analyst in their verification, since the level of coverage is set at the process level. Also, although it is a recommendation of the test process, we do not always have a test strategy in place. Even if it is, it may be incomplete or based on outdated assumptions. So to reduce the risk of insufficient testing, it is worthwhile to at least involve the business analyst in at least "random" quality control.

Such checking can, of course, be done after testers have completed the test specification. However, it can also be performed at the test development stage, which reduces the risk of delivering a test specification with the wrong level of quality. Moreover, if there is a sufficiently precise and complete requirements specification in the project, it is possible to replace the precise test specification with general test conditions referring to the detailed requirements. In this situation, a business analyst could help make sure that the test conditions properly cover the specified requirements.

What else can a business analyst support test design with? He can, of course, perform quality control after the fact, and he can help design test cases. But we can also change the approach a bit and adopt the practice of making requirements specification and test specification activities in parallel. In other words, the analyst works on the requirements specification, and the testers develop the tests in parallel. The form of documentation is not important here; the practice itself is key. Thus, a tester designing potential test scenarios is able to catch possible gaps and errors in the requirements, so that the analyst can fix these errors and ultimately deliver a reasonably complete and accurate requirements specification.

Still another approach, widely known from agile practices, is that the requirements specification in some way includes test scenarios—an example of such an approach is Behavior Driven Development and the related Gherkin technique that allows the specification of an acceptance scenario according to a specific syntax. Acceptance scenarios created in this way are relatively easy to convert into specific test cases. Ideally, a business analyst and a tester work on the acceptance scenarios, thus minimizing the risk of missing important situations, exceptions, or assumptions. An additional benefit is that once the requirements specification is completed in this way, we have both the requirements specification itself and the initial test specification.

An example of a requirement with acceptance criteria in Gherkin format worked out with the tester is shown below:

As a logged-in user, I want to be able to change my current password to be able to change my password for security reasons.

Actor: Any user of the system

Business scenario

1. The user logs into the system.
2. The user selects the "Change password" option in the user panel.
3. The user enters the current password in the form and enters the new password two times (in two input fields).
4. If the old password was correctly verified and the new password meets the standards, a message about the successful password change appears and a confirmation email is sent to the user's email address.
5. If the old password was incorrect or the new password does not meet the standards, a message appears asking to re-enter the data.

Acceptance scenarios in Gherkin

Scenario 1. Possibility to change the password

Given I am a logged-in user

When I choose the option "Change password" in the user panel

Then the system takes me to the password change form

Scenario 2. Entering a new password: positive scenario

Given I am on the password change form page

When I enter the old password correctly and two identical new passwords that meet the requirements AND I click the "Change password" button

Then the system displays the message "password has been changed" AND sends a confirmation email to the email address

Summary

6

The work of a business analyst is all about working with people, their visions, problems, needs and requirements. In order to ultimately find the right solution, we need to understand their thinking, their doubts and concerns about the planned change or transformation.

Stan Bühne, Managing director, IREB® GmbH

Dear reader, this is the end of this publication. In it, I have presented a handful of recommendations and practices gathered over many years of experience by myself and those I have had the pleasure of working with. I would like to conclude with a concise list of key recommendations to help you improve your business analysis practices.

Listen Very often, to understand a problem, all you need to do is stop talking and listen to what others have to say. Remember that in an analytics project, your job is, among other things, to gather information from different sources and different perspectives. Only by doing so will you be able to propose solutions that will actually improve the organization's operations.

Ask Questions Challenge the status quo. Ask for opinions and insights; ask about seemingly obvious aspects. Ask even when you think you know the answer. If, through questions, you are able to spark reflections on the part of your stakeholders that allow you to discover at least one area for improvement, that will be a huge success.

Build Relationships You are taking part in designing changes that affect people. It is their way of working or functioning in their personal lives that you will change. You work with people on the concept of change. In the project team you will work with people. The recipients of the results of the initiative are people. Every business is about people. One of the pillars of a successful business analyst's work is the ability to build relationships and

K. Zmitrowicz, *Business Analysis Done Right*,
https://doi.org/10.1007/978-3-031-62194-9_6

engage stakeholders—without this, even rich methodological, tooling. or engineering skills may not be enough to achieve the objective of the project.

Plan Planning may not be a particularly inspiring activity, but it allows you to organize your knowledge of what you want to achieve and the means to do so. By planning, you will thus verify your own assumptions and find out what you don't yet know. Without a plan, you don't know where you're going—so how will you know that you've already achieved your objectives?

Be Precise Defining needs, objectives, and requirements is the art of precise word usage. Be aware that in communication about a planned business change, every word matters—the consequences of misunderstanding can be many.

Write. Draw Present information in visual form. This will give you and the people you are working with a chance to validate your understanding of a topic, find gaps, and detect potential errors in thinking. What is written down can be verified. What exists in your mind is just a mental model.

Think in Terms of Systems An organization is a business system and should be viewed as such. A system operating in a specific environment, pursuing a specific objective. If you don't understand how the system works, how can you make valuable changes to it?

Think Holistically The change you are working on does not exist in isolation—it is part of the entire business ecosystem. You want to design changes that will bring value; you want to know how your change affects the rest of that ecosystem—view organizations holistically. Before you start focusing on the details, consider the big picture.

Study. Learn Don't assume you know the answers to everything. Draw knowledge—from the stakeholders you work with, from your team members, from others in the community. Business analysis is such a broad area, intertwined with other areas such as strategic management, solution design, systems engineering, and manufacturing, to name just a few, that there are a whole host of areas you don't know in depth, or haven't even heard of. Contrary to what you might think, you don't necessarily need to know all these areas—that's why we work in teams, so that their members complement each other's knowledge and competencies. However, it is important that you are learning all the time—including understanding others and yourself.

References

Alexander, Ian, and Beus-Dukic Ljerka. 2009. *Discovering Requirements: How to Specify Products and Services*. Wiley.

Alexander, Ian. 2002. *Writing Better Requirements*. Addison Wesley.

Atlantic Systems Guild Ltd. 2019. Volere. [Online] 2019. https://www.volere.org/templates/volere-requirements-specification-template/. Accessed 17 Feb 2024.

Brandenburg, Laura. 2009. Bridging the gap. [Online] 10 2009. https://www.bridging-the-gap.com/about-bridging-the-gap/business-analyst-manifesto/. Accessed 23 Jan 2024.

Cambridge University Press & Assessment. 2024. Cambridge Dictionary. [Online] 2024. dictionary.cambridge.org. Accessed 17 Feb 2024.

Cockburn, Alistair. 2000. *Writing Effective Use Cases*. 1st ed. Addison-Wesley Professional.

Cohn, Mike. 2004. *User Stories Applied: For Agile Software Development*. Addison-Wesley.

Fowler, Martin. 2003. *UML Distilled: A Brief Guide to the Standard Object Modeling Language*. Addison Wesley.

Gilb, Tom. 2015. *Competitive Engineering*. Elsevier.

———. 2019. *Value Requirements: Critical Stakeholder Objectives Engineering.*

———. 2021a. *Quanteer. How to Quantify Values.*

———. 2021b. *Stakeholder Engineering.*

———. 2021c. *SUCCESS: Super Secrets & Strategies for Efficient Delivery in Projects, Programs, and Plans.*

———. 2023. *Cost Engineering.*

Glinz, Martin, et al. 2022. *Certified Professional for Requirements Engineering. Handbook.* IREB.

Gorschek, Tony, et al. 2007. Industry evaluation of the Requirements Abstraction Model. *Requirements Engineering* 12: 163–190.

Gorschek, Tony, and Wohlin Claes. 2006. Requirements Abstraction Model. *Requirements Engineering* 11 (1): 79–101.

Hermes, Michelle. 2014. BA Times. [Online] 4 5 2014. https://www.batimes.com/articles/the-world-s-theory-the-history-of-business-analysis-evolution-of-the-business-analyst/. Accessed 30 Jan 2024.

IEEE. 1998. *830-1998 - IEEE Recommended Practice for Software Requirements Specifications*. IEEE.

IIBA®. 2015. *A Guide to the Business Analysis Body of Knowledge (BABOK® Guide) v. 3.0*. Toronto: International Institute of Business Analysis.

Incose. 2023. Guide to the Systems Engineering Body of Knowledge (SEBoK). [Online] 15 1 2023. https://sebokwiki.org/wiki/Guide_to_the_Systems_Engineering_Body_of_Knowledge_(SEBoK).

K. Zmitrowicz, *Business Analysis Done Right*,
https://doi.org/10.1007/978-3-031-62194-9

IREB. 2023. IREB Roundtable – How to Write good Requirements. [Online] 28 06 2023. https://youtu.be/m_JFdblX4KU?feature=shared. Accessed 19 Feb 2024.

———. 2024. *Certified Professional for Requirements Engineering Foundation Level, v3.1.1*. IREB.

ISO. 2014. *ISO/IEC 25000:2014 Systems and software engineering Systems and software Quality Requirements and Evaluation (SQuaRE)*. ISO.

ISO/IEC. 2017. *ISO/IEC 20246:2017 Software and Systems Engineering Work Product Reviews*. ISO.

ISO/IEC/IEEE. 2018. *ISO/IEC/IEEE 29148:2018 Systems and Software Engineering*. ISO.

ISTQB®. 2023. *Certified Tester Foundation Level Syllabus v4.0*. ISTQB®.

Jacobson, Ivar, and Cockburn Alistair. 2024. *Use-Case Foundation*. 16 02 2024.

Jacobson, Ivar. 1992. *Object-Oriented Software Engineering: A Use Case Driven Approach*. Addison-Wesley.

Jacobson, Ivar, Booch Grady, and Rumbaugh James. 1998. *The Unified Software Development Process*. 1st ed. Addison-Wesley Professional.

Knowledge Based Systems Inc. (KBSI). 2023. IDEF. [Online] 17 1 2023. https://www.idef.com/.

Kopczyńska, Sylwia, Nawrocki Jerzy, and Ochodek Mirosław. 2018. An Empirical Study on Catalog of Non-functional Requirement Templates: Usefulness and Maintenance Issues. *Information and Software Technology*. 11: 75–91.

Kosarenko, Yulia. 2019. *Business Analyst: A Profession and a Mindset*.

Laguna, Fabricio. 2023. The Brazilian BA. [Online] 7 3 2023. https://thebrazilianba.com/2023/03/07/the-business-analysis-mindset-in-an-approachable-and-charming-way/. Accessed 5 Feb 2024.

Malotaux, Niels. 2011. N R Malotaux. [Online] 11 2 2011. https://www.malotaux.eu/index.php?id=aphorisms. Accessed 22 Jan 2023.

Mitchell, Ronald K., Bradley R. Agle, and Donna J. Wood. 1997. Toward a Theory of Stakeholder Identification and Salience. *The Academy of Management Review* 22: 853–886.

OMG. 2010. *Business Process Model and Notation (BPMN)*. OMG.

———. 2015. *Business Motivation Model*. OMG.

Paul, Debra, and Cadle James. 2020. *Business Analysis*. 4th ed. BCS Learning and Development Ltd.

Podeswa, Howard. 2023. RE-Magazine. [Online] 22 03 2023. https://re-magazine.ireb.org/articles/why-your-agile-organization-needs-a-high-performing-requirements-engineering-competency. Accessed 30 Jan 2024.

PWN. 2024. Słownik języka polskiego PWN. [Online] 2024. https://sjp.pwn.pl/. Accessed 27 Jan 2024.

Robertson, James, and Robertson Suzanne. 2018. *Business Analysis Agility: Delivering Value, Not Just Software*. 1st ed. Addison-Wesley Professional.

Robertson, Suzanne, and Robertson James. 2012. *Mastering the Requirements Process: Getting Requirements Right*. 3rd ed. Addison-Wesley Professional.

Scaled Agile, Inc. 2022. SAFe 6.0. [Online] 13 03 2022. https://scaledagileframework.com/safe/. Accessed 17 Feb 2024.

Thomas, Philippa, Paul Debra, and Cadle James. 2012. *The Human Touch*. BCS, The Chartered Institute for IT.

Tomaszewski, Tomasz, and Paprocki Matt. 2023. ProductCraft. [Online] 24 09 2023. https://www.productcraft.pro/p/podstawy-okr-dla-product-managerow. Accessed 15 Feb 2024.

Weese, Susan A., and Wagner Terri. 2000. *CBAP / CCBA Certified Business Analysis Study Guide*. Wiley.

Wiegers, Karl, and Beatty Joy. 2014. *Specyfikacja oprogramowania*. In *Inżynieria wymagań. Wydanie III*. Gliwice: Helion.

Wiegers, Karl, and Hokanson Candase. 2023. *Software Requirements Essentials. Core Practices for Successful Business Analysis*. Addison-Wesley.

Wiegers, Karl. 2023. *Software Requirements*. 3rd ed. Microsoft Press.

———. 2024. Use Cases: The Business Analyst's Best Friend. [Online] 1 2 2024. https://medium.com/analysts-corner/use-cases-the-business-analysts-best-friend-375e06a7e428. Accessed 2 Feb 2024.

Yourdon, Edward. 1997. *Classics in software engineering*. Yourdon Press.

Żeliński, Jarosław. 2015. IT Consulting. [Online] 26 8 2015. https://it-consulting.pl/2015/08/26/modelowanie-biznesowe-czyli-sterowanie-i-mechanizmy/. Accessed 07 Jan 2023.